A CONSPIRACY IN THE U. S. ACADEMIC— GOVERNMENTAL COMPLEX ON EINSTEIN'S RELATIVITIES?

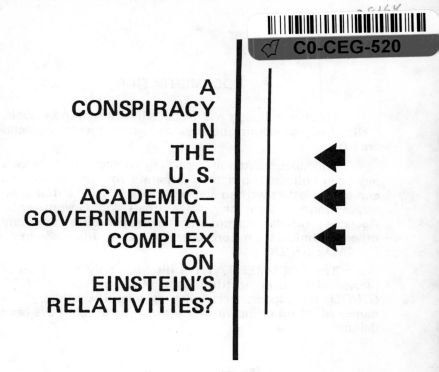

In a witty and anectodic style, IL GRANDE GRIDO provides a relentless probe into the scientific ethics and accountability of individual scientists, administrators and officers at several universities, governmental agencies and professional associations.

Some of the questions raised by IL GRANDE GRIDO:

HOW MANY HUNDREDS OF MILLIONS OF FEDERAL RESEARCH CONTRACTS WOULD BE LOST BY THE ACADEMIC—GOVERNMENTAL COMPLEX FROM THE POSSIBLE INVALIDATION OF EINSTEIN'S RELATIVITIES?

WHAT ARE THE RISKS FOR THE SECURITY OF THE U.S.A. WHICH WOULD RESULT FROM MANIPULATIONS OF BASIC PHYSICAL KNOWLEDGE PERPETRATED BY LEADING PHYSICISTS AT LEADING INSTITUTIONS?

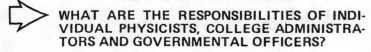

WHAT ARE THE RESPONSIBILITIES OF INDIVIDUAL PHYSICISTS, COLLEGE ADMINISTRATORS AND GOVERNMENTAL OFFICERS?

DOCUMENTATION

This book depicts real facts. All names of individuals, institutions, academic societies and governmental agencies are real.

The documentation regarding all factual statements has been collected into three separate volumes comprising copies of: letters written and/or received by the authors; referees' reports from physical journals and Governmental Agencies; official documents; newspaper clips; and any other documentation corroborating statements made in *IL GRANDE GRIDO*.

The DOCUMENTATION discloses only the names of individuals and/or institutions probed in *IL GRANDE GRIDO* for aspects pertaining to scientific ethics. The names of all other individuals and/or institutions have been deleted.

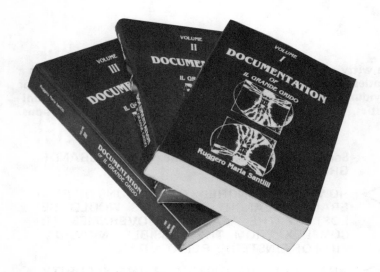

1132 pages total. Copyright © 1984 by Associazione Erida, Rome, Italy. The three volumes are not currently available. A limited edition is scheduled for production in 1985. ISBN 0–931753–01–7 (set of three volumes).

Translations of this book into the following
languages are either under way
or under organization

Italian
French
German
Spanish
Russian
Japanese
Chinese

Contact Alpha Publishing for the
availability of a translation in
the desired language

or

for the availability of
translation rights.

HISTORY OF U.S. PRINTINGS

First printing: October, 1984

Second printing: November, 1984

IL GRANDE GRIDO

Ethical probe on Einstein's followers in the U.S.A. *—An Insider's View*

Ruggero Maria Santilli

1984
Alpha
Publishing

Cover design by the artists

Bianca and Gianni Pardi
Viale Mazzini 115, I—67039 Sulmona, Italy

ISBN 0—931753—00—7

Library of Congress Cataloging in Publication Data

Santilli, Ruggero Maria, 1935-
    Il grande grido.

    Bibliography: p.
    1. Physics--United States--Moral and ethical aspects.
2. Science and ethics. I. Title.
QC28.S33   1984   174'.953'0973   84-24604

Produced by

ALPHA PUBLISHING
897 Washington Street, Box 82
NEWTONVILLE, MA 02160—0082, U.S.A.

Special discounts are available for the purchase of
this book in sufficient quantities. Contact the
Sales Department of Alpha Publishing for details.

This book is printed simultaneously in
the U.S.A. and abroad.

This copy has been printed in the U.S.A.

TABLE OF CONTENTS

FOREWORD

Dear Fellow Taxpayer,

I am an Italian physicist who, back in 1967, decided to follow the footsteps of Enrico Fermi, and left Italy to place his best energies and capabilities at the service of America. At the time of this decision, I was unaware of the fact that scientific ethics in the U. S. physics community had declined since Fermi's time. Following my arrival here, I have observed and experienced a further deterioration of scientific ethics. A series of more recent episodes has created my conviction that it is time for the U. S. society to confront and contain the problem of scientific ethics in physics. In fact, the lack of vigilance on ethical issues may well constitute a threat to our free societies.

In this book, I present my case to the best of my recollection and documentation. In Chapter 1, I present the background scientific issues in a way as understandable to the general audience as possible. In Chapter 2, I review my personal experiences with primary U. S. Universities, Federal Laboratories, Journals of the American Physical Society, and Governmental Agencies. Finally, in Chapter 3, I pass to the constructive part, the submission of a number of recommendations aimed at containing ethical problems in physics.

This book has been conceived and written for you, fellow taxpayer, wherever you are. In fact, when (and only when) ethical problems have been brought to the attention of the general public, the U. S. have proven the capability of undertaking all the necessary corrective measures in a way unmatched by other Countries. Lacking sufficient exposure to the general public, ethical problems remain generally ignored, as we all know well.

I am confident that all necessary or otherwise possible, corrective measures will be undertaken also for the problem of ethics in physics as soon as it is sufficiently exposed to the general public. This book brings the reader through a dark tunnel only because at the end I see light.

My task is that of providing you with sufficient information on the problem as well as on its implications for our societies. The decision regarding possible corrective measures is yours. The initiation of the distribution of this book signals the completion of my duty. Its continuation, if any, is now in your hands, fellow taxpayer.

I should also indicate from the outset that the problem

of scientific ethics considered in this book does not refer to stealing money, or the like.

The problem is instead of much more insidious nature and consists of manipulatory practices on truly fundamental physical issues perpetrated by overlapping rings of academic—financial—ethnic interests in the highest levels of the physics community. As such, the problem is potentially much more damaging to society than ordinary crime, as I hope to indicate in detail throughout this presentation.

Needless to say, the problem may well be of global nature and not only localized in the U.S.A. [in fact, in one of the appendices I present comments regarding scientific ethics at the largest european physics laboratory, the C.E.R.N. in Geneva, Switzerland]. Nevertheless, I pay taxes in the U.S.A. and, thus, I shall be primarily concerned with the U.S. profile. The problem of scientific ethics in other Countries is the concern of the taxpayer in those Countries.

I had several motivations for undertaking this rather unpleasant and uneasy task. They grew in time to such a point to render the completion of this book unavoidable, at whatever personal cost.

The first motivation originated from my children. I am now the father of two American children. My silence would have made me an accomplice in unethical practices at the foundation of physical knowledge which, as such, constitutes a threat to my children's future.

The second motivation originated from my fellow scientists scattered throughout the world. Even though their interest toward America has declined considerably in recent decades, as well known, they still dream in considerable numbers of following, like myself, the footsteps of Enrico Fermi. I felt a duty of telling them my story, so that they can have a true account of what it really means attempting to become a member of the contemporary U. S. academic community (and what are the implications for their families), particularly if they have creativity and independence of thought.

In short, I felt obliged to illustrate that, in my personal view and experience, under the deceptive vest of democratic peer review, the current U.S. academic community in physics is a most totalitarian (and internationally powerful) scientific organization which imposes a most questionable form of slavery, that of the human mind; the whole thing accomplished with our money, fellow taxpayer!

The third and perhaps most important motivation originated from my love for this beautiful Country. I would like to differentiate here my distrust of the U.S. academia from my love and respect for America, to which I have dedicated the best years of my life. At any rate, facts speak for themselves, by illustrating that, while the U.S. physics community has been hostile to me, America has been quite generous indeed.

At a deeper analysis, this book is the best form of appreciation I can provide the U.S.A. Rather than being weakened, the U.S. society can emerge stronger from a moment of critical examination of one of its most vital structures, the free pursuit of novel physical knowledge.

At any rate, I could not have possibly remained in the U.S.A. while silently watching its scientific future being jeopardized by rather unprecedented extremes of scientific—academic—ethnic greed.

Owing to its riches, this Country can well afford paying $ 1,000.00 for a military gasket that is normally worth $ 1.00 on the commercial market. But insufficient vigilance or excessive leniency on the ethics of basic research may well prove to be self—destructing.

A few additional, introductory comments may be of value for the appropriate perspective in the reading of this presentation.

During my European studies, from the elementary school up to the graduate school in theoretical physics, I had to study a number of ancient and contemporary languages. Nevertheless, whether you believe it or not, I never sat in an English class. I learned English by studying papers and books in mathematics and physics.

As of now, I have written a number of papers and monographs in English, but they are all of technical nature, and, as such, with emphasis on mathematical—physical elaboration and with the language reduced to an absolute minimum.

This work, instead, demands a literary knowledge of the English language which I simply do not have. The book is therefore written in "broken English", as I know well. At any rate, I see no need for linguistic perfection to convey the desired message, and for this reason I have absteined from the use of professional English editors.

Also, the language I have selected is as crude as possible. I have also eliminated in the final version of the manuscript all those calls to history, literature and art that render pleasant the reading of a book. The reasons are obvious. This books deals with seemingly dishonest episodes perpetrated by academicians. The matching of these episodes with historical, literary or artistics calls would have been offensive to the latters.

All names of individuals and institutions appearing in this book are real. The fact described are also real to the best of my recollection and documentation. Only the names of the innocent and of the victims of manipulatory academic practices have been withheld and are indicated with capital letters (such as A.A.A., B.B.B., etc.).

All statements of Chapter 2 are documented to my best.

Such documentation, being rather large, has been collected in three separate volumes.

If some of my statements are incorrect or erroneous, I beg the interested reader to provide me with the contrary evidence. I shall than take all necessary corrective measures, beginning with all needed apologies.

Ruggero Maria Santilli
The Institute for Basic Research
96 Prescott Street
Cambridge, Massachusetts 02138, U.S.A.

EDITORIAL NOTE: The writing of this book was initiated on January 9, 1984. The typesetting of the initial parts was initiated on March 19, 1984. The final parts of the manuscripts were released for typesetting on July 25, 1984. Possible subsequent editions of this book will outline, in Appendix C, all relevant events following July 25, 1984, jointly with any needed clarification and/or errata—corrige. Individual and/or institutions wishing to have their statements printed in Appendix C of subsequent editions, are encouraged to contact the author and/or the publisher.

CHAPTER 1

THE SCIENTIFIC CASE

1.1: THE LIMITATIONS OF EINSTEIN'S IDEAS IN FACE OF THE COMPLEXITY OF THE UNIVERSE.

The existing scientific literature contains a considerable number of theoretical, experimental and mathematical elements according to which:

1) Einstein's special relativity is exactly valid for particles which can be effectively approximated as being point–like while moving in empty space conceived as a homogeneous and isotropic medium.

This is the arena of the original conception of the special relativity, as clearly expressed by Einstein himself in his limpid writings.

Typical examples of exact validity of the special relativity are given by the peripheral electrons of the atomic structure, or by electrons and protons moving in particle accelerators;

2) Einstein's special relativity is only approximately valid (that is, strictly speaking it is violated) for extended particles/wave–packets under the short range interactions responsible for the nuclear structure, called strong interactions.

Evidently, these physical conditions are broader than those of the original conception. Rather than being diminished by the advancement of physical knowledge, the stature of Albert Einstein is therefore magnified by the physical intuition and scientific honesty that led him to state as clearly as possible the physical arena of applicability of his ideas.

Thus, according to the information under consideration, the special relativity is exact for the motion of the center–of–mass of a proton in a particle accelerator, but the same relativity is expected to be violated in the interior of the proton itself, or when the same proton exits the particle accelerator, and enters within the intense, short range, force fields in the vicinity of a nucleus.

3) **Einstein's general theory of gravitation is intrinsically erroneous and incompatible with nature.**

Thus, while the special relativity may still be considered as approximately valid in the interior of a hadron, the information under consideration excludes even the approximate character of the general relativity because of a number of inconsistencies we shall review in Section 1.5.

The historical roots of the limitations.

Let me say from the outset that the above elements are not of my own invention. In fact, they have been known in academic circles before I initiated any research activity.

As a matter of fact, most of the scientific scene characterized by points 1), 2), and 3) above reached me when I was a high school student in a small, but fascinatingly beautiful town in the Appennines, renouned for its schools and called the "Athens of the Sannium" (the town is Agnone in the Province of Isernia, Italy).

The information of the unsettled character of Einstein's ideas reached my high school mind with an impact that I still remember, because of the credibility of its authors. For instance, I still remember vividly when in the 50's I read the passage in the "Lecture Notes in Nuclear Physics" by Enrico Fermi [1], who stated, when referring to the nuclear forces and their range (which is of the order of 10^{-13}cm = 1 Fermi),

". . . .there are doubts as to whether the usual concepts of geometry hold for such region of space."

My high school knowledge of geometry was sufficient to see that doubts on conventional geometries necessarily imply doubts on Einstein's special relativity, owing to the deep interplay between geometry and dynamics identifiable already at the level of high school courses.

I subsequently discovered that the literature on the limitations of Einstein's relativities was rather vast. In fact, the limitations could be often traced back to names in the history of physics, and carry names such as the legacies of Langrange, Hamilton, Liouville, Jordan, Pauli, Fermi, Cartan, and others, as we shall see.

My lifelong programs of study and research.

The information was sufficient to create an uncontainable interest in this truly fundamental problem of contemporary knowledge. I therefore decided to become a physicist and to devote my life to the study of the issue. For this purpose, I resolved myself, first, to reach in Italy the most advanced possible technical preparation in pure and applied mathematics and in theoretical physics, and then move to the U.S.A. for the actuation of my research program. I did complete the first part of my program, by obtaining in 1966 the (Italian equivalent of the) Ph. D. in theoretical physics at the University of Turin. I did move to the U.S.A. soon thereafter. But in over sixteen years of attempts, I have been able to realize my research program only minimally, despite efforts to the limit of my capabilities.

The hostility I have encountered in the U.S. physics community.

This book is, in essence, a report on the rather extreme hostility I have encountered in U.S. academic circles in the conduction, organization and promotion of quantitative, theoretical, mathematical, and experimental studies on the apparent insufficiencies of Einstein's ideas in face of an ever growing scientific knowledge.

The hostility originated within vested, academic—financial—ethnic interests who apparently oppose the conduction of the studies for the sole pursuit of personal gains, in disrespect for the interests of America, as well as of the society at large.

In this chapter, I shall summarize the state of the art of Problem 1), 2) and 3) above. My personal experiences will be reported in Chapter 2.

The nontechnical character of this presentation.

I must stress that, under no circumstance this presentation can be considered as technical. It is a mere indication of the essential ideas which, as such, should be understandable to all.

I shall however indicate some of the technical literature to permit the interested, but yet uninformed scientist to acquire the necessary knowledge for ethically sound judgments. The quotation of relevant literature is also necessary to minimize the not unfrequent venturing of judgments by mumbo—jambo pseudo—scientists without technical knowledge of the background issues. In this way, physicists expressing their opinions can be subjected to a judgment of their technical knowledge and qualifications for this rather specialized field.

The technical literature directly or indirectly related to the problem considered is quite vast, and estimated to exceed the mark of 10,000 pages of printed research. My list of technical references cannot but be partial, and the interested colleague must do what all others in the field have done: spend several years of library search and study of the most advanced possible, relevant literature.

The unsettled character of available studies.

Despite their size, the available studies are inconclusive at this time. That is, we do not have conclusive evidence to claim that Einstein's special relativity is violated under strong interactions, and that the general relativity is incompatible with nature. We merely have a number of serious and authoritative reasons of doubts.

It should be stressed that the opposite view is also in the same situation. That is, we do not have at this time conclusive evidence that the special and general relativities are exactly valid. We merely have indications of validity.

In short, the scientific case underlying this book is, without any doubt, the most fundamental, basically unresolved problem of contemporary physics. The hostility I have encountered in academic circles appeared to be intended to suppress or otherwise jeopardize quantitative theoretical, mathematical, and experimental studies. These hostilities were perpetrated by renowned scholars, for the apparent purpose of preventing the achievement of progress in the field.

It is hoped that coordinated research on the limitations of Einstein's ideas will indeed be properly funded, and conducted as soon as the information on the currently deprecable state of research in the field has reached the general public.

An illustration of the direct implications for you, fellow taxpayer, of the problem of validity or invalidity of Einstein's ideas: the controlled fusion.

The historical dispute between Galilei and the Catholic Church whether or not our Earth is moving, had no practical implications for the people of that time. In fact, it took centuries of developments of the seeds planted by Galilei to reach technological applications.

The situation nowadays is fundamentally different than that at Galilei's times. In fact, the problem of the validity or invalidity of Einstein's ideas for strong interactions has direct implications for all our lives, as well as the lives of our children.

Einstein's ideas are the true, ultimate foundations of contemporary physics. Studies on their limitations, and possible generalizations may therefore have such scientific, economic and military implications as to dwarf most of the research currently preferred by leading academicians, and therefore funded by governmental agencies.

As a preliminary illustration of the implications of Einstein's ideas, consider the current efforts to achieve the controlled fusion, that is, the laboratory production of bound states of protons and neutrons under controlled conditions with a positive energy output.

It is evident that the characteristics of protons and neutrons play a fundamental role in a problem of this nature. For instance, one of the aspects currently studied is magnetic confinement of the plasma of particles. In turn, such confinement is evidently dependent on the values of the intrinsic magnetic moments of the particles.

Now, Einstein's special relativity characterizes the proton and the neutron as massive points. But points, being dimensionless, cannot be deformed. This implies the constant character of the intrinsic characteristics for the particles. It follows that, according to Einstein's special relativity, the values of the intrinsic magnetic moments of the protons and neutrons under the conditions of the controlled fusion are the same as those under other physical conditions (say, of electromagnetic type).

But, according to incontrovertible experimental evidence, the proton and the neutron have a charge distribution which is extended in space and whose dimension is of the order of one Fermi. The assumption of the extended character of the particles evidently implies the possibility of deformations under sufficiently intense external fields and/or collisions. In turn, deformations of the charge distribution are known (from classical electrodynamics) to imply an alteration of the value of the magnetic moments. Quantitative studies have indicated (see Section 1.6) that about 1% deformation of shape can imply 50% and more alteration of the value of the magnetic moments.

But the conditions of the controlled fusion are similar to those considered here. We therefore see the possibility that the intrinsic magnetic moments of protons and neutrons (as well as other characteristics) may change when the particles perform the transition from long range electromagnetic interactions (as experimentally detected until now) to the conditions of the controlled fusion. In turn, such alterations would have far reaching implications for the achievement of magnetic confinement and for other aspects of the controlled fusion, beginning with the engineering design of the magnetic bottle, let alone theoretical considerations.

The implications of Einstein's special relativity for the controlled fusion are now identifiable. If the theory is assumed to be strictly valid under strong interactions, as currently believed in leading academic circles, the protons and neutrons preserve all their intrinsic characteristics under the fusion conditions. If these characteristics are instead altered, a suitable generalization of the special relativity is unavoidable, as we shall see.

To put it bluntly, possible deviations from the special relativity under strong interactions may have a crucial role for the achievement of controlled fusion. At the extreme, a number of scholars (including myself) believe that the insistence on the strict validity of the special relativity under strong interactions may well prevent the achievement of the controlled fusion.

Some preliminary elements on academic interests suffocating at birth certain undesired experimental resolutions.

I should stress here that the hypothesis of the possible alteration of magnetic moments under nuclear conditions is not mine. In fact, it was conceived in the early stages of the theory as one possibility to interpret the total nuclear magnetic moments (which are still far from being understood despite over half a century of research).

In fact, in book [2] in nuclear physics by Blatt and Weisskopf, one can read on p. 31: "It is possible that the intrinsic magnetism of a nucleon [i.e., a proton or a neutron] is different when it is in close proximity to another nucleon." Similar statements can also be found in other well written early treateses in nuclear physics, such as that by Segrè [3].

Subsequently, studies of the hypothesis were reduced up to the current status of virtual complete silence in the technical literature, despite its manifest plausibility and its equally evident, rather large implications of scientific as well as societal character.

The reasons for such an unusual occurrence are known in academic corridors, but unspoken. They are due to the fact that, alterations of magnetic moments generally imply deviations from Einstein's special relativity because they are due to deformations of the charge distribution. In turn, such deformations generally imply the breaking of a central component of Einstein's special relativity, the symmetry under rotations.

The understandability of fundamental physical issues, with consequential capability by the taxpayer to identify manipulatory academic practices.

In short, one does not need a Ph. D. in theoretical physics to understand the essential physical ideas, and therefore appraise possible underground academic manipulations. In fact, everybody can see that a spherical charge distribution deformed by collisions and—or external fields is no longer rotationally invariant. This deformation is the fundamental physical point here. The alteration of the magnetic moments, on one side, and the violation of Einstein's special relativity, on the other side, are mere technical consequences.

In my view, the reason why no significant research on the hypothesis has been conducted, despite its manifest plausibility and evident relevance, is that its primary implication (the possible invalidation of Einstein's special relativity under strong interactions) is damaging to the vested, academic—financial—ethnic interests currently controlling the U.S. physics. In fact, after several years of efforts, I have encountered nothing but hostility and interferences in the study of the hypothesis, by exhausting all possible avenues for an orderly conduction of the needed research. At any rate, the lack of cooperation by Victor F. Weisskopf and his associates at the Massachusetts Institute of Technology is established beyond reasonable doubt, as reported in Section 2.2.

To this writing, the exact validity of Einstein's special relativity under strong interactions continues to be imposed in the typical way of all totalitarian regimes, via shear power of authority and the suppression, dismissal or disqualification of dissident views, in fundamental disrespect of the most elemental human and scientific values.

Silence as complicity in scientific crimes.

I hope, fellow taxpayer, you begin to see the tip of the iceberg that forced me to bring the situation directly to your attention.

I am sincerely convinced that the continuation of the current academic status on Einstein's ideas has such scientific, economic and military implications for our free societies to qualify silence as complicity in manipulating fundamental human knowledge, that is, complicity on scientific misconduits.

It is time to identify publicly the responsible academicians, administrators and governmental officers and expose them to the societal judgment.

1.2: THEORETICAL, MATHEMATICAL, AND EXPERIMENTAL MEANS TO ASSESS EINSTEIN'S IDEAS

Predictably, no scientifically meaningful assessment of Einstein's ideas can be conducted without a comprehensive analysis encompassing theoretical, mathematical and experimental aspects. This is due to the fundamental role of the ideas in all these aspects.

The fundamental character of Galilei's relativity for an appraisal of Einstein's ideas.

As soon as the consideration of a research program of this nature is initiated, one sees that the analysis cannot be limited to Einstein's ideas per se, but must initiate at the level of their own foundations, Galilei's relativity, that is, the relativity for point–like particles moving in vacuum at speeds that are small when compared to that of light.

In fact, Einstein's special relativity essentially generalizes Galilei's relativity to speed of the order of that of light. Einstein's theory of gravitation considers a further generalization, this time of geometric nature, via the transition from a flat to a curved space, but always in such a way to seek compatibility with the Galilean relativity.

As a result of this long historical process, the Galilean, the special and the general relativities have emerged to be deeply inter-related and mutually compatible. It then follows that the identification of insufficiencies of Galilei's relativity necessarily implies, for consistency, the existence of corresponding insufficiencies at the level of the special and of the general theory. Viceversa, insufficiencies independently identified at the levels of the special and/or of the general relativity must admit, also for consistency, corresponding, physically meaningful insufficiencies at the level of the Galilean relativity.

The need for classical and quantum mechanical studies of the problem.

At a deeper analysis, one can see that the entire process of critical examination of the Galilean–special–general relativities must be repeated twice, the first time for the classical description of our macroscopic environment, and the second time for the quantum mechanical counterpart at the level of particle physics.

The important point is that the scientific process can be initiated at the level of the physical reality of our environment. It is this ultimate origin that renders the expected limitations of Einstein's ideas, understandable by the general audience, without any need of graduate studies in theoretical physics.

It should be stressed that, even though the classical–macroscopic framework remains fundamental on conceptual [as well as technical] grounds, the quantum mechanical analysis is particularly important for the experimental resolution of the issues. In fact, most of the experiments needed to test Einstein's ideas call for beams of particles and other means that are typical of quantum mechanics.

As a first indication of the vastity, complexity and diversification of the problem considered, we can therefore say that scientifically meaningful assessments of the Galilean–special–general relativities can be done only upon completing the analysis at both levels, the classical and the quantum mechanical one.

The need for a vast program of research in pure mathematics.

As soon as a research program of this nature is initiated one can see a host of rather fundamental implications at the level of pure mathematics.

As an indication, Galilei's relativity is a manifestation of a certain type of algebras [the Lie algebra] and of a certain type of geometries [the symplectic geometry]. No advance on the physical issues is possible without the identification of the needed generalization of these mathematical tools.

To put it differently, the identification of insufficiencies of Galilei's relativity essentially means the identification of physical systems and conditions broader than those permitted by Galilei's relativity. But then, no physically meaningful elaboration of these broader systems can be conducted without a corresponding generalization of the underlying mathematics.

The dual analysis of the Galilean–special–general relativities at the classical and quantum levels, must therefore be complemented by a rather vast [and truly intriguing] program of research at the pure mathematical level. Only in this way, the physicist is provided with the rigorous mathematical tools needed for quantitative treatments.

The manifest need for a comprehensive experimental program.

Needless to say, the above theoretical and mathematical studies must be completed by a comprehensive experimental program. In fact, the only way final conclusions are reached in physics is the experimental way.

In particular, the experimental program cannot be limited to the formulation of suitable experiments that are feasible in currently available laboratories, and implies much more profound issues.

At this point, the fellow taxpayer is encouraged to meditate a moment on the fact that contemporary physical experiments no longer have the dials for visual measurements used up to the early part of this century. Today, a particle experiment is run, in its physical part, say, in an underground tunnel in Illinois; the information is fed into a computer, say, in Long Island; and the elaboration of the data is conducted, say, by a team in Berkeley, Cambridge and Paris.

Thus, the experimental program needed to achieve the future resolution of the validity or invalidity of Einstein's ideas is per se, highly complex and diversified, as well as deeply dependent on the preceding theoretical and mathematical research.

First, there is the need to formulate direct experiments on

the exact or approximate validity of the special relativity under strong interactions [Section 1.1]. By recalling that virtually all contemporary measures in particle physics are done via external electromagnetic interactions, one can see the need of a new generation of experiments, those capable of achieving direct measures under external strong interactions.

But this is not all. The experimental data are today elaborated via the use of theoretical tools that, in general, are dependent on Einstein's ideas in a truly essential way, as it is typically the case for contemporary high energy scattering experiments. It is then evident that the "experimental results" cannot be claimed as providing final evidence on the basic assumptions. In fact, if these assumptions are changed or modified, the numbers expressing the "experimental results" change, as already shown in the technical literature [See, later on, Section 1.7]. Jointly with the formulation of new, direct experiments, there is therefore the need to re—examine the very ways in which experiments are conducted these days and the "experimental results" claimed.

In conclusion, the research on the assessment of Einstein's ideas soon becomes so technically involved on all fronts, to be not only beyond this presentation for the general public, but also beyond professional physicists and mathematicians without a specific expertise in the field.

The need for a strict definition of experts in the problem of the validity or invalidity of Einstein's ideas.

In closing this section, permit me to warn the fellow taxpayer against false experts, no matter how renowned their academic affiliations are, whenever facing judgments on the scientific topic of this book.

Recall that "experts" in a given physical or mathematical field are individuals who have published in refereed journals at least a few papers, specifically, in the field considered. Thus, to qualify as "experts" on the possible insufficiencies of Einstein's ideas, physicists and mathematicians must have published at least some papers in the field considered.

If a guy has published even a large number of papers on Einstein's ideas, but without a mention of their expected insufficiencies and limitations, that guy does not qualify as "expert" in the topic of this chapter.

Besides, if a guy has published several papers on the validity of Einstein's ideas, he/she has manifest, vested, interests in their validity. As such, that guy is the very least qualified for expressing objective judgments on the limitations of the ideas.

The need to insist in requiring proofs of qualifications to

all physicists expressing judgment in the field.

At the risk of being pedantic and repetitive on this impoi c-
ant point, I must urge the fellow taxpayer most warmly to ask
the documentation of qualification of expertise to anybody expressing judgment on the topics of this chapter that is, to ask not
only the references to published articles, but most importantly,
the indication of the specific passages where the expected limitations of Einstein's ideas are explicitly presented and analyzed.
Lacking these latter essential elements of qualification, judgments may well be a powdery mask for inepts, no matter how
high the scholar is on the academic ladder.

It is hoped that the fellow taxpayer can acquire in this way
the necessary elements to distinguish between ethically and scientifically sound scientists, who generally express cautious views,
and dishonest academic barons, who usually venture judgments
because of academic—financial—ethnic motivations, without any
documented expertise in the field, and in total disrespect of the
pursuit of novel scientific knowledge.

1.3: THE AGING OF GALILEI'S RELATIVITY IN CLASSI-CAL MECHANICS

As a result of a scientific process initiated with Galilei's
Dialogus de Systemate Mundi of 1638 [4] and then continued
by Newton [5] and other founders of contemporary science, we
have reached the rather sophisticated, current formulation of
Galilei's relativity in classical, Newtonian, mechanics (see, for
instance, ref.s [6,7]). Nevertheless, the ultimate physical foundations remain those of centuries ago, the description of the
dynamical evolution of massive points.

**An arena of unequivocal applicability of Galilei's re-
lativity in classical mechanics.**

In fact, Galilei's relativity describes systems of particles
which

1) can be effectively approximated as being point—
    like (that is, without space dimension);

2) move in vacuum (empty space) assumed to be
    homogeneous and isotropic; and

3) are such that relativistic, gravitational, and quantum mechanical effects are ignorable (that is, the speeds are much smaller than that of light; the space has null curvature; and the masses of the objects are such to render ignorable effects due to their individual particle constituents).

An illustration of the physical arena of applicability of Galilei's relativity is given by our solar system in Newtonian approximation, in which the sun, our earth and all planets and satellites are approximated as massive points (see Figure 1.3.1).

GALILEAN SYSTEMS

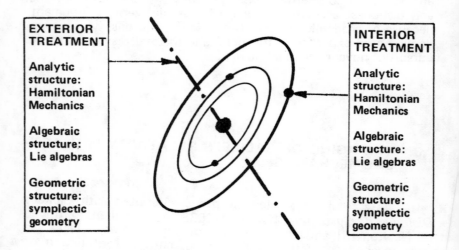

EXTERIOR
TREATMENT

Analytic
structure:
Hamiltonian
Mechanics

Algebraic
structure:
Lie algebras

Geometric
structure:
symplectic
geometry

INTERIOR
TREATMENT

Analytic
structure:
Hamiltonian
Mechanics

Algebraic
structure:
Lie algebras

Geometric
structure:
symplectic
geometry

Figure 1.3.1. A schematic view of a system characterized by Galilei's relativity, the solar system in Newtonian approximation which verifies conditions 1), 2) and 3) of the text. The relativity describes not only the center—of—mass of the solar system in its evolution within our galaxy, but also the dynamical evolution of each constituent. The description is achieved via the form invariance of the equations of motion under the so—called Galilean transformations in Euclidean three—dimensional space and time. They are the largest possible set of linear transformations interconnecting inertial reference systems, that is, observers not experiencing accelerations or any external force. The Galilean invariance of the equations of motion leads to ten conservation laws, those of the energy (one), of the total linear momentum (three), of the total angular momentum (three) and the uniform motion of the center—of—mass (three). In this way, physical conservation laws are reduced to primitive, abstract, mathematical laws of invariance under the (Lie) group of Galilean transformations, by achieving a symbiotic reduction of three underlying methodological tools: Hamiltonian mechanics, Lie's theory, and the symplectic geometry.

An arena of inapplicability of Galilei's relativity.

The physical arena characterized by conditions 1), 2) and 3) above also identifies the limitations of the relativity. In façt, Galilei's relativity is unable to provide meaningful treatments of systems of particles which

1')   cannot be effectively approximated as being point— like;

2')   move in a physical medium (gas, liquids, etc.); and

3')   are such that relativistic, gravitational and quantum mechanical effects are ignorable as in 3).

A typical example is given by a satellite during re—entry. As well known, when the satellite orbits around earth in empty space, its actual size and shape do not affect the dynamical evolution. As a result, the satellite can be effectively approximated as a massive point concentrated in the center—of—mass. Galilei's relativity then strictly applies.

However, when the same satellite penetrates the Earth's atmosphere, its actual size and shape affect the dynamical evolution directly. Under these conditions, the satellite cannot any longer be approximated as a massive point and Galilei's relativity becomes inapplicable. In fact, insistence on its applicability would lead to "perpetual motion" types of academic abstractions (such as the orbiting of the satellite within our earth's atmosphere with a conserved angular momentum and consequential lack of decaying of the orbit).

The mathematical roots of the inapplicability.

At a deeper analysis, the insufficiencies originate at the mathematical foundations of the relativity, that is, the analytic, algebraic and geometric methods in their so—called canonical realization. In fact, condition 1) essentially implies a local— differential geometry, that is, a geometry characterizing ordinary differential equations, which are the equations of motion of the centers—of—masses. On the contrary, condition 1') calls for a suitable nonlocal/integral geometry, that is, a geometry yet to be constructed by pure mathematicians (beginning from its topology), which characterizes equations of motion involving not only ordinary local terms for the centers—of—masses, but also integral terms computed on the surface—shape and/or volume of the objects.

A fully similar situation occurs in the transition from condition 2) to 2'). In fact, empty space can be safely assumed (for all Newtonian approximations) as being homogeneous and isotropic, while the Newtonian time, with its immutable character is evidently isotropic (again, at the Newtonian approximation). It is known that these conditions imply Galilei's relativity. In fact, the homogeneity and isotropy of space imply the exact character of the central part of the Galilei as well as of all relativities, the symmetry under rotations and translations in space. The isotropy of time implies the symmetry under translations in time. Additional technical steps imply the symmetry under the remaining component of the Galilean transformations the so—called velocity transformations (for technical details, one can consult, for instance, ref.s [6,7]). In turn, these symmetries imply the ten celebrated Galilean conservation laws (Figure 1.3.1).

In the transition to condition 2'), motion in physical media, the situation becomes profoundly different. In fact, as everybody knows, physical media such as our atmosphere are not homogeneous or isotropic. This implies the manifest breaking of the symmetry under rotations which, in turn, is a necessary condition for a representation of the decay of the satellite's orbit, that is, for the nonconservation of the angular momentum. Technical arguments then imply the breaking of the entire relativity [10].

In conclusion, conditions 1') and 2') complement each other into the same results, the inapplicability of Galilei's relativity for the broader physical conditions considered, with the consequential need for a suitable generalization.

The process of closing a nonconservative system into an isolated system inclusive of its environment.

The analysis cannot be halted at the level of the satellite. In fact, we must complement the nonconservative satellite with its environment, which has absorbed in various forms its loss of energy, in such a way to reach a closed system, that is, a system whose total energy is conserved. The issue is whether during this process we recover Galilei's relativity, in which case its loss at the constituent level would be of lesser significance.

Inspection of nature soon reveals that in the process of closing a nonconservative system into a broader conservative form inclusive of its environment, the ten total conservation laws for the center—of—mass are recovered, but Galilei's relativity remains inapplicable.

The understanding of this occurrence can be reached by comparing a Galilean system, such as our solar system, with a non—Galilean one, such as our earth, we considered as isolated from the rest of the universe to achieve closure.

In the case of the solar system, the validity of Galilei's relativity originates at the level of its planetary constituent

(Figure 1.3.1). The validity of the relativity for the system as a whole is then consequential.

In the case of our Earth, Galilei's relativity is inapplicable to its constituents, such as a satellite during re—entry, and such inapplicability persists in the transition to the earth as a whole, trivially, because the inapplicability is unaffected by our shifting the observation from the satellite to the center—of—mass motion of the entire earth.

Dynamical origin of the breaking of Galilei's relativity: the contact/nonpotential/nonlocal forces.

Nature therefore indicates, quite forcefully, that the validity of total conservation laws of an isolated system, by no means, necessarily implies the exact validity of Galilei's relativity (as erroneous stated or implied in a number of contemporary books of theoretical physics), because the same laws are admitted also by systems which are intrinsically non—Galilean.

We reach in this nontechnical way the ultimate dynamical foundations of the problem, the nature of the acting forces (or interactions). It is generally assumed that total conservation laws occur because the internal forces are of the so—called conservative type, that is, of action—at—a—distance type derivable from a potential energy. A typical example of a conservative force is the gravitational force responsible of the solar system (in Newtonian approximation).

Non—Galilean systems such as our earth admit instead internal forces that are conceptually, physically and mathematically more general than those of the solar system. They are called of contact type to express the actual, physical, contact among extended objects (these forces are evidently absent for point—like, Galilean particles, trivially, because they have no dimension in space and, thus, they cannot have contact effects). Second, the forces are called of nonpotential type. In fact, the notion of potential energy has no physical basis for them, because of the lack of distance which is essential to define it. Finally, the forces are called of nonlocal type, to express the fact that they do not occur at a point, but rather at a surface or volume, exactly as it is the case for the satellite during re—entry. As a result, the forces are called of contact/nonpotential/nonlocal type [10, 12] or of follower type, particularly in engineering [13]. At a deeper analysis, the forces are also of non—Hamiltonian type, in the sense that they violate the conditions for the applicability of the entire mechanics at the foundation of Galilei's relativity, Hamiltonian mechanics [9].

Once the nature of the forces acting on the satellite during re—entry is understood, the inability to recover Galilei's relativity in the closure of the system into a conservative form is consequential. In fact, our shifting of the observation from the open—nonconservative satellite to the closed system constituted by the entire earth, leaves the nature of the forces unaffected: the forces are of non—Galilean type prior to closure and remain of non—Galilean type after closure of the system.

The identification of the nature of the acting forces also permits the understanding that the inapplicability of Galilei's relativity originates at the mathematical foundation of the theory. In fact, not only the equations of motion are noninvariant under Galilei's transformations, but the underlying mathematical structures are inapplicable. I am referring here to the inapplicability not only of Hamiltonian mechanics, but more specifically of the Lie algebras and of the symplectic geometry (Figure 1.3.1).

The fundamental notion of closed non—Hamiltonian systems as forcefully established by nature.

We reach in this way a notion which is at the foundation of the studies presented in this chapter, from the Newtonian, to the quantum mechanical ones. I am referring to "closed/non—Hamiltonian systems", that is, systems which, when seen from the outside, verify all conventional conservation laws of total quantities, but their structural equations are of non—Galilean type.

The systems were identified, apparently for the first time, in memoir [14] and then studied by a number of authors (see, e.g., ref. [15]). For a review, the reader may consult monograph [10].

The approximation of the integral forces via power series in the velocities permits the regaining of the locality of the theory, that is, its definition at a set of isolated points. But the Galilean noninvariance as well as the general non—Hamiltonian character persist , all in a way compatible with conventional total conservation laws. This local approximation is also useful to illustrate the mathematical consistency of the theory via readily solvable equations (see Figure 1.3.2 for more details).

Generalization of Galilei's relativity for closed non—Hamiltonian systems.

As a result of a considerable number of contributions in mechanics, algebras and geometries beginning from the past century, a generalization of Galilei's relativity for closed non—Hamiltonian systems has been submitted in ref. [8] , and worked out in monographs [9, 10, 11, 12] .

The generalized relativity consists of two formulations. The first (tentatively called "Galilei—isotopic relativity" for cer-

NONGALILEAN SYSTEMS

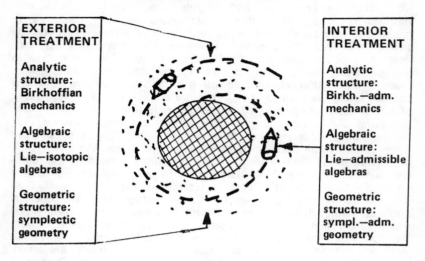

EXTERIOR TREATMENT		INTERIOR TREATMENT
Analytic structure: Birkhoffian mechanics		Analytic structure: Birkh.–adm. mechanics
Algebraic structure: Lie–isotopic algebras		Algebraic structure: Lie–admissible algebras
Geometric structure: symplectic geometry		Geometric structure: sympl.–adm. geometry

Figure 1.3.2. A schematic view of systems, called closed/non–Hamiltonian, which are outside the technical capability of Galilei's relativity. They are given by systems such as our Earth which, when considered as isolated, verify all total conservation laws of the conventional Galilei's relativity (Figure 1.3.1), but the internal forces violate the conditions for the applicability of the mathematical foundations of the relativity (analytic mechanics, Lie algebras and symplectic geometry in canonical realizations). While Galilei's relativity can treat only systems that are of local and potential nature, the internal forces of non–Galilean systems such as our Earth are of nonlocal/integral and of non–potential/noncanonical/non–Hamiltonian type due to motion of extended objects (such as satellites) moving within material media (such as our atmosphere). The consistency of our mathematical description of closed non–Hamiltonian systems is readily established [10, p. 235]. In fact, the conventional, total conservation laws imply only seven conditions on the internal forces, thus permitting multiple infinities of consistent, non–Hamiltonian equations of motion. Two generalizations of Galilei's relativities have been submitted in ref.s [8, 9, 10, 11, 12] for closed/non–Hamiltonian systems under the approximation of nonlocal internal forces via power series in the velocities, in which case locality is regained, but the nonpotential/non–Hamiltonian character persists. The first generalized relativity (called Galilei–isotopic) is conceived for the exterior treatment [9, 10], while the second (called Galilei–admissible) is conceived for the complementary interior treatment of open–nonconservative constituents [8, 11, 12]. Both generalized relativities are based on the central idea of all relativities, the identification of symmetries for the invariant descriptions of the equations of motion. Nevertheless, the objectives are different for the exterior and the interior case. In the former, the symmetry is used to characterize total conservation laws under non–Hamiltonian internal forces, while in the latter, the symmetry is used to characterize time–

rate–of–variations of physical quantities, the systems being nonconservative by conception. Rather profound conceptual differences also exist between the conventional and the generalized relativities. In the conventional relativity, one assumes the underlying symmetry, Galilei's symmetry, and restricts the systems to verify such symmetry. This attitude generally results in the exclusion of systems of the physical reality, inasmuch as only very few Newtonian systems verify Galilei's relativity. In the generalized Galilei–isotopic relativity, the attitude is reversed, inasmuch as one first assumes the equations of motion in their most general possible form, and then seeks its symmetry according to a method called of Lie–isotopy which is based on the generalization of the unit of Galilei's symmetry, while leaving all other aspects unchanged (see ref. [10] for the general lines and the subsequent ref.s [18, 19] for the detailed techniques). While Galilei's transformations are unique, there exist multiple infinities of Galilei–isotopic transformations because of the multiple infinities of contact/non–Hamiltonian forces (which are represented by the multiple infinities of possible generalized units). Also, while Galilei's transformations are linear, the Galilei–isotopic ones are generally nonlinear (although expressible in a formally linear, isotopic, form which suggested the name of Galilei–isotopic relativity). Finally, while Galilei's transformations connect inertial frames, the Galilei–isotopic transformations connect noninertial frames (recall that inertial frames are a conceptual abstraction and do not exist in the physical world). Despite all these and additional differences, Galilei's and Galilei–isotopic relativities coincide at the level of abstract, coordinate–free, algebraic–geometric formulations, by therefore resulting to be characterized by different realizations of the same abstract mathematical structure. This latter property is truly fundamental for the studies presented in this chapter. In fact, the same situation will be found at the relativistic and quantum mechanical levels.

---

tain technical reasons) is conceived for the exterior treatment, in which case the emphasis is on the achievement of conventional, total, conservation laws under non–Galilean internal forces [9, 10].

The second formulation (tentatively called Galilei–admissible relativity) is conceived for the complementary interior treatment of each constituent, such as a satellite during re–entry. In the latter case, the emphasis is in the maximal possible time–rate–of–variations of physical quantities under the most general possible external forces [11, 12].

The underlying generalizations of Hamiltonian mechanics.

The generalizations were permitted by the previous construction of two complementary generalizations of Hamiltonian mechanics for closed and open systems, called Birkhoffian and Birkhoffian–admissible mechanics for certain historical reasons related to ref. [16]. In turn, the two mechanics were permitted by two, progressive generalizations of Lie's theory, the first of the Lie–isotopic type and the second of the more general Lie–

admissible type. The underlying geometry in the former case resulted to be of conventional symplectic type [17], although realized in its most general possible form, while that of the latter case (called symplectic-admissible) is under investigation. Both generalized mechanics verify the so–called theorems of direct universality, that is, the capability of representing all Newtonian systems considered (universality) in the frame of the experimentalist (direct universality). By comparison, Hamiltonian mechanics is capable of representing in the frame of the observer only a rather small class of Newtonian system.

Also, both the Birkhoffian [10] and the Birkhoffian–admissible mechanics [12] preserve their structure under the most general possible transformations. By comparison, Hamiltonian mechanics preserves its structure only under a special class of transformations (called canonical). In particular, the Birkhoffian–admissible mechanics is a covering of the Birkhoffian mechanics which, in turn, is a covering of the Hamiltonian one.

Status of the studies.

Despite these advances, I must stress that, by no means, the studies are final. In fact, despite the number of independent contributions in several theoretical and mathematical aspects, the studies are essentially at the beginning. Nevertheless, we can claim today:

a) the unequivocal existence in our classical, macroscopic reality of closed–isolated systems whose internal dynamics is beyond Galilei's relativity (such as our Earth);

b) the consistency of our nonlocal mathematical representations as well as of their local approximation via power series in the velocities; and

c) the expectation of the consequential existence of suitable generalizations of Galilei's relativity, for which the generalized relativities submitted in ref.s [8, 9, 10, 11, 12] may be useful working grounds.

Independence of the proposed generalizations of Galilei's relativity from those worked out by Einstein.

Note that the proposed generalizations of Galilei's relativity are basically independent from those worked out by Einstein. In fact, the former generalizations are characterized by structurally broader forces, while the latter generalizations are characterized by other physical rules, such as relativistic speeds or curvature. This independence has been implied in the preceding analysis by keeping conditions 3) unaltered.

The independence of the generalizations of Galilei's relativity under consideration from the Einsteinian ones is evidently of utmost importance. In fact, it opens up a new, virtually endless, scientific horizon for potentially fundamental, novel advancements (Figure 1.3.3). At the same time, the independence is at the foundation of the limitations of Einstein's ideas, as we shall see.

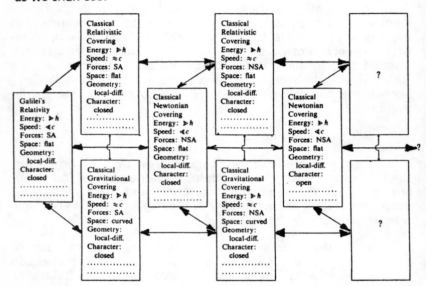

Figure 1.3.3. A reproduction of the figure of page 250 of ref. [10] illustrating the absence in physics of terminal theories. The first column depicts the conventional Galilei's relativity in Newtonian mechanics where: $\hbar$ is Planck's constant; c is the speed of light; and SA stands for selfadjointness, that is, the verification of the conditions for the forces to be of potential type [8]. The second column depicts the generalizations of Galilei's relativity proposed by Einstein's. As well known, the generalizations were intended to admit relativistic effects due to speed and gravitational effects due to curvature of space, but not more general forces. The relativity of the third column is the first conceived for the treatment of systems which are still purely Newtonian, yet of non–Galilean and non–Einsteinian type because of structurally more general forces of nonselfadjoint (NSA) type, that is, of contact/nonpotential type, as incontrovertibly established in the physical reality. In turn, the mere plausibility of the generalization of the third column implies the expectation of relativistic and gravitational generalizations of Einstein's relativities depicted in the fourth column, with additional chains of generalizations in sight. We can therefore conclude by saying that the lack of terminal character of Einstein's ideas can be identified in a rather forceful way via the mere inspection of the Newtonian reality of our environment.

Some, rather frequent, dishonest comments intended to suppress the need for suitable non—Einsteinian generalizations of Galilei's relativity.

I would like to close this section by providing the fellow taxpayer with some elements of judgment to identify dishonest academic postures in regard to the research reviewed in this section.

The fact that Galilei's relativity is violated in the classical physical reality of our environment is an absolutely incontrovertible fact. The relativity necessarily implies the conservation of the energy and other physical quantities. The insistence on its validity would imply the existence of the perpetual motion in our environment. Again, the proposed generalized relativities are conjectural, tentative and yet incomplete. But the insufficiency of Galilei's relativity for the description of our Newtonian environment is absolutely out of the question.

Whenever confronted with this reality, and with efforts in attempting generalizations, dishonest academicians generally venture rather incredible (at times hysterical) mumbo jumbo talks.

The most plausible reason why these academicians dismiss the violation of Galilei's relativity in our environment is due to the fact that such violation implies a corresponding violation of Einstein's special relativity (Section 1.4), as well as some irreconcilable inconsistencies of Einstein's general relativity (Section 1.5).

These occurrences must be expected from the deep inter—connections and mutual compatibilities among the Galilean, the special, and the general relativities (Section 1.2).

The purpose of this book is to stimulate the taxpayer to initiate actions aimed at an improvement of ethics in physics, and of accountability in the use of public funds.

Along these lines, it is important that the taxpayer is informed in more details of the arguments by which academic barons attempt to suppress the invalidity of Galilei's relativity in Newtonian mechanics.

Approach an academician with documented record of vested interests in Einstein's ideas. Present the equations of motion of any system of our environment, such as the damped pendulum, the damped giroscope, etc. All these equations violate Galilei's relativity in a manifest way (see ref. [10], pp. 344—348 for a treatment and classification). Ask them to reconcile this reality with the validity of Galilei's relativity.

One answer I have heard countless times is that the violation is "apparent" (sic), in the sense that if the equations are subjected to an appropriate transformation, the validity of Galilei's relativity is regained.

Fellow taxpayer, do not be blinded by this type of academic talk with a mask of technical vest. You are the observer watching the decay of the pendulum (that is, the NON—conservation of its energy) or the decay of the gyroscope (that is, the NON—conservation of its angular momentum). Any relativity, to be applicable, must hold in the frame of the observer, that is, in your frame, and not in another hypothetical frame. At any rate, explicit calculations are possible (and I have done them, see ref. [10], p. 246) to prove that, in general, the transformed frame in which Galilei's symmetry might be recovered is generally nonrealizable with experiments because it would imply accelerating all your laboratory equipments into a logaritmic orbit spiraling throughout the Milky Way!

In short, when academic barons suggest you to change reference frame to regain Galilei's relativity, chances are that the guys are asking you to sail with your equipment throughout our galaxy so that they can protect vested academic—financial—ethnic interests.

Another mumbo—jumbo comment I have heard countless times, is that the forces causing the breaking of Galilei's relativity are themselves "apparent" (sic!), because, the argument goes, when the systems considered (damped pendulum, damped gyroscope, satellite during re—entry, etc.) are reduced to their elementary particle constituents, the potentiality of the force is regained in full, and so is the strict validity of Galilei's relativity.

This second argument is much more dishonest than the former, in my view, for numerous reasons.

First, you have presented the academician ONE single equation describing very well the decaying of the angular momentum of the gyroscope, etc. With the argument above, the academic baron is essentially telling you that this is wrong. What you should do instead is to replace your single equation with multi—gillions of many different equations for all the elementary constituents of your system. You do not need a Ph. D. in theoretical physics to see that, while you could compute numbers with the original, single, Galilei—non—invariant equation, you have lost all computational capability whenever you (try to) replace it with a very large number of different equations.

In short, chances are that the academic baron is asking you to renounce all your computational capability in engineering, so that he/she can serve vested academic—financial—ethnic interests. And, do not forget, fellow taxpayer, that any physicist proposing this is fully aware of the implications. It is all done in full consciousness!

But this is only the beginning of the story. The argument of reducing Newtonian systems to elementary constituents in the hope of regaining conventional relativities is plagued by so many technical inconsistencies to truly render it dishonest, particularly when ventured verbally, without the backing of published papers.

Regrettably, this general presentation is not conducive to technical treatments. Nevertheless, permit me to recall that the forces experienced by the damped oscillator, by the damped gyroscope, by the decaying satellite, etc., are of generally non—Hamiltonian and non—canonical type. This implies that the time evolutions of the systems are generally of noncanonical type. Now the description of the elementary constituents demands quantum mechanics (Section 1.6) and, for any conventional relativity to hold, the time evolutions must be of the so—called unitary type.

The technical inconsistency under consideration here is that a classical noncanonical time evolution cannot be reduced to a collection of unitary ones, no matter how many you have of them. In fact, at the classical limit of the quantum description, unitary laws will always recover potential forces, and you will never be able to recover the true, actual, real NON—potential/NON—Hamiltonian force of your system.

These things are taught in undergraduate studies of physics and, as such, are well known, and otherwise must be assumed as known by anybody venturing judgments on the "apparent" character of the invalidation of Galilei's relativity in our environment. It is their widespread knowledge that renders unavoidable the raising of ethical issues.

Recommendation to the taxpayer of asking for suitable qualifications by scholars dismissing the limitations of Einstein's relativity.

My first suggestion to the fellow taxpayer is the following. Whenever academicians dismiss or otherwise minimize the invalidation of Galilei's relativity in our reality, the fellow taxpayer should ask for their curriculum and see the papers and books published by the guys. If these papers are heavily dependent on Einstein's ideas, the most probable reasons for the attitude is the protection of vested, academic—financial—ethnic interests, in disrespect of the pursuit of new scientific knowledge.

My second suggestion is the following. Whenever an academic baron tells you that your classical, non—potential, non—Galilean systems can be reduced to a large collection of potential Galilean, elementary, constituents, ask reference to proofs of consistency of the reduction printed in refereed articles. If the baron does not provide such evidence, his dishonesty is established beyond a reasonable doubt. The guy is quite likely acting to protect vested interests.

My list of inconsistencies in the (sometimes frantic) attempts by corrupt academicians to retain old ideas at any cost, could go on and on, but I do not want to bore you.

The story of governmental pressures on NASA regarding the prediction of the location of impact of Skylab during its re–entry.

The following story may be quite instructive. I have heard it in academic corridors, and I do not know whether it is true or false. The story is related to the re–entry of Skylab on Earth of a few years ago. Recall that, during the last days prior to impact, NASA did not know where the station would fall. NASA merely knew a strip several hundred miles wide around the entire Earth in which the impact would occur. But the Kremlin was well within such a strip and, thus, it was within the area of impact.

Owing to this occurrence, high governmental officers exercised pressures on NASA scientists to have them sharpen their prediction and calculate more precisely where Skylab would indeed fall.

Whether this is true or not, the press coverage of the episode documented quite well that NASA was indeed under severe pressures to predict the point of impact, and that every possibility was indeed attempted. Now, NASA had at its disposal the best possible scientists, the most powerful computers and the most elaborate sensors on board Skylab that kept sending down, up to the last hours, all sort of data on pressure, temperature, density, etc.

As well known, despite these massive means, NASA was unable to predict the point of impact during the last days of re–entry of Skylab.

As a result, the story goes, pressures on NASA scientists grew and grew by the hour to predict the location of impact. At one point, a high governmental officer urged a NASA scientist at the Johnson Space Center in Texas to call in academician experts in relativities, at which, so the story goes, the NASA scientist promptly replied:

"If a professor comes here with his relativities, he will be chased out of NASA's premises."

The appraisal of our current knowledge provided by the re–entry of Skylab.

The story, whether true or only imagined, is very instructive. Relativities provide the ultimate characterization of dynamics. The governmental officer was therefore well informed of physics, and the recommendation to call in experts in relativities was therefore fully sound. But the reply by the NASA scientist was equally sound.

While orbiting in empty space, Skylab was a true Galilean system. In fact, its shape and dimension did not affect its dynamical evolution. Under these conditions, Galilei's vision was correct: Skylab could be well approximated as a massive point. The applicability of Galilei's relativity was consequential. This implied the capability of predicting with extreme accuracy the location of Skylab in empty space and in time.

But, once within Earth's atmosphere, Skylab was no longer a Galilean system because the actual size, shape and structure of the station affected directly the re—entry trajectory. This means that Skylab was experiencing contact forces of nonlocal/integral type inasmuch as they were generated at its entire surface. A system of this type is fundamentally outside the technical capability of Galilei's relativity, as well as of Einstein's special relativity, and Einstein's general relativity, as we shall see. In fact, the strict applicability of these relativities would have implied the conservation of the angular momentum, that is, according to the professor, Skylab would have continued to orbit indefinitely within our atmosphere!

This is the reason why the NASA officer would have chased the professor out of NASA's premises. All his/her voluminous books on Einstein's relativities, not only would have been useless, but would have implied ridiculous consequences.

In short, we have reached, today, an extremely advanced knowledge on systems verifying conditions 1), 2) and 3) at the beginning of this section (point—particles moving in empty space). NASA's exploration of the solar system proves that such knowledge permits predictions of extremely high accuracy. Nevertheless, we have virtually no knowledge on the more general systems 1'), 2') and 3'), i.e., for extended objects moving within a resistive medium.

Preliminary elements on the opposition by S. Coleman, S. Glashow, S. Weinberg and other senior scientists of Harvard University against non—Einsteinian generalizations of Galilei's relativity.

In 1977, I was visiting the Department of Physics at Harvard University for the purpose of studying precisely non—Galilean systems. My task was to attempt the generalization of the analytic, algebraic and geometric methods of the Galilean systems into forms suitable for the non—Galilean ones.

The studies began under the best possible auspices. In fact, I had a (signed) contract with one of the world's leading editorial houses in physics, Springer—Verlag of Heidelberg, West Germany, to write a series of monographs in the field (that were later published in ref.s [9] and [10]. Furthermore, I was the recipient of a research contract with the U. S. Department of Energy, contract number ER–78–S–02–4720.A000, for the conduction of these studies.

Sidney Coleman, Shelly Glashow, Steven Weinberg, and other senior physicists at Harvard opposed my studies to such a point of preventing my drawing a salary from my own grant for almost one academic year.

This prohibition to draw my salary from my grant was perpetrated with full awareness of the fact that it would have created hardship on my children and on my family. In fact, I had communicated to them (in writing) that I had no other income, and that I had two children in tender age and my wife (then a graduate student in social work) to feed and shelter.

After almost one academic year of delaying my salary authorization, when the case was just about to explode in law suits, I finally renceived authorization to draw my salary from my own grant as a member of the Department of Mathematics of Harvard University.

But, Sidney Coleman, Shelly Glashow and Steven Weinberg and possibly others had declared to the Department of Mathematics that my studies "had no physical value". This created predictable problems in the mathematics department which lead to the subsequent, apparently intended, impossibility of continuing my research at Harvard.

Even after my leaving Harvard, their claim of "no physical value" of my studies persisted, affected a number of other scientists, and finally rendered unavoidable the writing of IL GRANDE GRIDO.*

The details of the story are presented in Section 2.1, while the documentation is available from the publisher of this book. In this way, the taxpayer will be provided with all the necessary elements to decide on his/her own whether S. Coleman, S. Glashow, S. Weinberg and other officers of Harvard University acted in good faith, or their actions were intended to protect vested, academic–financial–ethnic interests in disrespect of their scientific accountability in the use of public funds.

---

*S. Glashow and S. Weinberg obtained the Nobel Prize in physics in 1979 on theories, the so–called unified gauge theories, that are crucially dependent on Einstein's special relativity; subsequently, S. Weinberg left Harvard for The University of Texas at Austin, while S. Coleman and S. Glashow are still members of Harvard University to this writing.

1.4: THE AGING OF EINSTEIN'S SPECIAL RELATIVITY IN CLASSICAL MECHANICS.

The lack in physics of terminal theories.

Physics is a science that will never admit terminal theories. No matter how valid Einstein's ideas are for contemporary physics, generalized theories will one day be constructed for physical conditions broader than those currently known. It is only a matter of time. It is evident that, the sooner these generalizations are constructed, the better for the advancement of human knowledge. It is also evident that such generalizations will not be constructed overnight. As history of physics teaches, the generalizations will be the result of a long scientific process of trials and errors, presentation of plausible ideas, and their critical examination by independent researchers. Therefore, the sooner the scientific process is initiated, the better.

These facts are well known. They are demanded by scientific ethics as well as the need for scientific accountability vis—a—vis the taxpayer supporting the research. In fact, today we could be using the special relativity under physical conditions for which it is fundamentally insufficient, with consequential waste of public money.

The reality of the situation in U. S. physics departments and research institutions could not be more removed from the above ethical guidelines.

Vested, academic—financial—ethnic interests on Einstein's ideas.

To understand the ethical status in the field, one must recall that Albert Einstein has been the biggest dispenser of academic chairs in the history of physics, of course, not personally, but via his ideas. This has created immense ethnic, financial and academic interests that will be manifestly damaged by any generalized theory. Even the consideration of the limitations of the special relativity, let alone open studies on its generalization, are damaging to vested interests.

This book is intended to be a documentation of the rather extreme, at times hysterical oppositions, obstructions, interferences, manipulations, and shear dishonest actions I have personally experienced in the U. S. physics community while attempting to conduct a critical examination of the limitations of Einstein's ideas and their possible generalizations.

The understanding is that I am not alone. In fact, the methods of suppression at birth of undesired advances in physical knowledge appear to be practiced across all segments of the physics community, from the assignment of jobs, to the publication of papers, and to funding of research programs.

By publishing this book, I also hope that other colleagues with similar experiences will come out and expose specific names to the societal judgment. In fact, dishonesty feeds on silence, which, as such, is complicity.

This book is solely dedicated to the presentation of my own experience. I shall be silent on the experience by others known to me. In fact, it is up to them to speak out and identify seemingly dishonest academic barons operating under public financial support.

But, let us proceed in an orderly fashion. To judge whether or not dishonesty does indeed exist in U. S. basic research, it is essential to know first the scientific profile. Only then, individual actions and reactions can be properly appraised.

Outline of the status of our knowledge on the special relativity.

To put it in a nutshell, the current state of the art of our knowledge in regard to the special relativity in classical mechanics is the following:

A)   A physical arena of unequivocal validity of the relativity is solidly established;

B)   Broader physical conditions of insufficiency of the special (as well as general) relativity have been identified;

C)   Studies on the generalizations of the special relativity for the broader physical conditions considered have already been initiated by a number of independent scholars, with particular reference to the generalization of the underlying mathematical tools (mechanics, algebras and geometries). The understanding is that the currently available generalizations are tentative. Nevertheless, they constitute valid working grounds for interested young minds of all ages.

In short, we are at the beginning of the scientific process indicated earlier. The fellow taxpayer should keep in mind that the studies under consideration in this section, being classical, constitute only half of the needed studies, the remaining half being the quantum mechanical ones (see Section 1.6). In turn, the ultimate experimental resolution of the problem is expected to occur precisely within a quantum mechanical setting.

Nevertheless, the classical studies remain essential for any meaningful scientific program and, for this reason, they are simply unavoidable. At any rate, classical studies constitute an excellent introduction to the much more advanced and abstract issues in particle physics.

An arena of unequivocal validity of the special relativity in classical mechanics.

The historical contributions by Lorentz [22], Poincaré [23], Einstein [24], and others that were termed "Einstein's special relativity" identified quite clearly the physical conditions of conception and validity of the relativity. These conditions were reproduced in the early treateses in the topic, such as that by Bergmann [25] (see the title of Chapter VI). Regrettably, the same conditions were subsequently suppressed in more recent treateses, such as those by Weinberg [26], Misner, Thorne and Wheeler [27], or the more recent book by Pais [28]. In this way, the special relativity has acquired the character of universal applicability that is tacitly implied in contemporary presentations.

When interested in the limitations of the special relativity, young minds of any age are therefore urged to consult the original contributions of the builders of the theory, rather than the contributions of their followers.

Stated in a way as simple as possible, the special relativity is incontrovertibly valid for systems of particles verifying the following conditions:

I)   The particles can be well approximated as being point—like;

II)   The particles move in empty space assumed as homogeneous and isotropic; and

III) Gravitational and quantum mechanical effects are ignorable.

Thus, Conditions I) and II) remain exactly the same as Conditions 1) and 2) for the validity of Galilei's relativity (Section 1.3), while only Condition 3) is broadened into III) to permit speeds of the order of that of light. These occurrences should be expected. In fact, the preservation of Conditions 1) and 2) in the relativistic generalization of Galilei's relativity constitute the premises for the compatibility of the two relativities.

Conditions I) and II) are not merely conceptual, because they have deep technical implications. The point—like character of the particles permits the use of local geometries, algebras and topologies. The homogeneity and isotropy of empty space implies the validity of a central component of the special relativity, the rotational symmetry. The special relativity itself is finally reached from Conditions I) and II) via the imposition of the constancy of the speed of light in vacuum for all inertial observers.

The hystorical, fundamental role of Lorentz and Poincaré in the construction of the special relativity.

The special relativity is fundamentally dependent on transformations discovered by Lorentz [22] for the case without translations, and by Poincaré [23] for the more general case inclusive of translations. These transformations are today called Lorentz and Poincaré transformations.

There is no doubt that the mind who mastered the reduction of available knowledge into one, single, physical theory, the special relativity, was that of Einstein. Nevertheless, the appropriateness of the terms "Einstein's special relativity" have been repeatedly questioned throughout the years because of the fundamental value of the contributions by Lorentz and Poincaré.

For these reasons, a terminology more ethically appropriate I shall adopt hereon for scientific profiles is that of "Einstein—Lorentz—Poincaré relativity" (ELP—relativity) or "special relativity" for short. The terms "Einstein's special relativity" will be used in political parlance.

Once an arena of unequivocal applicability of the special relativity is known, the identification of broader physical conditions suggesting possible generalizations is consequential.

In the following, I shall consider first physical conditions broader than II). Conditions broader than I) will be considered subsequently.

The plausibility of small anisotropies of space.

Consider Condition II). Inspection of our macroscopic environment clearly supports the hypothesis of the homogeneity of empty space. However, the hypothesis of joint isotropy is not equally tenable. This is due to the fact that empty space is far from being "empty". It is in actuality a rather complex medium transmitting all electromagnetic interactions, as well as permitting the existence of elementary particles as some form of dynamical oscillation. As a result, a number of possibilities exist whereby homogeneity can be assumed as exact (for all practical purposes of our current knowledge), but isotropy is only approximate.

As an illustration, it is possible that the violent process of creation of the universal via the primordial explosion (called "big bang") may well have created an anisotropy along the direction of explosion, and that anisotropy is sufficiently small to have escaped current experimental observations until now.

Numerous additional arguments of plausibility of a sufficiently small anisotropy of space exist in the literature, but they are ignored here for brevity.

The generalization of the special relativity for homogeneous but anisotropic spaces by Bogoslovsky from the U.S.S.R.

If space is homogeneous but anisotropic, even in a very small amount, the Einstein—Lorentz—Poincaré relativity is invalid on strict scientific grounds. A suitable generalization would then be needed for systems of point—like particles moving in a homogeneous but anisotropic space.

Such a generalized relativity has already been constructed in 1977 by Bogoslovsky [29] in all essential elements. Very regrettably, these intriguing studies have been ignored in the virtual totality of the contemporary physical literature.*

The generalization of ref.s [29] is technically based on the replacement of the space underlying the special relativity, the Minkowski space, with the more general Finsler spaces (see, for instance, ref. [30]) which are precisely capable of representing homogeneous but anisotropic media. The generalized relativity then follows by imposing the constancy of the velocity of propagation of light. This leads to a generalization of the fundamental transformations by Lorentz and Poincaré.

The notion of covering theory.

Recall that a physical theory is a "covering" of another one when: (a) the former theory applies for physical conditions broader than those of the latter; (b) the former theory is based on mathematical tools structurally broader than those of the latter; and (c) the former theory contains the old one as a particular case.

The generalized relativity of ref.s [29] is a covering of the special relativity. In fact, it applies for broader physical conditions (anisotropic space); it is based on broader mathe-

---

*Owing to this silence, particularly in recent books and technical reviews, it is virtually impossible to identify other contributions in the problem, unless one spends years of library search. I would therefore gratefully appreciate the indication of any contribution, specifically devoted to the generalization of the special relativity, that preceded or followed the studies of ref.s [29]. I am referring to generalizations for point—like particles moving in a homogeneous but anisotropic medium, in which gravitational and quantum effects are ignorable. Attempts trying to render the special relativity compatible with a possible anisotropy of space are of no scientific relevance when compared to suitable generalizations.

matical tools (Finsler spaces); and it recovers the special relativity identically whenever the anisotropy is put equal to zero.

In the traditional style of physical advances, the relativity of ref.s [29] is dependent on the preceding work by Lorentz [22], Poincaré [23] and Einstein [24]. For this reason, I shall call the generalized relativity under consideration here the "Bogoslovsky—Einstein—Lorentz—Poincaré relativity", or B E L P —relativity for short.

Scientific implications of Bogoslovsky's studies.

The practical implications of the B E L P —relativity are quite intriguing indeed. in fact, the generalized relativity is consistent with most of the predictions of the special relativity. The primary deviations occur for speeds approaching that of light in vacuum. In fact, the predictions of the gerneralized and of the special relativities regarding the speed dependence of mass, time, length, etc. coincide up to sufficiently high values of speeds and then diverge.

The only possible scientific conclusion at this time is that the B E L P —relativity is mathematically consistent, plausible, and not disproved by available experimental evidence up to the very high speeds achieved in particle accelerators.

If the ELP—relativity is exactly valid, the mass of the accelerated particles will tend to infinity with the approaching of the speed of light, as well known. If, on the contrary, infinities do not exist in the universe, and the B.E.L.P—relativity is correct, we should expect deviations from the predictions of the ELP—relativity beginning with a certain, hiterto unknown, value of speed (see Figure 1.4.1 for more details).

The invalidation of the special relativity implied by the inapplicability of Galilei's relativity in Newtonian mechanics.

The possible anisotropy of space and the Bogoslovsky— Einstein—Lorentz—Poincaré relativity are only the tip of the iceberg. In fact, we have learned in Section 1.3 that particles can be conceived as moving in empty space only under rather special circumstances. A more general physical situation is that of extended objects moving in material media. In this case, the inhomogeneity and anisotropy of the medium is incontrovertibly established by experimental facts. The inapplicability of the Einstein—Lorentz—Poincaré relativity then follows from that of Galilei's relativity.

Invalidation arguments based on the instantaneous character of contact interactions among extended objects.

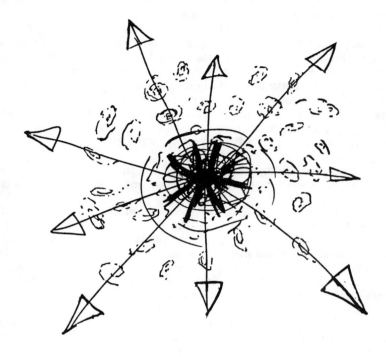

Figure 1.4.1. A schematic view of the primordial explosion (the "big bang") that lead to the creation of the universe as seen by us. It is possible that such explosion created an anisotropy of the space characterized by the direction of propagation of the galaxies, and that such anisotropy is sufficiently small to have escaped detection until now. A number of additional arguments in other branches of physics (e.g., thermodynamics, or particle physics) also lead to a conceivable anisotropy of space. In turn, such anisotropy, if confirmed, would lead to the invalidation of the Einstein—Lorentz—Poincaré relativity at the speed of light, while the same relativity remains valid for speeds sufficiently smaller than that of light. A generalization of the special relativity for anisotropic space has been worked out by the U.S.S.R. physicist Bogoslovsky [29]. Intriguingly, the generalized and special relativities have exactly the same predictions for a range of speeds varying from zero up to relativistic speeds. The predictions of the two theories then diverge with the approaching of the speed of light. Lack of studies on the issue, particularly in the U.S.A., prevent any resolution of the validity or invalidity of the studies of ref.s [29]. The only scientific conclusion we can reach at this moment is that the special relativity is valid up to the very high speeds attained in particle accelerators. No scientific conclusion is possible at this time for speeds very near that of light.

The same conclusion can be reached in a virtually end-less variety of ways. For instance, it is known that the notion of simultaneity is outside the context of the Einstein—Lorentz—Poincaré relativity. But then, this evidently implies the inability of the relativity to incorporate the contact/nonpotential/non-local interactions of our real world (Section 1.3). In fact, these interactions demand the actual contact of the objects. They are therefore instantaneous by nature and, thus, outside the special relativity. As a result, and as easily predictable, the forces char-acterizing the inapplicability of Galilei's relativity, characterize also the inapplicability of the special relativity.

Invalidation arguments based on the deformable, rota-tionally—noninvariant character of extended objects.

A further equivalent way of reaching the same conclusion is the following. Another limitation of the special relativity fully identified in the original treatments, but avoided in more recent ones, is the inability to represent deformable objects. In fact, the special relativity is applicable only to absolutely rigid bodies, while no relativistic formulation of the entire branch of engineering known as the theory of elasticity has ever been a-chieved.

It is evident that perfectly rigid objects are a mere aca-demic abstraction. In the real world, all material objects are elastic. Evidently, the amount of deformation may vary from one object to another and from one physical condition to an-other. But the existence of the deformation itself is absolutely out of question.

This deformation implies the incontrovertible invalida-tion of the Einstein—Lorentz—Poincaré relativity. The oc-currence can be proved in a variety of ways with a minimum of high school mathematics.

Consider a particle moving in empty space at sufficient-ly high (relativistic) speeds. Suppose that the particle is per-fectly spherical and with unit radius (say, one cm). In three—dimensional Euclidean space, the sphere is represented by $R' R = xx + yy + zz = 1$, where R is a column with values (x, y, z); R' is its transpose (a row with the same values); x, y, z are the (Cartesian) coordinates of a generic point of the sphere with center at the origin of the reference system; and 1 represents the unit radius.

Under the conditions considered, the special relativity is strictly verified. In fact, the sphere is a particular case of the Minkowski invariant $X'mX = xx + yy + zz - tc^2t$ where X is a column with elements (x,y,z,ct): X' represents the trans-pose of X; m is the Minkowski metric (a four—by—four diagonal matrix with elements $m = diag(+1, +1, +1, -1)$ and zero elsewhere); t represents time; and c represents the speed of light in vacuum.

The Poincaré transformations are the most general possible, linear transformations $Y = AX$ preserving the Minkowski invariant, $Y'mY = X'mX$, while the Lorentz transformations are the most general possible ones without translations. Note in particular, the rotational symmetry originating from the perfectly spherical shape of the particle.

Suppose now that, at a certain value of time, the particle experiences a deformation of its shape due to sufficiently intense external forces or collisions. Assume the simplest possible deformations, those into the ellipsoids $R'gR = xa_1 x + ya_2 y + za_3 z = 1$ where g is a three–by–three diagonal matrix with elements $g = diag(a_1, a_2, a_3)$ given by positive definite quantities representing the three characteristic axis of the ellipsoid.

The invalidation of the special relativity under the broader physical conditions considered is then incontrovertible for a number of independent, but concurring reasons, such as the breaking of the rotational symmetry, the loss of the Minkowski invariant, etc.

At any rate, the proof can be conducted by any high school student. When the spherical particle is deformed into an ellipsoid, the Minkowski invariant must be replaced by the more general one $X'GX = xa_1 x + ya_2 y + za_3 z - tc^2 t$ where G is now a four–by–four diagonal matrix with elements $G = diag(a_1, a_2, a_3, -1)$. Then, the Lorentz transformations produces two effects on the generalized invariant $X'GX$. First, they alter the shape of the ellipsoid, and, second, they alter the value of the speed of light in vacuum. In this way, the insistence in the preservation of the special relativity for deformed spheres implies the violation of two of its basic postulates, that of form–invariance, and that of constancy of the speed of light.

Needless to say, the considerations above have been specifically selected for the nontechnical level of this book. The technical treatment can be presented in rather sophisticated theoretical language (via the embedding of the deformed sphere in Euclidean space of the so–called SO(3) symmetry, into the covering complex space of the so–called SU(2) symmetry, and then extending the results to the covering of the Lorentz group, the so–called SL(2.C) group).

The taxpayer, however, should dismiss these technical aspects. They may have a value in satisfying academic wishes and preferences, but the physical roots of the invalidation of the special relativity remain the same as those in the rudimentary considerations presented above.

Invalidation arguments based on the locally varying character of the speed of light.

A further way of reaching the same conclusion is by examining the basic postulates of the Einstein—Lorentz—Poicaré relativity and comparing them with nature. As recalled earlier, the relativity is based on the constancy of the speed of light. But, as everybody knows, the speed of light is not constant in the real world. Not at all. In fact, such speed has a complicated functional dependence on a number of physical characteristics, beginning with the frequency f of light itself, and continuing with characteristics of the medium in which the propagation occurs, such as: local coordinates r ; time t ; density d ; etc. We must therefore assume that the speed of light is a function of the type $c = c(f, r, t, d, . . .)$. .

The question is then: does the special relativity apply to the speed of light as it actually occurs in nature, that is, with a complex functional dependence on local physical characteristics? The answer is NO! In fact, the Lorentz transformations are generally unable to preserve the value of such a locally varying speed, contrary to the very fundamental postulate of the relativity itself.

It is evident that there is no contradiction here with the celebrated Michelson—Morley experiment. In fact, this experiment was intended to treat the speed of light in vacuum [25]. We are referring here to a different physical arena, such as light traveling in a region of space occupied by a variety of adjoining, transparent substances, such as air, ice, glass, oil, water, etc.

Complementarity of all invalidation arguments.

Equally evident is the complementarity of the deformation of physical objects with the dependence of the speed of light on local physical conditions. In fact, they both refer to the need to generalize the basic Minkowski invariant via structures at least of the type $X'GX = R'gR - tC^2t = xa_1 x + ya_2 y + za_3 z - tC^2t$ where we assume hereon that X is the column with elements (x, y, z, t); G is the diagonal matrix with elements a_1, a_2, a_3, and $-C^2$, all depending on local physical characteristics, that is, $G = G(X, \dot{X}, d, . . .)$.

The space part $R'gR$ of the generalized separation then permits the description of extended, deformable particles, as well as motion within inhomogeneous and anisotropic media, while the time part tC^2t represents the locally varying speed of light.

The four—dimensional space with points $X = (x, y, z, t)$ equipped with the invariant $X'GX$ can be conceived as an isotope of the Minkowski space and, for this reason, it is called the

Minkowski—isotopic space [32]. This isotopy is useful for constructing the new space—time symmetries (see below).

A non—Einsteinian generalization of the special relativity for extended, deformable particles moving within inhomogeneous and anisotropic media.

A generalization of the Einstein—Lorentz—Poincaré relativity for the more general physical conditions under consideration here, has been submitted in ref.s [32, 33] following preparatory works in ref. [31] as well as previously quoted references by the same author. We are referring to a generalized relativity for systems of particles which:

I')   cannot be effectively approximated as being point—like, thus demanding a suitable representation of their extended and therefore deformable character;

II')   move in physical, generally inhomogeneous and anisotropic material media; and

III')   gravitational and quantum effects are ignorable as in III).

The generalized relativity is then reached by imposing the local invariance of the locally varying maximal speed of propagation of causal signals. More explicitly, such speed is assumed as varying from one space—time point to another, as indicated earlier. Thus, the invariance is referred to the value of the maximal speed at each space—time point (local invariance).

Also, the speed of light is replaced in the generalized relativity of ref. [32] with the "maximal speed of propagation of causal signals", that is, of signals verifying the principle that effects do not precede the cause in our time arrow. This is recommended when the generalized relativity is applied to the interior of hadronic matter (such as a nucleus). In fact, light cannot propagate within these media (whose density is among the highest known in the universe). Light is then replaced by any causal signal, such as the collision of a particle on one point of the surface of a nucleus, and the subsequent, consequential process of emission of other particles in another point of the surface of the same nucleus.

The central part of the non—Einsteinian generalization of the special relativity: the explicit construction of the generalized Lorentz and Poincaré transformations.

The most important part of the generalized relativity of ref. [32] is constituted by the techniques permitting the explicit construction of the generalized Lorentz and Poincaré transformations that apply for conditions I'), II') and III'). These techniques are based on the so—called Lie—isotopic generalization of Lie symmetries which were proposed, apparently for the first time, in memoir [8], subsequently outlined in monograph [10], and more recently re—elaborated in papers [18, 19]. The main ideas are simple and deserving an outline.

The fundamental transformations of the special relativity, the Lorentz or Poincaré transformations, are representations of corresponding Lie groups, called Lorentz and Poincaré groups (see, for instance, ref. [6]). The special relativity is based on the postulate of invariance of nature under these groups of transformations.

Now, all (continuous) Lie groups in their current formulation are constructed from an element called the unit element. For the case of the Lorentz and Poincaré transformations in Minkowski space—time, this unit is the four dimensional unit matrix I having all +1 in the main diagonal and zero elsewhere, $I = \text{diag}(+1, +1, +1, +1)$.

The Lie—isotopic generalization of Lie symmetries permits the generalization of the Lorentz and Poincaré groups for all physical conditions I'), II') and III') via the replacement of their unit I into the generalized unit $\hat{I}$ given by the inverse of the metric G of the separation considered earlier, $X'GX$, while all other aspects of the original groups remain essentially unchanged.

A number of theorems then ensure that the generalized transformations emerging from this procedure (called in ref. [31] Lorentz—isotopic and Poincaré—isotopic transformations) leave invariant the new separation $X'GX$. Theorems aside, it is known that Lie groups leave invariant the unit in a trivial way. Exactly the same property holds when the theory is expressed in terms of the more general unit $\hat{I} = G^{-1}$. The invariance of all possible metrics G is then a trivial consequence.

In particular, the generalized transformations can be explicitly computed for each given physical condition via the sole knowledge of the metric G.

Direct universality of the generalized Lorentz and Poincaré transformations.

It has been proved [33] that the Lorentz—isotopic and Poincaré—isotopic transformations provide the form—invariance of the generalized separations $X'GX$ for all possible metrics G (universality) in the space—time coordinates X of the experimenter (direct universality).

It should be also indicated that the sole restrictions on the metrics G are those of being, real—valued, symmetric, nonsingular and of verifying certain continuity conditions. The important point is that the underlying geometry, and, most importantly, the functional dependence of G on local quantities are completely unrestricted by the Lie—isotopic theory.

Thus, while the special relativity is based on one, unique, type of transformations (the Poincaré transformations for the most general possible case inclusive of translations), the generalized relativity of ref. [32] applies for each of the multiple infinity of physical conditions I'), II') and III'), that is, of possible, different metrics G.

The local isomorphism between the Poincaré—isotopic group and the conventional group.

The Minkowski metric m = diag(+1, +1, +1, −1) and the generalized metric here considered, G = diag(a_1, a_2, a_3, $−C^2$) are equivalent from an abstract topological viewpoint, in the sense that, in both cases, the first three diagonal elements are positive definite, while the fourth elements are negative definite.

This equivalence has far reaching implications. In fact, it implies that the Poincaré—isotopic group is locally isomorphic to the conventional Poincaré group. This property is proved for the Lorentz—subcase in ref. [32] and the full proof is worked out in detail in ref. [33].

A necessary condition for the achievement of such isomorphism is that the generalized transformations are expressed via the Lie—isotopic theory (that is, via associative products of the type A∗B = AGB, G = fixed, with Lie—isotopic product A∗B − B∗A, while the conventional Poincaré group is expressed via conventional associatives products AB with conventional, attached, Lie product AB − BA .   (See Section 1.8 for more details).

We recover in this way a fundamental aspect of the Galilean studies of Section 1.3.

Recall that, for the Newtonian case, the generalized mechanics (Birkhoffian mechanics) coincides with the conventional mechanics (Hamiltonian mechanics) at the level of abstract, coordinate—free geometric formulations. The two mechanics emerged as being different realizations of the same geometric axioms (those of the symplectic geometry [17]). Hamiltonian mechanics is the simplest possible realization (called canonical), while the Birkhoffian mechanics was constructed as the most general possible realization of the same axioms [10].

In the transition to the applicable Newtonian relativities, the situation was predictably equivalent. In fact, the Galilei—isotopic and Galilean relativities admit one, single, abstract, geometric—algebraic formulation (technically realized by imposing that the Galilei—isotopic group is locally isomorphic to the conventional Galilei group [18, 19]).

The situation at the level of the generalization of the special relativity under consideration here is equivalent, as it must be for unity of physical thought as well as self—consistency and mutual compatibility of the different layers of analysis.

In fact, we have generalized the Minkowski invariant from the form $X'mX$ applicable for point—like particles moving in empty space, into the form $X'GX$, $G = G(X, \dot{X}, \ldots)$, for ex-tended—deformable particles moving within inhomogeneous and anisotropic material media. The generalization implies a cor-responding one for the transformations, because the Poincaré transformations that leave invariant the separation $X'mX$ must be generalized into the Poincaré—isotopic transformations for the invariance of $X'GX$.

The important point is that, despite these differences, the Poincaré—isotopic group and the conventional Poincaré group admit one, single, unified, abstract, geometric—algebraic struc-ture. The latter group is the simplest possible realization, while the former group is the most general possible one.

The scientific implications of this result are far reaching. In fact, the result relegates the problem of space—time symmetry breaking to mere semantics. The Poincaré symmetry can be con-sidered broken for invariant $X'GX$ only when realized in the simplest possible way (that with the simplest possible associa-tive product AB and attached Lie product $AB - BA$). How-ever, if the symmetry is realized in a sufficiently more general way (that with the associative isotopic product $A*B = AGB$, with attached, Lie—isotopic product $A*B - B*A$), then the Poincaré symmetry is still exact for the generalized invariant $X'GX$, and no breaking of the ultimate axiomatic foundations has actually occurred. The only condition needed is that indi-cated earlier, the positive—definite character of the first three elements a_1, a_2, a_3, of the metric G, and the negative—de-finite character of the fourth element $-C^2$.

The implications for academic politics are truly substan-tial. As we shall indicate better in Section 1.6, a main reason for opposing studies on the possible invalidation of the Poin-caré symmetry in the interior of strongly interacting particles (hadrons) is the expectation of the consequential invalidation of the currently central hypothesis of particle physics, that yet unidentified particles called "quarks" are the constituents of hadrons. In fact, quarks are a representation of the Poincaré group.

The local isomorphism between the Poincaré—isotopic and the conventional Poincaré group renders this expectation without scientific value. In fact, it implies the possibility that quarks can exist exactly as conceived today, even if the special relativity and the Poincaré symmetry are broken in the interior of hadrons.

The only difference would be in regard to the realization of the theory, which would acquire a generalized character in the interior of hadrons as compared to the conventional character for the description of the exterior dynamics. In turn, these differences, as we shall see in Section 1.6, rather than being a drawback to quark theories, appear to permit the resolution of some of their most fundamental open problems (such as the confinement of quarks and the identification of their own constituents with physical particles).

The covering character of the generalized relativity over the special relativity and that worked out by Bogoslovsky.

The generalized relativity of ref. [32] is a covering of the special relativity in the sense indicated earlier in this section. In fact, the former relativity applies to a physical arena broader than that of the latter; it is based on more general mathematical tools; and it recovers the special relativity identically, whenever the original physical conditions are recovered identically.

Intriguingly, the generalized relativity of ref. [32] is also a covering of the Bogoslovsky—Einstein—Lorentz—Poincaré relativity [29]. This can be seen from the fact that the generalized invariant $X'GX$ admits the Finsler's invariant as a particular case (but the inverse is not generally true).

This situation was expected, because physical conditions I'), II') and III') are broader than those of ref. [29]. The mathematical methods of ref. [32] (Lie—isotopy) are also broader than those of ref.s [29] (which are conventionally Lie). The covering character of the former relativity over the latter must then occur for consistency.

As a further comment, it should be mentioned that the generalized relativity of ref.s [32, 33] is non—Einsteinian in the sense that it is not necessarily of the type of Einstein's general theory of gravitation. In fact, physical conditions I'), II') and III') are not related to gravitation. At any rate, the metric G is generally dependent on local velocities. As well known (see, for instance, ref. [27]), such a dependence is excluded in the Riemannian geometry of the general relativity.

Intriguingly, the methods of Lie—isotopy are applicable also to the case when G is the metric of Einstein's theory of gravitation, thus permitting the construction of the explicit form of the general coordinate transformations that leave invariant current gravitational theories. In fact, as indicated earlier, the Lie—isotopic theory demands no restriction on the functional dependence of the metric, thus permitting the gravitational case as a particular case.

The predictions of the generalized relativity that are confirmed by experimental evidence.

To this writing, some of the predictions of the generalized

relativity of ref. [32] are verified, others are plausible but experimentally unverified.

First, the generalized relativity recovers the well known Cerenkof effect in water. This is a physical condition concerning ordinary electrons which, in water, can travel faster than the speed of light in the same medium, thus emitting the bluish light visible in the pool of nuclear reactors. In fact, the speed of light in water is of the order of 2/3 that in vacuum, while ordinary electrons can travel in the same medium much faster than 2c /3. This case, which is fully established, is naturally represented by the generalized relativity of ref. [32] (see Figure 1.4.2 for more details).

The possibility of breaking the speed of light as the barrier of maximal possible speed in the interior of protons and neutrons, or in the core of stars.

As a complement to the Cerenkof light, the generalized relativity predicts maximal speeds C of causal signals higher than that of light in vacuum, in which case ordinary particles such as electrons, could travel at speeds higher than c . It is well known that such an occurrence is impossible for the original physical conditions I), II) and III) of the special relativity. Nevertheless, the occurrence has been proved as possible for generalized conditions I'), II') and III').

The possibility of ordinary massive particles (such as electrons) being accelerated beyond the speed of light in vacuum was predicted, apparently for the first time, in ref. [31] as a consequence of contact/nonlocal/nonpotential forces due to motion of extended particles within material media. In fact, these forces, having no potential energy, have dynamical implications fundamentally different than those of the action—at—a—distance, potential forces of the special relativity.

A typical arena for the realizations of conditions I'), II') and III') indicated in ref. [31] is that of the structure of strongly interacting particles (hadrons), such as proton, neutron, pions, etc. In fact, experimental evidence establishes that the wave—packets of the constituents of these particles must be in a state of mutual penetration and overlapping one within the space occupied by the other. The motion of each constituent can therefore be conceived as occurring within a medium constituted by other particles (the hadronic medium), thus resulting exactly in conditions I'), II') and III').

As a consequence, generalized relativity [32] predicts the possibility that the constituents of hadrons could be massive particles traveling at speeds higher than that of light. It should be stressed that these deviations from the special relativity are conceivable only in the interior of a hadron while the center—of—mass of the same particle remains strictly conformed to the

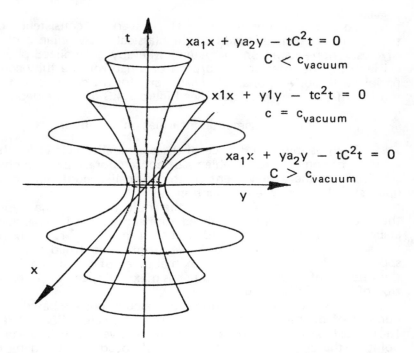

$$xa_1x + ya_2y - tC^2t = 0$$
$$C < c_{vacuum}$$

$$x1x + y1y - tc^2t = 0$$
$$c = c_{vacuum}$$

$$xa_1x + ya_2y - tC^2t = 0$$
$$C > c_{vacuum}$$

Figure 1.4.2. A reproduction of Figure 1, page 553, of ref. [32]. The central cone depicts the celebrated cone of light of the special relativity. The deformed cones are those predicted by the proposed covering relativity. The inner cone represents the case when the speed of light is smaller than that in vacuum because of propagation in transparent media such as water. In this case, ordinary particles such as electrons can propagate faster than light itself. This case is experimentally established and known as the Cerenkof effect. The outer cone is a prediction of the generalized relativity conceivable mostly for the physical conditions in the interior of strongly interacting particles or in hadronic matter, such as in the interior of a neutron or of a star (Section 1.6). In this latter case, the speed C is higher than that of the light in vacuum, c. In summary, the central prediction of the special relativity regarding c as the maximal possible speed of causal signals is tenable only under the conditions for which the special relativity was conceived, conditions I), II) and III) of the text. The surpassing of the speed c by physical, causal signals becomes conceivable for more general physical conditions. In turn, this opens up a truly vast horizon of potentially fundamental advances in numerous sectors of theoretical and applied physics. The currently available experimental information, even though far from a conclusive character, is encouragingly in favor of the hypothesis [31], that the maximal speed in the interior of hadronic matter is different than that in vacuum. It is given by recent re–elaborations of the dependence of the mean life of unstable hadrons in flight at different energies, which show quite clear deviations from the predictions of the special relativity (see ref.s [35, 36, 37]). These experimental aspects are considered in detail in Section 1.7.

special relativity.

To put if differently, ref. [31] proved the consistency of the relativistic generalization of the classical, Newtonian notion of closed/non–Hamiltonian system, whereby generalized physical laws for the interior of a proton or a neutron are fully compatible with conventional relativistic laws for the center-of–mass motion of the same particle. (See Figure 1.4.3 for more details).

Preliminary experimental information of support.

The possible significance of these generalized views for the solution of some of the problems of contemporary particle physics (such as the achievement of the so–called confinement of quarks) will be indicated in Section 1.6.

We here limit ourselves to the indication that the hypothesis of ref. [31] was submitted to a subsequent independent elaboration by De Sabbata and Gasperini in ref. [34]. By using the so–called gauge theories, these authors identified the first specific value $C = 75c$ as the maximal speed of causal signals for the interior of a hadron and, thus, as maximal speed of propagation of hadronic constituents.

As stressed by the authors, the calculations are based on a number of plausible assumptions. Thus, the value $75c$ of ref. [34] must be considered as merely indicative. The important point is the confirmation of a maximal speed greater than c. The actual value of the speed is of subordinate physical relevance.

Currently available re–elaboration of the data on the behaviour of the mean life of unstable hadrons at different energies appear to confirm the relativity of ref. [32]. In particular, the re–elaboration of the data on the mean life of charged pions ånd kaons by Nielsen and Picek [35] have confirmed the apparent existence of deviations from the special relativity, and, in particular, from the Minkowski separation X'mX. The applicability of the generalized relativity of ref. [32] is then consequential.

Independent but equivalent results have been achieved by Aronson et al [36] for the mean life of the neutral kaons. Additional, independent studies by Huerta and Lucio [37] also confirm the same findings of ref.s [35, 36]. Further studies can be found in ref. [38].

It should be stressed that all studies [35, 36, 37] are preliminary. The final resolution of the issue demands the conduction of a comprehensive experimental program, including the repetition of the direct measures of the mean life of unstable hadrons at different energies. These experimental aspects will be considered in more detail in section 1.7.

What is important for this presentation is that the deviations from the special relativity of ref.s [35, 36] as well as others not quoted here for brevity, are all particular cases of the

NONEINSTENIAN SYSTEMS

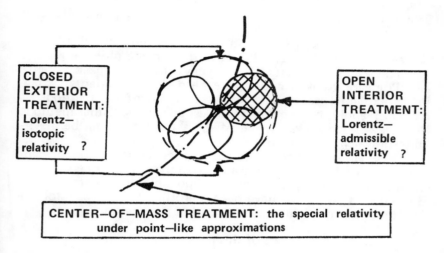

CLOSED EXTERIOR TREATMENT: Lorentz—isotopic relativity ?

OPEN INTERIOR TREATMENT: Lorentz—admissible relativity ?

CENTER—OF—MASS TREATMENT: the special relativity under point—like approximations

Figure 1.4.3. A pictorial view of the relativistic extension of the Newtonian notion of closed/non—Hamiltonian system (Section 1.3), worked out in ref.s [31, 32, 33]. The system is assumed to move in empty space. Its center—of—mass is therefore restricted to verify the special relativity, that is, to verify the conventional Minkowski invariant $X'mX$ described in the text. The constituents of the same system, however, are permitted to verify a dynamics fundamentally more general than the special relativity, that is, to verify the generalized invariant $X'GX$ also described in the text. It follows that the speed of the center—of—mass is bound by c, the speed of light in vacuum, while the maximal speed C of the constituents depends on local physical conditions (coordinates, velocities, density, etc.), but is otherwise unrestricted. Studies have furthermore indicated that, under contact/non potential/nonlocal forces, the speed C of the constituents can exceed the speed of light in vacuum. This is due to the fact that contact forces are capable of accelerating particles without any potential energy by assumption (the interaction being of contact type). This implies an alteration of the conventional relativistic dynamics and, thus, of the maximal speed. The achievement of a maximal speed C higher than c is then only a question of proper local physical conditions. As an example, consider a proton moving in the high vacuum chamber of a particle accelerator. As such, the proton experiences only action—at—a—distance, potential forces (of electromagnetic type). The special relativity then applies for all speeds achieved so far (see earlier remarks for speeds very close to that of light). Thus, when seen from an outside observer, the proton verifies the special relativity. Nevertheless, its constituents can verify the structurally more general relativity of ref. [32]. In particular, they can travel at speeds higher than that of light in vacuum. This latter possibility, rather than being far—fetched, is supported by preliminary experimental information (see Section 1.7 for details). In particular, rather than being against established knowledge in particle physics, the hypothesis appears to permit the resolution of some of the vexing open problems in quark theories, such as the achievement of a strict confinement of quarks and the identification of their constituents with physical particles (see Section 1.6 for these latter issues).

---

generalized separation $X'GX$ of the relativity submitted in ref. [32].

Evidently, we do not know at this moment whether or not generalized relativity [32] is verified in the physical reality. Nevertheless, we can state that, whenever the generalized Lorentz and Poincaré transformations are needed for invariants $X'GX$ in an explicitly computed form, the Lie—isotopic methods of ref. [32] apply, by providing the desired results. Other methods that may be conceivably identified in the future will be inevitably equivalent to those of ref. [32].

To state it differently, the explicit construction of generalized Lorentz and Poincaré transformations for each element of the multiple infinity of possible invariants $X'GX$, $G = G(X, \dot{X}, d, . . .)$, have been identified in ref. [32] for the first time, and this is the priority of that publication.

The incompleteness of this presentation.

It should be stressed that, by no means, this presentation is exhausting all mathematical, theoretical and experimental studies on the limitations and possible generalizations of the special relativity.

As a result, this presentation is grossly deficient in completeness. I would like to apologize to all authors for my inability to present a comprehensive review of their work. In fact, such a presentation would have been so voluminous, to call for a separate book.

Nevertheless, I would like to encourage authors to keep me informed of their past and forthcoming contributions on the limitations and possible generalizations of the special relativity. In fact, numerous editorial initiatives are under way at the Institute for Basic Research, in Cambridge, U.S.A., such as the possible organization of reprint volumes on all these studies. The availability of the information could therefore offer the possibility of remedying the deficencies of this presentation at some future time.

The interruption of the research.

Paper [32] is a summary letter, as one can see. The extended presentation of the generalized relativity is contained in manuscript [33] which is yet untyped to this writing.

It is significative here to note that the research on the topics presented in this section (as well as others) was interrupted for the writing of this book, and this included the interruption in the completion of paper [33] which is perhaps the most important one of my research life.

The reasons for such a rather extreme sacrifice are numerous. The first reason is due to my conviction that, lacking a serious consideration and containment of the problem of ethics in the U. S. physics, studies on the generalizations of Einstein's relativities constitute mainly a waste of time. Whenever the attempts to suppress them fail, the studies are generally discredited at birth in academic corridors.

In particular, I do not foresee the possibility that the U. S. physics community can undertake the comprehensive experimental program needed for a scientific resolution of the issue, unless the problem of ethics in physics is first tackled in a serious way.

Another reason for the interruption of the research is due to the termination of my research support from the Department of Energy, as well as the rejection of each and every one of the considerable number of inter—related research grant applications filed by our Institute on behalf of internationally renouned, senior, mathematicians, theoreticians and experimentalists.

Most distressing is the language of the referee reports used by governmental agencies for the rejection of all these applications, such as "trash", and other offensive language we shall review in detail in Section 2.5.

The historical legacies of Lagrange, Hamilton and Liouville.

The limitations of the special relativity in classical mechanics are not of my own invention. They are deeply rooted in the history of physics. In fact, they are a modern day version of legacies of the founding fathers of science that have remained opened to this day.

Some of the legacies directly related to the limitations of the special relativity are those of the founding fathers of analytic mechanics, Lagrange and Hamilton, and of a founding father of statistical mechanics, Liouville (see, for instance, memoir [39], Section 2.1).

Contemporary analytic mechanics is based on equations called precisely Lagrange's and Hamilton's equations. When these equations are formulated for three—dimensional Euclidean space and time, they constitute the analytic foundations of Galilei's relativity. When the same equations are formulated for Minkowski space—time (in a special version due to subsidiary constraints), they provide the foundations of the special relativity.

In all cases, the equations are based on the knowledge of the total energy of the system, that is, the sum of the kinetic energy and the potential energy of all action—at—a—distance forces.

In the preceding section, we have shown that the breaking

of Galilei's relativity in Newtonian mechanics is due to the fact that Newtonian forces, in general, are not derivable from a potential, and they are of potential type only in special cases.

In the transition to the breaking of the special relativity, the dynamical origin is essentially the same. In fact, it is associated to contact effects (deformations, motion in resistive media, etc.) which do not admit a potential energy.

The knowledge of the total energy is then insufficient to represent the system in its entirety owing to the presence of internal nonpotential interactions that are outside the capabilities of the Hamiltonian function (Figures 1.3.2 and 1.4.3).

This situation implies the inapplicability of the analytic foundations of the Galilean and of the special relativity, because Lagrange's and Hamilton's equations of the contemporary literature are unable to represent the equations of motion in their entirety.

The situation is not new. In actuality, it was known before the conception of the special relativity, and, predictably, it was identified by Lagrange and Hamilton themselves. For these reasons, the case is known under the name of "legacy of Lagrange's and Hamilton's" (see ref. [39], p. 1700).

I took my Ph. D. in theoretical physics in the town (Torino, Italy) where Lagrange lived and wrote his most important papers. Being interested in mechanics, it was my duty to study Lagrange's original work (some of which was published in Italian).

Unlike numerous contemporary physicists (see below), Lagrange was fully aware of the fact that part of the forces of the physical world are of potential type and part are not. For this reason, he formulated his famous equations with external terms representing precisely the nonpotential forces. It has been only since the beginning of this century that Lagrange's equations have been "truncated" with the removal of the external terms, by acquiring the form generally used in the contemporary physical (and mathematical) literature.

The situation for Hamilton's equations is similar. In fact, the equations were also originally written with external terms. Only since the beginning of this century the external terms have been "truncated", by restricting the representational capabilities to systems with only potential forces.

The legacy of Lagrange and Hamilton is now clear. In fact, whenever the external nonpotential terms are re—established according to their original conception, the invalidation of the Galilean and of the special relativity follows from numerous technical reasons independent of those indicated earlier (for instance, external terms in Hamilton's equations imply a violation of the Lie character of the theory; see ref. [8], p. 300).

The legacy of Liouville is the statistical counterpart of that of Lagrange's and Hamilton's. For brevity, the interested reader is referred to ref. [39] , p. 1702.

The attitude of ethically sound scholars toward the limitations of the special relativity.

The situation depicted in this section is routinely accepted by all ethically sound scholars.

As limpidly expressed by Einstein himself, the special relativity was specifically conceived for point−like particles moving in empty space. As a consequence, the relativity is intrinsically unable to describe extended−deformable particles moving within inhomogeneous and anisotropic material media.

Physicists interested in the advancement of scientific knowledge are expected to disagree on the appropriate form of generalization. But the insufficiency for extended−deformable particles of a relativity conceived for point−like particles is out of the question for all ethically sound scholars.

The posture of dishonest academic barons in face of the limitations of Einstein's special relativity.

Unfortunately, the acknowledgment of the limitations of the special relativity is the exception, and the suppression of the information, or its distorsion or adulteration is more likely the rule, particularly in high ranking academic circles in the U.S.A.

My hope is that the fellow taxpayer will initiate actions aimed at a containment of academic dances perpetrated with the intent of protecting vested interests, in disrespect of the proper use of public funds.

The elements to corner the corrupt academic baron have already been provided for the classical profile of the problem (see Section 1.6 for the quantum mechanical one).

Suppose an academician tells you that Einstein's special relativity is perfectly fine in classical mechanics and that its alleged limitations are nonsensical.

Then the fellow taxpayer is recommended to ask the same academician to prove that the special relativity can describe the re−entry of satellites in Earth's atmosphere. The academic baron at this point will likely retort by saying that this is not a relativistic system, that is, the speeds are minimal; Newton's equations of motion are enough; and there is no need to use the special relativity.

Fellow taxpayer, I beg you not to be blinded by these academic dances of mumbo−jumbo talk. An essential part of the special relativity is the Galilean particularization for low speeds. All low speed systems violating the Galilean relativity constitute direct violation of the special relativity. Period! The rumors emanating from the vocal cords of the academic baron have therefore no scientific meaning.

You should then insist and not leave the issue open—ended. Consult an engineer or a military expert on drag (such as satellites and missiles in atmosphere). Ask these applied scientists the equations of motion describing the system (you will generally see integral equations approximated via power series expansions in the velocities which have lately reached the fifth and even the sixth power). Confront the academic baron with these equations and ask him/her to prove their compatibility with Einstein's special relativity. Chances are that, at the very sight of these equations, the academic baron will remain speechless. His scheme to protect vested academic—fincanical—ethnic interests in disrespect of human values is then proved beyond a reasonable doubt.

The satellite during re—entry is only one case. Numerous other ways to confront seemingly dishonest academicians have been provided in these pages, such as: particles experiencing deformations; the motion of extended objects within inhomogeneous and anisotropic, material media; the dependence of the speed of light on local physical quantities; etc. All these classical phenomena are simply outside the technical capabilities of the special relativity. Period! The efforts to retain old knowledge as much as possible and at whatever cost is nothing but a manifestation of scientific dishonesty.

A small "pearl": the episode of my visit to L. C. Biedenharn at Duke University.

The following small "pearl" may be appropriate for the closing of this section.

In spring 1981, I decided to visit Larry C. Biedenharn, Jr., of the Department of Physics of Duke University in Durham, North Carolina. My primary motivation was of experimental character. In fact, while under a research contract with the Department of Energy, I was studying the problem of testing the possible alteration of the magnetic moments of nucleons under the condition of the controlled fusion (Section 1.2) via the so—called neutron interferometric techniques.

As indicated earlier, the alteration of the magnetic moments is expected to be due to the breaking of the rotational symmetry. In turn, the ultimate physical origin of such a breaking can be seen in the non—conservation of the angular momentum of a satellite during re—entry.

L. C. Biedenharn is a leading expert in the rotational symmetry, having published two monographs in the field [20, 21] and many different articles. I had met him the first time at a Conference in Coral Gables, Florida, in 1968. Our contacts had then increased in time. In 1978, Biedenharn had accepted my invitation to become a member of the Editorial Council of a

Journal in theoretical physics and applied mathematics (called the "Hadronic Journal") I had organized while at Harvard. Our relationship at that time could not possibly be more cordial, cooperative, and mutually respectful.

My tasks in visiting Biedenharn at Duke were: (a) to analyze the dynamical origin of the breaking of the rotational symmetry in classical mechanics; (b) to review the on—going studies on the generalizations of the rotational symmetry for systems with non—conserved angular momenta, and, most importantly, (c) to review with him in detail certain particle experiments via neutron interferometry that were apparently indicating a breaking of the rotational symmetry in quantum mechanics. In particular, as we shall see in Section 1.7, the confirmation o r disproof of these experiments would resolve the crucial problem of alteration of the magnetic moments under the fusion conditions.

The schedule of my visit had been all prepared in advance, and consisted of arrival in the morning, deliver a seminar in the afternoon, and then spend the following morning in technical discussions on the experimental test of the rotational symmetry in particle physics.

I therefore drove one and one—half days with the old Cadillac of the Hadronic Journal, to reach Durham, N. C. from Boston, MA. My arrival was on schedule. At the time of my seminar, I noted a rather unusual lack of physicists in an otherwise well populated department. In fact, only three people entered the conference room, L. C. Biedenharn, one of his friends (of whom I do not remember the name) and A. A. A., a young European physicist then visiting Duke University.

My seminar lasted well below 60 seconds. I began by recalling the Skylab re—entry and by drawing an idealized trajectory on the blackboard expressing the decay of the angular momentum, with consequential, manifest breaking of the rotational symmetry. At these latter words, I was attacked in a hardly believable way, primarily by Biedenharn's friend although Biedenharn himself participated with evident side on the criticisms. A. A. A. was so shocked by the situation that he remained totally silent for the entirety of the episode.

The criticisms were those reported earlier in Section 1.3. All my attempts at bringing Biedenharn and his friend to scientific reasons were shattered by an ever increasing tone of their voices.

At one point, at the peak of his furor, Biedenharn's friend lost control of himself, and unmasked the true reason of his criticism. In fact, I still remember when, turning his head toward Biedenharn, he acknowledged that the breaking of the rotational symmetry for the satellite during re—entry is a starting point for insufficiencies of Einstein's special relativity!

A constructive scientific process genuinely intended for

the pursuit of novel physical knowledge was naive and laughable under these circumstances. I broke the chalk and terminated this useless session.

I then drove to my hotel with A. A. A. where I expelled some of my rage. Once alone, A. A. A. asked me questions. Being employed under a contract with the U. S. Government, I could not lie. At any rate, this young fellow was capable of smelling problems miles away. In this way a European physicist became aware that considerable public sums were used by the Department of Physics of Duke University on research projects crucially dependent on the exact validity of the rotational symmetry in particle physics. The manifestly uncooperative attitude during my efforts to appraise the limitations of the symmetry, and the continued use of public funds while the symmetry is manifestly broken in our classical world, created an evident problem of scientific accountability at Duke University.

On the subsequent morning, I cancelled the research session, and left as early as possible, with the firm determination never to return to Duke University.

A few years later, as reported in Section 2.5, more serious episodes forced me to ask Biedenharn to terminate all scientific and human contacts.

1.5: THE INCOMPATIBILITY OF EINSTEIN'S THEORY OF GRAVITATION WITH THE PHYSICAL UNIVERSE.

Academic politics in gravitation.

I believe that, among all branches of contemporary physics, the general theory of relativity is, by far, the most controlled by vested, academic—financial—ethnic interests and, therefore, it is the least scientifically sound.

I have written only one paper in gravitation, ref. [40], and soon thereafter I decided to abstein entirely from any additional contribution in the field. This decision was the result of rather incredible excesses I have personally experienced in the denial of incontrovertible physical evidence, and in the lack of scientific process of due examination and rebuffal of published critical studies.

Contemporary views on gravitation are, therefore, the most representative of the current totalitarian condition of the U. S. physics. The views are simply imposed via shear academic power and control of the various aspects of research (jobs, papers, grants).

Predictably, among all the branches of physics supported by governmental agencies, gravitation is, by far, the most questionable. In fact, to the best of my knowledge, governmental agencies continue to disperse public funds to leading academicians on gravitational theories that have been proved to be fundamentally inconsistent in refereed technical journals, while these critical studies continued to be totally ignored.

This situation, which is per se distressing, is compounded by the virtual total lack of any possibility of improvement of the scientific accountability in the use of public funds. In fact, governmental agencies act on the basis of peer reviews by leading scholars in the field. In turn, these leading scholars have proved beyond a reasonable doubt their lack of cooperation and desire to initiate a scientific process in technical journals of due examination of the inconsistencies of Einstein's gravitation accumulated in the recent decades. Such a very tight governmental—academic circle then implies the continuation of the status quo ad infinitum.

Owing to this situation, the most drastic possible recommendations of this book have been made precisely for the funding of research in gravitation. In fact, in Section 3.3, I have recommended the initiation of class actions against federal agencies by organized groups of taxpayers to halt the monopolistic funding of models proved to be inconsistent in refereed journals. The circles of governmental—academic interests are such that, lacking suitable class actions, the unperturbed dispersal of public money in seemingly erroneous theories, and the suppression of potentially fundamental advancement, will continue indefinitely.

The purpose of this section is to provide the taxpayer with elements of judgment whether this situation is real or only imaginary. For this purpose, we must first clear Albert Einstein of any wrong doing, the responsibility of the situation being exclusively in the hands of academic barons currently in control of the field. We shall then go at the roots of the technical problem, by comparing current views in gravitation with the physical reality.

As the taxpayer will see, the basic ideas are readily understandable with a minimum of openmindedness toward science, and without any need of a Ph. D. in gravitation.

The ethical and scientific stature of Albert Einstein.

Albert Einstein has reached a towering stature in history, not only because of his physical intuitions, but also because of his scientific and human integrity.

Such an integrity transpares from his writings to this day in a number of ways, beginning with the identification of the limits of applicability of the theories he considered, and then passing to a critical self—examination of the results. By comparison, most of the contemporary papers and books in physics lack even the intention of implementing this ethical process, let alone its realization.

In the preceding section, I have recalled the identification by Einstein of the physical arena of applicability of the special relativity. In regard to his general theory, Einstein used to compare the left—hand—side of his gravitational equations to the left wing of a house made of "fine marble", and the right—hand—side of his equations to the right wing of a house made of "base wood".

This was one way to express his uneasiness, that is, the existence of yet unsettled problems. As we shall see in a moment, subsequent studies proved Einstein's doubts to be correct, by therefore confirming his ethical and scientific vision.

Einstein was also known for having stated that the society of true researchers has very few members at all times. This statement could not be more significative for the contemporary U. S. physical community!

The separation of the problem of gravitation into an exterior and an interior part.

Astrophysical bodies, such as the sun, the planets, and far away stars, consist of a region of space occupied by the bodies themselves, and the surrounding space permeated by their gravitational field. The former region characterizes the interior problem of gravitation, while the latter region characterizes the exterior one.

This distinction is evident. The interior region is the minimal surface where the totality of the mass lies. As a result, it is the region where the gravitational field is expected to originate. The exterior region is that experiencing the propagation of the field.

This distinction of gravitation into an exterior and an interior problem was fully identified in the early stages of the theory, although the distinction has progressively disappeared in subsequent treatments, up to the current condition of virtual complete silence in the contemporary literature.

In this presentation, I shall return to the original conception of the theory, and consider separately the two problems.

The main ideas of the general theory of relativity for the exterior gravitational problem.

By putting aside technical aspects, Einstein's gravitational equations represent the equality of two quantities. The left—hand—side (called Einstein's tensor G_{ij}) characterizes the curvature of space via a suitable geometric structure, as one form of representing the presence of gravitation (see, for instance, ref.s [26, 27]).

The right—hand—side represents all possible sources of the field, that is, mass (expressed via the matter tensor M_{ij}), and total electromagnetic quantities such as total charge, total magnetic moment, etc. (represented via the electromagnetic tensor T_{ij}).

The equations are then given by $G_{ij} = k(M_{ij} + T_{ij})$, where k is a certain constant (inessential for this presentation). Since the theory considered here is purely classical, contributions from short range, particle interactions are ignored.

When studying the exterior problem of gravitation, the mass contribution disappear and the equations reduce to the simpler form $G_{ij} = kT_{ij}$. In fact, as recalled earlier, mass is contained in the interior problem.

Finally, when the total electromagnetic quantities of the body considered are null (null total charge, null electric and magnetic moments, etc.), the term T_{ij} is also null. Einstein's equations then reduce to the form, $G_{ij} = 0$.

We reach in this way a most representative hypothesis of Einstein's general theory of relativity, that the gravitational field has no source in the exterior problem considered. It is a purely geometric quantity represented by the local curvature of space (or metric).

At any rate, even when the total charge and magnetic moment are not null, their contribution is truly minimal, particularly when compared to that of the mass. As such, it can be ignored in first approximation. The equations $G_{ij} = 0$ then hold for the exterior problem of virtually all astrophysical bodies.

A typical example is the gravitational field of our earth. As we all know, the intensity of its magnetic field is truly small, particularly when compared to the value of the total mass of our planet. As a result, the contributions, say, in the moon's orbit due to the earth's magnetic field is ignorable. A similar situation holds for earth's total charge. The reduced equations $G_{ij} = 0$ therefore represent the true, ultimate, foundations of Einstein's gravitation.

The irreconcilable incompatibility of Einstein's exterior gravitation with the charged structure of matter and Maxwell's electromagnetism.

Consider an astrophysical body with null total electromagnetic phenomenology. Even though the total charge is null, that body is made up of a very large number of elementary charges of opposite sign.

This charge structure of matter begins to manifest itself at the level of the structure of the atoms composing the body. In fact, as we all know, atoms are composed of peripheral electrons of negative charge and of a nuclear structure of positive charge.

The charge structure of matter manifests itself a second time in the structure of the nucleus, which is composed of protons (positively charged) and neutrons (neutral).

The same charge structure finally manifests itself a third time, at the level of the structure of each nuclear constituent. In fact, recent experiments in particle physics have established that protons and neutrons are composite states of charged constituents.

The theory of electromagnetism, called Maxwell's theory, establishes beyond any possible doubt that, even though the total charge of the astrophysical object is null, the electromagnetic field (say, E_{ij}) due to the oppositely charged constituents is not null. Explicit calculations show that, such a field E_{ij} is so large, that can conceivably account for the entire (gravitational) mass of the object. Einstein's equations $G_{ij} = 0$ must then be replaced with the equations $G_{ij} = kE_{ij}$.

The only possibility for this field to be very small (and, thus, ignorable) is to have a sufficiently small number of charged constituents moving at sufficiently small speeds. These conditions are not verified in astrophysical bodies.

The only possibility for this field to be identically null is when all charges are superimposed in the same point without relative motion. These conditions are also not realized in ordinary astrophysical bodies.

We must therefore recognize the existence of an electromagnetic field due to the charged constituents of matter that, not only is large, but it can be so large to account for the total mass of the object, that is, its total gravitational field.

This situation establishes the irreconciliable incompatibility of Einstein's entire gravitational theory with Maxwell's electromagnetism.

The invalidation begins with the exterior gravitational equations for the bodies with null total electromagnetic data, $G_{ij} = 0$. In fact, a null, total electromagnetic field for the charged constituents of the body, $E_{ij} = 0$, would require a radical revision of Maxwell's electromagnetism, contrary to over one century of experimental verifications.

The invalidation then continues for the case of bodies with non—null total electromagnetic data (i.e., a non—null total charge and magnetism), $G_{ij} = kT_{ij}$. Even though the addition of the tensor T_{ij} representing these total quantities is correct, the lack of the tensor E_{ij} for the charged constituents persists, by keeping in mind that E_{ij} is much bigger than T_{ij}, as indicated earlier.

To put it differently, in order to achieve consistency with the physical reality, it is not sufficient to consider only the total values of charge and magnetism. Instead, a consistent theory must consider the contributions due to charges and magnetic mo-

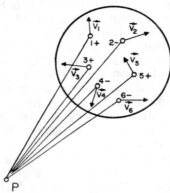

Figure 1.5.1. A reproduction of Fig. 1, p. 111 of ref. [40] illustrating the invalidation of Einstein's gravitation due to the charged structure of matter. The figure provides a schematic view of one neutron as a collection of charged constituents in highly dynamical conditions. Even though the total charge is null, at a point P outside the neutron the electromagnetic field due to the charged constituents is far from being null. Calculations conducted in ref. [40] for the simpler case of the neutral pion indicate that this electromagnetic field can be so large to account for the entire gravitational mass of the particle considered. An extrapolation to astrophysical bodies then leads to the presence of a large electromagnetic field which is missing in the right–hand–side of Einstein's gravitation, as well as in the virtual entirety of current extensions (e.g., of gauge type) and generalizations (e.g., of supersymmetric type). All these models have been proved to be incompatible with the charge structure of matter. Despite a considerable propagation of the information via distribution of preprints, reprints, letters, etc., the inconsistency has been ignored since its appearance, and continues to be ignored in contemporary papers, books and research contracts in gravitations. Any evidence to the contrary would be gratefully appreciated.

ments of each individual constituent of the body (or at least approximate them via suitable statistical means). Once this more appropriate approach is followed, the contributions due to total charge and magnetic moment follow as a consequence.

Finally, the invalidation involves the ultimate foundations of the theory, the interior equations $G_{ij} = k(M_{ij} + T_{ij})$, as indicated below in more details.

The incompatibility of Einstein's gravitation with Maxwell's electromagnetism was established in paper [40].

The litany of theoretical and experimental inconsistencies of Einstein's exterior gravitation identified by the U. S. physicist H. Yilmaz.

The invalidation of Einstein's gravitation due to the charged structure of matter is only the beginning of the problematic aspects.

A truly considerable number of additional, independent inconsistencies have been identified by the U. S. physicist H. Yilmaz (see ref.s [41—48] and quoted papers).

These deficiencies are of both theoretical and experimental character. In fact, the studies identify additional, inconsistencies of the right—hand—side of the equations (that made of "base wood" according to Einstein himself). In addition, and most importantly, the studies disprove beyond a reasonable doubt that the theory verifies the celebrated gravitational tests, contrary to a rather popular belief.

The deficiencies of Einstein's gravitation focused by Yilmaz were long suspected, as well as, at times, considered in incidental ways. Yilmaz has been the first, to my best knowledge, to articulate them into a coordinated construction encompassing all possible aspects. Also, Yilmaz has not limited the analysis to unproductive criticisms, but has worked out a significant generalization of the theory.

Quite intriguingly, Yilmaz's studies [41—48] are in agreement with the invalidation of the right—hand—side of Einstein's equations studied in ref. [40].

Since the financial and ethical implications of Yilmaz's studies are considerable, it is important for the fellow taxpayer to have an outline of them.

Yilmaz's submission of papers to the Hadronic Journal.

I first met Yilmaz back in 1979 when I was a member of the Department of Mathematics of Harvard University. He came to visit me in my capacity of editor in chief of the Hadronic Journal.

Among his several papers in gravitation, Yilmaz did submit and publish a number of papers in the Hadronic Journal [44, 45, 46]. This gave me a rather unique, dual opportunity, the first, as an individual physicist who has studied his work, and the second, as an editor who has contacted referees, studied their reports, consulted them by phone for elaboration and proof of their statements, etc.

The academic politics on Yilmaz's research.

This situation has also given me a direct, rather unique experience of the decaying of ethics in the U.S. physics. Renowned physicists currently controlling gravitation are generally uncooperative and some become even hysterical at the very mention of the studies. My insistence in due scientific process of critical examination of dissident views and presentation of counter—criticism in published articles,has generally failed.

After almost one quarter of a century from their original publication [41], "leading" physicists in gravitation still continue to ignore completely Yilmaz's work, that is, they continue to ignore research challenging their own work.

Almost needless to say, nobody is asked to accept passively Yilmaz's theory or any theory for that matter. Nevertheless, physicists working in conventional gravitational models under federal support have a strict ethical duty, first, to quote Yilmaz's work, and then to disprove it. Yilmaz's work invalidates conventional models, that is, it challenges the ultimate reasons for the granting of federal support to begin with. Silence on his work is therefore strictly unethical.

I often wandered why this silence has been kept for so long. One possible explanation is due to the fact that no counter—criticism truly exists on Yilmaz's work to this writing. I am not referring to counter—criticism ventured in academic corridors, or in adulterated reviews of research grant applications. I am referring to serious counter—criticism published in refereed journals.

Central aspects of Yilmaz's analysis.

The central aspects of Yilmaz's critical examination of Einstein's studies are the following.

1) Einstein's assumed that matter only is responsible for space—time curvature. The stress—energy of the gravitational field itself was omitted from both the conceptual structure of gravitation and its mathematical realization;

2) Einstein did not equip his gravitational theory with a clear, unique, operational procedure for measurement which is compatible with that of the special relativity.

From these two basic deficiencies, a number of physical mismatches and inconsistencies follow throughout the entire theory, to the point of rendering it unusable for a genuine representation of gravitation.

Inability of Einstein's gravitation to recover the Newtonian description of the planetary motion.

The omission of stress—energy (represented with the tensor t_{ij}) implies the inability of the gravitational equations to recover the Newtonian description of the planetary orbit. This point has been proved by Yilmaz beyond a reasonable doubt in paper [46], although the arguments are included in his earlier work.

The fellow taxpayer should recall the fundamental character of the Galilean—Newtonian description of planetary systems, stressed in Sections 1.2 and 1.3. In fact, no gravitational theory can be considered valid unless it is compatible with the Galilean—Newtonian description. After all, this description is established by centuries of experimental observation. All other theories, including the general theory, are mere refinements. Yilmaz has essentially proved that the nonrelativistic limit of Einstein's general relativity is not Newtonian mechanics, but the so—called Hooke's mechanics. This is a mechanics in which the sun has infinite inertia, and the law of action and reaction is generally absent.

This point can be anticipated by any physicist with a minimum of knowledge of both Newtonian mechanics and Einstein's general relativity. The former is centrally dependent on the capability to represent orbital motion via Hamilton's equations (Section 1.3). On the contrary, the latter is known to lack a consistent Hamiltonian formulation (e.g., because the Hamiltonian is, in general, identically null). The incompatibility of the two theories is therefore predictable. Yilmaz has been the first to prove it in all necessary technical details.

Incompatibility of Einstein's gravitation with the special relativity.

One of the main properties of the special relativity is the capability of providing a consistent relativistic generalization of the Galilean relativity (this is the reasons why the special relativity, when inapplicable, can be at most claimed to be approximated, but not as being "wrong").

In particular, the special relativity succeeded in achieving a consistent relativistic formulation of the conservation laws of total energy, linear momentum, angular momentum, charge, etc.

Another point achieved by the special relativity is the proper generalization of the process of radiation of electromagnetic waves, for instance, by an accelerating electron. This is an historical success of the special relativity inasmuch as quantum mechanics had to be constructed precisely in order to understand the lack of radiation from the electrons of the atomic structure.

Yilmaz has achieved a proof beyond reasonable doubts that Einstein's general relativity is unable to reach these fundamental physical properties at the relativistic limit of null curvature. I am differentiating here the nonrelativistic/Newtonian limit of the preceding comments from the relativistic setting under consideration here.

More specifically, Yilmaz has proved that the general relativity is unable to recover the energy—momentum conservation laws of the special relativity. Only the rest—mass conservation law is recovered by Einstein's gravitation, but this is known to violate the special relativity. Yilmaz has furthermore proved that the origin of this occurrence is, again, the lack of the stress—

energy tensor in the right–hand–side of the gravitational equations.

Yilmaz has furthermore proved that the general relativity is unable to provide a proper representation of the phenomenon of radiation of energy, already within a curved framework, with consequential inability to recover the relativistic treatment of radiation for null curvature. Yilmaz has also established that this additional inconsistency is, again, due to the lack of the stress–energy tensor.

Incompatibility of Einstein's gravitation with experimental tests on gravitation.

In the Newtonian mechanics there are three kind of masses, the "inertial mass", the "passive gravitational mass" and the "active gravitational mass". They are all equal among themselves. This property is called in the literature the "strong principle of equivalence".

Yilmaz has proved that the general relativity violates the identity of the active and passive gravitational masses of the same body, and that this is due, again, to the lack of stress–energy tensor in the right–hand–side of the equations.

One of the most visible and important consequences is the inability of Einstein's gravitation to represent the experimental information on the perihelium of Mercury, contrary to a long standing claim by vested interested in the field.

According to historical experimental evidence accumulated throughout the centuries, the perihelium of Mercury advances 575" per century. The first point the fellow taxpayer must know is that the major portion of this advancement, 532", is fully representable by the Galilean–Newtonian formulation of gravitation. In fact, an advancement of 532" per century has long been established as being due to the Newtonian perturbation of the other planets (mostly Jupiter and Venus).

The problem facing Einstein was the representation of the remaining 43". Yilmaz has essentially proved that Einstein's gravitation does recover the small, relativistic correction of 43", but it is unable to represent the primary, nonrelativistic contribution of 532"!

The ultimate reasons can now be seen from the known lack of a Hamiltonian formulation of the general theory of relativity, which implies the lack of a Hamiltonian formulation at the Newtonian limit. In turn, this implies the inability to represent the primary contribution of 532".

This logical line of scientific thought has been bypassed until now via quite involved argumentations aiming at the derivation of a consistent Newtonian–Hamiltonian formulation, from an inconsistent gravitational–Hamiltonian one. Yilmaz has however proved that these salvage attempts are per se plagued by a host of direct and indirect inconsistencies. The simple scientific truth is that the general theory of relativity violates the Hamiltonian character of mechanics. Period.

But this is only the beginning of the experimental insufficiencies identified by Yilmaz. Another insufficiency is the inability to provide a consistent interpretation of the celebrated bending of the light rays when passing near the surface of the sun, the earth or any other astrophysical body. This is due to the inability of the theory to achieve the identity of the passive and active gravitational mass. As a result, the currently available "explanation" of the bending of the light rays, when worked out in details, implies an infinite value of the mass of the attracting body, contrary to the finiteness of the masses in the physical reality.

Numerous additional experimental inconsistencies have been identified by Yilmaz, but they are omitted here for brevity.

Incompatibility of Einstein's gravitation with quantum mechanics.

This additional incompatibility has been known for decades. It is due to numerous technical problems in achieving a consistent formulation of Einstein's equations in the formalism of quantum mechanics (operators acting on Hilbert spaces; see next section).

This additional incompatibility acquires particular relevance in this presentation because it completes the range of incompatibilities of the theory with the remaining branches of physics describing orbital motion.

In fact, from the studies under consideration it emerges that Einstein's general theory of relativity is incompatible with Maxwell's electromagnetism, it is incompatible with the Galilean—Newtonian formulation of planetary motion and its experimental data; it is incompatible with the special relativistic formulation of dynamics; and, finally, it is incompatible with the quantum mechanical formulation of the same dynamics.

Yilmaz has, of course, considered the latter incompatibility. His contribution is the identification of the origin of the incompatibility which, again, has resulted to be the lack of stress—energy tensor of the gravitational field in the right—hand—side of Einstein's equations.

Yilmaz's "new theory" for the exterior problem of gravitation.

By far the most important contribution by Yilmaz has been the construction of a significant generalization of Einstein's gravitation for the exterior case. In fact, as it is the case in any valuable scientific occurrence, the identification of the insufficiency of Einstein's theory was merely introductive to the constructive part.

In essence, Yilmaz has generalized Einstein's field equations $G_{ij} = 0$ described earlier into the more general form $G_{ij} = k\, t_{ij}$, where t_{ij} represents the stress—energy tensor of gravitation, and k is a suitable constant.

Yilmaz has therefore proved that the generalized theory (which he calls "the new theory") is compatible with:

1) the Galilean—Newtonian description of planetary dynamics;

2) the special relativistic description of planetary dynamics;

3) the generalization of planetary motion offered by quantum mechanics.

The capability of Yilmaz's new theory of being consistent with available experimental evidence on gravitation is then a consequence. I remember, both as a physicists and as an editor, to be keenly interested in inspecting, verifying, and re—verifying the experimental consistency of Yilmaz's new theory. My original doubts had to give the way to the physical evidence originating not only from my own study of the issues, but also from (ethically sound) referees of his articles submitted for publication to the Hadronic Journal.

The technical reasons for such, rather astonishing successes of Yilmaz's theory are, again, conceptually simple (although predictably involved on technical grounds). The addition of the stress—energy tensor t_{ij} to the right—hand—side of the equations essentially implies the regaining of a consistent Hamiltonian formulation, that is, the theory can be consistently represented via the knowledge of the total energy of the system, when properly expressed in a curved space—time.

Such Hamiltonian character has first the merit of permitting a ready compatibility with the Galilean—Newtonian description of the orbital dynamics. In fact, the theory was consistently Hamiltonian to begin with, and remains Hamiltonian at the nonrelativistic level. Most importantly, this implies the capability of the new theory to represent consistently the Galilean—Newtonian contribution of 532" per century in the advancement of the perihelium of Mercury, as well as all other nonrelativistic experimental data.

Secondly, the Hamiltonian character achieves compatibility with the special relativity, including the relativistic formulation of conservation laws, the gravitational extension of the famous formula $mc^2 = E$, etc. Again, the special relativity is of Hamiltonian character (although of a particular type due to contraints). The important point is that such character persists in the transition from the special to Yilmaz's new theory, while it is violated in the transition from the special to Einstein's theory.

Most importantly, this latter consistency permits the achievement of a representation of the relativistic correction to the Newtonian experimental data, such as the representation of the additional 43" per century in the advancement of the perihelium of Mercury.

Finally, the restoration of the Hamiltonian character of the theory permits Yilmaz's new theory to achieve compatibility with quantum mechanics. This can also be understood by the general public without the need of graduate studies in theoretical physics. As all other branches of physics considered here (such as Galilean and relativistic mechanics), quantum mechanics is fundamentally dependent on the Hamiltonian character of the theory. In fact, most of the known methods of quantization are dependent on the existence of a Hamiltonian description. Lacking a consistent Hamiltonian formulation, Einstein's theory resulted to be incompatible with quantum mechanics. Owing to the presence of a consistent Hamiltonian description, Yilmaz's new theory, instead, is compatible with quantization.

Limitations of Yilmaz's revision of Einstein's exterior gravitation.

It is the fate of all physical theories to possess specific limitations, insufficiencies and drawbacks. As predictable, Yilmaz's revision of Einstein's exterior gravitation does not escape this fate.

To the best of my understanding, the major problematic aspect of Yilmaz's approach is that it is not fully compatible with the electromagnetic fields E_{ij} of the charged structure of matter. In fact, owing to certain technical reasons, Yilmaz's stress—energy tensor t_{ij} cannot be identified with E_{ij}, i.e., $t_{ij} \neq E_{ij}$. This signals the lack of terminal character of Yilmaz's approach as predictable. In fact, his equations for the exterior problem, $G_{ij} = k\, t_{ij}$ (for null, total, electromagnetic fields T_{ij}), need a suitable modification of the right—end—side to incorporate the tensor E_{ij}.

Despite this limitation, Yilmaz's approach remains preferable over Einstein's theory. In fact, Einstein's equations for the exterior problem (also for the case $T_{ij} = 0$) read $G_{ij} = 0$, by therefore resulting to be "irreconcilably incompatible" with the charged structure of matter, as stressed earlier. Yilmaz's revision $G_{ij} = k\, t_{ij}$ is manifestly better, e.g., because the tensor t_{ij} may well incorporate at least part of E_{ij}.

A number of additional problematic aspects also exist for Yilmaz's approach, but they are of technical nature and not conducive for this presentation.

NEWTONIAN LEVEL	GALILEAN RELATIVITY
RELATIVISTIC LEVEL	EINSTEIN– LORENTZ– POINCARÉ RELATIVITY
GRAVITATIONAL LEVEL	EINSTEIN– YILMAZ RE- LATIVITY ?

Figure 1.5.2. A schematic view of the status of our classical descriptions of particles that can be well approximated as massive points while moving in empty space, at the nonrelativistic, relativistic and gravitational levels. Each level is characterized by the applicable relativity. Also, the relativity of each level is a covering of that of the preceding level in the sense indicated in Section 1.4. The fundamental relativity is the Galilean one, followed by the Einstein–Lorentz–Poincaré relativity for speeds approaching that of light which, in turn, is a particular case of Yilmaz's revision of Einstein's exterior gravitation. While the Newtonian and the relativistic levels are fully resolved to this writing (for the physical conditions considered here), the gravitational level is, by far, unresolved, as elaborated in the preceding text for the exterior problem (see below for additional problematic aspects related to the interior problem).

The possible elimination of the problem of unification of gravitation and electromagnetism.

As well known, the problem of the unified theory vexed Einstein in the last year of his life. As also well known, Einstein failed to reach a solution of the problem. After Einstein's death, numerous additional attempts were made throughout a number of decades without major results.

The combination of the research of ref.s [40] and [41–48] apparently removes the existence of the problem.

Again, the conceptual bases are simple and understandable to all. As indicated before, Einstein did not consider the charged structure of matter in his gravitational theory. This led him to the inconsistency pointed out earlier, but also to a fundamental misrepresentation of the problem of unification.

Owing to the way gravitation had been approached, Einstein faced two different fields, the gravitational and the electromagnetic fields (plus short range, quantum mechanical interactions here ignored). Along these lines, it was rather natural to look for the "unification" of the two fields into a single entity.

When the problem of gravitation is approached as in this section, beginning with the primary contribution from the electromagnetic field of each matter constituent, the perspective of the problem is fundamentally changed.

In fact, the studies of ref. [40] were presented as a theory on the "origin of the gravitational field". Most importantly, the contributions from the charged constituents of matter resulted as being able to account for the entire gravitational mass of the bodies. This implied the possibility to "identify" the electromagnetic and the gravitational field. Under these conditions, their "unification" becomes not only unnecessary but actually meaningless.

More particularly, paper [40] proposed a theory whereby the gravitational field is identified with (a particular form of) the electromagnetic field of the charged constituents of matter, plus short range particle contributions. The curvature of space—time is a mere consequence of the intensity of the electromagnetic field of the matter constituents.

Short range, particle contributions must evidently be taken into account, but they are a consideration of the interior problem (see below). So far, we have considered only the exterior problem. It is evident that, at large interplanetary distance, only the long range electromagnetic field of the matter constituents is present in a direct form.

I have halted, years ago, the research on this possible resolution of the historical problem of unification, and no active studies have been conducted by other researchers along the same lines to my knowledge.

The reasons for the truncation of research of such manifestly relevant character have been indicated earlier.

Physical resolutions cannot be achieved alone. They demand a scientific process involving the entire physics community in the sector, and comprising a variety of steps, such as: verbal consultations with colleagues; constructively critical analysis of preliminary results; constructive refereeing processes in the submission of papers and of federal grant proposals; achievement of consensus on the conduction of new experiments; etc.

In my personal opinion and experience, each of these essential aspects is unrealizable in contemporary U. S. physics for all research that is contrary to vested, academic—financial—ethnic interests.

In fact, all my attempts to contact leading U. S. physicists in gravitation for advice and constructive criticisms have resulted in failure after failure repeated over a rather extended period of time. Whether intended or accidental, this has the result of suppressing, jeopardizing or discouraging any study that might even remotely lead to a generalization of Einstein's idea.

Scientific accountability in gravitation research.

Physical research is (hypothetically) based on freedom, but also implies precise responsibilities of scientific and societal character.

Whenever a physicist uses public funds, he automatically acquires a direct responsibility of societal character known as scientific accountability.

Among the multiple duties of scientific accountability there is that of taking in due consideration ALL dissident views on his/her own research. This duty alone is of multiply nature. In fact, it demands the quotation of the dissident views in ALL scientific material, from grant applications, to papers, to books, to talks, etc. Furthermore, it demands publication of disproofs of dissident views whenever the later are published in refereed journals.

The dimension of the ethical responsibility of researchers using public funds evidently varies from case to case. There is first the case of initiation of dissident views published, say, only once or just appeared in print. It is understandable that in this case researchers may not necessarily be aware of dissident views on their work. Then, there is no violation of scientific ethics, provided the researchers, when informed of the dissident views, acquire a documented record of active cooperation, examination and eventually disproof also in refereed journals.

To be repetitive in this crucial aspect of scientific ethics, when dissident views are published in refereed journals or other equivalent scientific vehicles, counter—criticism cannot be limited to exchange of informal letters, or to corridor's talks, but MUST be presented in the same scientific vehicles of the original criticism: refereed publications.

It is evident that the problem of ethics grows with time. In fact, when the original dissident views have been published, republished, treated, and retreated by an increasing number of independent authors, the problems of scientific ethics and accountability grow proportionately.

The tactics used by leading gravitational experts to avoid knowledge of dissident views.

Yilmaz's new theory, by now, has been published, and quoted in papers spanning about one quarter of a century.

It is evident that, under these circumstances, Yilmaz's studies constitute a sizable problem of ethics for ALL physicists conducting research in Einstein's gravitation under public support. The ignorance of Yilmaz's studies simply magnifies the ethical problems.

As well known, corrupt academicians are masters in denying knowledge of undesired lines of research. Such denial, however, is simply untenable for the case of Yilmaz's studies for any physicist who can qualify him/herself as an "expert" in gravitation. This is due to the following reasons.

Authors of dissident views generally enter into a progressive and intensive propagation of the information of their work. The first action is that of mailing a preprint to most of the leading physicists in the sector asking for advice in the revision and completion of the manuscript.

When this first step remains without acknowledgments, the action is generally continued by mailing copy of the reprint of the published version of the paper, and again asking for the courtesy of comments. The assumption is that academicians are generally very busy and do not visit libraries. They must therefore receive directly on their desk copies of papers presenting criticisms of their work.

But, academicians do not read papers (or at least so they claim whenever convenient, just to claim the opposite one minute thereafter, whenever they need qualifications for passing judgment . . . .). As a result, the original mailing of preprints, followed by the mailing of the reprints, is generally complemented with a third action consisting of a letter summarizing the essential elements of the dissident views, and, again, asking for the courtesy of counter—criticisms whether or not these (by now published) views have sense.

The understanding is that, if the academicians do not read preprints and reprints, they may well read a nice, personalized, individualized letter. Right? Wrong! Academicians do not read even letters addressed to them, of course, when containing undesired scientific lines. At least this is a logical conclusion whenever you see that their subsequent papers are totally silent on published dissident views.

At this point, the dishonesty of the academicians can be considered as proved beyond any reasonable doubt. Then, what do you do? Dishonesty feeds on silence which is, therefore, complicity. So, you decide to talk. But to whom? You cannot approach other academic barons because the loyalty of academic alliances is known to be so strong to dwarf that in organized crime.

These are the roots of the problem of ethics in U. S. physics. These are also some of the reasons why this book was written.

To my knowledge, Yilmaz and/or his friends (including myself) have exhausted all possible or otherwise conceivable means for the propagation of the information on the studies. As a result, no true expert in the field can claim lack of their knowledge at this time.

I have followed the iterim of exhaustive information on dissident views not only for the case of the invalidation of Einstein's gravitation due to the charged structure of matter, but also in other cases. (See, for instance in Section 1.6 the case of the paper of criticism on quarks distributed in 15,000 copies).

The roots of the ethical problem in U. S. gravitation.

Let us now focus our attention on the problem of ethics in gravitation caused by:

1) the publication in refereed technical journals of a truly considerable number of independent invalidations of Einstein's gravitation for over one quarter of a century;

2) the rather sizable propagation of the information to individual researchers in the field done independently by Yilmaz, myself and others; and,

3) the rather complete silence in technical papers, books and talks by leading U. S. physicists in gravitation on the above problematic aspects.

No physicist who is mentally sound will ever ask passive acceptance of these invalidations. But then, no physicist who is ethically sound can continue to ignore them for decades after decades.

But after decades and decades of impunity, there are no reasons to expect changes in the behaviour of governmental—academic circles. After all, why should an academician change his/her posture if he/she continues to enjoy governmental support? Similarly, why should governmental agencies change their own posture if they continue to receive positive reviews by leading peers?

These are the reasons why I have recommended the fellow taxpayer in Section 3.4 to organize class actions aimed at the truncation of the use of public money in the unilateral funding of research on Einstein's gravitation without any consideration of its published inconsistencies.

The uncooperative attitude by S. Deser, A. Pais, S. Weinberg, and J. A. Wheeler from the U.S.A. and Y. Ne'eman from Israel.

I am a physicist. As such, I am primarily interested in constructive research and not in seeking unnecessary scandals that are damaging to all, beginning with myself.

Thoughout the years, I have therefore attempted anything in my power to implement an orderly scientific process, but I have failed.

Even as recently as early 1984, I was still hoping that leading U. S. physicists in gravitation could be brought to scientific reasons; that an orderly scientific process of resolution of the inconsistencies of Einstein's gravitation could be initiated; and that I would have found myself without reasons to write IL GRANDE GRIDO, or at least avoid the writing of this section in gravitation.

Facts proved that my hopes were unfounded.

On January 3, 1984, I wrote a letter to the following lead-
ing physicists in gravitation: Stanley Deser of Brandeis Univer-
sity; Abraham Pais of Rockefeller University; Steven Weinberg of
The University of Texas at Austin; John A. Wheeler also of The
University of Texas at Austin; and Yuval Ne'eman of Tel–Aviv
University in Israel.*

As one can see from the Documentation (p. II–708), the
letter was written in a way as respectfully as possible; it summarized the scientific lines of this section; it included the most recent preprint and references; and concluded with its most important point: asking for assistance in the organization and conduction of a workshop on all views, in favor and against, the problematic aspects of Einstein's gravitation, and in the publication
of its proceedings.

The rationale of the proposal was that the most effective
way to initiate the orderly resolution of the issue was precisely
via an international workshop with the participation of experts
of different views.

All the physicists indicated above answered with a few, dry
lines without any scientific content. None of them indicated interest in the organization of the workshop, and some of them did
not even acknowledge the petition for its organization.

At the same time, owing to the current totalitarian nature
of the U.S. physics, the organization of a workshop without the
participation of leading experts in the field has no true weight in
the community.

The inclusion of this section on gravitation in this public
appeal was therefore unavoidable. My gentle and respectful call
for due scientific process to Deser, Pais, Weinberg, Wheeler and
Ne'eman was my very last try.

**The refusal by the Department of Physics of Boston Col-
lege to list a seminar by H. Yilmaz in the Boston Area
Physics Calendar.**

As well known, the Boston area is populated by universities, colleges and research laboratories. *The Boston Area
Physics Calendar* is a weekly list of all seminars in mathemati-

---

*
Y. Ne'eman was selected for the mailing of the letter dated January 3,
1984, because, even though he conducts research outside the U.S.A., he
has used a considerable amount of money of the U.S. taxpayer both directly (via federal contracts from the international branch of the National
Science Foundation dealing with U.S.A.–Israel exchanges) and indirectly
(via financial support from U.S. Departments of Physics he has visited
throughout the past decades, said support being drawn from governmental
contracts). As a result, Y. Ne'eman has acquired a direct scientific accountability with the U.S. taxpayer for his gravitational research.

cal, theoretical and experimental physics, as well as philosophy of science. The Calendar is a very useful guide for all scholars in the area, including visitors. Listings in the Calendar require the mailing or phoning of the information.

Production of the calendar is done by a local Physics Department, which generally changes from one academic year to the next. Subscriptions are granted upon paying a yearly fee.

The production of the Calendar for the current academic year (1983—1984) is done by the Physics Department of Boston College, Chestnut Hill, MA. The editorial responsibility of the calendar rests with S. Lynch, an employee of Boston College, under the supervision of the current chairman of the Physics Department, R. A. Uritam.

Following the publication of his article [46], in early March 1984, H. Yilmaz came to visit me in my capacity of President of the Institute for Basic Research. He wanted to deliver a talk along the lines of his studies entitled "Problematic aspects of the general relativity for planetary orbits". He therefore asked my assistance for the organization of the seminar at our institute in the hope of receiving constructive criticisms, in the interest of a resolution of the historical open problems reviewed in this section.

The seminar was set for March 26, 1984. I therefore wrote a letter to S. Lynch providing the information needed for the listing with copy to Yilmaz. The letter was mailed as a regular first class mail on March 7, well in time for the listing of March 26. The Calendar for the week of March 26—30 DID NOT contain the listing of Yilmaz's seminar because, as indicated by Ms. Lynch, my communication had arrived late for the listing!

We therefore rescheduled the seminar for April 16, 1984. A new communication dated March 27, 1984, was mailed to S. Lynch, this time via certified letter, return receipt requested, with copy to R. A. Uritam as chairman of the Physics Department of Boston College. The Calendar for the week April 16—21, 1984, arrived at the I.B.R. on April 11, 1984. TO MY ENOURMOUS SURPRISE YILMAZ'S SEMINAR HAD NOT BEEN LISTED! The calendar contained no mention of it. The listing had been simply suppressed without any communication whatsoever to our Institute or to Yilmaz (Doc. pp. I—197—211).

I immediately wrote a certified letter, with return receipt requested to Father Donald J. Monan, President of Boston College,* asking for a public investigation of the case, with the soliciation to terminate the employment of all persons responsible for the occurrence.

---

* See Doc. p. I—211. Father Monan never acknowledged my letter. One of the first copies of IL GRANDE GRIDO was therefore mailed to the State Department of the Vatican in Rome, Italy, with an accompanying report.

By no means, the fellow taxpayer should think that this is an isolated occurrence. Not at all. In fact, the episode is nothing but a continuation of similar episodes occurred while the Calendar was produced by the Physics Department of Tufts University, as we shall see in detail in Section 2.1. The only difference is that the former episodes have much more serious elements of possible discrimination of research under governmental support (in fact, the seminars refused for listing were under contract with the U. S. Department of Energy!).

The questions raised by Yilmaz's case are evidently endless. Did Boston College act alone, or was the decision to refuse the listing reached under consultation and possible complicity of other local departments? As we shall see in Section 2.1, at the time of the incidents with Tufts University, the chairman of that physics department disclosed that the prohibition to list I. B. R. seminars under D. O. E. support had been voiced by senior members of the Department of Physics of Harvard University. Any investigation of Yilmaz's case must therefore clarify, in a way as open to the public as possible, whether or not Harvard University and /or other local colleges were also responsible.

I hope the fellow taxpayer will not be blinded by "explanations". The Boston Area Physics Calendar has been published since its inception in a very informal (simply typed) way, without ever indicating restrictions for listing, and with the illusory face of democracy. At any rate, restrictions in the listings would invalidate the very title of "Boston Area Physics Calendar".

Since the Boston College (as well as Tufts University) never released any indication of the reasons for the lack of listings, we are currently unaware of covert legal aspects. But, fellow taxpayer, bear in mind that, even assuming that Boston College and the other local universities will one day be claimed to be right by a Court of Law, the episodes are and will remain strictly undignifying for America! If nothing else, where is the alleged, traditional, scientific hospitality in the U.S.A.?

The refusal by Boston College (and Tufts University) to list seminars by renowned scholars is only one of the too many episodes providing a clear, cold blood, identification of the decaying status of the U.S. physics community.

But why reach such hysterical extremes? The most plausible reasons are obvious to me. The physicists who suppress due scientific process are not stupid or uneducated. They are fully aware that Yilmaz's criticisms of Einstein's ideas are correct and incontrovertible. This is why they retort to covert suppression of scientific process. They have no other choice. It is all done in full knowledge, in plain daylight, and, most regrettably, with our own money.

I hope, fellow taxpayer, you begin to see the reasons why, by being silent, I could not look at my children with clear eyes.

Enough is enough. The control of science by such academic—financial—ethnic greed in the U.S.A. has simply passed the limits of human decency, and must be halted at whatever cost. Only the accomplices can tolerate it.

The irreconciliable invalidation of Einstein's gravitation for the interior problem.

Despite their number, diversification and relevance, all the invalidation arguments considered until now constitute only half of the presentation. In fact, the arguments deal exclusively with the exterior problem of gravitation. The remaining half is evidently that of the interior problem.

The irreconciliable invalidation of Einstein's equations for the interior problem of gravitation is established quite forcefully by the mere inspection of physical reality, not that of far away stars (as preferred by several academicians), but instead that of our earth.

Interior trajectories are those within our atmosphere, or, more generally, those of extended objects moving within a resistive medium, such as satellites during re—entry.

As indicated in the preceding sections, these systems violate the foundations of the Galilean and of the special relativity. The violation of the general relativity is a mere consequence.

When approximated via local power series in the velocities, the equations of motion are simply outside the technical capabilities of the general relativity. Any other view is a mere attempt to manipulate fundamental human knowledge.

It is sufficient to recall the episode of Skylab during re—entry (Section 1.3). No matter what treatment is used, the general relativity simply cannot represent this motion in any meaningful way (this was the reason why the NASA scientist would have chased out of NASA premises the professor expert in current theories of gravitation . . . .).

What Einstein did for the interior problem was to assume an idealized situation whereby astrophysical bodies are made up of massive points, much along the conceptual lines of the special relativity. The important aspect (that re—inforces rather than weakens Einstein's ethical stature) is that he stressed the limited capability of the theory.

The responsibility of bringing the theory to the current religious level lies entirely in his followers.

It is evident that, for the idealized body made up of massive points, the action can only be at a distance, whether in flat or curved space—time. But nature is much more complex than that. In fact, the forces of the physical reality are not necessarily of action—at—a—distance type.

Simple inspection of our environment proves it, by establishing the irreconcilable inability of the general theory of relativity to represent the physical reality of the interior problem of gravitation.

The invalidation of the Riemannian geometry for the interior gravitational problem.

All dynamical formulations are based on a given geometry. This is the case also of Einstein's gravitation. Its underlying geometry is called Riemannian and essentially consists of mathematical formulations suitable for the representation of a curvature in space—time. The geometry is of the so—called local and differential character, in the sense recalled in Section 1.3.

To avoid an insidious misconception, we must now go back and reconsider first the exterior problem of gravitation. Then we shall consider the interior problem on a comparative basis.

Einstein's biggest contribution to gravitation has been the left—hand—side of his equations for the exterior case. It introduced for the first time the Riemannian geometry for the treatment of gravitation.

The aspect that must be clarified to avoid unnecessary misrepresentations, is that the Riemannian geometry is fully valid for the exterior problem of gravitation. In Einstein's own words, the left—hand—side is the left wing of the house made of "fine marble". All criticisms reviewed above deal exclusively with the right—hand—side of the equations, that is, with the source terms.

The physical reasons of consistency can be readily understood. When considering the exterior gravitational problem, whether in flat or curved space, we are dealing with objects moving in empty space. Then (see Section 1.3), the actual shape and structure of the bodies do not affect the dynamics. The bodies can therefore be approximated as being massive points, along Galilei's vision. Under these conditions, the geometry can indeed be local and differential.

The selection of the Riemannian geometry is then a mere technical consequence.

In the transition from the exterior to the interior problem, the situation becomes fundamentally different. In the interior problem, we do not have any more points moving in empty space. We have instead extended objects experiencing contact effects besides action—at—a—distance ones. This is the case for satellites during re—entry, or for the atoms in the interior of the sun, or for neutrons in the interior of a neutron star.

In every case, we have objects with a finite, extended, character experiencing collisions with other extended objects. These phenomena simply cannot be reduced to massive points. A study of the situation soon reveals that the primary characteristics of the Riemannian geometry, its local and differential characters, fail to be effective for the new physical situation considered. In fact, interior trajectories such as those of satellites during re—entry, demand integro—differential equations, that is, equations having integral and differential terms. The applicable geometry is then expected to be of at least integro—differential type, although a full integral geometry is expected to be more appropriate (Section 1.8).

Mathematical studies on the construction of such geometries have already been initiated in the mathematical literature. Nevertheless, to my best knowledge, we do not possess to this writing a generalization of the Riemannian geometry which, on one side, constitutes a generalization of the Riemannian one, and, on the other side, permits an effective treatment of the interior problem of gravitation. Indications of suitable geometries would be gratefully appreciated.

Lacking the underlying geometry, we simply have no way to construct a meaningful gravitational theory for the interior problem.

In short, for the exterior problem, we do have a promising theory: Yilmaz's revision of Einstein's theory. For the interior problem, instead, we have no consistent theory to this writing. This is the reason why, in my own solitary efforts, I had to start with the attempt to generalize Galilei's relativity. The corresponding generalization of the special relativity (also for interior trajectories) is the second problem. The achievement of a consistent generalization of Einstein's interior gravitation can be tackled only upon achieving consistency in the preceding two layers of physical reality.

The legacy of Cartan.

The invalidation of the general theory of gravitation in the interior problem is not my own invention. Instead, it was identified by one of the founders of geometry, Cartan, and is known today as the "legacy of Cartan" (see, for instance, ref. [39], page 1712).

In fact, Cartan had indicated that the Riemannian geometry is unable to recover Newton's equations of motions at the limit of null curvature. This is evidently due to the infinite variety of possible Newtonian forces with arbitrary functional dependence in the velocities and other physical quantities, when compared with rather restricted rails of the Riemannian structure.

It is very regrettable that the legacy of Cartan is ignored in the virtual totality of scientific literature in gravitation except rare occasions.

The incompleteness of this presentation.

As done for the relativistic case, I must stress again the incompleteness of this presentation and apologize with all authors I have regrettably not quoted at this time.

NEWTONIAN LEVEL	GALILEI– ADMISSIBLE RELATIVITY ?	
RELATIVISTIC LEVEL	LORENTZ– ADMISSIBLE RELATIVITY ?	
GRAVITATIONAL LEVEL	LOCALLY LORENTZ– ADMISSIBLE RELATIVITY ?	

Fig. 1.5.3. A schematic view of the insufficiency of our current knowledge for the classical description of extended–deformable particles moving within inhomogeneous and anisotropic material media, as typical for all levels of interior trajectories, the Newtonian, the relativistic and the gravitational one. None of the relativities for the exterior case (Figure 1.5.2) is now applicable because of inconsistencies pointed out in the text. Only very preliminary and tentative studies are available at this writing for the applicable relativity. In the exterior case, a central problem is the interpretation of the stability of the orbit of particles under central–force fields. This stability is interpreted via the conservation of the angular momentum which, in turn, is represented via the symmetry under rotations. The Lorentz symmetry follow for the relativistic extension. As a result, a necessary condition for an exterior gravitational theory to be consistent is that it is locally–Lorentz, that is, it recovers the special relativity in the neighborhood of each space time point. In interior trajectories, the central problem is the representation of time–rates–of–variations of angular momenta due to contact effects in such a way to admit the conventional conservation as a particular case. A conjecture to develop a generalization of Galilei's relativity along these lines (called Galilei–admissible relativity) has been submitted in ref. [8]. The corresponding relativistic case has been touched in ref. [12]. The gravitational case has not been considered so far, to my best knowledge. One aspect is however known. Any gravitational theory, to be physically meaningful for the interior case, cannot be locally–Lorentz in character, that is, it MUST NOT admit the special relativity in the neighborhood of each point. In fact, such locally–Lorentz character implies, in particular, the local validity of the conventional rotational symmetry, that is, the local conservation of the angular momentum. The incompatibility of the general relativity for interior trajectories (such as Skylab during re–entry) is therefore due precisely to the locally–Lorentz character of the theory. If the conjecture of building a Galilei–admissible relativity will be proved meaningful, and admitting of a relativistic extension, then, the interior gravitational theory can be constructed accordingly, that is, by searching for a theory that is locally–Lorentz–admissible in character. Note that Yilmaz's "new theory" holds only for the exterior problem. In Section 1.6.1, I shall outline the inconsistencies of the reduction of the non–Hamiltonian interior trajectories of the real world to Hamiltonian trajectories of the constituent particles (which is at the basis of the current, widespread use of the Riemannian geometry for the interior problem).

However, unlike others, I am fully cooperative for the

remedial of my faults. I therefore invite all interested authors to let me know of their work on the limitations of conventional, exterior and interior gravitational theories. I shall than take all the necessary initiatives for their proper quotation in future work. At the Institute for Basic Research in Cambridge, we are interested in organizing reprint volumes of all relevant articles in the problems considered in this section. It will be my duty to make sure that all relevant articles brought to my attention are reprinted or at least properly quoted in such review volumes.

A first group of contributions here considered relevant are those identifying explicitly the limitations of available gravitational theories.

A second group of relevant contributions are those generalizing available exterior gravitational theories along the lines considered in this section, Yilmaz's revision of Einstein's gravitation (with corresponding revisions of gauge, supersymmetric and other models).

A third group of relevant contributions are those treating conceivable generalizations of the interior gravitational problem along the lines indicated earlier, that is, in such a way to achieve the capability of crude, but meaningful treatments of interior trajectories (satellites during re—entry, damped oscillators, decaying spinning tops, etc.).

Need for the taxpayer to exercise care in the acceptance of views by so—called "experts".

If you submit to The Physical Review a paper on the inconsistencies of Einstein's gravitation, the editors will inevitably send your paper to the leading "experts" in gravitation at leading colleges (Harvard University, the Massachusetts Institute of Technology, Yale University, and a few others). The rejection of the paper is then inevitable.

If you submit a research grant application to Governmental Agencies (such as the National Science Foundation or the Department of Energy) also on the limitations of Einstein's gravitations, you would also be waisting your money and time. The application would also be submitted to leading "experts" at leading institutions. The chances of acceptance are so minute to be ignorable.

This is the way U. S. physics is structured and operates at this time

Dear fellow taxpayer, you can do much better in the selection of "experts" and in the verification of their qualifications PRIOR to accepting their judgment.

To be qualified "experts on the limitations of Einstein's gravitation", physicists must have a record of publication of papers in refereed journals specifically in the limitations themselves.

Therefore, fellow taxpayer, PRIOR to accepting judgments on the inconsistencies of current gravitational theories, I urge you to ask for documentation of qualification. If the guy presents you a long list of publications in famous journals, do not be blinded. Keep going. Ask first for inspection of at least ONE publication in a refereed journal, and then request that passages be shown to you containing explicit words such as "invalidations", "inconsistencies", "incompatibilities" of Einstein's gravitation and similar sentences. If these physical problems are not addressed directly and explicitly, chances are that you are not facing a scientist.

Of course, ethically sound scholars in conventional gravitation do exist in the U.S.A. When consulted in the limitations of their own work, these people generally identify explicitly in the report their vested position, and stress the partial value of their view, of course, in favor of old ideas. Judgments of this clean type should indeed be considered and respected. The point is that no mature judgment can be achieved based only on them. Judgments by true experts in the inconsistencies of Einstein's gravitation, remain the most important ones.

After all, the formers discourage, while the latters promote advancements of physical knowledge.

Comments on the books in gravitation by Weinberg, by Misner—Thorne—Wheeler, and by Pais.

As indicated earlier, a most distressing aspect of gravitational literature is the lack of quotation of the problematic aspects of Einstein's general theory, which therefore acquires the artificial vest of perfection and terminal character.

In turn, the presentation of fundamental physical theories without the joint treatment of their limitations is one of the most antiscientific possible practices, inasmuch as it can assassinate at birth all sparks of creativity, particularly in young readers. As such, possible scientific services are overshadowed by the antiscientific aspect of preventing or otherwise discouraging advances.

This is by and large the status of the virtual totality of books in gravitation written by contemporary leading experts (evidence of the erroneous nature of this statement would be gratefully appreciated).

This presentation would have no value without specific cases of physically identified authors.

Among a variety of choices, I would like to comment on the following three books.

In 1972, I was intensely involved in the preparatory work of paper [40] (which was subsequently printed in 1974). The appearance at that time of book [26] in gravitation by S. Weinberg, then at Harvard University, was for me a rather shocking experience. I had been warned by B.B.B., a graduate student in physics who had attended the lectures on gravitations by Weinberg. At that time,* B.B.B. was also interested in fundamental open problems of gravitation. He communicated to me a sense of anguish in listening to Weinberg's lectures because of the presentation of Einstein's theory with a sort of an iron curtain of totalitarial validity, without a spark of possible fundamental advances. The reading of Weinberg's book confirmed these feelings. Most distressing for me was the presentation of the terminal character, not only of the general theory of relativity, but also, and primarily that of the special relativity. I subsequently learned that B.B.B. and myself were not the sole people to read Weinberg's book with a sense of distress. In fact, I now know of a number of authors who have quoted Weinberg's book essentially along these critical lines. But, in 1972 Steven Weinberg was a distinguished professor of physics at Harvard University. I therefore kept my impressions to myself and remained silent.

Only one year passed and then there was the appearance of the rather massive book in gravitation by Charles W. Misner of the University of Maryland, Kip S. Thorne of the California Institute of Technology, and John A. Wheeler, then at Princeton University (ref. [27]).

At that time, I was working at the final drafting and re—drafting of paper [40] as well as at the preliminary elements of monograph [11].

Again, I was shocked by the presentation of Einstein's special and general relativities as terminal descriptions of nature, without any meaningful hint of their limitations.

Perhaps too pessimistically, I recalled B.B.B. who had left physics in the meantime, and I imagined a negative impact of book [27] in the minds of countless young readers throughout the world.

This time I decided to initiate at least some action of containment of the scientific damage I was expecting from book [27]. I therefore began the drafting of a critical analysis of ref. [27], that was subsequently published in 1978 in Section 3.4 of ref. [11], page 458 and following.

Prior to releasing the criticism for printing, as scientific ethics demands, I did mail a preliminary copy of the manuscript to each of the three authors.

Regrettably, I have lost the correspondence with the passing of time. Nevertheless, I recall lack of reception of any acknowledgment by W. Misner. I also remember a rather cooperative attitude expressed by the remaining two authors, K. S.

---

*
B.B.B. subsequently abandoned physics for business. I regretted dearly the loss for physics of his young mind which was one of the sharpest and most inquisitives I ever met. Who knows how many other young minds have left the pursuit of novel scientific knowledge for other, more rewarding lives? What an immense loss for America as well as for the human society.

Thorne and J. A. Wheeler, which I report here with sincere pleasure.

But, by far, the most shocking experience was the reception of the more recent book [28] by Abraham Pais of Rockefeller University. As one can see, the manuscript was written some twenty years ago. I have no doubt that, if published at that time, the book would have been scientifically valuable and appropriate.

But the publication of the same book twenty years later had, for me, a most distressing effect. The book is a presentation of Einstein's theories without any mention of the limitations and inconsistencies that have been accumulated during the past twenty years. For instance, book [28] does not quote critical literature on Einstein's theories, such as Yilmaz's work [41—48].

I still remember quite vividly the evening of 1982 when, back home from a long day of study, I found among my mail Pais' book. By scanning through the various sections and the literature, it took me minutes to realize the potentially immense damage to the advancement of human knowledge, if not the creation of a modern obscurantism, that can be promoted by Pais' book, especially at a time in which courageous scientists throughout the world are resolving some of the limitations of Einstein's relativities.

I therefore went into my room, I locked the door, and, with this book on my knees, I cried.

Note added in proof: the generalization of Einstein's gravitation for the interior problem by the Italian physicist M. Gasperini.

Upon completion of the typesetting of this section, I received a paper by the Italian physicist M. Gasperini entitled "A Lie—admissible theory of gravity", ref. [50], with complementary comments presented in ref. [51].

Gasperini has essentially initiated the generalization of Einstein's interior gravitation indicated as lacking in this section, that incorporating all possible Newtonian systems, as needed for realistic trajectories in the interior problem of gravitation.

In fact, Gasperini's interior gravitation is, first of all, of open/non—conservative character and, second, it is locally Galilean—admissible in the sense of ref. [8], as well as locally Lorentz—admissible in the sense of ref. [12]. As such, Gasperini's relativity enjoys the direct universality of all physical theories possessing a Lie—admissible structure. By comparison, the representational capabilities of Einstein's interior gravitation is of extremely minute nature (in fact, it can represent only interior trajectories of "perpetual—motion—type"). The non—incremental advance from Einstein's to Gasperini's interior relativity is then evident.

1.6 THE AGING OF GALILEI'S AND EINSTEIN'S RELATIVITIES IN PARTICLE PHYSICS.

Scientific, economic and military implications of the validity or invalidity of Einstein's ideas in particle physics.

By far, the most important implications of the validity or invalidity of Einstein's ideas occur in particle physics.

Scientifically, we are talking about the ultimate foundations of current physical knowledge, with a direct or indirect bearing on numerous branches of science, such as theoretical biology or solid state physics.

Economically, Einstein's ideas are known to be at the basis of the nuclear energy and other aspects. Their possible generalization can conceivably permit the discovery of new, more efficient forms of energy currently unthinkable. After all, strongly interacting particles (hadrons) are the biggest energy reservoir known to mankind. With fission and fusion we have barely touched the surface of this reservoir.

Militarily, the implications are equally far reaching. It is today generally believed that only a few nuclei are fissionable and therefore usable to build bombs. If suitable generalized views are valid in the interior of hadrons, new, currently unthinkable weapons could be possible.

Dear fellow taxpayer, I detest weapons as much as you do. But, the security of my children depends on the military strength of America. The inclusion of a military profile in this presentation has been rendered necessary by the rejection of research projects submitted by the Institute for Basic Research to U.S. military agencies (the Defense Advance Research Project Agency—DARPA—and others). The limited information (evidently without any detail) presented in this book is known by a number of foreign physicists. While the U.S. government is apparently not interested in military applications originating from generalizations of Einstein's ideas in the interior of hadrons, other governments may think otherwise. Besides an ethical profile, there is an evident aspect of national security. When vested academic—financial—ethnic interests on Einstein's ideas endanger or jeopardize even minimally the security of this Country, I cannot be silent.

In this section, I shall attempt an outline of the central aspects underlying the above profiles.

Regrettably, all contemporary treatments of particle physics depend on abstract mathematical formalisms in a truly essential way. All nontechnical reviews are therefore inherently deficient. This review is no exception.

The fellow taxpayer, however, should not feel discouraged by the abstract content of this section. In fact, the ultimate physical ideas remain accessible to all. In turn, an understanding of the basic ideas and of their plausibility (and not of their mathematical treatment) is essential to achieve a mature judgment of the problem of ethics in the scientific, economic and military sectors of the U.S. physics.

Central aspects of nonrelativistic and relativistic quantum mechanics.

Quantum mechanics (see, for instance, the book by Dirac [52]) is often differentiated into nonrelativistic and relativistic formulations. The former is characterized by the applicable relativity, the Galilean one, while the latter is characterized by the special relativity. All formulations are quantum mechanical in the sense that they are characterized by local—differential operators acting on a particular type of carrier spaces called Hilbert spaces (par contre, the corresponding classical formulations are expressed via ordinary functions of local variables).

The formulation of the relativities via operators on Hilbert spaces implies a number of principles which are typical of the particles world, such as: Heisenberg's uncertainty principle (expressing our inability to measure jointly positions and momenta of particles with unlimited precision); Pauli's exclusion principle (expressing the impossibility that more than one identical particle with half—odd—integer spin occupies the same state with given quantum numbers); and others. It should be recalled that the mutual compatibility and inter—dependence of the various parts of quantum mechanics are so rigid, that deviations from any principle would necessarily imply deviations from the underlying relativities, and vice versa.

The mathematical structure of quantum mechanics is characterized by local—differential operators, say, A,B,C, . . .acting on Hilbert spaces over complex numbers. Operators essentially represent physical quantities such as coordinate r, momentum p, energy H, etc. The multiplication of operators is the ordinary product AB verifying the associative rule $(AB)C = A(BC)$. The set of all possible operators A,B,C, . . .equipped with the product AB is called the enveloping associative algebra. Said algebra permits, for instance, the calculation of squares of operators (say, $p^2=pp$) which, in turn, are generally needed to compute physical quantities (such as, for instance, the kinetic energy $T = pp/2m$).

Most important equations representing the dynamical evolution of quantum mechanical particles are given by the celebrated Heisenberg's equations. They can be written for an arbitrary physical quantity operator A as $i\hbar\dot{A} = AH - HA$, where: H is the total energy; AH is the associative product considered earlier; AH—HA is the Lie product attached to the enveloping algebra (see also Section 1.4); and $\hbar$ is Planck's constant.

All space—time symmetries, including the Galilean and the Lorentzian symmetries, are expressed via groups of transformations of the so—called unitary type. They are given by operators of the type $U = \exp(iwA)$ verifying certain conditions.

Whether in nonrelativistic or relativistic mechanics, the time evolution is represented by the unitary transformation $U = \exp(itH)$ where t is time and H is the total energy. For infinitesimal values of time, the unitary time evolution yields precisely Heisenberg's equations which, as such, acquire a fundamental character not only for the representation of the dynamical evolution, but also for the characterization of the structure of the applicable relativities.

An arena of unequivocal applicability of quantum mechanics: the atomic structure.

An arena of unequivocal applicability of quantum mechanics is well known. It is given by systems of particles under electromagnetic interactions, that is, particles which:

A)   can be effectively approximated as being point—like;

B)   move in empty space conceived as homogeneous and isotropic; and are such that

C)   gravitational effects are ignorable.

On a comparative basis with the arenas considered in the preceding sections, we have essentially permitted "quantum effects", that is, processes of emissions and absoption of energy in discrete amounts that are multiples of Planck's constant $\hbar$.

An illustration of the arena considered is given by the atomic structure. After all, we should not forget that the mechanics was conceived and constructed, specifically, for the understanding of the atomic structure, and for that structure it resulted to be correct beyond the best expectations of its builders.

Doubts on the exact validity of quantum mechanics for the nuclear structure.

One of my first duties as a graduate student in theoretical physics was to conduct an in depth study of the application of quantum mechanics to the atomic structure. During these studies, I was soon fascinated by the beauty of the theory as well as by the amount of direct experimental verification, that still impress me to this day.

During the same program, I had subsequently to study the application of quantum mechanics to the different physical arena of the nuclear structure. This time, however, I experienced considerable uneasiness which has remained with me to this day. The reasons are due to the fact that the physical conditions of the nuclear structure are profoundly different than those of the atomic structure. Even though the approximate validity of quantum mechanics in nuclear physics is, and should remain, unquestionable, the problem of its exact validity remains basically open.

The physical differences between the atomic and the nuclear structure are well known (although rarely emphasized in the contemporary technical literature). The mutual distances of the peripheral electrons in the atomic structure are so large, that the size of their wave—packets can be ignored. In the transition to the nuclear structure, the situation is different. In fact, the constituents of nuclei (protons and neutrons) have extended charge distributions and wave—packets whose size is of the order of 10^{-13}cm. Nuclear volumes are also known. Simple calculations then show that the constituents of nuclei are so close together to be actually in (average) conditions of mutual overlapping of about 1/1000 parts of their volume.

This situation has implications at all levels of study. In fact, while quantum jumps of energy can be readily justified in the atomic structure owing to the distance among stable orbits and their occurrence in empty space, the visualization of the same situation in nuclear structures creates uneasiness. Even though stable orbits may be somewhat conceived, quantum jumps of energy similar to those of the atomic structure are not possible, trivially, because the nuclear volume is filled up with hadronic matter. The nuclear constituents are not, therefore, "free to jump" from one orbit to another. In short, the extended character of the constituents of nuclei and their conditions of mutual penetration creates doubts on the final character of the truly central notion of quantum mechanics, the "quantum" of energy.

Most significantly, while the atomic two—body, the hydrogen atom, admits an infinite, discrete, spectrum of excited states, the corresponding nuclear two—body, the deuterium, has revealed no excited state at all, by therefore resulting to be one, single, unique structure. This differentiation alone was, for me, sufficient to warrant the search for a generalization of quantum mechanics, inasmuch as the nuclear emphasis is in the suppression of the atomic spectrum of energy.

The dynamical roots of possible departures from quantum mechanics: nonlocal effects due to mutual wave overlappings of wave—packets of particles.

Once the conditions of mutual penetration of the wave—packets of protons and neutrons are truly considered, they imply the lack of applicability of the mathematical foundations of quantum mechanics, let alone the mechanics itself. In fact, the conditions imply the presence of contact interactions which do not admit potential energy (Section 1.3), and thus, cannot be mediated by particle exchange, that is, by exchange of discrete amounts of energy. In turn, contact interactions have a number of implications, such as: the inability to represent the system considered via only one operator, the total energy operator (Hamiltonian); the inapplicability of the local—differential character of the underlying geometry in favor of nonlocal/integro—differential generalizations, etc.

This process of critical examination of the validity of quantum mechanics in nuclear physics should not be misrepresented. In fact, the approximate validity of the mechanics in the arena considered is and remains out of the question. After all, the successes of quantum mechanics in nuclear physics are well known. The problem that is open at this time is the possibility of corrections in the quantum mechanical description of nuclei. Said corrections are expected to be essentially small in value because the conditions of mutual penetration of nuclear constituents are small, as recalled earlier. However, the implications of the corrections would be far reaching, because they would imply a generalization of the ultimate physical and mathematical foundations of the theory.

The expected insufficiencies of quantum mechanics for the interior of hadrons.

In the transition to the problem of the structure of neutrons, protons, and all hadrons, the departures from quantum mechanics are expected to increase. In fact, all strongly interacting particles possess a size which is of the order of magnitude of the range of the strong interactions, about 10^{-13}cm. This implies that the constituents of hadrons are expected to be in conditions of mutual penetration much greater than those of the nuclear constituents. As an example, for a proton and an electron to reach a bound state of the order of the size of the neutron, the two particles must be in conditions of total mutual penetration and overlapping of their wave—packets. The departure of these physical conditions from those of the hydrogen atom are then clear.

It is evident that, while conceivable deviations from conventional relativities and quantum mechanics can be at best small for the nuclear structure, they can be much greater for the hadronic structure.

If we pass to the problem of the structure of the core of stars, say, undergoing gravitational collapse, deviations from quantum mechanics are expected to be maximal, not only because of the additional presence of gravitational effects, but also because of the maximization of the conditions of mutual overlapping of the particles, that is, of the departures from the

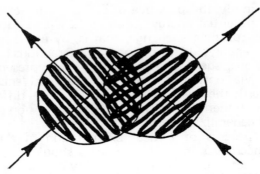

Figure 1.6.1. A reproduction of Table 5, p. 1214 of ref. [53] intended to illustrate the insufficiency of point—like abstractions of particles for a deeper understanding of strong interactions. According to a rather wide-spread view in contemporary physics, the entire universe can be reduced to a collection of points (resulting into the so—called local theories), with only action—at—a—distance interactions (resulting into theories of potential type). According to this view, the entire universe can be described by only one quantity, the Lagrangian or the Hamiltonian, defined locally, at a collection of distinct points. In fact, all known interactions are today reduced to local—differential and potential treatments. I am referring to electromagnetic, weak, strong and gravitational interactions. Now, the existence of interactions that can be effectively treated via these local—differential and potential techniques is unquestionable, as typically the case of the electromagnetic interactions. However, the existence of interactions which are structurally beyond local—differential and potential techniques is equally unquestionalbe. This is typically the case for the strong interactions whose range is exactly of the order of magnitude of the size of all hadrons, 10^{-13}cm. The diagram above therefore depicts the conditions of mutual penetration of the wave—packets of particles which are necessary to activate the strong interactions. It is then evident to all that wave—packets in conditions of deep mutual penetration cannot be effectively reduced to isolated, dimensionless points, unless extremely crude descriptions are desired. The diagram above therefore identifies the insufficiency of the contemporary reduction of the universe to a collection of isolated points (locality) with only action—at—a—distance interactions (potentiality), in favor of suitable, non—local/integro—differential generalizations. Regrettably, the mere view of the experimental reality depicted by the diagram above generally creates semi—hysterical reactions by physicists with vested interests in local/potential models; by therefore precluding the implementation of a constructive scientific process of trial and error in the selection of the appropriate generalizations. In fact, the diagram presents a visible illustration of the lack of exact character for strong interactions of the most essential structures of contemporary particle physics, the special relativity, quantum mechanics and Lie's theory. Note that the symbol of the I.B.R. is given precisely by two overlapping circles representing hadrons under strong interactions.

---

atomic structure (see Figure 1.6.1).

A dominant physical characteristic of all strongly interacting systems is therefore that motion cannot be conceived as occurring in vacuum, because it occurs in a material medium consisting of other hadrons, called "hadronic medium" [14]. It is evident that this medium is not, in general, homogeneous or isotropic, thus implying the breakdown of the prerequisites for the applicability of the Galilean and special relativities, exactly along the corresponding occurrences in classical mechanics (Section 1.3 and 1.4).

The proposal to construct hadronic mechanics as a generalization of quantum mechanics specifically conceived for strong interactions.

The considerations above identify the following arena of expected insufficiency of quantum mechanics. It is given by systems of extended particles/wave–packets which:

A') cannot be effectively approximated as being point–like;

B') move in inhomogeneous and anisotropic hadronic media; and are such that

C') gravitational effects are ignorable.

A proposal to construct a generalization of quantum mechanics for the broader physical conditions A'), B'), and C') was submitted in memoir [14]. The name of "hadronic mechanics" was recommended for the new mechanics to emphasize the intended applicability of the generalized mechanics only to the hadronic phenomenology, as well as to stress the medium in which motion occurs, the hadronic medium.

Hadronic mechanics was recommended to be a "covering" of quantum mechanics, that is: to apply for physically broader conditions; to possess a mathematically broader structure; and to admit quantum mechanics not only as a particular case, but also in first approximation. The latter requirement is evidently essential to recover the known achievements of quantum mechanics in particle physics (see Figure 1.6.2 for more details).

A comprehensive mathematical, theoretical and experimental program was initiated on the construction of the hadronic generalization of quantum mechanics, as we shall review below in this and the remaining sections of this chapter. Despite these efforts, it must be stressed that the studies are at the beginning and far from being conclusive.

What we can claim today is the mathematical existence and self–consistency of hadronic mechanics, but we do not have conclusive evidence of its effectiveness for the representation of nuclei, hadrons and stars.

The situation for quantum mechanics is essentially the same.

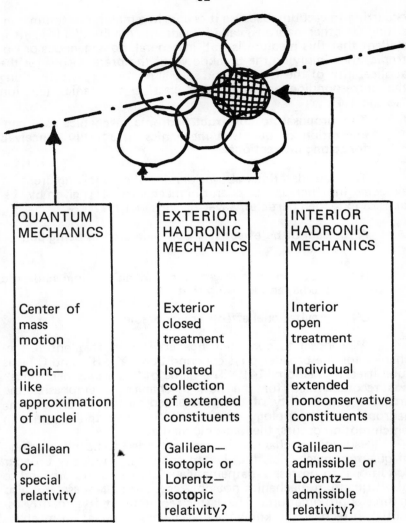

QUANTUM MECHANICS	EXTERIOR HADRONIC MECHANICS	INTERIOR HADRONIC MECHANICS
Center of mass motion	Exterior closed treatment	Interior open treatment
Point— like approximation of nuclei	Isolated collection of extended constituents	Individual extended nonconservative constituents
Galilean or special relativity	Galilean— isotopic or Lorentz— isotopic relativity?	Galilean— admissible or Lorentz— admissible relativity?

Figure 1.6.2. The three conceivable layers of the descriptions of a system of strongly interacting particles, such as a nucleus or a hadron. First, one can consider the system as moving in empty space under long range electromagnetic interactions. In this case, the system can be approximated as being a massive, charged, point. The theory is purely Hamiltonian, that is, the knowledge of only the total energy H is sufficient to characterize the time evolution of an arbitrary (total) physical quantity A according to the celebrated Heisenberg equations, which I write in the form $idA/dt = A*H - H*A$, where $A*H = A(1/\hbar) H$, and the products are the ordinary associative products. Quantum mechanics then strictly applies, with the underlying Galilean and special relativities. Their time component is given by the exponentiated form of Heisenberg's equations, which I write in the form $A' = \exp(itH/\hbar) A \exp-(itH/\hbar)$. The same mechanics and underlying physi-

cal laws are today assumed as valid also for the characterization of the structure of strongly interacting systems. Quantum mechanics, however, can only represent protons and neutrons (and their constituents) as massive, dimensionless points, as well known. As a result, quantum mechanical models of nuclei are intrinsically unable to represent the extended character of the nuclear constituents and related phenomenology (such as the possible deformability of neutrons and proton when within a nuclear structure, with consequential alteration of their magnetic moments; see below in the main text). Greater insufficiencies occur for the problem of the hadronic structure (see below). In the hope of reaching advances in these latter problems, the construction of a generalization of quantum mechanics under the name of "hadronic mechanics" was suggested in memoir [14]. An objective was that of achieving, in due time, an operator version of the closed, non–Hamiltonian systems of our Newtonian reality, such as our Earth (Section 1.3), where the contact, non–Hamiltonian, internal forces are precisely a representative of the extended character of the constituents. Besides possible new insights in strong interactions, hadronic mechanics could then permit the attempt of regaining the currently lacking unity of physical and mathematical thought (see below in the main text). As well known, under point–like approximation of hadrons, quantum mechanics can characterize both a strong system as a whole and each of its open constituents. Under contact/non–Hamiltonian internal forces among extended constituents, the situation resulted to be different inasmuch as a formulation effective for the exterior, closed, treatment resulted to be not necessarily effective for the characterization of each individual open constituent much along the classical counterpart. The construction of hadronic mechanics was therefore recommended along two different, yet complementary branches, one for the exterior treatment of isolated strongly interacting systems, and one for the complementary interior treatment of each individual open constituent. The emphasis in the former case is therefore in the achievement of total nonconservation laws under non–Hamiltonian internal forces, while the emphasis in the latter case is in the maximization of the nonconservation of the physical characteristics of each constituent, evidently, as a condition to maximize the internal interactions. The exterior–closed treatment was restricted to possess the same mathematical structure (Lie–isotopic theory) of its classical counterpart, the Birkhoffian mechanics [10], while the interior–open description was restricted to possess the same mathematical structure (Lie–admissible theory) of the classical Birkhoffian–admissible mechanics [12].

EXTERIOR, LIE–ISOTOPIC BRANCH OF HADRONIC MECHANICS.

An important element of quantum mechanics is the unit. This is an element I of the operator algebra verifying the rules $IA = AI = A$ for all operators A, where the product is the trivial associative product recalled earlier in this section. This unit has fundamental physical relevance inasmuch as it represents Planck's constant. The mathematical relevance is equally fundamental, because Lie's theory, space–time symmetries, and conventional relativities can be constructed beginning from the unit element. A central idea of hadronic mechanics is that of generalizing the unit element I into nontrivial operator forms. For the case of the exterior–closed branch, the generalized unit can be written $\hat{I} = g^{-1} \neq \text{diag}(1,1,1,...) \hbar$, and follows from the generalization of the conventional associative product AB of quantum mechanics into the form $A*B = AgB$, $g = $ fixed, for which $\hat{I}*A = A*\hat{I} = A$. The product $A*B$ is an isotope of AB in the sense that it preserves the original associative character of the envelope. The new envelope is then called "isoenvelope". The generalization of the quantum mechanical unit implies the consequential generalization of the totality of the theory. In fact, the antisymmetric product attached to the isoenvelope is now given by $A*B - B*A$ and it is still Lie. Physically, this implies the generalization of the fundamental dynamical equations, Heisenberg's equations, into the isotopic form $idA/dt = A*H - H*A = AgH - HgA$ first proposed in ref. [14], p. 752. One can see the need of two quantities to characterize a strong system, the total energy operator H and the isotopic operator g, the latter one representing precisely the internal non–Hamiltonian forces. When $\hat{T} = I\hbar$, $I = diag(1,1,1,....)$, hadronic mechanics recovers quantum mechanics identically. When $\hat{T}$ is close to $I\hbar$, we have small deviations from quantum mechanics (as conceivable in the interior of nuclei) otherwise we have finite deviations (as conceivable in the interior of hadrons and of stars). The generally non–local integro–differentive operator $\hat{T} = g^{-1}$ can therefore be conceived as a generalization of Planck's constant $\hbar$ for particles under mutual wave–overlapping. The total energy is trivially conserved because of the antisymmetry of the product, $idH/dt = H*H - H*H = 0$. The conservation of other total quantities then follows much along conventional lines. In this way hadronic mechanics achieves total conservation laws under non–Hamiltonian internal forces, as desired. Quantum mechanics admits a single infinity of possible models, those characterized by the all possible Hamiltonians H. The exterior branch of hadronic mechanics admits a double infinity of possible models, those characterized by all possible Hamiltonians H and isotopic operator g which must therefore be selected from experimental information on the system considered. The isotopic generalization of Heisenberg's equations admits a consistent exponentiation into a group of non–unitary transformations called unitary–isotopic. In turn, this implies the generalization of the Galilean and special relativities, beginning with their time component, from the conventional unitary form recalled earlier, to the generalized form $A' = exp(iH*t)Aexp(-it*H)$. The generalization is called Lie–isotopic because it preserves the essential axiomatic structure of Lie's theory. The underlying carrier space of quantum mechanics, the Hilbert space, is also subjected to an axiom–preserving generalization, resulting into a structure called isohilbert space. The quantum mechanical action $A\psi$ of operators A on elements ψ of the Hilbert space is generalized into the isotopic form $A*\psi$ resulting into a generalization of all the remaining parts of quantum mechanics such as Schroedinger's equations, eigenvalue equations, operations on Hilbert spaces, observables, etc. [77]. The compatibility of the exterior branch of hadronic mechanics with the center–of–mass, quantum mechanical treatment has been recently established [55]. I am referring to the proof that generalized quantum mechanical laws for the interior nuclear and hadronic problem (such as generalized Heisenberg's uncertainties) are compatible with conventional quantum mechanical laws for the center–of–mass treatment (such as conventional uncertainties). As a result, the validity of quantum mechanics for the dynamical evolution, say, of one proton in a particle accelerator constitutes no evidence whatsoever for the validity of the same laws for the interior structural problem.

INTERIOR LIE–ADMISSIBLE BRANCH OF HADRONIC MECHANICS.

The physical requirement of reaching the nonconservation of physical quantities of ONE individual constituent, is permitted by a dual generalization of the quantum mechanical unit, one for the product to the right, $I^{\triangleright} = f^{-1}$

and one for the product to the left, $\triangleleft_l = g^{-1}$, $g \neq f$. In turn, this implies two different isoenvelopes, one for the action to the right $A \triangleright \psi = Af\psi$, and one for the action to the left $\psi \triangleleft A = \psi gA$. Physically, the cases describe evolutions moving forward and backward in time. The cases are therefore connected by time reversal. One reaches in this way a further generalization of Heisenberg's equation of the type $idA/dt = A \triangleleft H - H \triangleright A = AgH - HfA$ first proposed in ref. [14], p. 746, which is called of Lie—admissible type for certain mathematical reasons (see Section 1.8), where H now represents only the energy of the individual particle considered. Its nonconservation then follows from the lack of antisymmetry of the product, $idH/dt = H(g-f)H \neq 0$. A similar situation occurs for other quantities under the evident condition that these internal nonconservations must be compatible with total conservations.. The Lie—admissible generalization also admits an exponentiation into the form $A' = \exp(iH \triangleright t)A \exp(-it \triangleleft H)$ which is now no longer of Lie character. This suggested the construction of a further, Lie—admissible generalization of the Galilean and special relativities [14], this time for the characterization of one nuclear or hadronic constituent (rather than a strongly interacting system as a whole). The underlying mathematical structure is called a Lie—admissible bi—module [86—88]. The generalization of the remaining aspects of the Lie—isotopic formulations into the more general Lie—admissible form is then consequential. For a review, the interested reader may consult ref. [78]. Despite its abstract mathematical structure, the interior Lie—admissible branch of hadronic mechanics essentially consists of an algebraically consistent re—formulation of the nonunitary time evolutions conventionally used in quantum mechanical treatments of open, nonconservative, particle reactions. These latter transformations can be written $A' = \exp(i\mathcal{H}t)A \exp(-it\mathcal{H}^{\dagger})$, where $\mathcal{H}^{\dagger}$ is the so—called hermitean conjugate of $\mathcal{H}$. Their infinitesimal version is given by $idA/dt = A\mathcal{H}^{\dagger} - \mathcal{H} A$, and does not characterize a consistent algebra owing to its trilinear character. The decompositions $\mathcal{H}^{\dagger} = Hg$, $\mathcal{H} = fH$, $H = H^{\dagger}$, $g^{\dagger} = f$, then implies the Lie—admissible form above which restores the bilinearity of the product and the consistency of the algebra. The regaining of a consistent algebra implies the possibility of physical calculations that would be otherwise difficult or impossible [59]. Note that the interior branch of hadronic mechanics is intrinsically irreversible, in the sense that the time evolution of each constituent is generally non—invariant under time inversion even when its Hamiltonian H is time—reflection invariant. Such time—reflection—asymmetry generally disappears in the transition to the exterior, Lie—isotopic form (see below the comments on the origin of irreversibility. Particularly important is the "direct universality" of hadronic mechanics established in 1979 (ref. [39], p. 1820). I am referring to a theorem stating that, under sufficient topological conditions, all possible, generally nonunitary time evolutions can be written in the Lie—admissible form indicated above. The Lie—isotopic and the conventional, quantum mechanical forms are then trivial particular cases. Also important is the property that hadronic and quantum mechanics admit a single, unique, abstract mathematical structure. In fact, the isotopic products are associative in the same measure as that of the conventional product; the isohilbert spaces are Hilbert; etc. Quantum mechanics is the simplest possible realization of these mathematical axioms, while hadronic mechanics is the most general possible realization. The understanding is that a generalization of quantum mechanics is applied only when warranted by sufficient physical conditions. The abstract unification of hadronic and quantum mechanics is the operator counterpart of the corresponding classical occurrence, the unification of Hamiltonian and Birkhoffian mechanics into single, abstract, Lie/symplectic structures. This property therefore confirms the achievement of hadronic mechanics as an operator version of Birkhoffian mechanics.

APPLICATIONS, DEVELOPMENTS AND COMMENTS. The hadronic generalization of quantum mechanics was suggested for the representation of the possible alteration of the intrinsic magnetic moments of protons and neutrons when under sufficiently intense fields and/or collisions, for the possible identification of the origin of irreversibility, for the possible identification of the hadronic constituents with physical, experimentally detected particles, and other primary applications reviewed in the main text. A number of additional applications have also been initiated in the literature, such as the hadronic generalization of gauge theories, of quantum field theory, of the interior gravitation, and others. The theoretical physicists who have primarily contributed to the construction of the hadronic mechanics following proposal [14] are the following: R. Mignani (Italy), G. Eder (Austria), A. Kalnay (Venezuela), M Gasperini (Italy), C. N. Ktorides (Greece), J. Fronteau and A. Tellez—Arenas (France), P. Caldirola (Italy), A. Jannussis (Greece), M. Nishioka (Japan), J. Lohmus, M. Koiv and L. Sorgsepp (U.S.S.R.), Chun—Xuan Jiang (China), E. Kapuscik (Poland), A. Schober and R. Trostel (West Germany), and others. A primary mathematical contribution has been provided by H. C. Myung (U.S.A.). Other mathematical contributions will be listed in Section 1.8. Experimental contributions will be identified in Section 1.7. Regrettably, U.S. governmental agencies rejected a considerable number of research grant applications for the construction of the hadronic mechanics filed over a three year period (from the founding of the I.B.R. in 1981 until 1983). Even grant applications for possible military developments were rejected (see below). A plea to all primary U.S. private foundations resulted to be a total waste of time and money. As a consequence of these rejections, all physical research on the hadronic mechanics has been halted in the U.S.A., but it is continued abroad at a fast growing pace. In fact, at the time of writing this page (May 15, 1984) there is absolutely no U.S. physicist working on the construction of the hadronic mechanics, to my best knowledge (I have myself halted all research in the sector, as indicated earlier). Even the conduction of scientific meetings (Conferences, Workshops and research sessions) have all been moved abroad, evidently, because of the financial impossibility of their conduction in the U.S.A. This condition is per se instructive. In fact, the fellow taxpayer can readily compare the large number of reserach contracts along minute incremental advances on established trends, versus the evident fundamental relevance in the construction of a new discipline. This suppression of research via the systematic prevention of funding is however only part of the issue. To achieve a mature judgment of the current condition of basic physical research in the U.S.A., the fellow taxpayer must be informed of the remaining facets, such as the impossibility of publishing articles in the hadronic mechanics at the journals of the American Physical Society, the impossibility of obtaining jobs, the refusal of academic hospitality for the mere needs of library facilities, and numerous other aspects reviewed in Chapter 2.

The first quantitative predictions of hadronic mechanics in nuclear physics: alterations of spin and magnetic moments under intense, external, strong collisions.

As recalled in Section 1.1, early studies in nuclear physics lead quite naturally to the hypothesis that the value of the magnetic moments of protons and neutrons change in the transition from the electromagnetic to the strong interactions. The hypothesis emerged quite naturally from the fact that total nuclear magnetic moments still escape full understanding [2,3]. As also recalled in Section 1.1, studies of the hypothesis were subsequently halted, apparently because of its implications for academic politics, despite the manifest plausibility and the eqally manifest relevance for controlled fusion and other aspects. To this day, the magnetic moments of protons and neutrons have been measured and re-measured countless times, but all times when the particles move in empty space under long range electromagnetic interactions, while no measures of the same quantitity under strong nuclear conditions exist

The studies of the hypothesis were resumed in memoir [14] according to the following main lines.: Quantum mechanics represents protons and neutrons as points which, being dimensionless, cannot be deformed, thus preserving their intrinsic characteristics for the life of the particles. The constancy of the magnetic moments (and all other intrinsic characteristics) then follows under any possible external field.

Memoir [14] suggested the construction of the hadronic generalization of quantum mechanics for the purpose of representing protons, neutrons and all hadrons as they actually are in the physical reality, extended particles with a charge distribution of about two Fermis. The representation of hadrons as extended implies the consequential possibility that they can experience deformations under sufficiently intense external fields and/or collisions. In turn, such a deformation of shape necessarily implies the alteration (called "mutation" in hadronic mechanics) of the magnetic moments.

These results were reached in memoir [14] via the hypothesis that the intrinsic angular momentum (spin) of proton, neutron, and the hadron in general, may experience deviation-mutation from the conventional quantum mechanical values under sufficiently intense collisions with other particles, much along the established classical counterpart. The alteration of spin would then imply the necessary alteration of the magnetic moment.

These are evidently the most general conceivable conditions for the mutation of magnetic moments of hadrons, with nontrivial consequences. In fact, the alteration of spin ½ of the proton or the neutron would imply their lack of strict verification of Pauli exclusion principle, trivially, because the particles are no longer exact fermions. In turn, mutation of spin implies corresponding deviations from the Galilean and special relativities. For these reasons, ref. [14] promoted the test of the special relativity and Pauli principle beginning from the title.

The assistance by distinguished U.S. mathematicians, such as H. C. Myung and others (see Section 1.8), permitted the initiation of quantitative studies [60,61]. The first contact with experiments occurred in paper [62], where the use of available experimental data permitted the fit with the (average) value of spin 0.49777 for neutrons under strong nuclear interactions due to Mu-metal nuclei. In the hope of minimizing possible misrepresentations, it was stressed in the literature, beginning with ref. [14], that the conceivable value of spin 0.49777 was specifically intended for neutrons under the OPEN NONCONSERVATIVE conditions caused by EXTERNAL NUCLEAR INTERACTIONS, and that conventional total value of angular momentum are recovered if one considers the system neutron-nucleus.

These remarks are important, not only to identify the proper conditions for meaningful experiments, but also to maximize the conditions for the mutations of spin and magnetic moments predicted by hadronic mechanics (see Section 1.7).

The second quantitative predictions of hadronic mechanics in nuclear physics: alteration of magnetic moments while preserving conventional values of spin.

In the preceding paragraph, I have reported the state of the art in the problem of mutation of spin and of magnetic moments as of August 1980.

Fundamental advances in the problem were subsequently achieved by the Austrian physicists G. Eder, a senior expert in nuclear physics (see his book [63]). His most important contribution, presented in articles [64, 65, 66], is that the magnetic moments of protons and neutrons can mutate while preserving the conventional value of the spin of the particles. In addition, Eder reached a specific, quantitative, prediction of 1% mutation ("fluctuation" in his words) in the angle of spin precession for neutrons in the intense electromagnetic fields in the vicinity of silicon nuclei (see ref. [65], p. 2031).

Thus, prior to Eder's contributions, the emphasis was first on the mutation of spin under external strong interactions, with consequential mutation of magnetic moments. Eder showed that the mutation of magnetic moments can also occur under sufficiently intense, but purely electromagnetic interactions, without the necessary presence of the strong. In this latter case, the values of spin can remain the conventional ones.

Eder's studies opened up a new experimental orizon we shall review in the next section. At this moment, we indicate the following hierarchy of descriptions and related experimental verifications.

First, we have protons and neutrons (as well as any other hadron) moving in empty space under interactions that do not imply an appreciable deformation of their shape. Under these conditions, the particles can be well approximated as being point–like. Quantum mechanics then strictly applies, jointly with the preservation of conventional values of the magnetic moments. A large body of experimental verifications exist for these conventional conditions, as generally reported in nuclear physics books.

Second, we have the conditions discovered by Eder, whereby the value of the spin of protons and neutrons remains ½, but the value of the magnetic moments is altered because of deformations of the shape of the particles and other dynamical effects. Since the value of the spin is not changed, the protons and neutrons under these conditions are expected to obey Pauli's exclusion principles. The mutations can be measured directly via the so–called neutron interferometer experiments. Most importantly, the predictions of hadronic mechanics are well within available experimental capabilities. Even more importantly, the cost of the experiments is truly minimal (in the range of $ 50,000) particularly when compared to the large costs of current high energy experiments (that can reach millions of dollars).

Third, we have the full case of memoir [14], interactions and/or collisions sufficiently more intense than those of the preceding level, to cause an alteration of the value of the spin, with consequential mutation if the magnetic moments and departures from Pauli's exclusion principle. These latter predictions can be today tested via the scattering of sufficiently energetic neutrons on tritium and other means, as we shall see in the next section.

Hadronic regeneration of space–time and internal symmetries that are quantum mechanically broken.

One of the biggest misrepresentations of the studies on the construction of hadronic mechanics is the alleged intention of the theory to "break" fundamental space–time and other symmetries. This misrepresentation generally occurs because of lack of knowledge of the available literature (or because desired for reasons of academic politics).

The reality is the opposite of that. Hadronic mechanics offers genuine possibilities of regenerating space–time and other symmetries that are broken at the level of quantum mechanics.

The rotational symmetry is the best illustration of this occurence. Consider a proton or a neutron, and assume that they are perfectly spherical (which is already debatable to begin with), i.e., they have the structure discussed in Section 1.4: $R'R = xx + yy + zz = 1$. In this case, the conventional rotational symmetry is exact.

Suppose now that the particles experience a deformation of their shape due to external forces and collisions, as indicated earlier. Assume the simplest possible deformations, those into ellipsoids. Then the sphere is replaced by the equations also considered in Section 1.4: $R'gR = xa_1x + ya_2y + za_3z = 1$, where the a's are positive—definite quantities expressing the three principal axis of the ellipses, and the metric g generally depends on all possible local quantities, such as coordinates R, speeds $\dot{R}$, etc., $g = g(R, \dot{R}, \ldots)$.

Under these conditions, the rotational symmetry is manifestly broken. After all, the symmetry was conceived for point—like particles. For extended—deformable particles, ethically sound physicists may disagree on the appropriate generalization, but not on the breaking of the conventional rotational symmetry at the quantum mechanical level.

The main idea of the generalized rotational symmetry suggested by hadronic mechanics for extended—deformable particles is the following. It is that given by the Lie—isotopic generalization of Lie's symmetries discussed in Section 1.4. It begins with the generalization of the associative algebra, from the trivial form AB of quantum mechanics to the less trivial form $A*B = AgB$ of hadronic mechanics, where g is precisely the metric of the deformed shape of the particles. It then implies the generalization of each and every aspect of the conventional rotational symmetry, from the unit, to the group structure, to the Lie algebra, to the representation theory, etc., as presented in ref. [19, 32, 54].

Most important is the property that the isotopic rotation group is locally isomorphic to the conventional group [54]. Thus, the ultimate, axiomatic foundations of the symmetry remain exact in the transition from the perfect sphere to the ellipsoids, and only specific realizations are broken.

In this way, the "breaking of the rotational symmetry" is reduced to the level of mere academic parlance without a true scientific value. In fact, the abstract rotational symmetry cannot be considered broken for the ellipsoids. Only its realization in the structurally most simple possible form is broken, that via the trivial associative product AB. On the contrary, if the same symmetry is realized in the less trivial way, then it is exact, as proved for the isotopic product $A*B = AgB$.

This illustrates the possibilities offered by hadronic mechanics of regenerating exact space—time and internal symmetries that are quantum mechanically broken, that is, that are violated when realized in their simplest possible way.

Apparently, this feature is not restricted to the rotational symmetry, but extends to other space—time and internal symmetries, including the so—called discrete ones (see below).

In fact, the regeneration of the exact character of the symmetry via the Lie—isotopic generalization has been proved for the following additional cases of continuous transformations:

—   the Lorentz symmetry [32] ;

—   the so—called unitary symmetries, as studied by the Italian physicist R. Mignani [67] ;

—   the so—called gauge symmetries, as studied by the other Italian physicist M. Gasperini [68] ; and others.

The case of discrete transformations will be considered in the next paragraph.

These discoveries are not purely formal, because they have a number of implications for experiments.

In fact, an experiment "to test the breaking of the rotational symmetry" can be deprived of true physical contents, unless properly conceived, and the results expressed with care.

This situation is evidently due to the preservation of the abstract axioms of the rotational symmetry in the deformation of the sphere, while the explicit forms of conventional and isotopic rotations are basically different, as they must be.

The situation becomes even more delicate when passing to the special relativity. In fact, the underlying axiomatic structure remains unchanged in the transition from the conventional to the isotopic relativity, as reviewed in Section 1.4. In particular, the abstract structure of the Lorentz symmetry is preserved.

Despite that, we can have massive, ordinary particles moving inside hadronic matter at speeds exceeding that of light in vacuum (Section 1.4).

As a result, we can speak of a "breaking of the special relativity" in the sense that: the explicit form of the conventional Lorentz transformations no longer provide the invariance of physical laws; the speed of light in vacuum is no longer the upper bound for causal signals; etc. Nevertheless, the terms "breaking of the Lorentz symmetry" have no scientific meaning.

Use of hadronic mechanics for the identification of the origin of irreversibility in nature.

The most visible and perhaps most fundamental problematic aspect of quantum mechanics is its incompatibility with the established irreversibility of the macroscopic world. I am referring to the fact that the Newtonian and statistical layers of the physical reality violate the invariance under time inversion (which is an example of discrete transformation), while quantum mechanics is intrinsically reversible, that is, its structure is invariant under time inversion, as well known in the technical literature.

Inspection of our environment establishes the incontrovertible irreversibility of the classical reality. In fact, if the time–reversal symmetry was exact in our Newtonian environment, a phenomenon such as a bullet breaking through a wall should admit its time–reversed image, the automatic regeneration of the wall and the expulsion of the bullet without firing a shot!

The existence of irreversibility in statistical mechanics is equally established by incontrovertible evidence. In the ultimate analysis, entropy is a manifestation precisely of the irreversible character of the physical world.

On the contrary, currently preferred quantum mechanical treatments are reversible, as well known.

The lack of unity of physical and mathematical thought is then self–evident.

Hadronic mechanics permits new frontiers in this truly fundamental, open problem, by recovering the unity of physical thought via a unique mathematical structure that applies at all levels of treatment, whether in Newtonian, or statistical, or particle mechanics.

The fundamental question is the origin of the irreversibility in classical and statistical mechanics. Once this origin is identified jointly with its abstract mathematical structure, the particle description MUST be adapted accordingly. The other approach, that of attempting compatibility of a reversible particle description with macroscopic irreversibility cannot but be plagued by a host of inconsistencies (Figure 1.6.3).

Compatibility of the reversibility of the center–of–mass descriptions of particle interactions with the irversibility of the interior dynamics.

At this point, we must clear a basic, rather widespread misrepresentation. It is generally believed that the reversibility of the center–of–mass description of high energy particle collisions implies the reversibility of the particle reaction considered.

Nothing could be more fallacious than that.

The fellow taxpayer can readily understand the point, and see the implications for scientific accountability (see next paragraph), by ignoring complicated papers in high energy physics, and going back to the observation of our Newtonian environment.

Look at our earth. Its interior trajectories, such as that of Skylab during re–entry (Section 1.3), are generally irreversible. Nevertheless, the motion of the center–of–mass of earth within the solar system is fully reversible. This illustrates the physical reality according to which the reversibility of center–of–mass descriptions, by no means, implies the reversibility of interior processes.

THE PROBLEM OF UNITY OF PHYSICAL AND MATHEMATICAL THOUGHT

SYSTEM	POINT—LIKE PARTICLES	EXTENDED PARTICLES IN CLOSED—CONSERVATIVE TREATMENT	EXTENDED PARTICLES IN OPEN/NONCONSERVATIVE TREATMENT
UNIFYING MATHEMATICAL STRUCTURE	LIE ALGEBRAS [74]	LIE—ISOTOPIC ALGEBRAS [8]	LIE—ADMISSIBLE ALGEBRAS [75]
NEWTONIAN DESCRIPTION	HAMILTONIAN MECHANICS [6]	BIRKHOFFIAN MECHANICS [10]	BIRKHOFFIAN—ADMISSIBLE MECHANICS [12]
STATISTICAL DESCRIPTION	HAMILTONIAN STATISTICS [76]	PRIGOGINE'S STATISTICS [71]	STATISTICS BY FRONTEAU, TELLEZ—ARENAS ET AL. [69,70]
PARTICLE DESCRIPTION	QUANTUM MECHANICS [52]	EXTERIOR BRANCH OF HADRONIC MECHANICS [77]	INTERIOR BRANCH OF HADRONIC MECHANICS [78]

Figure 1.6.3. One aspect of contemporary theoretical physics which is carefully avoided in orthodox presentations, is the lack of unity of physical and mathematical thought, with such inconsistencies and incompatibilities in the transition from one layer to another, to create a clear problem of scientific ethics (see next paragraph). Newtonian and statistical mechanics are intrinsically irreversible, that is, they violate the symmetry under inversion of time, as established by trajectories in our atmosphere, the notion of entropy, and countless other phenomena. The ultimate physical origin of such irreversibility is well established and consists precisely of the contact/non-local/non—Hamiltonian forces considered throughout this presentation. This physical reality at the Newtonian and statistical levels is contrasted with quantum mechanics which is intrinsically reversible, as well known. The incompatibilities of quantum mechanics with the preceding descriptions are such to constitute a second litany (besides that for Einstein's gravitation of Section 1.5). To avoid excessive length, I merely recall here the following facts, well known to every physicist: (a) irreversible Newtonian trajectories are generally non—Hamiltonian; (b) reversible quantum mechanical trajectories are Hamiltonian; and, consequently (c) the reduction of classical irreversible trajectories to a large collection of quantum mechanical, reversible trajectories is strictly inconsistent. Period! Thus, the reduction of Skylab to a large collection of reversible, quantum mechanical constituents is intrinsically inconsistent because of the non—Hamiltonian character of the former system versus the strictly Hamiltonian character of the latters. The only classical and Newtonian descriptions truly compatible with quantum mechanics are those depicted in the figure (Hamiltonian mechanics and statistics). But they are generally reversible, to begin with. Besides, they represent only part of the systems and, as such, are not suited for an overall view on the unity of physical thought and underlying mathematical structures. Hadronic mechanics was proposed

in ref. [14] also in the hope of regaining, in due time, the currently missing unity of physical and mathematical thought. In fact, the mechanics is, first of all, differentiated into one branch for the exterior/conservative treatment, and a different, but compatible branch for the complementary open/nonconservative problem. Secondly, each of these branches is constructed in such a way to possess exactly the same mathematical structure of the corresponding statistical and Newtonian layers of description. Only the verification of this rule can avoid fundamental inconsistencies, as occurring in current physical theories. Intriguingly, all the formulations of the second column can be constructed via the use of the transformation theory applied to the corresponding formulations of the first column. For instance, the structure of Birkhoffian mechanics can be reached via non—canonical transformations of Hamiltonian mechanics [10]. Similarly, the structure of Prigogine's statistics [72] and of the exterior branch of hadronic mechanics [79] can be obtained via non—unitary transformation of corresponding statistical and quantum mechanical settings. After all, as stressed throughout this text, the Lie and Lie—isotopic descriptions can be reduced to the same, abstract, realization—free axioms. The true novelty of description from an axiomatic viewpoint is that depicted in the third column. This can be readily seen from a mathematical point by the fact that Lie—admissible formulations cannot be reached via suitable transformations of the Lie—isotopic ones, thus establishing their novel character [79]. As a result, the true, ultimate, physical and mathematical description, from which all the others can be derived, are those for the OPEN conditions. Closed—conservative descriptions constitute an academic abstraction because no system can be truly considered as isolated in the universe. In regard to irreversibility, the emphasis on open/nonconservative conditions becomes essential not only for the theoretical description, but also for the conception and realization of experiments (Section 1.8). When additional branches of sciences are included in this overall view, the findings above are strengthened, rather than weakened. For instance, a theory of gravitation for the interior problem, to be meaningful, must represent the trajectory of Skylab (at least qualitatively!). This means that it "must" be locally Galilean—admissible [12], owing to the direct universality of the Lie—admissible formulations for Newtonian systems (as a consequence of which, other results are necessarily equivalent to the Lie—admissible treatment). If we include theoretical biology, the situation is more reinforced. It is well known in the specialized literature that neural systems are strictly non—Hamiltonian, thus in line with the second and third column of the diagram, but not with the first. We can therefore conclude by saying that **the entirety of science has now an established non—Hamiltonian structure, including Newtonian mechanics, statistical mechanics, interior gravitation, theoretical biology, etc., not to mention mechanical engineering. The only and last branch of science that still remains stubbornly anchored to Hamiltonian descriptions (or equivalent lagrangian ones) is particle physics (inclusive of nuclear physics), despite a litany of manifest inconsistencies, let alone an evident lack of unity of physical and mathematical thought.** This situation is a central motivation for writing this book. In fact, the thesis submitted to the U.S. taxpayer for his/her own independent judgment is that this stubborn misoneism is a manifestation of the scientific obscurantism imposed for decades in the U.S. physics by vested, academic—financial—ethnic interests surrounding Einstein's ideas. To abandon the Hamilto—ian—Lie descriptions in favor of broader physical—mathematical theories implies a necessary abandonment of Einstein's relativities in favor of suitable generalizations, with a manifest damage to said interests. The most visible and rumorous illustration of this situation is provided in Section 2.4 It regards an incredible stubborness of the Journals of the American Physical Society to publish a paper on the views presented in this paragraph (which was then readily published in Europe, ref. [59]. Every possible effort on my part, including the written request of resignation of two editors, the filing of documented reports to high governmental officers, etc. proved to be totally fruitless. After over one year of useless fights, I wrote to the editor in chief of the A.P.S. that I had been forced "to cross the Rubicon". This book IS my Rubicon.

To put it differently, we have a situation similar, and actually complementary to that for relativities. The validity of Galilei's relativity for the center—of—mass of earth, by no means, is evidence of the validity of the same relativity for the interior trajectories. At a deeper study, it emerges that the departures from Galilei's relativity in the interior problem constitute precisely the physical origin of the irreversibility of Newtonian mechanics. It could not be otherwise for a truly considerable number of technical reasons (such as the fact that Galilei's relativity is characterized by canonical transformations, while irreversible trajectories are generally non—canonical).

In the transition to particle physics, the situation is expected to be the same on conceptual grounds. This is the reason for the insistence that hadronic mechanics provides a nuclear (and hadronic) structure model as an operator version of our earth.

We know now that the validity of the Galilean (or the special) relativity for the center—of—mass motion of, say, a nucleus, by no means, is evidence of the validity of the same relativity for the interior dynamics. We therefore construct a structure model of the nucleus in such a way to admit interior irreversible processes, while possessing a time—reversible center—of—mass motion. This is precisely the hadronic model proposed in ref. [14] (see Figure 1.6.2).

The experimental implications are intriguing, inasmuch as they imply the lack of conclusive character of all experiments on irreversibility conducted until now for the closed—conservative approach, that is, in the center—of—mass system, as we shall see better in the next section.

Hadronic mechanics and its underlying mathematical structures can therefore provide the identification of the ultimate origin of irreversibility of the universe which, according to Tellez—Arenas [70] and others, is given precisely by the contact/non—local/non—Hamiltonian interactions, whether for Newtonian systems moving within a resistive medium, or for the collision of molecules, or for the mutual penetration of the wave—packets of hadrons.

To summarize, the center—of—mass trajectories of nuclear (as well as particle) reactions is expected to be time—reversal invariant in the conventional quantum mechanical sense.

The hadronic—isotopic description of the same reactions, with internal non—Hamiltonian effects, is also expected to be time—reversal invariant, of course, in the associative—isotopic sense indicated earlier.

The ultimate manifestation of irreversibility is therefore seen in OPEN/NONCONSERVATIVE nuclear (and particle) reactions. But then, I do not need experiments for that. In fact, all these dynamical evolutions are non—unitary and, as such, intrinsically irreversible [59]. Their extension into a closed form inclusive of the external systems cannot but preserve the internal irreversibility, thus reaching the nuclear structure provided by hadronic mechanics.

We essentially have a situation similar to the closing of Skylab into an isolated system, inclusive of earth atmosphere (Section 1.3). Such closure simply cannot change the intrinsic irreversible character of Skylab.

The same situation is expected to occur in nuclear (and particle) physics. No more, no less. Experiments can only provide the quantitative resolution of the internal irreversibility.

But, again, the existence of an internal irreversibility in systems under strong interactions should remain out of the question.

The deprecable condition of scientific ethics in irreversibility.

As everybody can see, the ideas on irreversibility summarized in the preceding paragraph are so simple, to be understandable by everybody.

The same ideas, however, encounter extremes of opposition by leading physicists in leading U.S. institutions, as we shall see. In fact, the central episodes of Section 2.4 are related to questionable editorial actions aimed at preventing the appearance of the ideas in the journals of the American Physical Society. I am referring not only to theoretical studies (Section 2.4), but also to experimental studies by international teams of experimentalists (Section 1.7). As as shall see, the publication of the same papers in European Journals was routinely done without difficulties, We are therefore facing, specifically, a problem in the U. S. Physics.

It is time to point out openly and plainly the most plausible reasons for these obstructions in due scientific processes. The final judgment, of course, belongs to the fellow taxpayer.

Stated in a nutshell, the time—reversal symmetry is one of the foundations of Einstein's special relativity. In fact, the fundamental invariant of the special relativity, the Minkowski form $X'mX$, $X = (R,ct)$, $m = diag(+1,+1,+1,-1)$, considered in Section 1.4, is left invariant by the change of the direction of time, that is, by the replacement of t with —t. Evidently, the time—reflection symmetry affects the structure of a rather fundamental part of the relativity, the time evolution. As evident from the preceding sections, the representation of irreversibility in Newtonian and statistical mechanics has requested the generalization of the time evolution. The need for the construction of suitable generalizations of Einstein's special relativity is then a mere consequence.

To put it different, a further incontrovertible invalidation of Einstein's special and general relativities is given precisely by the irreversibility of the physical world.

The most plausible reasons for the current difficulties in establishing a corresponding irreversibility in particle physics is now evident. Such irreversibility would establish the invalidation of Einstein's special relativity with consequential, manifest damage to vested, academic—financial—ethnic interests. It is always the same, ultimate, root of the ethical problem in U.S. physics.

Again, there are means for the fellow taxpayer to separate corrupt academic manipulations, from physical truths, without the need of a Ph.D. in physics.

For this, the fellow taxpayer is asked to contact any nuclear physicist, or to consult any (well written) textbook in the field, and identify the equations for dissipative nuclear processes or for all particle processes involving the loss of energy (such as for beams of protons or neutrons interacting on an external, fixed target).

All these processes are represented by non—unitary time evolutions, as well known. In turn, all these time evolutions are intrinsically irreversible, and strictly in conflict with Einstein's special relativity (which demands unitary laws, as a necessary condition to admit a Lie structure).

The reformulation of non—unitary time evolutions via the Lie—admissible/hadronic form is useful for the reasons indicated earlier, including: (a) the regaining of a consistent algebraic structure; (b) the regaining of the capability to achieve numerical predictions for all quantities essentially dependent on the consistency of the underlying algebra; and, last but not least, (c) the possibility of initiating the generalization of Einstein's special relativity for open, irreversible particle reactions (via the generalization of the currently used, one side, modular—unitary realization of the Poincaré group into the most general covering known at this time, that provided by the Lie—admissible bimodules; see the mathematical section later on).

The point which is relevant here, is that the irreversibility IS NOT a consequence of the Lie—admissible re—formulation of non—unitary time evolutions. In fact, the irreversibility is intrinsic in the original formulation. The Lie—admissible re—formulation merely maximizes the visibility of the violation of the time—reflection symmetry (precisely via the differentiation of the right and left modular action).

The violation of Einstein's special relativity is therefore already there, printed in the books and articles. The violation itself IS NOT quoted because of apparent political reasons. But the authors of those books and articles know well that, whenever the unitarity of the time evolution is gone, the special relativity is also gone.

When such open/nonconservative conditions are closed into a conservative—isolated form, the internal irreversibility persists with the inevitable breaking of the special relativity. In fact, the change of observational frame simply cannot alter the physical reality.

The following incidental note may be instructive. Another discrete symmetry, which is also part of Einstein's special relativity, is the space inversion, that is, the change of the space coordinates R into the form —R. This discrete transformation also leaves invariant the basic Minkowski separation of Section 1.4, X'mX.

The possibility of violating the space—reflection symmetry in particle physics (called parity) was conjectured in the U.S.A. by T. D. Lee and C. N. Yang a number of decades ago, and subsequently confirmed experimentally in certain (weak) interactions (see book [80]).

The incidental note I would like to bring to the attention of the fellow taxpayer is that, after some initial opposition, the violation of parity was indeed accepted by leading physical circles in the U.S. On a comparative basis, the violation of time—reflection symmetry continues to be opposed, decade after decade.

The most plausible reasons for this rather awkward occurrence (recall that the irreversibility cannot be denied for dissipative nuclear and particle treatments!) is, again, the vexing ethical problem of vested interests on Einstein's ideas.

The violation of parity does not directly affect the structure of the special relativity. As a result, models treating parity violation in weak interactions have been constructed in such a way to verify (at least the authors believe*) Einstein's special relativity. The same thing simply cannot be done for irreversibility. The violation of Einstein's special relativity in this case

---

* I believe that parity violation alone implies the invalidation of the entire special relativity. Apparently, the same view is shared by a number of other independent physicists. The reasons are due to the fact that parity—violation has been merely "described" until now, via semi—empirical, quasi—pheomenological models. If the "dynamical origin" of the breaking is instead considered, the invalidation of the entire special relativity then becomes unavoidable. In fact, such dynamical origin seems to be precisely the internal, contact/non—local/non—Hamiltonian effects due to mutual wave—overlappings.

is too apparent to be disguised via artificial manipulations.

Silence, suppression of evidence, and other questionable practices, then appear to be preferred in academia.

In this case too, the entanglement of the situation at the governmental—academic complex is such that no self—corrective procedure appears possible. Again, editors (governmental officers) will keep sending out papers (grant applications) to leading physicists in the field at leading U.S. institutions for the so—called "peer review". In turn these "peers" will continue to reject papers (grants) supporting the irreversibility in nuclear and particle physics. The scientific obscurantism in the sector is therefore expected to continue indefinitely.

The only hope is for the taxpayer to intervene and organize suitable actions aimed at preventing the dispersal of public funds in academic, corporate and military research on reversible models which ignore the critical literature in the field.

Expected contributions of hadronic mechanics to hadron physics.

The contributions of hadronic mechanics in hadron physics are expected to be more fundamental than those in nuclear physics. This is due to the fact indicated earlier that the approximate validity of quantum mechanics in nuclear physics is out of question, thus relegating the role of hadronic mechanics to possible refinements and deeper understandings of results achieved via the use of quantum mechanics.

In the transition to hadron physics, we cannot exclude the possibility of finite departures from quantum mechanics due to the much greater conditions of mutual penetration of the wave—packets of the constituents, when compared to the nuclear conditions. As a consequence, we expect the possibility of achieving resolutions that have been prohibited until now by quantum mechanics.

Recall that the primary and, by far, most fundamental achievement of quantum mechanics in nuclear physics was the identification of nuclear constituents with physical particles (protons and neutrons).

Despite massive efforts, the application of quantum mechanics to hadron physics has not provided until now the final identification of the hadronic constituents with physical particles, that is, particles identified via direct experiments.

As well known, hadrons are today thought to be composed of some sixteen different particles called quarks, and their sixteen different antiparticles (with the possibility of additional quarks and antiquarks in sight).

This hypothesis, even though of proved physical relevance, has not resolved the identification of hadronic constituents with physical particles for numerous reasons, such as:

(a) Quarks are not produced free in the spontaneous decays of unstable hadrons; they are also not produced in hadronic collisions up to the highest possible energies attained in particles accelerators; and they have not been detected via any additional experiment until now, despite a rather large search.*

(b) Since quarks are not produced free in the spontaneous decays, they are thought to be "confined" in the interior of hadrons. Despite additional, also massive efforts, a theoretical model of confinement of quarks has not yet been achieved to this writing. In particular, a strict form of confinement of quarks, that with an identically null probability of tunnel effects of free quarks, is impossible whenever quantum mechanics is assumed as exactly valid in the interior of hadrons. This is due to the fact that, according to quantum mechanics, the probability of tunnel effects of free constituents of a bound state cannot be rendered identically null, irrespective of the potential barrier used.

(c) Quarks are today no longer considered as being elementary. A central open problem of current quark theories is precisely that of identifying the constituents of quarks with more elementary particles.

A primary objective of hadronic mechanics is to achieve, in due time, the identification of hadronic constituents with physical particles. Furthermore, these physical constituents should be such to be consistently identifiable as the quark constituents. Finally, the constituents should be such to permit the achievement of a strict confinement of quarks in the interior of hadrons, with an identically null probability of tunnel effects.

---

*Note that, the conceivable experimental detection of only one quark would leave the problem of hadronic constituents still fundamentally unresolved, because of the need to identify experimentally each of the conjectured sixteen different quarks and each of the sixteen different antiquarks. It is appropriate to recall here the known historical case when the experimental detection of the neutron was not considered evidence for the existence of the antineutron, which had to be detected independently. The need to follow exactly the same scientific rules for each quark and for each antiquark is then evident. Experimentalists have reported intriguing indications of measurement of fractional charges (which are one of the penculiarities of quarks). However, these measures alone, even if confirmed, by no means constitute evidence of the experimental detection of quarks, because of the need to measure jointly all the rather numerous additional characteristics of quarks (mass, spin, parity, magnetic moments, and others).

The three historical rules emerged from the resolution of the structure of atoms and nuclei.

The resolution of the problem of the structure of atoms identified three fundamental rules.

RULE 1:   The atomic phenomenology demands different, yet compatible models: a first model for the classification of atoms into families (the famous Mendeleyev table); and a different, yet compatible model for the structure of each individual atom of a given family.

RULE 2:   The atomic constituents can be produced free either spontaneously, or via suitable bombardment of the atomic structure.

RULE 3:   The number of atomic constituents increases with mass.

In the transition from the atomic to the nuclear structure, history repeated itself.   The three fundamental rules resulted to be fully verified, except some technical modifications.

In fact, the model of so—called unitary classifications of nuclei cannot produce a meaningful nuclear structure, which is instead interpreted via different models.   Similarly, the nuclear constituents can indeed be produced free either spontaneously, or via suitable bombardments.   Finally, the number of nuclear constituents also increases with mass, exactly as it is the case at the nuclear level.

For additional remarks along these lines, the interested reader may consult the introductory parts of ref.s [14, 11, 49].

Use of the hadronic mechanics for the construction of a structure model of hadrons along the three historical rules of atoms and nuclei.

Hadronic mechanics was proposed for the purpose of attempting a structure model of hadrons exactly along the historical Rules 1, 2 and 3 emerged from the nuclear and atomic structures.

For this reason, the available models of unitary classification of hadrons into families were assumed as being of terminal charactr [14,11,49].   The desired structure model was then restricted to achieve compatibility with such classification, exactly along the dychotomy classification/structure of the atomic and nuclear phenomenology.

Second, the constituents of hadrons were assumed to be suitably selected, massive particles produced free in the spontaneous decays.   In turn, each particle was subjected to the same reduction, until reaching electrons and positrons as the ultimate constituents. As now familiar, it was at this point that the construction of a generalization of quantum mechanics resulted to be necessary. In fact, we have a clear cut situation: either quantum mechanics is strictly valid in the interior of hadrons, in which case hadrons "cannot" be composed of massive particles produced in the spontaneous decays; or a suitable generalization of quantum mechanics holds in the interior of hadrons, in which case the consistency of the proposed structure model is reduced to the construction of an adequate covering mechanics.

Thirdly, and perhaps most importantly, the model was restricted to verify the rule of increase of number of constituents with mass.

The notion of hadronic constituents (called "eletons" and "antieletons") as characterized by hadronic me—chanics.

A primary hypothesis for the development of hadronic mechanics was the identification of the constituents of hadrons with the ordinary electrons and positrons (see ref. [14], Section 5).

While electrons are at the large mutual distances of the atomic structure, the same electrons, to be hadronic constituents, must be in a state of complete mutual penetration and overlapping of their wave—packets, each one moving within the medium constituents by the wave—packets of all the other constituents. In fact, the size of the electron's wave—packets is exactly of the order of magnitude as that of all hadrons (one Fermi). This results in motion within the hadronic medium, with consequential need to achieve a generalization of quantum mechanics capable of incorporating, not only the potential interactions of the atomic structure, but also the contact/non—potential/non—local interactions due to motion within hadronic matter. This second aspect was also fully identified in the original proposal [14]. In particular, the Lie—isotopic generalization of Heisenberg's equations was proposed for the exterior treatment of electrons and positrons in conditions of total mutual penetration, while the broader Lie—admissible generalization was suggested for the treatment of each electron while moving within the sea of all other constituents.

These broader dynamical conditions generally imply an alteration of the intrinsic physical characteristics of electrons and positrons (as well as of all other particles under similar physical conditions). In fact, rest mass, intrinsic angular momentum, parity, charge and magnetic moments of one electron while totally immerged within hadronic matter are not expected to be necessarily identical to the corresponding values when the same electron moves in empty space under long range electromagnetic interactions. All available experimental information on the intrinsic characteristics of the electrons is restricted to the latter conditions, while we have absolutely no direct experimental information on the measurement of the same characteristics when the electron is inside hadronic matter. At any rate, the reader can easily visualize the distorsion of the wave–packet of the electrons and positrons in the transition from motion in vacuum to motion within hadronic matter. The alteration of the physical characteristics due to this distorsion is then a mere technical consequence.

This additional aspect was also identified in the original proposal [14]. Electrons were called "eletons" when inside hadrons as one way to stress the deviations from their physical characteristics when in empty space. Today we know that the notion of eleton is one of the most technically involved objects of theoretical physics (a right and left, bi–representation of a Lie–admissible generalization of the Lorentz algebra acting on a bi–modular isohilbert space).

In particular, a progressive chain of "mutations" of the intrinsic characteristics were suggested as possible in ref. [14], beginning with minimal mutations (say of the magnetic moment only) for miminal conditions of wave–overlapping, and then passing to the mutation of additional characteristics for deeper departures from the atomic conditions.

Preliminary bound states of eletons and antieletons obeying the covering hadronic mechanics were also worked out in ref. [14] in a rudimentary local approximation, thus establishing the plausibility of the theory for light mesons and for the neutron (see below).

The reconsideration of these structure models of hadrons via the advances on hadronic mechanics made since 1978, had to be interrupted for the reasons indicated earlier.

The studies on the identification of electrons and positrons as the quark constituents as well as on the achievement of a strict confinement of quarks had also to be interrupted for the same reasons. The resumption of the research is not foreseeable at this time.

Identification of the constituents of the neutral pion with one electron and one positron obeying hadronic mechanics.

Consider the problem of the structure of the lightest known hadron, the neutral pion. If quantum mechanics and conventional relativities are assumed as strictly valid in its interior, a structure model of the neutral pion as a bound state of one electron and one positron is not possible for the following reasons.

Consistent, quantum mechanical, bound states of two particles (such as the hydrogen atom or the deuterium) have a total energy that is smaller than the sum of the energies of the constituents, including rest energy and kinetic energy. The loss of energy is the so—called binding energy. This property is well known.

An aspect that is not well known, even in the technical literature, is that when the sum of the rest energies of the constituents is much smaller than the desired total energy of the bound state, quantum mechanical equations become generally inconsistent in the sense of admitting only complex values of total energies.

This is essentially the case for the neutral pion as a bound state of one electron and one positron. In fact, the total energy of the neutral pion is 135 bigger than the sum of the rest energies of the assumed constituents. Under these conditions, quantum mechanical, physically meaningful bound states are unknown. For a study of the problem, the interested reader may consult Appendix A of ref. [40] and references quoted therein.

If contact interactions are admitted in the interior of the neutral pion because of the conditions of mutual penetration of the wave—packets of the constituents, the bound state of one electron and one positron is capable of representing all known characteristics of the neutral pion, such as: mass, mean life, spin, space and charge parity, electric and magnetic moments, etc. See in this respect Section 5.1 of ref. [14]. A pictorial view is presented in Figure 1.6.4.

The historical hypothesis on the structure of the neutron as a bound state of one proton and one electron.

The first hypothesis on the structure of the neutron was that it is a bound state of one proton and one electron. The hypothesis was based on the experimental observation that the neutron, when isolated, is unstable and decays precisely into one proton and one electron plus a massless neutrino. It was then rather natural to assume that the massive constituents of the neutron are the stable particles produced in its spontaneous decay.

The hypothesis had to be subsequently abandoned because of a number of technical difficulties in recovering all the characteristics of the neutron, such as:

1) The model is unable to recover jointly the rest energy and the mean life of the neutron. In fact, to recover the rest energy, the peripheral electron becomes so energetic that the mean life of the system is much too shorter than that of the neutron (about 15 minutes). Vice versa, if the neutron mean life is recovered, there is no sufficient internal energy to reach the neutron rest mass;

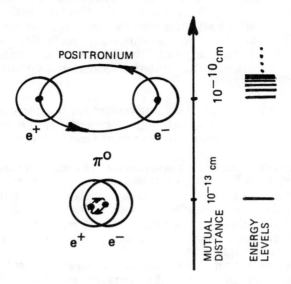

Figure 1.6.4. A schematic view of the hypothesis submitted in ref. [14], see pages 827 and following, according to which the lightest known hadron, the neutral pion, is a bound state of one electron and one positron under conditions of mutual overlapping down to the dimension of 1 Fermi. The admission of contact/nonpotential/nonlocal forces, and the use of hadronic mechanics permit the recovering of all known characteristics of the pion, such as, mass, spin, mean life, radius, electric and magnetic moments, space and charge parity, etc. [14]. Intriguingly, according to the hypothesis, the neutral pion results to be a positronium compressed down to the dimension of 1 Fermi. Recall that, when at sufficiently large mutual distances, one electron and one positron can be bound together to form the lightest known atom, the positronium, which possesses the typical, infinite, discrete spectrum of the atomic structure. Hadronic mechanics predicts the existence of an additional bound state of one electron and one positron,this time when the particles are in conditions of deep mutual overlapping. Apparently, only one such bound state is stable, resulting in the single, unique bound state that is typical of two—body nuclear states (such as the deuterium which, as recalled in the test, has no exited states). Recall that, in quantum mechanics, particles with spins can be bound together in two different ways, in the so—called singlet state (with spins antiparallel) and the triplet states (with spins parallel). It was stressed in ref. [14] that the latter bound states are highly unstable when the particles are bound one within the other, owing to the need of wave—packets rotating one against the other. For the same reason, the state of singlet is the only one expected to be stable, trivially, because the rotation of wave—packets would now be in phase, much along the coupling of gears. The unstable character of triplets states was considered per se sufficient to warrant the construction of a suitable generalization of quantum mechanics. The physical foundation of the model is the fact that the neutral pion decays spontaneously into one electron, one positron and a (massless) photon.

2)   The model does not recover the total spin of the neutron. This is due to the fact that the proton, the neutron and the electron, all have the same spin ½. Now, according to quantum mechanics, two spin ½ particles can only produce a bound state with integer spin, but not the needed value ½ for the neutron.

3)   The model does not reproduce the correct values of electric and magnetic moments of the neutron, as well as other difficulties of lesser relevance.

Hadronic mechanics apparently permits the resolution of all these difficulties. The understanding is that the studies are at the beginning and so much remains to be done prior to claiming any final conclusion, whether in favor or against the model.

The first difficulty is readily solved by contact/nonpotential/nonlocal forces via a mechanism similar to that of the hadronic structure model of the neutral pion.

The remaining difficulties are apparently resolved by the hypothesis that electrons experience an alteration of their intrinsic characteristics in the transition from motion in vacuum, to motion within hadronic matter, thus becoming "eletons".

The alterations were called "Lie—admissible mutations" or "mutations" for short, to indicate the transition from the mathematical theory applicable under electromagnetic interactions, Lie's theory, to the covering theory suggested for strong interactions, the Lie—admissible theory. The understanding is that, when eletons exit hadronic matter and return to motion in vacuum, they reacquire their known quantum mechanical characteristics.

The mutation of spin of the electron into that of the eleton can be readily visualized. Recall that the proton is about 1840 times heavier than the electron. It can therefore be considered as being at rest in first approximation. This means that the electron must penetrate inside a virtually stationary proton by therefore being forced to follow its intrinsic rotation.

These physical conditions have a number of consequences. First, they imply the lack of existence of the triplet state (with parallel spins) as a stable bound state (Figure 1.6.4). In fact, it would imply wave—packets continuously rotating one against the other. The only stable state is that with spins antiparallel called singlet, much along the coupling of gears. In fact, the model was called of "gear type".

Secondly, since the electron is forced to rotate "in phase" with the intrinsic rotation of the proton, the spin of the electron is forced to assume a value compatible with these physical conditions. In particular, the mutated value of the spin can apparently assume the value zero which, as such, permits to recover the value ½ of the spin of the neutron, as desired.

The massless neutrinos,* which also have spin ½, according to the hadronic model under consideration, are the particles produced by the electron when existing the proton and returning to the conventional dynamical conditions known until now, including its value ½ of spin.

It was also indicated in ref. [39] that the mutation of the spin of the electron, from the value ½ to the value zero, may be in the final analysis a mere illusory effect in the following sense. Consider an observer ideally located at the center of the proton. Then, for that observer, the peripheral electron may appear as having null spin owing to the phase conditions of rotations needed for stability (see Fig. 8, p. 1971), of ref. [39]). For an outside observer, the same electron has both an intrinsic angular momentum and an orbital one.

Thirdly, an alteration of the intrinsic angular momentum of the electron implies that of electric and magnetic moments. In turn, these latter mutations are used to resolve problematic aspects 3).

The ideas outlined above are essentially those known in 1979, ref. [39], p. 1968. Since that time, the studies of hadronic mechanics have made considerable progress. The model can be studied today via quite sophisticated means (see Figure 1.6.5).

---

*According to the model of ref.s [14, 39], the massless neutrino is not a constituent of the neutron, nor of any hadron. This position was assumed because of the extremely low capability for neutrinos to interact with matter. In fact, highly intense beams of neutrinos from the sun and outer space cross the entire earth continuously, without being scattered (our entire earth is said to be "transparent" to neutrinos). This situation suggested the assumption that only electrons and positrons are the ultimate, elementary constituents of hadrons (with the proton being a separate problem —see below). I must quote, at this point, intriguing studies by the U.S. physicist A. O. Barut [81], according to which the neutron is a bound state of one proton, one electron and one neutrino. Apparently, Barut has reached a mechanism for binding the otherwise elusive neutrinos within hadronic matter. Barut's efforts are more generally oriented toward the possible identification of quarks with physical, already known particles. As such, the studies are commendable, in my view. I regret to report, however, the considerable lack of interests in these studies by "leading quarkologists" in the U.S.A., for a number of technical reasons, besides the problem of binding neutrinos inside hadrons (such as the fact that the charge and other quantum numbers of quarks cannot be identified with those of protons, electrons and neutrinos). The connections between Barut's hypothesis [81] and that I submitted in ref. [39] are quite intriguing. In essence, Barut's model can be formulated via a fully conventional, quantum mechanical theory. In fact, the additional presence of the neutrinos avoids the crucial problematic aspect 2) regarding the recovering of the spin of the neutron. Nevertheless, I believe that Barut's model can be subjected to an isotopic lifting within the framework of hadronic mechanics, thus achieving compatibility with ref. [39].

For completeness, it should be indicated that the mutation of the spin of the electron into that of the eleton is not expected to be the only possibility to reach the neutron spin. In fact, recent studies by the Indian physicists P. Bandyopadhyay and S. Roy [82] have indicated the possibility that the "angular" momentum may assume half–odd–integer values when particles are moving in a hadronic medium. This possibility is strictly precluded for motion in empty space, as stressed in all textbooks of quantum mechanics. It is evident that, if angular momentum can assume the value ½ for one electron bound within a proton, that electron can preserve the value ½ of spin to achieve the spin ½ of the neutron.

Electrons, however, would still need an eletonic form owing to the need to exhibit mutations of the intrinsic magnetic moments in order to represent the total electric and magnetic moments of the neutron (see Figure 1.6.5 for additional comments).

The structure model of the remaining hadrons.

As recalled earlier, the lightest known, strongly interacting particle is the neutral pion. The immediately next particles in the value of the rest mass are the positively or negatively charged pions. By keeping in mind the historical rule of the increase of the number of constituents with mass, the charged pions were assumed as being bound states of three eletons and antieletons (two mutated electrons and one mutated positron or two mutated positrons and one mutated electron, depending on total value of the charge). Thus, in the transition from the neutral to the charged pions, one additional constituent was assumed within the context of hadronic mechanics (by comparison, the number of constituents remains the same within the context of quark models, not only for all pions, but also for all light mesons).

The next particles in the scale of mass, neutral and charged kaons, were assumed as bound states of mutated pions and mutated eletrons. Subsequent particles were then conceived as having a similar model. A special case is that of the proton which, owing to its stability, may well constitute the most complex structural problem of contemporary physics. After all, bound states of particles and antiparticles, whether conventional or mutated, are expected to exhibit the typical instability of the particle world.

The above model, (submitted in ref. [14], Section 5) has remained mostly unexplored until now, except isolated instances, such as the studies by Jiang, Chun–Xuan [83], a physicist from the People's Republic of China, and Z. J. Allan [84], a chemical engineer from Switzerland.

No conclusion can therefore be reached at this time,

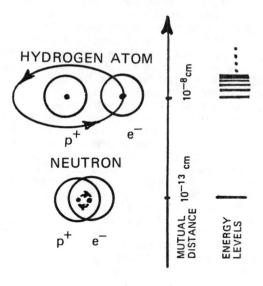

Figure 1.6.5. A schematic view of the hypothesis submitted in ref. [14] and subsequently elaborated in more detail in ref. [39], pages 1968–1974. As well known, when at sufficiently large mutual distances, one proton and one electron can bound together to form the hydrogen atom, with the familiar, infinite, discrete, spectrum of exited states. Hadronic mechanics predicts that the ordinary neutron is an additional bound state of one proton and one electron, this time bound together one inside the wave—packet of the other, in full analogy to the case of the positronium—neutral pion of Figure 1.6.4. Intriguingly, we have again one single, unique, bound state for two—body nuclear phenomenology. In turn, the absence of exited states appears to be crucial for the resolution of the problem of hadronic constituents of the remaining hadrons. The equations of structure of the model of the neutron considered here are similar to those of the neutral pion, as far as energy considerations are concerned. Nevertheless, additional technical difficulties emerge, particularly due to spin, electric and magnetic moments, and other aspects. The resolution of these difficulties is apparently permitted by the notion of eletons [Figure 1.6.4], that is, by the alteration of the intrinsic characteristics of ordinary electrons and positrons in the transition from motion in empty space, as in the atomic structure, to motion within hadronic matter, as necessary for the hadronic structure. In turn, this alteration is relevant for numerous other aspects, such as the identification of quark constituents, the achievement of their strict form of confinement, etc. These were essentially the main lines known in 1979. The model can now be re—inspected via the more recent advances due to the Lorentz—isotopic relativity [32] and the mathematical structure of hadronic mechanics [55]. The isotopic structure of the mechanics can be made to coincide with that of the Lorentz—isotopic relativity. This essentially implies the identification of the fixed operator g of the associative—isotopic product of operators, $A*B = AgB$, with the generalized metric

G of the Lorentz—isotopic relativity (see Section 1.4). The invariance of the model under the Lorentz—isotopic transformations is then ensured by construction. The selection of the generalized metric G for the interior of the neutron then constitutes the first degree of freedom of the hadronic description. An additional degree of freedom is given by the tensorial product of the (iso—)representation of the Lorentz—isotopic group identified in ref. [55]. The achievement of a total spin ½ is then consequential. Conventional total spins are computed via products of conventional representations of the rotation (or the Lorentz) group. In the transition to hadronic mechanics, the space—time symmetry groups are subjected to a first generalization; the representations of these groups are also of generalized character; and their tensorial products exhibit a third degree of freedom. The combined use of all these novel degrees of freedom permits the achievement of a total hadronic spin ½ from the bound state of two particles of original, quantum mechanical, spin ½. Note that the isotopic theory of rotations may well permit half—odd—integer angular momenta, exactly along the lines suggested by Bandyopadhyay and Roy [82]. To put it differently, at the covering isotopic level, the alternative of mutating the spin of the electron down to zero, or that of assuming angular momentum ½, may well turn out to be equivalent. Regrettably, the studies on the re—examination of the historical model of structure of the neutron had to be interrupted, among others, for the writing of this book, without any prediction of their possible resumption. Existing governmental support was truncated, while all applications submitted and re—submitted to governmental agencies for the development of hadronic mechanics and its applications over a three year period were rejected, including those for possible military applications (Section 2.5). This implied the impossibility of hiring physicists with the necessary expertise in nuclear physics.

---

whether in favor or against the model.

The conceivable military applications of the hadronic generalization of Einstein's ideas.

I do not know whether or not the neutron is truly a bound state of one proton and one electron. The only thing I am sure of is the necessity of resolving the issue either in favor or against the historical hypothesis. Besides evident scientific motivations, there are non—trivial military aspects which cannot be treated too lightly.

The military establishment in the U.S.A. believes that only a few nuclei are fissionable and therefore usable for weapons. If the neutron is a bound state of one proton and one electron, virtually all nuclei could be artificially "disintegrated" therefore resulting in a new generation of weapons.

Evidently, I cannot disclose technical details here. Nevertheless, there are aspects that the fellow taxpayer has the right to know. The first, is the existence itself of conceivable military applications of the studies reported in this section. I am referring to "disintegration" of matter that, to my best knowledge, would originate in the interior of nuclei, would be activated at a distance, and would not require mass thresholds.

The second point the taxpayer has the right to know is that this "disintegration" of matter is prohibited if Einstein's special relativity is exactly valid in the interior of nuclei, hadrons and (locally) of stars. In fact, the "disintegration" becomes conceivable only when suitable generalizations of the special relativity are assumed as valid for strong interactions (such as the generalization worked out by the U.S.S.R. physicist, Bogoslovsky [29], or the more general one of Lie–isotopic type I recently proposed [32]; see Section 1.4 for details). We could therefore face a typical case whereby vested academic–financial–ethnic interests on Einstein's ideas constitute a potential threat to the security of the U.S.A.

A further aspect the fellow taxpayer has the right to know is that the "disintegration" here considered is not permitted by the current military research known to the general public under the name of "star wars". In fact, these weapons are essentially based on lasers and other beams which lack the physical characteristics needed to initiate a disintegration process in the interior of nuclei. Nevertheless, owing to its potential capability of being activated at a distance, the "disintegration" of matter here considered is fully aligned with the "star wars" objectives.

Evidently, such "disintegration" could have non–military, economic-scientific applications in a number of fields such as energy or crystallography or neural surgery. The elaboration of these aspects is avoided here owing to the need of the prior disclosure of technical details.

At the risk of being pedantic, I must stress that I am merely referring to theoretically conceivable military applications. Whether or not these applications are indeed possible and technically feasable, it is unknown at this time.

I have been aware of these military possibilities since I suggested the construction of the hadronic generalization of quantum mechanics back in 1978 [14] while at Harvard. Nevertheless, since I detest weapons, I kept them for myself. A chain of events forced the changing of my stand on the matter.

My doubts began in 1979 when the resumption of the studies on the historical hypothesis on the structure of the neutron was discussed at a meeting at Harvard (see Section 1.9), and subsequently appeared in the Proceedings of the meeting (see later in ref. [124]). Even though military aspects were carefully avoided at the meeting, I realized that the same military ideas could well be conceived by other physicists throughout the world with manifest detriment to the U.S.A. In the subsequent years, the increase of the international efforts to construct the hadronic mechanics re–confirmed my doubts. Yet, I still kept silent on military profiles.

It was only in 1983 that specific circumstances finally urged the changing of my stand. I had eyewitnessed the rejection of a considerable number of research grant applications sub-mitted by our Institute to the U.S. National Science Foundations and the Department of Energy on non—classified profiles of the hadronic mechanics. It was therefore clear to me that, on one side, governmental agencies would continue to reject all grant applications filed by our Institute, while, on the other side, we would be forced to transfer abroad the physical research.

This is exactly what happened. In fact, all research acti-vities in the physical profiles of the hadronic mechanics are to-day conducted solely OUTSIDE the U.S.A. This refers not only to research by individual physicists, but also to all Conferences, Workshops, and research sessions planned by our group for the foreseeable future. They have been all moved abroad (see Sec-tion 1.9). This situation was readily predictable in 1983. In fact, N.S.F. and D.O.E. rejected not only all our research grant appli-cations, but also all our applications for support of Conferences and Workshops. Our group therefore had no other choice than move the meetings to more receptive countries.

In view of this scenario, and the evident potential damage to America, I felt compelled to make one last try: submit re-search grant applications to U.S. military agencies with a dis-closure of the conceivable new military applications. My hope was that these military profiles would break the apparent dead-lock against the funding of our research programs, and permit their continuation also in the primary, basic research sector.

On March 25, 1983, an I.B.R. application entitled "Stu-dies on hadronic mechanics" was formally submitted to Carl Romney, Deputy Director of the Defense Advance Research Project Agency (DARPA), which is the central research organi-zation of the Department of Defense (D.O.D.). A confidential memo elaborating further the possible military applications in-dicated here was submitted on June 20, 1983 also to Carl Rom-ney at DARPA.

Jointly, I prepared myself to apply for the U.S. Citizenship in order to be able to conduct classified research.

Regrettably, DARPA decided to follow the guidelines al-ready in force at NSF and DOE, that is, rejection of all I.B.R. applications. In fact, DARPA rejected or expressed no interests, not only for the primary application for the hadronic mechanics, but also for all remaining applications submitted by our Insti-tute. All this, despite the character of the applications manifest-ly aligned with the "stars wars" guidelines, the credibility of the investigators (mostly full professors with large scientific records), and the minimality of the funds that would have kept the pro-gram alive (about $ 70,000 per year).

The fellow taxpayer should know that the applications to DARPA were the VERY LAST planned by the I.B.R. As presi-dent, I am now operating the Institute under a formal decision NOT TO APPLY to U.S. governmental agencies for research support, and this decision will remain in force for as long as decided by the I.B.R. Board of Governors. Only formal invitations will be selectively considered.

For reasons of security, I have excluded in the Documentation of this book the entire file dealing with U.S. military agencies that were unsuccessfully approached by I.B.R. members and/ or by myself for research support, that is, not only with DARPA, but also with the research divisions of the Air Force and of the Navy.

An additional information is needed for the fellow taxpayer to reach a mature appraisal of the current funding of research in the U.S.A. It is the fact that no known or otherwise conceivable military (and/or economic) application exists for quark theories on hadronic structure. This situation should be compared with the structure model of hadrons reviewed in this section, for which considerable military (and economic) applications are indeed conceivable. Despite that, the former theories receive the totality of public funds in the sector, while no public funds whatsoever are invested in the latter theories.

The doubt persists in my mind that this rather ackward situation is due to the fact that the former theories are aligned with vested interests on Einstein's ideas, while the latter theories are not.

Violation of the three historical rules of atoms and nuclei by the quark models of hadronic structure.

As editor of a journal in theoretical physics, then a member of the Department of Physics of Harvard (we are talking of early 1978), I felt obliged to bring to the attention of the particle physics community the fact that quark models of hadronic structure violate all three historical rules which had resulted essential for the resolution of the structure of atoms and nuclei.

The introductory part of ref. [14] was in fact dedicated exactly to this issue, which was subsequently expanded in monograph [11], and later on reconsidered in paper [49].

First, one single model, the quark model, was assumed as resolving the totality of the hadronic phenomenology. To be explicit, the quark model was assumed as providing a classification of hadrons into families and, jointly, the structure of each individual member of a given family. This is evidently contrary to historical Rule 1.

Second, according to incontrovertible experimental evidence, the quark constituents are not produced free in any spontaneous decay or collision. This is evidently contrary to historical Rule 2.

Third, the number of quark constituents does not necessarily increase with mass, and actually remains the same for all members of the same family. For instance, according to the original quark models, one quark and one antiquark are the constituents, not only of the neutral pion, but also of the charged pions, as well as kaons and all other members of the so–called octect of light mesons. This is evidently contrary to historical Rule 3.

The clear validity of quark models for the hadronic classification and their problematic aspects when assumed as actual structure models.

I believe that the so–called unitary models (from which quarks originate) provide the final classification of hadrons into families. They are, therefore, the Mendeleyev table for hadrons. I clearly expressed this view in the locally quoted literature. The same view is shared by the majority of physicists.

All the reservations, problematic aspects, and shear inconsistencies originate when one assumes that the same models actually provide the structure of each individual hadron. Bluntly stated, the conjecture that quarks are the ultimate, elementary constituents of hadrons is afflicted by a litany of unresolved problematic aspects and shear inconsistencies.

Quarks are representations of the Lorentz group and of suitable, internal, unitary groups (such as the celebrated SU(3) group). the former part implies that quarks exist in our physical space—time, that is, they are physical constituents of hadrons. The latter part implies that they jointly possess an internal space producing the classification.

One of the biggest historical successes of atomic physics was the achievement by Bohr of equations of structure capable of representing ALL characteristics of the hydrogen atom, such as: size, charge, energy, exited states, etc. A similar situation occurred for the lightest known nuclear structure, the deuteron, even though available structural equations are often unsatisfactory (e.g., because of the general admittance of excited states contrary to experimental evidence).

In the transition to quarks, similar equations of structure are basically missing to this day. In fact, we do not have any equation of structure of the light mesons.

The technical difficulties are the same as those for the structure model of the neutral pion (rest mass of the constituent quarks much smaller than the total mass), but there are additional problems. In fact, a consistent equation of quark structure for the light mesons should contain only eight states, and all of them should have the proper values of the mass and other quantities. Structure equations of this type simply do not exist. The reason indicated in ref. [14, 49] as probable is precisely the violation by quark models of the three historical rules.

By comparison, the eletonic structure model, despite its

rudimentary character, achieved a consistent structure model of the pions since its initial proposal, by reproducing ALL intrinsic characteristics of the particles via structural equations of Bohr type. Apparently, this was possible because the model was constructed according to the historical rules.

Another problematic aspect of the quark models is that of confinement. If the taxpayer inspects the contemporary literature on quark theories (see, for instance, the quite readable review [85]), he/she will find the insistence of the construction of the structure model exactly according to the atomic structure and its underlying mechanics.

But, on strict scientific grounds, these assumptions imply the irreconciliable invalidation of the quark structure model (only, and not of the classification). In fact, the more the physicist insists on the compliance with quantum mechanics, the more evident is the existence of a finite, non—null, probability of tunnel effect for free quarks contrary to the experimental evidence.

I believe that this aspect alone has sizable ethical implications, and I shall dwell on them later on.

Par contre, the eletonic structure model resolves this problematic aspect. The free production of the constituents is assumed "ab initio" precisely because of the impossibility to confine physical particles within small regions of space.

The quark models of structure have been plagued by a considerable number of additional problematic aspects and/or inconsistencies, that either I noted on my own, or they were brought to my attention by ethically sound referees during my editorial functions.

One particular aspect (which is at the basis of an episode recalled at the end of this section) deals with the incontrovertible inconsistencies of certain nonrelativistic quark models that were fashionable in 1979—1980. I am referring to Galilean treatments of quark models, either per se, or as suitable limits of more general models.

As we shall see below, these models violated beyond any reasonable doubt numerous, independent, necessary, conditions for the applicability of the Galilean relativity.

By comparison, this additional inconsistency of quark structure models is resolved by the eletonic model. In fact, the latter model assumes the violation of Galilei's relativity and works out a suitable generalization.

To avoid excessive length, the interested taxpayer is referred to the locally quoted references for the remaining part of this third litany of problematic aspects (the first being that for Einstein's gravitation, and the second that for the origin of irreversibility).

In summary, there exist a considerable number of elements according to which the unitary classification of hadrons into families is of final physical character, but the joint quark models of structure of each individual element of a given family, are still inconclusive because afflicted by several, unresolved, fundamental problems when considered within the context of conventional quantum mechanics.

To avoid misrepresentations on the scientifically constructive intent of the above remarks, let me indicate that, even in case the quark hypothesis on the hadronic structure is invalidated by future evidence, this would basically leave unchanged the beautiful achievements of the theory. In fact, these achievements are essentially of classification nature, such as the prediction of new particles from the knowledge of existing ones. As a result, one cannot exclude the possibility of reformulating the theory at the pure classification level, via a suitable re—interpretation of the numbers currently attributed to quarks (for instance, the quantities currently thought to be the masses of the various quarks could, in the final analysis, result to be suitable parameters mixing different representations of the unitary groups, and the like).

Use of the hadronic mechanics for the identification of quark constituents with the ordinary electrons and positrons.

Incontrovertible experimental evidence establishes that the scattering of the (negatively charged)electrons on the (positively charged) positrons can produce all hadrons,

$$e^+ + e^- \rightarrow \text{hadrons}.$$

Vice versa, hadrons generally admit spontaneous, sequential decays whose ultimate, massive, elementary products are precisely electrons and positrons (plus the massless photons and neutrinos).

It is then rather natural to assume that the hadronic constituents in general, and the quark constituents in particular, are the ordinary electrons and positrons.

As well known, this hypothesis is inconsistent when conventional quantum mechanics is assumed as exactly valid in the interior of hadrons. However, the hypothesis can be consistent under a suitably generalized mechanics. In fact, the hadronic generalization of quantum mechanics has been proposed precisely to achieve a consistent structure model of hadrons whose constituents are the ordinary electrons and positrons.

In particular, hadronic mechanics can well "build" quarks as suitable granules of electrons and positrons, when in the conditions of deep mutual overlapping indicated earlier.

The main ideas are essentially simple. In conventional

quantum mechanics, electrons and positrons obey the Lorentz symmetry resulting into given, fixed, physical characteristics. Under the high nonconservative conditions due to motion within hadronic matter, the same electrons and positrons can be interpreted as verifying suitable Lie—admissible generalizations of the Lorentz symmetry.* In clustering these Lie—admissible mutations of electrons and positrons into granules, one can reach all physical characteristics of quarks, including their fractional charge.

In short, hadronic mechanics offers novel possibilities for the future resolution of the ultimate problem of hadronic structure: the identification of the hadronic constituents with physical particles.

Use of hadronic mechanics for the achievement of a strict form of quark confinement.

Academicians can manipulate their human academic environment, but not physical laws. If quantum mechanics is assumed as exactly valid in the interior of hadrons, the probability of tunnel effects of free quarks CANNOT be reduced to zero. As a result, the assumption of quantum mechanics and the achievement of a true confinement of quarks are intrinsically incompatible.

The best academicians can do is to minimize the probability of tunnel effects for free quarks (qualitative confinement) via the selection of suitable potentials. But the achievement of a strict confinement (identically null probability of tunnel effects for free quarks) is and will remain unachievable within the context of quantum mechanics. The phenomenon of barrier penetration is directly dependent on the basic laws of quantum mechanics and simply cannot be annulled without altering the same laws, that is, without subjecting quantum mechanics to a suitable generalization.

As a result, the generalization of the underlying mechanics is needed, not only for the identification of quark constituents with physical particles, but also for the resolution of the biggest problematic aspect of current quark theories: the achievement

---

*This is technically realized via two sequential generalizations. First the modular action of symmetry groups on the underlying carrier space (the Hilbert space) is lifted from the conventional modular form $A\psi$ to the isotopic form $A*\psi = Ag\psi$, where g is the isotopic operator indicated earlier in this section. This produces a Lie—isotopic generalization suitable for closed—exterior treatments [54]. Nonconservative conditions for each constituents are achieved via a differentiation between the right and left modular—isotopic action, thus resulting in the so—called Lie—admissible bimodules [86—88]. In fact, the differentiation implies the lack of conservation of physical quantities, trivially, because the product characterizing the time evolution is no longer antisymmetric (Figure 1.6.2).

of a strict confinement.

Again, hadronic mechanics appears to possess unique features for the achievement of a strict form of quark confinement.

The main ideas are simple and deserving an outline. Recall that quarks are representations of the product of two Lie groups, the Poincaré group and a suitable unitary group. The former acts in our physical space while the latter acts on a mathematical, internal space.

Assume now that hadronic mechanics is valid for the interior of hadrons, while conventional quantum mechanics continues to remain valid for the exterior case. This evidently implies a differentiation between the interior and exterior mechanics beginning from the fundamental physical principles (Heisenberg's uncertainty principle, Pauli's exclusion principle, etc.). The possibility of achieving a strict quark confinement is then consequential. For example, it can be achieved via differentiations between the interior and exterior dynamics such to render incoherent the related Hilbert spaces. In turn, this latter aspect can be achieved, for instance, via the realization of hadronic mechanics reached by the Argentinian physicist A. Kalnay [89—91] currently at the I.V.I.C. Institute in Caracas, Venezuela. In fact, Kalnay's mechanics has a phase space structure which is fundamentally different than that for the exterior conditions. A strict quark confinement is then expected.

It should be stressed that these results are conceivable without any alteration of the current quark theories, as far as their physical results are concerned. This is technically due to the fact that, according to hadronic mechanics, quarks would be realizations of suitable, Lie—isotopic generalizations of the Poincaré and unitary symmetries. Now, these generalizations have resulted to be locally isomorphic to the conventional ones (see ref. [32] for the Lorentz case and ref. [67] for the unitary one). In turn, this local isomorphism implies the possibility of preserving all essential quark characteristics under lifting.

I can therefore conclude by saying that a considerable number of seemingly independent aspects suggest the need to construct a generalization of quantum mechanics in the transition from the atomic to the nuclear—hadronic structures, with the understanding that quantitative predictions from quantum mechanics are expected to be minimal in the nuclear structure and higher in the hadronic structure. These elements range from the need to identify the origin of irreversibility, to the need for consistent bound states with very light constituents, to the need for a strict form of quark confinement.

Owing to the direct universality of the Lie—admissible algebras, the hadronic generalization of quantum mechanics is the structurally broader generalization available at this time. In fact, other generalizations proposed in the literature are all particular cases of hadronic mechanics. I am referring to the so—called supersymmetric, gauge, rigged and other extensions, as well as to nonlocal, nonlinear and discrete generalizations.

What is unknown to this writing is the particular form of realization of hadronic mechanics that actually holds within hadronic matter. This, however, is primarily an experimental problem, as indicated in the next section.

But the need for a generalization of quantum mechanics under strong interactions should be out of the question. After all, quantum mechanics is basically unable to represent the conditions of mutual penetration of wave—packets which are necessary to activate the strong interactions.

As stressed earlier in this section, particle physics is the last branch of science still anchored to Hamiltonian formulations, while all other branches have passed to structurally broader treatments, resulting in the current lack of unity of physical and mathematical thought.

When unity of science will be one day restored, this can only be done by abandoning Hamiltonian theories also in particle physics in favor of broader theories. The validity of hadronic mechanics within hadronic matter will then follow from its direct universality. It is only a matter of time.

I want to leave a record of this prediction in this book.

The incredible academic politics on quarks.

The word "quark" is an ultimate representative of huge, vested, academic—financial—ethnic interests in the entire U.S. physics, including the academic, corporate, and military sectors.

To understand this, the fellow taxpayer must be informed of a number of aspects, all concurring toward the same interests.

First and foremost, quarks are thought to obey Einstein's special relativity, or at least this is the official version imposed by academic barons in the field. The preservation of the relativity therefore puts quark theories aligned with all vested interests on Einstein's ideas.

Second, quarks are thought to obey conventional quantum mechanics or, again, this is the official version imposed by academic barons. As a result, quark theories are aligned with the vast interests surrounding quantum mechanics, including the corporate and military sectors.

Third, quarks are thought to be a manifestation of Lie's theory, or, again, this is the version imposed by academic barons. But Lie's theory is the hearth of contemporary mathematics (see Section 1.8). As a result, quark theories are aligned with the additional (not ignorable), vested interests in mathematics.

The combination of concurring interests in special relativity, quantum mechanics and Lie's theory, is the secret of the success of quark theories.

The achievement of such a vast combination of vested interests is all based on one central conjecture, that the quarks are point–like. In fact, as elaborated in this chapter, the assumption that quarks are point–like implies the validity of special relativity, quantum mechanics, and Lie's theory, beginning with the local–differential character of the underlying geometry, and then passing to the Hamiltonian character of the underlying mechanics.

The fellow taxpayer will remember the litany of inconsistencies of Einstein's gravitation (Section 1.5). The litany of inconsistencies of current quark theories is perhaps longer.

The hypothesis that quarks are point–like is purely political and deprived of true physical content. In fact, any person, to be a physicist, must know that: (a) quarks possess a wave–packet; (b) that wave–packet has the size of a hadron; and, therefore (c) the wave–packets of quarks must be in conditions of deep mutual penetration in the interior of hadrons. This activates directly the invalidation arguments of the locality of the theory (Figure 1.6.1).

As a result, the mathematical foundations of the special relativity, beginning with the local–differential character of the underlying geometry, cannot be exact for quarks.

Stated differently, "point–like wave–packets" may exist as a figment of academic imagination, but not in the real world.

But perhaps more evident is the invalidation due to lack of achievement of a strict form of confinement.

Recall that current quark theories are based on the assumption of quarks as physical constituents of hadrons which obey quantum mechanics, while no quark has ever been observed to date in the spontaneous decays of hadrons or in hadronic collisions up to the highest possible energies in available particle accelerators throughout the world. Now, one of the pillars of quantum mechanics is Heisenberg's uncertainty principle. According to this principle, when a quark is close to a potential barrier, it possesses a finite, non–null probability of being beyond the barrier (tunnel effect), that is, of being free, contrary to experimental evidence. The selection of an appropriate barrier can reduce the probability, but no theory can render it identically null, unless Heisenberg's uncertainty principle and other laws of quantum mechanics are abandoned in favor of suitable generalizations. But this implies abandoning quantum mechanics in favor of hadronic mechanics, as indicated earlier.

A point the fellow taxpayer has the right to know is that any quark model with a finite, non–null, probability of tunnel effect of free quark is intrinsically inconsistent. Period!

Another point the taxpayer must know is that orthodox papers on quark theories do not compute explicitly the probability of tunnel effect, to my best knowledge (evidence of the erroneous nature of this statement, and the reference to published articles with explicit calculations of the probability would be gratefully appreciated).

Also, the taxpayer should be cautious in accepting claims of "confinement" within the context of a quantum field theoretical description of quarks known under the name of "quantum chromodynamics" (QCD). In fact, the underlying equattions are, in general, nonlinear partial differential equations of unknown solution. In order to separate academic politics from the pursuit of physical knowledge, the achievement of a strict form of confinement must be first achieved at the level of quantum mechanics. Only thereafter the claims of having achieved confinement at the more general QCD level can be accepted by the scientific community at large, that is, including scientists not aligned with vested interests on quarks.

The problems of scientific accountability raised by this issue alone are staggering. Huge amounts of public funds are dispersed every year on quark models by the U.S. National Science Foundation, the Department of Energy, and other governmental agencies. A significant part of these funds have been spent for years, and continue to be spent to this day, on quark models that are intrinsically, demonstrably inconsistent. Yet, they are supported by leading "peers" in leading academic institutions and, as such, funded.

We are facing here tight governmental—academic circles much similar to those in gravitation and irreversibility, that is, without any foreseeable possibility of self—correction. Governmental agencies will continue to submit grant applications on quarks for review to leading experts on quarks at leading academic institutions. In turn, these "peers" will continue to ignore the lack of strict quark confinement. The governmental agencies will therefore continue to fund applications that are intrinsically inconsistent. After all, why should they change a routine happily followed for decades?

An outside intervention by the taxpayer is the only hope for scientific advances and for improvements of the scientific accountability in the sector.

The means are known. The methods to compute the probability of tunnel effect are taught in undergraduate courses in quantum mechanics. Most physics students are therefore able to compute the probability of tunnel effects for free quarks whenever the essential elements are given., that is, whenever the students know the mass of the quark, the explicit form of the "confining potential" and a few other data. If the probability of tunnel effect is "identically null", the model is consistent; otherwise, the model is inconsistent. Silence in the computation of this probability, as fashionable in the current technical literature, can only multiply the problems of accountability and resolve none.

A serious study of this ethical profile is recommended

here. If not conducted in the U.S., it will be likely conducted abroad.

The study should consider papers immediately following the original formulation in 1964 of the quark conjecture by the U.S. physicist M. Gell–Mann [92], and include papers up to the recent ones. All these papers carry their federal research contracts. The administrative profile can therefore be readily retraced, whenever needed. References to primary papers in the field are readily identifiable and need not be quoted here.

We are therefore talking about known papers in quark theories published under governmental support during the past twenty years. All these papers should be subjected to the calculation of the probability of tunnel effects for free quarks. They can be classified into three categories: the first, with a large probability of tunnel effect (this group contains most of the initial papers); the second with a small but non–null probability of tunnel effect; and the third with hopes of achieving a strict form of quark confinement.

The value of a study of this nature for future orientation and funding of research in the sector is evident.

Note that I am not recommending that research projects without strict confinement should remain unfunded. I am only insisting on the need of scientific honesty. Quark models with a "qualitative" confinement, that is, with a finite, non–null, probability of tunnel effect of free quarks contrary to evidence, should state so, clearly, in all printed papers. In turn, the clear identification of the problem is essential for its resolution.

Whether the current governmental funding of research in quark theories warrants or not an outside intervention by the taxpayer, one point should be crystal clear. The opinions by leading quark experts at leading U.S. institutions should remain what they are: opinions expressed by physicists with decades of vested interests in the dismissal of the problem of confinement. As such, the "peers" used by governmental agencies in grant refereeing are the very least qualified to pass judgment on the inconsistencies of their own grants.

The episode of the paper of criticisms on quarks I wrote at Harvard and distributed in 15,000 copies.

In anticipation of the more detailed report of Section 2.1, at the end of Section 1.3, I have presented a preliminary outline of the opposition I have encountered at the Department of Physics of Harvard University in 1977–1978 in the conduction of my research (need for experimental tests on the validity or invalidity of Einstein's special relativity and Pauli's exclusion principle in the interior of hadrons—see the title of memoir [14] written precisely at Harvard's physics department in early 1978).

After passing to the Department of Mathematics in June 1978, while regularly receiving my salary under my own grant from the Department of Energy (contract number ER—78—S—02—47420.A000 for the period June 1, 1978 until May 31, 1979), I thought that my problems were over for a while. I therefore plunged myself into the drafting and re—drafting of the monograph on the Birkhoffian generalization of Hamiltonian mechanics (subsequently published in 1982, ref. [10]).

But I was wrong.

In early 1979, Harvard filed a formal application to the Department of Energy for the renewal of my contract for one additional year (from June 1, 1979 until May 31, 1980). The application was filed after passing all the various layers of administrative approvals, from my department, to the office of the dean, and to the office of research contracts. In particular, the Department of Mathematics had approved the submission of the application to D.O.E. with my affiliation to the same department for one second year.

The D.O.E. promptly approved the application for funding under the new contract number AS02—78ER4742. The D.O.E. notification arrived jointly to Harvard's administration and to me. I felt reassured. At least I could feed and shelter my children and my wife (then still a graduate student) for one additional year, while doing research in physics. I therefore plunged myself into the studies for monograph [10] with renewed scientific ardor.

This happy status was short lived. One day in early April 1979, the chairman of Harvard's Department of Mathematics for that year, Heisuke Hironaka, came to my office.

Our relationship, at that time, was of utmost mutual respect and cordiality. I therefore invited Hironaka to sit in my sofa, and relax. He had visible difficulties in telling me what was going on. After some gentle pressures on my part, he came to the point, indicating that there were "insurmountable difficulties" for my staying one additional year at Harvard.

I reminded him that his department had formally approved the filing of my application to D.O.E., which had been subsequently approved by Harvard's administration and then funded by the D.O.E. He confirmed the awareness of these facts, but re—stressed the impossibility of my stay at Harvard for one additional year.

At one point, Hironaka stressed emphatically that I had to terminate my stay at Harvard at the end of the D.O.E. contract then in effect, that is, at the end of the following month.

I indicated to him that I had two children to feed and shelter and that, under no circumstances would I be able to find another job in such a short time. I also indicated to Hironaka that the attempt to transfer my contract to another university would raise a host of questions, beginning with the basic question: Why Harvard did not want to administer a contract that had already been formally filed and approved?

I therefore asked Hironaka to disclose the reasons of the "absolute impossibility" for my staying there one additional year with my own money, while giving to Harvard the gift of a significant amount of overheads.

I attempted to bring him to the reality of the inevitable consequences at the various levels, in Cambridge and in Washington, not to exclude evident legal implications. Also, the disclosure of the reasons for the "absolute impossibility" would have been important to attempt a friendly resolution of the case to the benefit of all people involved, including those opposing the continuation of my stay.

At one point, Hironaka finally ceased to resist, and told me what was going on. In essence, to draw my salary under the formally approved grant, I needed the renewal of my appointment there as a member of the Department of Mathematics. In turn, he had encountered "insurmountable difficulties" in reaching such a renewal. The senior high energy physicists at the Department of Physics of Harvard had reiterated (AGAIN!) their judgment of "lack of physical value" of my studies. In turn, this had created an evident, apparently intended deadlock at Hironaka's department. I was a theoretical high energy physicist and not a mathematician. As a result, the members of the mathematics department had to rely on the judgment of the senior high energy physicists at Harvard in order to reappoint me. The negative judgment at the physics department had therefore implied the consequential negative judgment at his department. In particular, the opposition at the physics department was so great to create an "absolute impossibility" for the renewal of my appointment.

I thanked Hironaka sincerely for the information (that I had suspected anyhow), and indicated that I would make one final attempt for an "orderly" solution of the problem within the mathematics department. Nevertheless, before he opened the door, I brought to his attention the extreme gravity of the occurrence.

That same night I initiated the writing of a paper of constructive critical examination of the litany of problematic aspects of the quark conjectures. The paper was subsequently completed in a preliminary form on April 19, 1979, under the initial title: "An intriguing legacy by Albert Einstein: the expected invalidation of quark conjectures". The paper was thereafter printed and distributed in 15,000 samples (as stated in the front page) thanks to funds and logistic assistance provided by the printer of the Hadronic Journal. The paper was subsequently subjected to a number of revisions, and finally printed with an expanded and edited title in *Foundations of Physics* in 1981 (see ref. [49]).

As everybody can see, the paper presents a litany of argumentations dismissing the possibility that quarks exist as conceived at that time at Harvard (as well as throughout the world), that is, as the ultimate, "elementary", and therefore indivisible constituents of hadrons. In particular, the paper re—stressed the final physical value of the theory for the Mendeleyev—type classification of hadrons and restricted the critical analysis only to the structural profile. The inspiration of the paper was constructive, as stated beginning from the abstract. The hope was that of stimulating a consideration of the problems by independent researchers in the field as a prerequisite for their solution.

The argumentations were those presented in this chapter, that is, the various reasons why we expect the lack of exact character of the special relativity in the interior of hadrons. But quarks are manifestations of the special relativity, as recalled earlier. Departures from the special relativity, if experimentally established, would then imply the impossibility for quarks to be elementary.

By April 28, 1979, the paper had been printed, and the distribution of the 15,000 copies had begun. I still remember car loads of boxes of individually addressed copies of the paper being distributed to Harvard University, M.I.T., Tufts University, Boston College, and the other universities of the Boston area, while heavy shipments were mailed to all other high energy research institutions throughout the world.

On April 29, 1979, I wrote a letter to all members of the Department of Mathematics at Harvard for an orderly solution of the case. The letter, written in the most respectful possible style, appealed to the scientific ethics of the addressees, as well as to the need for scientific freedom at Harvard.

At the subsequent faculty meeting, the Department of Mathematics formally approved the renewal of my appointment for one additional, but terminal year.

These are the events that forced me to interrupt the studies for monograph [10] and, against all my plans and wishes, forced me into the writing of a paper of criticisms on quarks.

Besides fulfilling the purpose of a scientific presentation of my views on quarks to the members of Harvard's mathematics department, paper [49] appears to have been totally useless on scientific grounds. In fact, the paper was never quoted by any physicist at Harvard, nor has ever been quoted in any paper on orthodox quark lines (evidence to the contrary would be gratefully appreciated).

To understand this occurrence, the taxpayer should know that: (a) no physicist in quark theories can claim lack of knowledge of the paper, owing to the quite unusual volume of distribution of the preprint, followed by the publication and subsequent mailing of reprints; (b) the idea that quarks cannot be elementary, but must be composite, is routinely accepted these days, as indicated earlier in this section; and (c) paper [49], even though unquoted, was and remains the first to present comprehensive argumentations on the impossibility for quarks to be elementary.

But, above all, the most distressing aspect is that the call launched by paper [49] (to test the validity of Einstein's ideas in the interior of hadrons) has remained unanswered to this day.

The moratorium of early 1980 in the publication of papers at the Hadronic Journal in non−relativistic quark theories.

Every relativistic model (that is, model verifying the special relativity) must admit, for consistency, a valid nonrelativistic limit (that is, a low speed limit verifying Galilei's relativity). The non−relativistic limit of quark theories (which are generally formulated within a relativistic setting) has therefore been studied since the early stages of the theory.

Severe doubts on excessive inconsistencies of non−relativistic quark theories had crossed my mind for years, and increased in time. One day, the issue exploded in my editorial hands in all its force.

In late 1979, I received a paper in non−relativistic quark theories submitted to the Hadronic Journal. At that time, my editorial office was room 435 of the Department of Mathematics at Harvard University.

I submitted the paper to two referees. The first was a leading expert in quark theory at a leading U.S. institution. The second was an applied mathematician, expert in nonrelativistic quantum mechanics, with a record of independence from vested interests on quark lines. The first referee recommended publication of the paper, while the second rejected the paper quite firmly.

The inability to resolve their differences forced me to implement a moratorium in the publication of papers in non−relativistic quark models. The case was reported in an open letter to editors of other Journals dated January 8, 1980, as well as in a following open letter to mathematicians interested in quantum mechanics dated March 19, 1980 (see Doc. p. I−316).

The main issues are the following. The non−relativistic limit of quark theories generally characterizes a Hamiltonian with a structure of the type: $H = aA(r) + bB(r)p + cC(r)p^2 + dD(r)p^4$ + higher powers in p, where: A, B, C, D are functions of coordinates r; p is the canonical momentum; and a, b, c, d are constants.

These models possess the following inconsistencies (mostly valid to this day).

(1) The models violate Galilei's relativity. Recall that the non−relativistic limit was studied precisely in the hope to reach a consistent Galilean setting as one element needed to

prove the consistency of the original relativistic formulation. Therefore, the violation of Galilei's relativity invalidates the very motivation of the study. The violation was proved beyond any reasonable doubt by the referee in applied mathematics. In essence, one of the necessary conditions for the verification of Galilei's relativity in quantum mechanics is the verification of the so—called Mackey's imprimitivity theorem [93]. In turn, this theorem is manifestly violated by all Hamiltonians with momentum powers higher than two.

(2)   The models violate the conservation laws of the total energy, linear momentum, angular momentum and other physical quantities. This second aspect was established, also beyond any reasonable doubt, by the necessary and sufficient conditions for given forces to admit a potential energy [9]. In fact, one theorem of this latter theory implies that the total energy is not conserved for all "potentials" with momentum powers higher than two. A similar situation occurs for all other physical quantities. In short, the models were intended to describe closed—isolated hadrons, but in actuality resulted to violate all total conservation laws. Of course, the Hamiltonian H(r,p) is conserved in time. The point is the H does not represent the total energy under the conditions considered. A similar situation occurred for other physical quantities.

(3)   The probability of tunnel effects for free quarks was excessively high. This third point was also proved beyond a reasonable doubt. It merely implied the use of actual physical quantities, rather than the canonical ones (that is, the use of the total nonconserved energy, rather than the conserved Hamiltonian, etc.).

A number of additional inconsistencies and problematic aspects also existed, such as the loss of the equivalence between the quantum mechanical, Hamiltonian and Lagrangian representations, the activation of the theorems preventing a consistent quantization, etc. For a review, the interested reader may consult paper [94].

It is evident that the problematic aspects of the papers were simply too big and too many to be ignored. There must be a limit beyond which leniency in scientific insufficiencies becomes complicity with aligned interests.

This is the reason why I imposed a moratorium in the field at the Hadronic Journal and, in addition, I felt obliged to bring my findings to the attention of the editors of other journals in particle physics. I did this in full knowledge that the information would be damaging to me, as it did! In fact, an anonimous referee subsequently rejected one of my research grant applications by quoting, among other things, precisely my open letter to the editors on this issue (see Section 2.5). Evidently, this referee was a quarkologist who felt threatened by my desire to do physics, rather than pursuing academic politics.

The reactions of the editorial community resulted to be a perfect image of the academic politics in the field. In essence, the editors of (U.S.) independent journals reacted with interest and cooperation, while those aligned or controlled by quark interests attempted to discredit my efforts, or to ignore them altogether.

For instance, the U.S. physicist David Finkelstein of the Georgia Institute of Technology, and editor of the International Journal of Theoretical Physics, reacted with keen interest. In particular, his constructive comments resulted to be invaluable in improving our understanding of the technical issues, and I shall remain always grateful to him for that.

Par contre, the U.S. physicist George L. Trigg of the American Physical Society, editor of Physical Review Letters (the leading journal of the society), reacted in a rather incredible way. I had mailed him (and to a number of other A.P.S. editors) all possible information, including copies of papers and of proceedings of workshops in related topics. His answer is reproduced below.*

PHYSICAL REVIEW LETTERS, Editorial Office, 1 Research Rd. Ridge, New York, N.Y. 11961, tel. (516) 924 5533

May 22, 1980

Dr. R. M. Santilli
Department of Mathematics
Harvard University
Cambridge, Mass. 02138

Dear Dr. Santilli:

Thank you for lending me the material from the workshop on Lie admissibility. I apologize for having kept it longer than the two weeks or so that you had suggested; I hope that this did not cause you any difficulties.

I find, to my regret, that my familiarity with modern abstract algebra is sufficiently sketchy that I was not really able to appreciate much of the argument. I cannot help feeling, however, that your campaign calls for much more drastic action than is really warranted. As you must be aware, this is not the first instance in which physics theory has made progress on the basis of questionable mathematics, nor is it likely to be the last. I do not mean in any sense to disparage the work that you and others are doing to try to provide a sounder basis; but I do not feel that a moratorium of any sort would be useful.

I thank you again for lending me the material, and I offer my wishes for success of the forthcoming workshop. I regret that my schedule does not permit me to attend.

Sincerely yours,

George L. Trigg
Editor

GLT/jaw

As one can see, Trigg dismissed the moratorium on grounds that the deficiencies were mainly of "questionable mathematics". Instead, the deficiencies were of purely physical nature and of primary physical relevance at that, such as: the invalidation of Galilei's relativity; the violation of the conservation of the total energy; the excessively high probability of tunnel effects of free quarks; etc.

The taxpayer can therefore draw his/her own conclusion. The fact remains that, at the Journals of the A.P.S., papers in non—relativistic quark theories continued to be printed without any consideration whatsoever or mention of the literature on the problematic aspects considered here. As far as the Journals of the A.P.S. were concerned, my efforts to stimulate a moment of reflection on the excessively big inconsistencies of non—relativistic quark models were a total waste of time.

Note that the scope of my action was not the suppression of research in the field. Not at all. Instead, the objective was the clear identification of open problems as a prerequisite for their solution.

It is hoped that the fellow taxpayer will remember this epidose when reading Section 2.4 on my experience with the journals of the A.P.S. In fact, all rejections of papers submitted to A.P.S. journals should be always compared to the quality and consistency of the papers routinely published, such as precisely the papers on nonrelativistic quark conjectures. I am referring to the rejection of the experimental paper on nuclear irreversibility by Phys. Rev. C, subsequentily published in Europe (ref. [105]), of the theoretical paper on hadronic mechanics and the possible internal irreversibility of strong interactions, rejected for over one year by Phys. Rev. Letters and Phys. Rev. D, subsequently published also in Europe (see ref. [59]), and too numerous other cases. All these rejections of papers not aligned with vested, financial-academic-ethnic interests on Einstein's ideas, should always be compared to the routine

publication of papers aligned with vested interests, irrespective of their inconsistencies and problematic aspects.

My invited talk at the 1980 Conference on Differential Geometric Methods in Mathematical Physics at the University of Clausthal, West Germany.

In early 1980, H. D. Doebner of the Theoretical Physics
Department of the University of Clausthal, West Germany, invited me to deliver a talk at the yearly *Conference on Differential
Geometric Methods in Mathematical Physics,* to be held at his institute the subsequent July.

The conference is generally attended by the leading experts in applied mathematics and theoretical physics. I saw a unique opportunity to draw attention on the limitations for strong
interactions of conventional algebras, geometries and mechanics.
My hope was that, in doing so, I could stimulate some of the best
minds toward the natural future step: the construction of suitable generalizations specifically conceived for the strong interactions.

I began my talk by projecting on the big screen of the conference room the symbol of this book: extended wave—packets
in conditions of mutual penetration and overlapping, as experimentally established for the strong interactions.

As stated during the talk, my task would have been accomplished if the participants had remembered the physical reality of
the diagram above, after the conference, when returning to their
research activities.

The diagram provides evidence of the lack of exact character of the algebras, geometries and mechanics used for the
strong interactions at that time, and continued to be used to this
day. As familiar from the preceding review, the diagram identifies the incontrovertible evidence according to which strong
interactions are non—local (that is, distributed throughout a finite volume of space), thus implying the insufficiency of all currently preferred geometries such as the symplectic geometry
(which are precisely of local—differential character). In turn,
this implies the insufficiencies of the Lie algebras, beginning with
the Lorentz and Poincaré algebras of the special relativity, because of the insufficiency of the underlying topologies and other

reasons. Finally, the diagram depicts the insufficiencies of currently preferred mechanics, because of the contact/non−Hamiltonian nature of the interactions.

To illustrate the implications to the conference participants, I outlined the status of our knowledge at that time on the expected deformation of the charge distribution of hadrons under external strong interactions, with the consequential mutation of the intrinsic magnetic moments, as reviewed earlier in this section. The quantitative treatment was conducted via the Lie−admissible generalization of the conventional, quantum mechanical, Lie treatment of the rotational symmetry. The embedding of the Lie treatment into a covering Lie−admissible one, was intended to represent the open/non−conservative character of one hadron under external strong interactions.

I concluded my talk with a review of the status of our experimental knowledge on the rotational symmetry which was intriguingly favoring the mutation of the magnetic moments as well as of the spin, although yet inconclusive (see next section).

The transparencies of my talk were subsequently expanded into a paper published in ref. [62].

One can imagine the reaction of the audience to my talk. Mathematicians there were heavily committed to the local−differential character of the geometry, while theoreticians had a known history of vested interests on Einstein's ideas. The very view of the diagram above, despite its incontroverible reality, was anatema for most of them.

I still remember S. Sternberg of the Department of Mathematics of Harvard University leaving the conference room as soon as the diagram above appeared on the big screen, and I began the presentation of the nonlocality of the strong interactions.*

Upon conclusion of my talk, I remember a vociferous intervention by Y. Ne'eman of Tel−Aviv University, Israel, who attacked the very idea of testing the rotational symmetry under strong interactions. My answer was that we had a duty to resolve the issue one way or the other, because of the fundamental character of the rotational symmetry, on one side, when combined with the plausibility of the deformations of extended hadrons, on the other side. At any rate, the idea that extended hadrons are absolutely rigid has no scientific value, while the breaking of the rotational symmetry for deformed charge distributions can be seen by all. But, all my argumentations (later continued in the corridor) were useless. As well known, Y. Ne'eman is a renowned expert in quark theories and Einstein's gravitation. The physical conditions of the diagram above undermine the ultimate mathematical foundations of both quark theories and Einstein's gravitation as elaborated thoughout this chapter. The possibility of establishing a constructive scientific dialogue be-

---

*When he subsequently delivered his own talk, I evidently made it a point in leaving the conference room soon after its initiation.

tween Ne'eman and myself proved to be nonexistent.

Another criticism that I still remember is that by I. Segal of the Department of Mathematics of the Massachusetts Institute of Technology who, in subsequent conversations, warned me against the study of the conditions of the diagram, because "it would open a Pandora's box." I told Segal that the conditions of the diagram were not of my own invention, and that we had an ethical duty to consider seriously Enrico Fermi and other founding fathers of strong interactions, who had established a record of the non—locality of the theory. Such an historical record could not possibly remain ignored. The sooner we study it, the better.

For fairness, I must report one voice of support during the discussion following my talk, by the Irish physicist C. C. C. He recalled to the audience that, under my assumptions (one hadron in the open/non—conservative conditions due to external strong interactions) "all conventional Lie symmetries are expected to be broken, including the rotational symmetry". But his voice was lost in the sea of oppositions.

More recently, while organizing, in late 1983, a workshop on hadronic mechanics to be held at the beautiful Villa Olmo, on the edge of the Lake of Como in Italy (Center Alessandro Volta) in 1984, I invited K. Bleuler of the University of Bonn, West Germany, to be a member of the Organization Committee jointly with several other distinguished mathematicians and physicists. Bleuler was one of the founders and co—organizers of the Clausthal Conference. He was present at my talk there in 1980 and fully aware of the issues. My invitation was motivated by the fact that hadronic mechanics uses, among other tools, a certain generalization of the inner product of the Hilbert spaces of quantum mechanics that had been identified in the early 50's. Bleuler was the last living physicist of the original group who had identified the generalization [95]. His participation in the Organization Committee of the Como Workshop on Hadronic Mechanics would have been scientifically invaluable, even without physically attending the meeting.

Bleuler never acknowledged my invitation, nor the gentle solicitation by the Workshop secretary. Evidently, a few words of declination of our respectful invitation would have been sufficient. I must denounce Bleuler's silence because strictly anticollegial and antiscientific. In fact, his lack of answer produced considerable delays in the completion of the formal announcement of the meeting, with evident scientific damage.

Nevertheless, I would like to take this opportunity to express my utmost gratitude and respect for H. D. Doebner. By permitting a presentation at the 1980 Clausthal Conference of the ultimate roots of the expected inapplicability of Einstein's ideas under strong interactions, he fulfilled in full his scientific accountability as a scientist and as a conference organizer. What happened afterward is the sole responsibility of the conference participants.

All in all, the experience of my participation at the Clausthal conference reinforced my conviction that the conduction of research on the expected invalidation of Einstein's ideas in the interior of hadrons is a total waste of time, and will remain a total waste of time until taxpayers intervene to force the implementation of strict scientific accountabilities in the sector.

This is why I halted all research, and considered my time better spent in writing this book.

Interruption due to the death of my mother.

On the afternoon of March 16, 1984, I received a phone call from Italy asking for my leaving immediately for Rome, due to a sudden illness of my mother who was dead at my arrival there the following morning. Work on this book was resumed on the afternoon of April 4, 1984.

She had gently followed and spiritually supported me throughout my life, and, in particular, during my difficult times recalled in Chapter 2. Monograph [10] on the Birkhoffian generalization of Hamiltonian mechanics was dedicated to her.

I wanted to have a record in this book of this unexpected event.

1.7: THE EXPERIMENTAL VERIFICATIONS OF THE VALIDITY OR INVALIDITY OF EINSTEIN'S IDEAS UNDER STRONG INTERACTIONS.

The approaching of the central ethical issues raised by IL GRANDE GRIDO.

The experimental tests on the validity or invalidity of Einstein's ideas under strong interactions (A) are fully within current technological capabilities, (B) are of quite moderate costs, particularly when compared to orthodox particle experiments, and last but not least, (C) the experimental information currently available, even though preliminary and still inconclusive, points quite clearly toward the violation.

Once the taxpayer has reached a sufficient knowledge of these aspects, a number of stormy questions follow quite naturally:

— *Why these fundamental experiments are not done?*

— *Why public money is spent in other experiments whose relevance is dwarfed by that of the tests on Einstein's theories?*

— *Who is behind this?*

— *What is the responsibility of presidents of national laboratories and leading colleges?*

— *Is there an organized conspiracy within the U.S. governmental—academic complex to impose a scientific obscurantism on Einstein's theories?*

and many, many more.

Information on the plausibility of the violation of Einstein's ideas has been provided in the preceding analysis. In this section, I shall provide the taxpayer with a review as simple as possible of the available experimental information.

But, upon achieving these tasks, my job would remain still incomplete. The same information can be reached by all people with scientific curiosity and time, trivially, because the information is available in research libraries.

To complete my job, I must present my experience as an insider. I must tell the episodes I have experienced during my (totally unsuccessful) attempts to have the governmental—academic complex at least consider the tests, let alone actually do them! Only then the taxpayer will have the elements to judge the gravity, depth and diversification of the questions above, and their potential implications for our societies.

Bits of the latter task have been occasionally included in the preceding sections. More detailed information will be presented in the next chapter.

The fellow taxpayer should be aware that the fundamental knowledge is and remains the scientific one. Only after achieving such a knowledge, the issues of scientific ethics and accountability can be truly mastered. As stated earlier, this chapter on the scientific profile is merely a guide throughout (part of) the technical literature. The taxpayer is therefore urged to complement this presentation with the reading of the quoted literature. Except the inevitable technical passages, most of the argumentations and conclusions are understandable by all. The reading of articles NOT authored by me is also essential to understand that, by no means, I am alone. On the contrary, I am only one among numerous scholars on the limitations of Einstein's theories scattered throughout the world.

The fundamental experiments by the Austrian physicist H. Rauch on the tests of the rotational symmetry under strong interactions.

Recall the prediction of hadronic mechanics, that the charge distribution of hadrons can experience deformations under sufficiently intense external fields, with consequential breaking of the rotational symmetry and, consequently, of the special relativity.

This deformation/rotational—Lorentz—asymmetry can be readily subjected to experimental measures. In fact, it implies a (necessary) alteration of the intrinsic magnetic moments of hadrons, while the intrinsic angular momentum (spin) can remain unchanged for sufficiently low energies.

Experimental measures directly relevant for the above prediction have been conducted by the Austrian physicist H. Rauch (director of the Atominstitute of Wien), and his associates. The measures have been conducted at the Laue—Langevin Laboratory in Grenoble, France, via the so—called neutron interferometers (see Figure 1.7.1 for more details). The experiments tested the rotational symmetry of neutrons under external fields. The first measures were conducted in 1975 [96]. The tests were then repeated in the subsequent years [97,98,99]. The latest available measures are given in ref. [100].

The main ideas of the experiments are so simply, to be understandable by all. The intrinsic magnetic moment of neutrons renders them similar to small magnets. Under an external magnetic field due to an electromagnet, neutrons therefore rotate. The value of the neutron magnetic moments in vacuum is known. Thus, the field of the external electromagnet can be calibrated for one, two, or more "spin flips" or complete rotations.

When a neutron beam propagates in vacuum under the long range action of the electromagnet only, no deformation of the charge distribution and mutation of the magnetic moment is expected. To realize experimentally the physical conditions for activation of hadronic mechanics, the neutrons must be brought within the intense fields in the vicinity of nuclei. In this case, Eder's calculations [65] show about 1% deviation in the intensity modulation, a value well within current experimental capabilities.

Rauch's team reached, rather accidentially, the physical conditions needed for hadronic mechanics. Indeed, they filled up with Mu—metal sheets the electromagnet gap. This was done by the experimenters to reduce the stray fields. In actuality, by letting the neutron beam to propagate within matter, they automatically reached the joint conditions of long range electromagnetic and short range nuclear interactions.

The first experiments [96] were conducted for neutron propagating in vacuum. Their results, therefore, have no value for hadronic mechanics. More recent experiments, however, have been conducted with the electromagnet gaps filled up with Mu—metal sheets. These are the relevant experiments here.

The best available measurements on the angle for two complete spin flips are the following [100] : 715.87±3.8 deg, that is, the minimal angle is 712.97 deg, while the maximal value is 712.07 deg. As a result, and according to the experimenter's own words, the measures "do not include the expected 720 deg within its simple error limits" (ref. [100], p. 730).

What does this mean? The answer is incontrovertibly clear for all ethically sound scholars: THE CURRENTLY AVAILABLE MEASURES BY RAUCH DO NOT CONFIRM THE PREDICTIONS OF QUANTUM MECHANICS IN THE BEHAVIOR OF THE FUNDAMENTAL ROTATIONAL SYMMETRY. In fact, to confirm orthodox theories, the measures should have been of the type, say, with maximal angle of precession 720.01 deg and minimal angle of precession 718.37 deg, thus including 720 deg. As remarked by the experimenter, the value 720 deg is instead OUT of the simple errors limits. Quantum mechanics is therefore not confirmed by the experiments as they stand now.

It is equally evident to all ethically sound scholars that Rauch's values [100] DO NOT confirm hadronic mechanics either. In fact, such a confirmation can only be claimed after repetition of the experiments in a substantial number of different realizations (see below).

In short, the experiments by H. Rauch and his team on the rotational symmetry of neutrons under strong and electromagnetic interactions, confirm the essentially open character of this fundamental problem of human knowledge. The lack of recovering of the angle of precession predicted by the exact rotational symmetry, confirms the plausibility of the deformation of hadrons with consequential alteration of their magnetic moments.

The need for the repetition of the experiments is then evident to all.

The needed tests are well known (see, for instance, ref.s [62,100]). They are as follows:

1) The first tests suggested are given by the repetition of measures [100] according to exactly the same set up as originally done, (two complete spin flips in both branches of the neutron beams), but with an improved accuracy. Apparently, the use

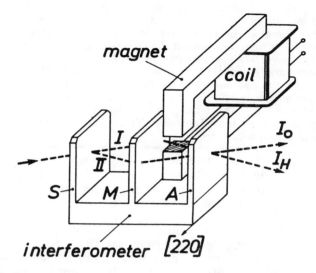

Figure 1.7.1. A schematic view of the neutron interferometers used in the tests [96–100] of the rotational symmetry under short range interactions. A low energy neutron beam originating from a nuclear reactor is subjected to a coherent spitting into two beams via perfect crystal, and then to a coherent recombination. An electromagnet acts on each or both branches of the beam thus inducing a precession in the orientation of spin. Some typical data are the following: beam cross section = 2×1.5 mm^2; crystal characteristic wavelength = 1.83 Å; magnetic induction needed to produce two complete spin flips = 7496 G. The stray fields for electromagnet gaps in air are rather pronounced, thus increasing the errors. The gaps are therefore filled up with Mu–metal sheets. This latter feature renders the experiment of fundamental character because it implies the test of the rotational symmetry under the long range magnetic forces of the electromagnet and the short range, intense fields in the vicinity of nuclei due to penetration of the neutron beams within the Mu–metal sheets. Under these latter conditions, hadronic mechanics predicts a deformation of the charge distribution of the neutron due to the intense nuclear fields. This deformation, in turn, (necessarily) implies an alteration (mutation) of the intrinsic magnetic moments. Still in turn, the alteration of the magnetic moment implies deviations from the angle of spin precessions predicted by the exact rotational symmetry. Explicit calculations conducted by Eder [65] predict about 1% deviations, The measures of the angle of spin precession are done via measures on the so–called intensity and polarization modulations. The experiments have been conducted by Rauch and his associates since 1975 [96–100]. The latest available measures [100] DO NOT contain the angle of the exact rotational symmetry (720 deg) in their simple errors limits. The measures are therefore encouraging in favor of hadronic mechanics, although, and this must be stressed here, they are inconclusive and in need of numerous verifications before reaching any conclusion. The measures, if confirmed by future tests, imply a direct violation of Einstein's special relativity. In fact, as reviewed in Section 1.4, the violation of the rotational symmetry implies the breakdown of the foundations of the special relativity, such as the alteration of the speed of light under a Lorentz

transformation. It should be stressed that the experiments reviewed here are not specialized to maximize the deformation—mutation effects. Rauch's tests can therefore be repeated to maximize the possible deformation—mutations. As final comments it should be indicated that neutron interferometric measures are known to be among the most accurate measurements throughout the entire experimental physics. This accuracy is mostly dependent on the low energy of the beam, which is therefore important for the experimental resolution of the possible mutation of the magnetic moment of hadrons. The tests of other predictions of hadronic mechanics demand sufficiently higher energies. This is the case of the tests for Pauli's exclusion principle (see later on).

of recent experimental advances could permit a decrease of the error by a facotr of 1/10. An improved accuracy of this type would be per se sufficient to resolve the issue.

2) The tests should be repeated with an increasing number of spin flips, say, 2, 4, 6, 8, 10, and more (apparently, currently technology could permit up to 50 spin flips). The comparative analysis of the various individual tests would then permit the elimination of possible statistical fluctuations, the identification of the linear or nonlinear behaviour of possible deviations with the precession angle, and other important aspects.

3) Each of the tests 2) should be finally repeated with a progressive increase of the width of matter penetrated by the neutron beam, say, 0.5 cm, 1 cm, 1.5 cm, etc. This latter specification is evidently important to maximize the physical conditions needed for a possible mutation of the magnetic moments. Progressive tests of the type suggested here would also provide additional information on the possible nonlinear behaviour of the mutation with the width of matter penetrated by the beam, and others.

A number of additional tests have also been suggested in the literature, such as repeat experiments 1), 2) and 3) with the electromagnet in only one branch of the neutron beam, with particles other than neutrons, etc.

The scientific implications of Rauch's experiments.

The scientific importance of Rauch's experiments is such to dwarf ALL other experiments in particle physics, without exceptions. It is of the essence that the fellow taxpayer understand the ethical implications originating from the suppression or even delays in the repetition of Rauch's experiment.

The rotational symmetry is the true, ultimate pillar of the entirety of our current description of the microscopic world. The central role of the rotational symmetry for the special relativity has been stressed beginning from Section 1.4. But this is only part of it. Each and every aspect of quantum mechanics is either directly or indirectly dependent on the rotational symmetry.

It is important that the taxpayer understands the lack of reciprocity of this occurrence. Take for example the discrete symmetries: space and time reflections. For the case of particles with spin, these symmetries are dependent explicitly on the rotational symmetry. Thus, if the rotational symmetry is broken, the space and time reflection symmetries must be broken too. The opposite situation, however, is not necessarily true, in the sense that the discrete symmetries can be broken, but the rotational symmetry can remain exact (or at least this is the thesis currently preferred in leading U.S. institutions). The reasons are identified in the additional components of discrete symmetries, besides those depending on the rotational symmetry.

A similar situation occurs for virtually all other aspects of nuclear physics, particle physics, statistical mechanics (including the controlled fusion!) and other branches of physics.

It is a truism to say that, if future experiments will confirm the breaking of the rotational symmetry, the virtual entirety of our contemporary description of the microcosm must be suitably generalized.

The low cost of Rauch's experiments on the rotational symmetry when compared to the costs of current particle experiments of lesser relevance.

The neutron interferometric measures on the rotational symmetry [100] can be repeated with expenses ranging from $ 50,000 to $ 100,000. This expenditure includes reactor time, salary for two experimentalists, and all other direct and indirect costs.

This cost takes into account the fact that all basic equipments are already available, such as the reactor to produce the neutron beam and the perfect crystal, while the measures can be reached within a period of time of the order of two months.

To understand these numbers, the fellow taxpayer should compare them with costs of other experiments in particle physics. These latter experiments typically involve teams of several dozen (or even hundreds) of experimentalists, working for extended periods of time (of the order of one year or more). The tests are done in particle accelerators, resulting in costs of the order of millions of dollars and more.

Whenever we shall enter into the problem of ethics and scientific accountability in the U.S. physics, the fellow taxpayer must remember this comparatively low cost of the test of the rotational symmetry, jointly with their comparatively more fundamental relevance.

In fact, owing to their low costs, financial reasons cannot be claimed in a credible way as the reasons for the lack of repetition of the experiments.

Once the taxpayer sees that, then he/she will be able to see beyond reasonable doubts that the lack of repetition of the experiments is due to mumbo—jumbo academic politics and maneuvring by vested interests.

The impossibility to repeat Rauch's experiments on the rotational symmetry since 1978.

As indicated earlier, the first measures by Rauch's team were conducted in 1975 [96] and then repeated in subsequent years. The last tests occurred in 1978 [99]. In fact, the best available measures [100] are a mere re—elaboration of the measures of 1978 due to the improvements of physical constants and other advances occurred in the meantime.

Since 1978, it has been impossible to repeat the measures, despite numerous attempts in two continents, as we shall review in detail throughout the rest of this presentation.

As a preview, the impossibilities included:

— the prohibition by the Laue—Langevin Laboratory in Grenoble, France, to repeat the measures in conjunction with an international conference in the field;

— the lack of interest and cooperation by the Massachusetts Institute of Technology despite its availability of all basic equipments;

— the rejection by E. T. Ritter, Director of the D.O.E. Division of Nuclear Physics, to fund the repetition of the measures via an Austria—France—U.S.A. collaboration;

and numerous other aspects the taxpayers of the U.S.A. and abroad MUST know.

These difficulties have been one of the ultimate motivations for writing IL GRANDE GRIDO. As evident, if the experiments could have been routinely done, the scientific issues underlying this book would have been resolved one way or the other, by therefore pre—empting the scientific motivations of this presentation.

The tests of Pauli's exclusion principle under strong interactions.

Recall that the magnetic moments could be altered by short range interactions without affecting the value of the spin [65], resulting in measures [100]. This situation, however, is expected to be only the first stage of a much deeper physical context.

In fact, under sufficiently higher energies and/or collisions, the value of the spin itself is expected to mutate, in which case the mutation of the magnetic moment would be a mere consequence.

The test of the possible mutation of spin can be done via the experimental verification of the validity or invalidity of Pauli's exclusion principle under strong interactions. This is the test submitted in memoir [14] which originated most of the theoretical studies reported in this book.

Quite encouragingly, the test of Pauli's principle is well within current technical feasibility. Also, it is of quite limited cost and of high accuracy inasmuch as it can also be done via neutron interferometers.

To avoid misrepresentations of this presentation, it should be indicated that no direct experimental measure of Pauli's exclusion principle exist to this day, and the information is strictly inconclusive.

Nevertheless, it is encouraging to see that the test has already been studied by experimentalists and considered as feasible via the scattering of neutrons on the nuclei of the tritium.

The main physical ideas are again simple and understandable to all. The core of the tritium is made up of two neutrons in the s—state with antiparallel spin, thus filling up all possible states. According to Pauli's principle, no additional neutron can therefore penetrate within such a core when in the s—wave state, contrary to our intuitions and expectations.

The experiment consists in having a beam of s—wave neutrons collide with the tritium. Pauli's principle can be tested via interferometric measures of the so—called scattering length which is one measure of the mutual penetration of wave—packets.

For sufficiently low energies of the incident beam, the validity of Pauli's principle is unquestionable. In fact, the preservation of the value ½ of the spin of the neutron for low energy nuclear phenomena is out of the question.

With sufficiently high energies, instead, the situation is expected to be different. Spin is nothing but an intrinsic angular momentum. As such, it is expected to alter in value (or fluctuate in Eder's words [65]) under sufficiently intense collisions. If this is indeed the case, neutrons with a value of the spin ½+ ϵ, where ϵ is near zero, are not exact Fermions, and Pauli's exclusion principle is not expected to be exactly valid, as suggested in ref. [14]. Sufficiently small deviations are then conceivable. These deviations result in a proportionately small penetration of the incident neutron within the tritium core,

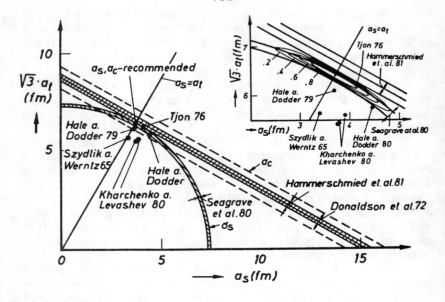

Figure 1.7.2. A reporduction of diagram 3, p. 731 of paper [100] on the experimental elaboration of the test of Pauli's exclusion principle under nuclear interactions done via the neutron—tritium scattering. The diagram summarizes most of the available experimental data (represented via lines) and includes also some theoretical estimate (represented via points). The value of scattering length a_c recommended in paper [100] as plausible under currently available data is indicated in the top—left part of the figure. Of course, there is no experimental evidence at this time favoring deviations from Pauli's principle. Nevertheless, the experimental resolution is well within current technical capabilities and simply requires the repetition of the experiment with neutron beams of sufficiently higher energy (see the test). The most encouraging aspect is the plausibility of the violation. This can be seen in a number of ways. In fact, the wave—packets of the incident neutrons become closer and closer to those of the tritium core with the repetition of the tests (see the insert of the figure). The possibility of overlapping, and thus violation of Pauli's principle, cannot be excluded with further tests specifically conceived for the purpose. The fellow taxpayer, however, can reach a true assessment of the situation via the fact that **all experimental and theoretical data presented in this diagram have been elaborated via the assumption of the exact validity of Pauli's exclusion principle.** Under these conditions, the results simply cannot test the (tacit) assumption in a true way. ALL data presented in the diagram above should therefore be re—elaborated via the use of hadronic mechanics and the assumption of a (small) violation of the principle. The two results should then be compared, and the emerging context be resolved by subsequent tests. Particularly for higher energies of the incident neutron beam, the elaboration of the data of the insert under the assumption of the validity of Pauli's principle has exactly the same credibility than that under the assumption of the violation (which could ALREADY show overlapping). Above all, the fellow taxpayer should keep in mind the religious—type—dogma underlying all this: the absolute constancy of the intrinsic angular

momentum of the incident neutron, irrespective of the impact and collisions with the tritium core. How can physicists believe in such absolute physical conditions and jointly expect no critical examination of their scientific ethics?

---

which is prohibited by Pauli's principle, as indicated earlier. This possible penetration can be measured via the scattering length.

In the experimenter's own words (ref. [100], p. 731):

> "The extracted singlet and triplet scattering lengths ($a_s = a_t$ & 3.70 fm) define a repulsive hard core radius which determines an overlapping region given by the radial mass distribution of the neutrons of the tritium nucleus outside the hard core radius. Within this region a partial violation of Pauli's principle can be assumed."

Again, these comments are inconclusive. The important point here is the technical feasibility of the experiment as well as the plausibility of deviations from Pauli's principle.

It should be indicated here for clarity that we do not possess at this moment the theoretical prediction of the threshold of energy which could initiate deviations from Pauli's principle. This is due to the fact that we have no direct experimental knowledge of the underlying forces, the contact/non–local/non–Hamiltonian ones. We have some knowledge for their representation (via isotopies and genotopies of conventional formalisms), but the "strength" of the forces for given physical conditions are unknown.

In different terms, the state of our knowledge regarding the contact/non–local/non–Hamiltonian forces is similar to that at the time of the discovery of the law $F = qq' / r^2$ by Charles Augustin de Coulomb in 1785. At that time, there was some idea regarding the physical law. However, quantitative predictions could be made only upon achieving an experimental knowledge of the value of the charges q and q'.

The situation regarding the contact/non–local/non–Hamiltonian forces due to mutual penetration of wave–packets is quite similar to the preceding one. In fact, we need at least some preliminary measures on the strength of the forces in at least one physical situation. Once this is achieved, then we are in a position to make quantitative predictions in different physical situations.

The tests of the mutation of magnetic moments and/or of spin could provide exactly this missing link. In fact, once achieved, the experimental knowledge could be extrapolated via the techniques of hadronic mechanics to other physical conditions, by therefore achieving the capability of quantitative prediction that is typical of physical theories.

The needed tests are evident (see, for instance, ref.s [14, 62, 100]). The interferometric measures of the scattering length of neutrons on tritium should be repeated with a progressive increase of the energy up to the highest possible value achievable with contemporary technology. A comparative analysis of the individual tests could then provide the currently missing link: the possible treshold of deviations from Pauli's principle. Jointly, the accuracy should be improved, as routinely done in each test.

Finally, and most importantly, the available experimental data should be re—elaborated under the assumption of a sufficiently small violation of Pauli's exclusion principle. The results should then be compared with those based on the exact validity of the principle. The need for the alternative elaborations is evident. In fact, it may well be that the experimental results of Figure 1.7.7 (lack of overlapping of the wave—packets of the incident neutron beam with the neutron core) are a mere consequence of the theoretical assumption in the data elaboration (exact validity of Pauli's principle).

The impossibility of conducting the test on Pauli's principle until now.

I published memoir [14] in the hope of stimulating a constructive scientific dialogue on this fundamental open problem of human knowledge. After its overwhelming experimental verification in the atomic structure, Pauli's principle was merely "assumed" as valid in the nuclear structure without any, even minimal, process of critical examination.

But, physics cannot be done on the basis of experimentally unverified assumptions. Owing to its fundamental character, the problem of validity or invalidity of Pauli's principle in the nuclear and hadronic structure must be subjected to suitably exhaustive, theoretical studies and experimental resolutions.

Despite this scientifically democratic but inquisitive attitude of memoir [14], the reaction of the community was generally that of complete ignorance, if not of hysterical opposition, except on rare occasions.

As an example, D. D. D., an internationally renown scientist, following the appearance of memoir [14] wrote me to terminate the scientific association we had at that time on grounds that there was no need to test Pauli's principle.

I accepted the termination of our association with pleasure, but I accused him of scientific corruption.

Memoir [14] did not recommend to verify the violation of Pauli's principle. Instead, it recommended the establishing of physical knowledge via experiments, irrespective of whether in favor or against Pauli's exclusion principle. As a result, the experimental proposal, when realized, could well CONFIRM the validity of Pauli's principle.

Any person opposing such experimental verification "must" be accused of scientific corruption. Otherwise, why should that person oppose experiments that may eventually confirm his/her views?

Numerous correspondence with experimental nuclear physicists in the U.S.A. and abroad indicated quite clearly that the possibility of testing Pauli's principle under strong interactions along the lines considered here were absolutely null. This correspondence has been lost with the passing of time (and my too numerous changes of office . . .). Lacking the documentation, I shall abstein from reporting it in this book. The illustration will be essentially restricted to a documented report of the reaction by the Massachusetts Institute of Technology (Section 2.2).

Mutatis mutanda, the substance of the matter is that, except the experimental consideration in the European paper [100], it has been impossible to reach even the "consideration" of the test of Pauli's principle under strong interactions in the U.S. physics. The possibility of the actual conduction of the experiment prior to the appearance of this book is absolutely null.

This situation should be compared with the ultimate essence of physics, that of conducting, repeating, and then doing again all necessary experiments to establish and then refine our physical knowledge. For instance, the magnetic moment of the neutron has been measured, remeasured, and then measured again countless times since the discovery of the particle. This is the reason why any physicist opposing the experimental test of Pauli's principle must be accused of scientific corruption.

But, fellow taxpayer, nuclear laboratories in the U.S.A. use hundreds of millions of our dollars in research projects crucially dependent on the exact validity of Pauli's exclusion principle under strong interactions, that is, on a religious dogma currently deprived of a direct experimental support. If the (generally small) deviations theoretically predicted in ref. [14] and experimentally indicated as plausible in ref. [100], are true, a significant portion of our money goes down the drain (that is, in the pockets of academic barons without true scientific output).

Again, as it was the case for governmental funding of manifest inconsistencies in Einstein's gravitation, statistical irreversibility, and quark conjectures, absolutely no self—correcting mechanism by the governmental—academic complex is conceivable without your intervention, fellow taxpayer.

Of course, academic barons have the right to voice their opinions on the lack of needs for the experimental verification of Pauli's exclusion principle under strong interactions. But this, if and only if they have no scientific accountability toward the taxpayer, that is, if and only if they use their personal money or money belonging to their colleges. Under no circumstances the voicing of such antiscientific opinions should be justified and, most importantly, should be permitted to continue under governmental support.

Experimental data on the mean life of unstable hadrons at different energies conducted in Denmark, Mexico, U.S.A. and other countries.

The experiments immediately following those on the rotational symmetry in the scale of absolute scientific values, are the measures of the mean life of unstable hadrons in flight at different energies which test the Lorentz symmetry (see Figure 1.7.3).

Recall that an unstable hadron, such as a charged pion or kaon, when moving within the high vacuum of a particle accelerator, must verify the special relativity, in the sense that its center—of—mass trajectories must conform to the physical laws of the special relativity, including the increase of mass with speed, the Lorentz contraction, etc.

Pions and kaons, however, are composed of particles with wave—packets in conditions of deep mutual penetration and overlapping, thus resulting into an internal non—local structure with consequential departures from the special relativity.

The problem considered in the preceding sections was that of ascertaining how deviations from the special relativity in the interior dynamics could manifest themselves to the outside world, while the center—of—mass trajectory is strictly conformed to the special relativity.

An answer known at this time is the behaviour of the mean life as a function of the energy of the particle. The reasons are evident. The mean life is directly dependent on the internal dynamics. If such a dynamics violates the special relativity, the behaviour of the mean life must deviate from the predictions of the special relativity.

Very intriguingly, ALL available re—elaborations of the experimental data on the behaviour of the mean life with energy show deviations from Einstein's ideas. The available studies are quite numerous, all concurring toward the same conclusion, and increasing in time.

Here I limit myself to recall the studies by the Danish physicist H. B. Nielson and his associates at the Niels Bohr Institute in Copenhagen [35]. These authors have essentially re—elaborated available experimental data on the charged pions and kaons. The data shows a clear variance in the structure of the space—time underlying the special relativity, the Minkowski space. In fact, the structure $X'mX$ indicated in Section 1.4, is shifted to the new structure $X'gX$, where $g = \text{diag}(1 + 1/3 a,$

1 + 1/3 a, 1 + 1/3 a, −1−a) and a = (−3.79±1.37) x 10^{-3} for charged pions, while a = (0.61±0.17) x 10^{-3} for charged kaons [35].

The direct universality of the Lie—isotopic relativity [32] can now be put to work. In fact, whether the parameter a is constant or a local function, the Lorentz—isotopic relativity applies, yielding the generalizations of the Lorentz transformations leaving invariant the quantity X'gX.

Note the differences in values and signs of the Lorentz breaking parameter a in the transition from pions to kaons. This is also fully in line with hadronic mechanics and the Lorentz—isotopic relativity. In fact, the two particles are expected to have basically different structures (in the sense of having different numbers of elementary constituents). In turn, these structural differences result in different Minkowski—isotopic spaces, those with different values of g.

The independent studies conducted by the Mexican physicists R. Huerta—Quintanilla and J. L. Lucio M. [37] have confirmed the above findings, by reaching the value a = (3.6±5.2) x10^{-3} for the case of muons.

Further independent studies have been conducted by the U.S. physicists S. H. Aronson, G. J. Bock, Hai—Yang Cheng and E. Fishback [36] on the behaviour with varying energy of all essential parameters of the neutral kaon including most importantly the mean life. As stated by the authors in the abstract of article [36] "The data suggest that these parameters may have an anomalous energy dependence", where in plain language the term "anomalous" means violation of Einstein's idea.

As a matter of fact, the violation indicated as possible by this latter study is much deeper than that of the preceding studies [35,36], because it predicts an energy—dependence of the mean life of the neutral kaon even for observers at rest with the particle. According to the special relativity, no such a dependence is possible for the rest frame.

The needed experiments are well known and definitely within current technical capabilities. They consist in the measuring of the mean life on unstable hadrons (at least pions and kaons) at a number of values of increasing energies. The comparison of the measures with the predictions of the special relativity will resolve the issue one way or another, at least up to the attained energies (see Section 1.6 on the possible breakdown of the special relativity at the speed of light in vacuum).

The experiments should also be repeated for leptons with the understanding that its composite character is unclear at this writing. In fact, the muons could be excited states of the electrons (as suggested by the Italian physicist Caldirola [58] and others), in which case no anomalous behaviour of the mean life is conceivable, trivially, because of the lack of nonlocal internal effects. Even if muons are indeed composite, they are not

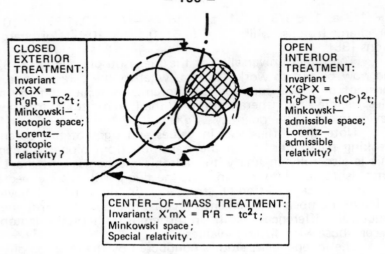

CLOSED EXTERIOR TREATMENT:
Invariant
$X'GX = R'gR - TC^2t$;
Minkowski–isotopic space;
Lorentz–isotopic relativity ?

OPEN INTERIOR TREATMENT:
Invariant
$X'G^{\triangleright}X = R'g^{\triangleright}R - t(C^{\triangleright})^2 t$;
Minkowski–admissible space;
Lorentz–admissible relativity?

CENTER–OF–MASS TREATMENT:
Invariant: $X'mX = R'R - tc^2t$;
Minkowski space;
Special relativity.

Figure 1.7.3. A schematic view of the currently available experimental information on the apparent validity in the interior of hadrons of suitable generalizations of Einstein's ideas, while the same ideas remain valid for the center–of–mass trajectories in vacuum. The information is based on the behaviour of the mean life of unstable hadrons at different energies [35–37]. The results are apparently in favor of the hadronic generalization of quantum mechanics due to internal, nonlocal/non–Hamiltonian effects originating from deep mutual penetration and overlapping of the constituents' wave–packets. This situation is depicted in the figure above by associating the conventional Minkowski space of the special relativity with the center–of–mass trajectory in vacuum, and the Minkowski–isotopic space [32] with the interior dynamics as suggested from experimental studies [35–37]. The contributions by hadronic mechanics to these latter studies are the following: (1) reconciliation of a generalized interior relativity with the conventional center–of–mass one [31,55]; (2) methods for the explicit construction of the generalized Lorentz transformations leaving invariant the Minkowski–isotopic separation (this is achieved via the methods of ref. [8, 10, 18, 19, 32, 33]); and (3) possibility of achieving a unified formulation of all seemingly different results of ref.s [35–37] as well as of others. But perhaps the most relevant contribution of hadronic mechanics is the possibility of regaining unity of physical and mathematical thought which is inclusive not only of the interior strong problem, but also of other fundamental aspects, such as the irreversibility of the real world, the noncanonical character of classical mechanics, the lack of local Lorentz character of the interior gravitational problem, etc. All these aspects can be unified via the Lie–admissible generalization of quantum mechanics for the open–nonconservative interior problem, with its Lie–isotopic counterpart for the complementary closed–conservative treatment. In fact, the unification is permitted by the abandoning of local/Hamiltonian/Lie formulations in favor of structurally more general formulations. In turn, the physical origin of the generalizations is given precisely by the nonlocal/non–Hamiltonian effects originating from deep overlapping of the wave–packets under strong interactions. The deviations from Einstein's ideas reported in ref.s [35–37] are precisely a manifestation of these effects. The historical roots of the occurrence are intriguing indeed. The founding fathers of the theory of strong interactions indicated quite clearly the intrinsically nonlocal character of the interactions due to the deep penetration of the wave—packets (which is generally absent under electromagnetic interactions). This legacy has been studiously ignored by vested interests for decades (see the episode of my talk at the Clausthal Conference at the end of Section 1.6). The studies reported in this chapter have taken the legacy seriously and identified preliminary (not necessarily unique), mathematical means for its quantitative treatment. Everything else is a consequence of that, including the Lie—admissible/Lie—isotopic generalizations of quantum mechanics, the identification of the physical and mathematical roots of anomalies [35—37], and the possible regaining of the unity of physical and mathematical thought. The most fascinating aspect is that these anomalies are without any possibility of achieving a credible reconciliation with the special relativity (as it was possible for the case of parity violation). To illustrate this point beyond a reasonable doubt, it is sufficient to note that **all anomalies [35—37] imply the abandonment of the speed of light in vacuum as the limiting speed of the universe, by therefore resulting to be a confirmation of prediction [31] and of the basic assumptions of the generalized relativity submitted in ref. [32, 33]** (see Section 1.5). This is an inevitable consequence of the alteration of the time component of the Minkowski metric which, as well known, characterizes precisely the maximal speed of causal signals. Thus, the experiments under consideration leave no room for manipulatory maneuvring due to academic greed. This ultimate resolutory character of the experiments is, of course, well known to vested interests and constitutes the most plausible reason for the impossibility of their repetition until now.

---

strongly interacting. This implies smaller conditions of internal mutation due to wave—overlappings [14] and, therefore, a lesser anomalous behaviour of the mean life. Despite these considerations, the analysis of ref. [36] (on the anomalous behaviour of the mean life of the muons) should be kept in mind.

Preliminary theoretical predictions of deviations have already appeared in the literature. For instance, the Canadian physicist D. Y. Kim [101] predicts a deviation of about 14.3% from the prediction of the special relativity for muons at 400 GeV. The results of the analysis appear to be readily extendable to hadrons. [As an important note, ref. [101] intended to stress the view that the experimentally established violations of discrete symmetries are due to the violation of the special relativity because they all originate from the nonlocality of the interior structure.]

The most important aspect is that **the experiments on the mean life of unstable particles are the most direct possible tests of the Lorentz symmetry for the interior problem, without questionable theoretical elaboration of the data.** In fact, the value of the energy produced by the particle accelerators can be identified in an incontrovertible way. The measures then reduce to those of mean life of the particles, from their production to their spontaneous decays. As one can see, no major theoretical elaboration is used, except those of routine experimental character (such as for the errors).

To understand the importance of this occurrence, the fellow taxpayer should compare it with that of other experiments in which the law to be tested is often used as a fundamental assumption in the data elaboration (see the case of Pauli's principle of Figure 1.7.2!). The experiments, here considered, therefore leave no room for attempts by vested interests to re—elaborate the data in such a way to reach compatibility with old doctrines.

The impossibilities to repeat experimental measures on the behaviour of the mean life of unstable hadrons at different energies.

All experimental studies [35—37] deal with "re—elaborations" of experimental data intended for different purposes. Differently stated, the experiments were authorized for objectives full aligned with vested interests. At the time of such authorization, it was apparently unknown that the same measures contained information on the apparent invalidation of Einstein's ideas. If this possibility had transpared even minimally, the chances of running the experiments would have been so minute to be ignorable.

This situation is established beyond a reasonable doubt by the fact that ALL APPEALS TO U.S. (AND FOREIGN) LABORATORIES TO REPEAT THE MEASURES OF THE MEAN LIFE OF UNSTABLE HADRONS AT DIFFERENT ENERGIES FILED BY INDEPENDENT SCHOLARS INCLUDING MYSELF, HAVE RESULTED TO BE COMPLETELY USELESS. (See Section 2.3 for details). Incontrovertible evidence proves that, despite these appeals, no experiment on the direct measure under consideration here is currently under way at U.S. National (as well as foreign) laboratories to this writing (April 16, 1984).

Again, the impossibility to repeat these truly fundamental tests has been another pivoting reason for writing IL GRANDE GRIDO. In fact, the experimental resolution of the issues would have voided the very motivation for writing this book.

The experimental tests of the reversible or irreversible character of nuclear interactions.

Additional, fundamental, experiments that must be brought to the attention of the taxpayer are those on the reversible or irreversible character of nuclear interactions.

Recall the predictions of hadronic mechanics indicated in Section 1.6, that: (A) the center—of—mass trajectories of strong systems are generally reversible; (B) the internal open processes are strictly irreversible; and (C) the complementary exterior—closed treatment can restore the time reflection symmetry under isotopy (by incorporating all time—asymmetric terms in the isotopic operator g of the abstract product A*B = AgB). In short, the most reliable way to test the reversible or irreversible character of strong interactions is to ensure the achievement of open/nonconservative conditions due to external strong fields. The reversibility of the closed—exterior treatment can be at best misleading (recall the Earth whose center—of—mass trajectory in the solar system is strictly reversible, while its interior trajectories are strictly irreversible).

Experimental studies of the issue conducted by a number of experimentalists have added further conditions for the a-chievement or meaningful tests, such as the lack of reliability of the so—called cross—sections. In fact, these quantities are averaged out over all possible states. In this way, their experimental information is reliable for other objectives (e.g., of statistical nature), but not for the time—reflection symmetry.

The same studies have identified that the most effective means to test the time—reflection symmetry in nuclear physics is via direct measures of the so—called polarization of the forward reaction and analyzing power of the backward reaction (see the readable review by the Canadian experimentalist R. J. Slobodrian [102]). If these quantities are equal, the time reflection symmetry is exact "under the conditions considered" (e.g., in the center—of—mass frame); otherwise, it is violated.

Note that time cannot be reversed in experiments. Thus, the tests deal with one given nuclear reaction, and its "time reversed image", that is, the reaction in which the original and final products are interchanged with respect to those of the original one.

An experimental collaboration Québec—Berkeley—Bonn reported in 1980 experimental measures of the difference between the polarization and analyzing power thus indicating the existence of irreversibility in nuclear reactions. Their findings were subsequently printed in 1981 (see ref. [103] and quoted papers).

Most importantly for this presentation, experiments [103] identified the origin of the irreversibility in the spin component of the nuclear force, thus indicating a possible direct connection with measures [100] on rotational—asymmetry (recall that the breaking of the rotational symmetry would imply that of the space and time reflection symmetries, although the opposite is not necessarily true).

As a result, measures [103], if confirmed, would have provided full experimental grounds for the regaining of unity of thought in physics, by identifying the origin of irreversibility in the most elementary layer of nature, and by promoting their unified treatment via suitable generalizations of currently relativities.

Measures [103], however, were not confirmed by independent experiments conducted at Los Alamos [104].

At the writing of this section, the experimental situation

is essentially unsettled either way. Following publication [104], the Los Alamos group has not repeated the experiment any more. Other experimentalists have conducted additional measures and dismissed the existence of irreversibility in nuclear physics. However, these latter measures do not appear to deal directly with polarization and analyzing power. As a result, their true implications for experiments [103] are unknown to me.

The Québec–Berkeley–Bonn experimental group has continued to be quite active in the conduction of new experiments, by confirming quite firmly their original findings (see ref.s [106–109] and quoted papers).

A comprehensive theoretical program had been prepared by the Institute for Basic Research in Cambridge for an in depth investigation of the problem by experts in the field. Regrettably, funding of the project was rejected by both the U.S. National Science Foundation and the U.S. Department of Energy. As a result, all research on the problem has been halted. The comments below are merely indicational.

The most unsettled aspect of all experiments [103–109] is the currently lacking identification of their nonconservative character. In fact, all experiments are intrinsically open because they deal with beams of nucleons on fixed "external" targets. It is evident that, under these conditions, the energy is not conserved, and the reactions are open.

The taxpayer should recall that, once this nonconservative character is identified, the experiments can only identify the "amount" of irreversibility. But the "existence" of the irreversibility is out of the question (e.g., because of the nonunitary character of the time evolution). This point is essentially presented in ref. [59], jointly with other aspects reviewed earlier.

Along the same lines, if measures [103–109] do indeed deal with center–of–mass treatments of nuclear reactions considered as closed and isolated, then the lack of irreversibility should be expected.

Note the need for comprehensive theoretical studies both in favor and against irreversibility, to avoid insidious interpretations of experimental results.

My coming of age as a physicist.

Physics advances by conjectures that slowly acquire the flavor of plausible theories, to become later physical truths when verified experimentally in all needed details.

Until a few years ago, when still a naive physicist to a considerable extent, I thought that academic manipulations could occur in physics only during the first stage, that of presentation of theoretical conjectures. But the experimental profile was still sacred to my naive thinking of that time.

I was wrong.

I later came to realize that academic manipulations do occur also in the experimental sector. At first, I thought that this regrettable human aspect occurred only during the process of consideration of the experiments, but not when the machines are eventually running.

I was wrong.

The more I familiarized with the experimental setting, the more I realized how easy it is to manipulate contemporary particle experiments except rare cases. In fact, the final "experimental numbers" are the results of numerous assumptions. Often, a minimal variation of only one of these assumptions is sufficient to product basically different "numerical" results.

I realized this as soon as I started reading experimental papers. But then, one question called for another. For instance, the deeper I read within the lines, the more I realized that, in general, only part of the underlying assumptions are fully reported in the final publications, while other assumptions are either reported in part or not reported at all.

It was only at that point that my childhood as a researcher terminated and I became an adult physicist. Today, I know that the credibility of "experimental numbers" in particle physics is primarily dependent on the ethical record of the experimenters. The experimental aspects appear to be of strictly secondary relevance.

The more fundamental the experiments are (with therefore deeper political implications), the more dominant is the ethical record of the experimenters over the technical stuff.

The apparent commissioning of the disproof of nuclear irreversibility.

The fellow taxpayer must know certain background facts underlying the conduction and publication of the opposing experimental results on irreversibility by the Québec—Berkeley—Bonn group [103] and by the Los Alamos group [104]. The information is mostly available in the papers themselves for everybody to read.

The case is quite intriguing indeed. Papers [103, 104] report measures of the same quantities of the same nuclear reactions, resulting into irreconciliably different results, one in favor and the other against nuclear irreversibility. As such, one of the two papers must be wrong. There simply is no room for compromise.

It should be noted for fairness that the Québec—Berkeley—Bonn group conducted several measures of both polarization of the forward reaction and analyzing power of the backward reaction in two different reactions, while the Los Alamos group repeated only some measures of polarization in only one reaction, and ignored the repetition of the remaining measures in the same as well as in the second reaction. Numerous additional differences also exist, but they are too technical for review in this general presentation and (regrettably) must be ignored here.

As one can see, paper [103] was submitted to the leading journal of the A.P.S., Phys. Rev. Letters, on August 8, 1980. The paper was published on December 21, 1981, that is, some 1½ years (or some 70 weeks) later.

This extremely long period of consideration is per se sufficient to justify a suspicious attitude toward the editorial board of the journal. In fact, we are talking about a letter journal that is expected to print important results in a matter of weeks.

To have means of comparison, the taxpayer should know that rebuffal [104] was printed in Phys. Rev. C (rather than in the Letters) in only sixteen weeks; or that experimental paper [110] co–authored by one of the editors of Phys. Rev. Letters, R. K. Adair, was printed in the same volume of ref. [103] in about fifteen weeks.

The suspicious attitude stimulated by the excessively long time of publication of ref. [103] is reinforced by a chain of elements the fellow taxpayer has the right to know for whatever their value.

The first idea that comes to mind when facing delays in publication of important results, is that, perhaps, major refinements occurred during the editorial consideration. This possibility is disproved by evidence for paper [103]. In fact, all the papers published by the authors prior to the appearance of ref. [103] or during its submission (see, for instance, ref.s [102, 106]) indicate quite clearly that all the essential results have remained unchanged during the long consideration process of paper [103].

But then, why did the A.P.S. delay a manifestly important paper for such a long period of time without any meaningful improvement occurring in the meantime?

My suspicion was reinforced by the reading of the paper and by the identification of its authors. In fact, one of the authors, H. E. Conzett, is a member of a U.S. National Laboratory, the Lawrence Berkeley Laboratory. I therefore thought that, perhaps, Conzett was a junior member there. To ascertain that, I did some research. It turned out that he was a senior member. I then did further research, by ascertaining that it was common practice by the journals of the A.P.S. to publish experimental papers released by senior members of U.S. national laboratories often without any refereeing at all.

I have no elements to know if and when this practice was halted. But the caliber, ethical record, credibility, and associations of the authors of paper [103] increased my suspicion.

In summary, the following facts are incontrovertible: 1) the A.P.S. kept letter [103] for about seventy weeks; 2) rebuffal [104] was published in sixteen weeks; 3) countermeasures [104] were not running at the time of the submission of paper [103] to Phys. Rev. Letters; 4) paper [103] was published only AFTER contrary measures [104] were available and duly quoted in the paper (see the explicit statement to this effect in page 1806); and 5) immediately after the appearance of rebuffal [104], the official position of the "establishment" in nuclear physics was that nuclear irreversibility had been "disproved" by measures [104] and did not exist!

All these facts created the rumor (I have heard in two continents) that rebuffal [104] had been "commissioned" by vested academic–financial–ethnic interests in the U.S. physics.

Whether this rumor is true or false is immaterial here. The important point is that the A.P.S., by permitting facts 1), 2), 3), 4) and 5) above, has rendered the rumor simply unavoidable.

To my knowledge, this book constitutes the first time the rumor appears in print. Besides the evident need to shed scientific light on the case, the objective of this presentation is to alert the U.S. taxpayer of the occurrence, so that all necessary or otherwise needed actions will be undertaken to prevent its repetition in the future. There is no doubt that the handling of paper [103] has damaged the credibility and ethical standards of the A.P.S. throughout the world.

According to all editorial practices, the Physical Rev. Letter should have: printed immediately paper [103] WITHOUT any reference to opposing data (which at the time of the submission had yet to start!!!), then follow with the publication of measures [104] as soon as available. To put it differently, the function of any journal is that of reporting all relevant results, without any editorial partisanship. Thus, the original measures [103] had exactly the same rights to be printed quickly as the opposing measures [104]. No more, no less. The long delay in the publication of measures [103], compared to the rapidity of publication of rebuffal [104], renders the suspicion of partisanship at the journals of the A.P.S. simply unavoidable. At any rate, a subsequent paper by the Québec–Berkeley–Bonn group confirming the original measures was rejected by Phys. Rev. C, although, it was routinely published by a European journal [105].

The rumors above are quite credible for anyone with a minimum of inside knowledge of the structure, organization and operation of the A.P.S. In fact, as publicly recognized, important papers must pass the approval of leading physicists at leading U.S. Institutions "in good standing with the A.P.S." (see Section 2.4 and related documentation). Translated in plain language, this means that paper [103] had been passed to representatives of the vested interests currently in control.

The halting of its publication for 1½ years was then a quite natural consequence.

Whatever the academic baron (tries to) say in his/her defense, facts persist: the rebuffal [104] was initiated considerably AFTER the submission of paper [103] which was permitted to appear in print only FOLLOWING the NEGATIVE results of the new measures.

But we are still at the beginning of the case. During the conduction of my own investigation of the case out of shear curiosity, I later discovered that E.E.E., a leading representative of vested interests opposing nuclear irreversibility, had left his campus and spent a considerable amount of time at Los Alamos during the running of measures [104]. This fact alone drove my hair into a state of extreme electrostatic stretch. E.E.E. is not an experimentalist (and, indeed, he is not one of the authors of paper [104]). Yet, he has a record of vested interests against nuclear irreversibility on all counts (academic, financial and ethnic). What was he doing at Los Alamos at that time? Was he there on other business, or to supervise measures [104]? Did the experimenters there have meetings with E.E.E.? And if so, what was the impact of E.E.E. in the final results? Also, who paid E.E.E.'s trip there, his college, Los Alamos, or his own government contract? Was he acting alone or was he representing other members of his circle of interests? The number of questions that crossed my mind, all unanswered, were endless.

One thing is sure: the presence of E.E.E. at Los Alamos at the time of measures [104] damaged the credibility of the experimenters.

But, we are still at the beginning of the case. Everything reported so far occurred prior to my direct, personal, contacts with members of both measures [103, 104]. The year 1981 was that of the founding of the I.B.R. (see the appendices). Our institute was interested in both measures. As I.B.R. president, I therefore issued invitations to both groups to deliver joint talks at one of our meetings.

The Québec—Berkeley—Bonn group was quite cooperative, by permitting my visual inspection of their equipment in Québec (a large van der Graph accelerator); by participating in our meetings, and being readily available for all criticism.

On the contrary, the Los Alamos group resulted to be quite distant, to use an euphemism. In fact, my sincere invitation for their sending a representative (under full financial support) to deliver a talk jointly with the opposing group, was rejected (actually it was ignored). At my phone call to ascertain whether the invitation had indeed arrived, I was told that the experimenters were then working on something different and were no longer interested in the problem of nuclear reversibility!

This drove, again, my hair into a stretch. Why were these people uncooperative? How could we possibly reach any genuine clue of the situation without putting the two experimental teams together and trying to understand their differences with open discussions (rather than papers)? I do not know the answer. But one thing was sure: the lack of participation of the Los Alamos group to our meeting, whether accidental or planned, had the net effect of preventing advances on the problem.

To have a deeper understanding of the situation, the fellow taxpayer must keep in mind the formal position in irreversibility by the "official U.S. physics" immediately following the appearance of paper [104].

At that time, the only direct measures of polarization and analyzing power were those of paper [103] and [104]. How could any physicist claim that any of them is right and the other is wrong? The only ethically sound conclusion was the open nature of the problem (as it remains to this day). Any claim that measures [104] were true and [103] were false was manifestly corrupt. Period!

I then attacked myself to my last hope, that foreign nuclear laboratories had kept independence of thought from their U.S. counterpart. Evidence shattered also this last hope. In fact, a quick scanning of conferences in nuclear physics abroad soon revealed total silence on the issue (a clear sign of dismissal of the very existence of the problem). Verbal communication with colleagues abroad then confirmed the dreadful reality: the official position of foreign laboratories was fully aligned with that in the U.S.A.

Fellow taxpayer, I am confused. I know that the above facts are true. The spider's web behind them is unknown to me. I can only recommend that you conduct a deep, deep, look at the case, if you care for this beautiful Land, for the preservation of its Institutions, and for what they mean to humankind.

Besides that, my best suggestions are those of Section 3.2: to have first the A.P.S. formulate and adopt a CODE OF ETHICS, and then have an appropriate, independent body to strictly enforce it.

Lacking a code of ethics, everything goes!

Of one thing I am sure: the handling of the experimental case of nuclear irreversibility by the journals of the A.P.S. has been questionable. Rushing the repetition of only a few of the measures conducted by the Québec—Berkeley—Bonn group, and then claiming lack of irreversibility has not been dignifying for the A.P.S. The scientific, economic and military implications of irreversibility are simply too big to justify such an insufficient approach to such a fundamental physical problem.

Note that the official position on the lack of nuclear irreversibility will stand forever, and no credibility will be given to research efforts attempting to show the open nature of the problem, . . . unless you, fellow taxpayer, intervene. This reality is well known to all researchers in irreversibility submitting papers to the journals of the A.P.S. or submitting grant applications to U.S. governmental agencies. I am one of them.

But, above all, one thing should constantly remain in your mind throughout the consideration of each and every aspect related to the case: **the establishing of irreversibility in nuclear reactions would imply the irreconcilable experimental invalidation of Einstein's ideas under strong interactions.** The need for vigilance on ethical issues is then evident to all.

High energy experiments and the nonpotential generalization of the scattering theory by the Italian physicist R. Mignani.

The fifth and last experimental aspect I feel obliged to bring to the attention of the taxpayer is the current situation in conventional high energy scattering experiments, those fully aligned with vested interests, and routinely done at national laboratories.

As an example, take the deep inelastic scattering of leptons on hadrons conducted a few years ago at the Stanford Linear Accelerator Center (SLAC) and then repeated elsewhere.

As it is the case of all experiments without exception, the SLAC experiments produced beautiful physical results. For instance, they provided experimental confirmation of the composite character of hadrons. This physical value is obvious, and it is not an issue here.

The relevant aspect is the objectivity of the "numerical" results. In turn, this objectivity is dependent on the way the data are elaborated.

The first, and most obvious thing is that the special relativity is routinely assumed at the foundation of the theoretical tools elaborating the data. This is perfectly admissible. After all, alternative theoretical tools based on a generalized relativity more suitable for the interior of hadrons are not available to this writing.

The point is that scientific caution should be exercised whenever considering "experimental results" which are directly dependent on the assumed relativity. To be specific, the SLAC experiments under consideration here concluded that hadronic constituents are point–like. The issue is how objective is this "experimental result"? The only possible answer is that caution should be exercised before assuming this result ad litteram. After all, the special relativity is fundamentally dependent on the point–like character of the particles, as stressed throughout this presentation. As a consequence, it is at best unclear whether the experimental result (point–like constituents) is a true experimental information, or it is a mere consequence of the theoretical assumption. One thing is sure: the experimental detection of extended constituents within hadrons would have been incompatible with the underlying special relativity.

Most generally, currently available experiments in hadron physics cannot be interpreted as providing "evidence" of the validity of Einstein's special relativity. Such a position has value only for academic politics. The reasons are incontrovertible: the special relativity is assumed as a central tool in the data elaboration of the experiments. The results, therefore, cannot test the assumptions. The experiments considered can, at best, provide elements of plausibility.

This is a case similar to that of Pauli's exclusion principle encountered earlier in this section (see Figure 1.7.2).

Particularly unreassuring is the current way experimental data are elaborated for hadron—hadron scattering, that via a theory known as "potential scattering theory". The very name of the theory implies the underlying central assumption: that the scattering is of potential/action—at—a—distance type. For electromagnetic interactions, the use of the theory is unquestionable, to my knowledge. However, the use of a potential scattering theory to elaborate strong interactions scattering experiments may well result to be insufficient if not inconsistent for the reasons indicated throughout this book.

The unreassuring aspect is that, if the potential scattering theory is insufficient, the numerical results are, at best, qualitative, and possibly wrong.

The construction of a nonpotential generalization of the potential scattering theory for strongly interacting particles with contact/non—Hamiltonian interactions due to mutual wave—overlappings, has been initiated by the Italian physicist R. Mignani in papers [111—113] as an important part of the hadronic generalization of quantum mechanics (Section 1.6). Even though the studies are predictably at the beginning, they have shown that the existence of a non—Hamiltonian component in the strong interactions implies the alteration of the central tool of the theory, the cross section [113].

The scientific and administrative implications of these studies are potentially far reaching. If Mignani's nonpotential scattering theory is correct, it implies the need to review virtually all high energy experiments on strong interactions whose numerical results have been reached via conventional cross sections.

It is hoped that this presentation has provided sufficient elements to illustrate the plausibility of the nonpotential nature of the strong interactions. The fellow taxpayer should then see the administrative implications for future funding of high energy scattering experiments.

That is my last hope.

U.S. governmental agencies do not see this. In fact, both the National Science Foundation and the Department of Energy rejected research grant applications filed by the I.B.R. to hire (U.S.) personnel for the study of Mignani's nonpotential scattering theory.

The fact that vested interests in the U.S. physics have benefited by the above rejections is beyond any reasonable doubt. In fact, the rejections have achieved in full the apparently intended or evidently consequential result: halt the research in this sensitive field [NOTE:Mignani's scattering theory is incompatible with Einstein's ideas, being based on suitable generalizations].

The issue pertinent to you, fellow taxpayer, is equally clear: has the decision to halt research on Mignani's scattering theory been in your best interest, that is, in the best possible accountability in the future spending of your money in the sector? The answer is equally clear: NO! There is no doubt that the investments of public funds in the use of the potential scattering theory for the data elaboration of strong interaction experiments is and will remain questionable until the studies rejected by N.S.F. and D.O.E. are conducted and the situation resolved either way.

In summary, there is a realistic possibility that hundred of millions of your money may be spent each year in data elaborations of particle experiments that are potentially inconsistent.

In the hope of minimizing misrepresentations, I want to stress that the rejection of the I.B.R. grant application does not create, per se, any ethical problem. After all, grant applications are routinely rejected every day. The ethical issue is created by the rejection of the I.B.R. applications WITHOUT the research being conducted at other institutions. The uniqueness of the I.B.R. applications, their rejection by governmental agencies, and the lack of conduction of the same research elsewhere, have implied the suppression of the investigations in the field. The ethical issue is created precisely by such an implied suppression of research, and not by the rejection of the I.B.R. applications. After all, if studies on Mignani's scattering theory and the possible insufficiencies of current data elaboration of scattering experiments were currently conducted, say, at Harvard University or at the Fermi National Acceleration Laboratory, the issue under consideration here would be nonexistent.

1.8: THE MATHEMATICAL RESEARCH.

The mathematical structure of physical theories.

In the preceding pages, I have attempted to present a known property, that physical theories constitute mere realizations of abstract mathematical structures. As a consequence, a true generalization of a given physical theory cannot be attempted, unless one identifies first the underlying generalized mathematical theory.

The mathematical structure of Einstein's ideas is the so—called Lie theory (including its diversification into algebras, groups and geometries). As a consequence, no true generalization of Einstein's ideas is conceivable, unless one identifies first at least a conceivable generalization of Lie theory, including its algebraic, group theoretical and geometrical formulations.

Viceversa, mathematical studies on possible generalizations of Lie theory are manifestly important, not only in pure mathematics, but also in theoretical physics. In fact, once a generalization of Lie theory has been identified in the mathematical literature, the construction of the corresponding generalization of Einstein's ideas is only a matter of time.

Lack of sufficient generality of the contemporary mathematical formulation of Lie's theory.

As soon as I was exposed to Lie theory during my graduate studies in theoretical physics, I noted the lack of its sufficiently general formulation. This occurrence is at the basis of the generalized relativities presented in this book and, as such, it deserves a few comments.

Very loosely speaking, Lie theory can be constructed via the so—called enveloping associative algebra [114]. This is an algebra with generic elements A, B, C, . . .and product AB verifying the associative law (AB)C = A(BC). The Lie algebra is characterized by the antisymmetric product attached to AB, the celebrated Lie product AB − BA [74]. Lie groups can be constructed via suitable power series expansions in the associative envelope (the so—called exponentiation) or other means [74]. The notion of the carrier space and field in which the theory is realized, and additional data, permit the identification of the underlying geometry (such as, the symplectic geometry [17]).

Physical applications, for instance, in quantum mechanics occur when interpreting the elements A, B, C, . . .as matrices (or operators). The time evolution of a generic physical quantity A is then given by Heisenberg's law idA/dt = AH − HA, where H is the total energy (Hamiltonian)and AH is the ordinary product of matrices (Section 1.6).

The lack of sufficient generality I noted in the late 60's is due to the fact that the product AB − BA is the simplest conceivable Lie product, because the associative envelope with product AB is the simplest possible envelope. In fact, I could identify nonassociative generalizations of the product AB in such a way that the attached antisymmetric product is still Lie. In this way I reached the existence of a more general formulations of Lie theory, that via nonassociative envelopes.

The Lie—admissible generalization of Lie algebras.

The first paper I wrote (jointly with others related to my Ph. D. thesis) was ref. [115] on the so—called Lie—admissible generalization of Lie algebras.

An algebra with generic elements A, B, C, . . .and abstract product, AxB, is called Lie—admissible when the attached product AxB — BxA is Lie. The important point is that the product AxB is not necessarily associative, that is, (AxB)xC ≠ Ax(BxC). The generalized character of the product AxB — BxA over the conventional form AB — BA, is then evident.

At the time of writing paper [115], the words "Lie—admissible algebras" were unknown in the physical literature. An inspection soon revealed that a nonassociative product AxB whose antisymmetric part AxB — BxA is Lie, was also unknown in all mathematical textbooks of the time I could inspect in research libraries. Owing to this situation, I was forced to spend a number of years of research in specialized mathematical libraries in northern Italy. I finally discovered that the algebras I was interested in had been identified by the U.S. mathematician A. A. Albert in 1948 [116] under the name of "Lie—admissible algebras" and thereafter ignored in mathematical circles to a considerable extent, with the sole exception of ref.s [116—117]. I published paper [115] only upon achieving such knowledge on prior contributions.

Some essential mathematical aspects of the Lie—admissible algebras.

By recalling the fundamental role of Lie algebras throughout mathematics, the mathematical possibilities of the Lie—admissible algebras are evident.

A first possibility is that of generalizing the enveloping associative algebras [75]. In fact, the associative product AB is one of the simplest possible particularizations of the nonassociative Lie—admissible product AxB. A second possibility is that of generalizing the Lie algebras themselves [8]. In fact, the Lie product AB — BA itself is one of the simplest possible particularlizations of the nonassociative Lie—admissible product, that is, we can have AxB = AB — BA. Also, Lie algebras are Lie—admissible, although the opposite property is not necessarily true, while the algebraic axioms of the Lie—admissible algebras (here ignored for simplicity) are a bona fide generalization of those of the Lie algebras. Additional possibilities are offered in other branches of mathematics, such as geometry or topology. More recent studies have indicated the possibility of generalizing the remaining aspects of Lie theory (this is the case of the generalization of Lie groups provided by the so—

called Lie–admissible bi–module [86–88]).

Mathematical studies of the Lie–admissible algebras have been conducted by the following scholars. G. M. Benkart, D. J. Britten, H. C. Myung, R. H. Oehmke, S. Okubo, J. M. Osborn, A. A. Sagle, M. L. Tomber and G. P. Wene from the U.S.A.; by Y. Ilamed from Israel; by S. Gonzales and A. Elduque from Spain; and others. A comprehensive list of mathematical studies on Lie–admissible algebras can be found in the three volumes of Tomber's bibliography and index [118].

Predictably, the physical applications of the Lie–admissible algebras follow as close as possible the above mathematical profile. In fact, the first physical application of the Lie–admissible algebras was their use to treat broken unitary symmetry [119], in which case they were used as generalized envelopes. The immediately next application was their use to characterize the time evolution of Newtonian systems [120], in which case they were used as bona fide generalizations of the Lie algebras themselves.

Additional physical applications followed the mathematical ones. For instance, the hypothesis on the generalization of the special relativity for open/nonconservative systems was submitted in monograph [12] only upon achieving a rudimentary identification of the geometry underlying the Lie–admissible algebras, the symplectic–admissible geometry. The same geometry was subsequently studied by another theoretician [50–51] to formulate a generalization of the available interior gravitational theories for the inclusion of the trajectories of the real world, those of non–Hamiltonian type (Section 1.5).

Further physical advances can be reached only when additional studies are conducted at the pure mathematical level, such as in the representation theory (this is particularly the case for the possible identification of the hadronic and quark constituents with electrons).

The mathematical relevance of the studies is so evident that needs no comments here.

The Lie–isotopic theory.

A "bonus" in the study of the Lie–admissible algebras is the identification of an intermediary generalization of Lie theory which, even though still Lie in character, is nontrivial. It is given by the construction of Lie's theory via an envelope with abstract product $A*B$ which is still associative, yet more general than the conventional one AB. This is the case of the product $A*B = AgB$, g = fixed, characterizing the hadronic generalization of quantum mechanics (Section 1.6). The formulation is called "isotopic" in the (Greek) sense of preserving the basic characteristics of the original formulation. In fact, the original product AB is associative, and so remains the product $A*B$. Similarly, the original product $AB - BA$ is Lie, and so remains the more general product $A*B - B*A$.

The Lie–isotopic theory emerges quite naturally in the study of the nonassociative Lie–admissible algebras. In fact, under certain conditions, the Lie algebras constructed via nonassociative envelopes with products AxB can be reformulated via associative–isotopic envelopes with products $A*B$, while leaving the Lie product unchanged, and I shall write $AxB - BxA = A*B - B*A$. The point is that this reformulation generally does not regain the simplest possible product $AB - BA$, that is, $A*B - B*A \neq AB - BA$. The need to formulate Lie theory via its most general possible associative envelopes, is then consequential.

It is evident that the isotopic generalization of the envelope of Lie's theory implies a corresponding generalization of the entire theory. The mathematical relevance of the generalization is evident, as illustrated in the preceding sections via the explicit construction of the symmetry transformations (invariance group) of a given n–dimensional metric space with metric g (achieved via the isotopic lifting of the orthogonal group in n–dimension, $O(n)$, and trivial unit $I = diag(1,1,1,...,1)$, into the isotope $\hat{O}(n)$ characterized by the generalized unit $\hat{1} = g^{-1}$; the invariance of g then follows because Lie theory leaves invariant the unit, whether in its conventional or in its isotopic form).

The needed mathematical research.

A comprehensive mathematical study on all possible generalizations of Lie theory is recommended here, under the proviso that the theory admits (a) a consistent generalized algebra; (b) a consistent generalization of the Lie transformation groups; and (c) a consistent generalization of the geometries underlying current Lie–Hamiltonian formulations.

The studies should begin with the Lie–isotopic reformulation of the contemporary Lie theory. This study is needed because several properties and theorems of the conventional formulation are not necessarily true for the Lie–isotopic one (for instance, a Lie algebra which is compact or semisimple when expressed via the conventional Lie product, does not remain necessarily compact or semisimple under Lie–isotopic reformulation).

The mathematical studies should then continue with the more general Lie–admissible theory in its various aspects (generalized algebras, groups and geometries), and then pass to conceivable other generalizations not necessarily of Lie–admissible type.

Also, all theories presented in this book are of local–differential (although non–Hamiltonian) type. Studies should also initiate for their nonlocal generalization.

One point should be clear. The depth and diversification of the physical application of Lie theory have been possible because of the availability of comprehensive mathematical studies in the field (often conducted by theoreticians). The need for similar, comprehensive research in the generalizations of Lie theory, is then evident for further physical advances.

Regrettably, ALL research grant applications filed over a three year period by the I.B.R. to U.S. governmental agencies (both civilian and military) on behalf of distinguished, senior mathematicians, have been systematically rejected, often against the recommendation of the referees, as we shall see in Section 2.5 (and in the Documentation of this book).

The doubt still persists in my mind that a relevant (if not determinant) factor in all these rejections was the knowledge that mathematical studies on the generalization of Lie's theory will inevitably imply a generalization of Einstein's theories.

1.9: IL GRANDE GRIDO.

The organizational efforts underlying the studies reported in this book.

Studies on the limitations and possible generalizations of Einstein's theories are definitely not a one man job. The studies presented in this chapter have been the result of a considerable organizational effort to coordinate the research by distinguished mathematicians, theoreticians and experimentalists.

I initiated these efforts back in 1977 with the founding of the Hadronic Journal (whose first issue was published in April 1978). This demanded first the raising of the necessary funds, and then the setting up of an adequate editorial organization. Today, thanks to all authors, editors, editorial advisors and referees, the Hadronic Journal has acquired a record of seven years of regular and successful publication, in the specialization originally planned: mathematical, theoretical and experimental papers on the limitations and possible generalizations of current relativities, mechanics and related mathematical structures. The understanding is that papers along conventional trends not only are welcome, but are often invited.

Once the Hadronic Journal was under way, I passed to the organization of the yearly *Workshops on Lie–admissible Formulations.* The first meeting was held at Harvard's Department of Mathematics in early August 1978 with three participants (including myself). The meeting resulted in papers [121–123] on mathematical studies of Lie–admissible algebras and their application to particle physics (field theory and Pauli's principle). The mathematical and physical foundations of the studies reported in this chapter were established in that year, such as: the direct universality of the Lie—admissible algebras in Newtonian mechanics; the main ideas of possible generalized relativities; the proposal to construct the hadronic generalization of quantum mechanics; etc.

The *Second Workshop on Lie—admissible Formulations* was held in August of 1979 at Harvard's Science Center. The meeting saw a considerable increase of participants, and resulted in the publication of two volumes of proceedings [124], one of review papers and one of research papers. With this second meeting, we succeeded in gathering mathematicians and theoreticians for one full week. Theoreticians would identify open physical problems, while the mathematicians would assist in the identification of applicable mathematical tools. The relaxed, friendly, and mutually respectful atmosphere permitted a number of mathematical advances, such as the identification of one of the most general forms of Lie—admissible algebras (by Y. Ilamed from Israel), or the continuation of the structure theory (by H. C. Myung, R. H. Ohemke, G. P. Wene from the U.S.A. and others). Some of the physical advances achieved at the meeting were: the proof of the direct universality of the Lie—admissible algebras in classical field theory (by J. A. Kobussen from Switzerland) and in statistical mechanics (by J. A. Fronteau and A. Tellez—Arenas from France, and myself); and other advances.

The *Third Workshop on Lie—admissible Formulations* was held in August 1980 at the new Harbor Campus of the University of Massachusetts in Boston. This time we succeeded in putting together in the same room for one full week mathematicians, theoreticians, AND experimentalists. The meeting resulted in the publication of three volumes of proceedings [125], one in pure mathematics, one in theoretical physics, and one in experimental physics and bibliography. The advances achieved at the meeting are too numerous to be outlined here.

The year 1981 saw a major thrust in the organizational efforts. Circumstances reviewed in the next chapter forced the founding of a new, independent, institute of research, the I.B.R. As a result of a considerable financial effort by individuals, a building was purchased in July 1981 within the compound of Harvard University (the "Prescott House") for the housing of the new institute which was formally inaugurated on August 3, 1981. The ceremony was attended by the governors, officers and advisors of the institute, as well as scholars from several countries (see the Appendix on the I.B.R.). Immediately after the inauguration, we had our *Fourth Workshop on Lie—admissible Formulations,* which saw further advances reported throughout this chapter (for instance, the discovery by the Austrian physicist, G. Eder of the possible mutation of magnetic moment while

keeping conventional values of spin, was presented at this meeting for the first time). The meeting resulted in a number of
papers published in mathematical and physical journals.

The advances achieved during the preceding years permitted the organization of a new series of meetings, this time of
formal character. In this way, we had our *First International
Conference on Nonpotential Interactions and their Lie–admissible Treatment,* held in early 1982 at the Universite d'Orléans,
France. This meeting saw a considerable increase in the participation (including participants from the U.S.S.R. and the People's
Republic of China), and resulted in the publication of four
volumes of proceedings [126] for some 1,700 pages of printed
research in mathematical, theoretical and experimental aspects
reported in this chapter. This new series is scheduled for continuation every few years. (The Second International Conference
is scheduled for early 1986 in Europe).

Our First International Conference made us aware of
having achieved the essential research objectives in classical mechanics. I therefore released for publication monographs [10,
12] outlining the primary results. This signaled the need for our
focusing of the efforts in the hadronic generalization of quantum
mechanics. For this purpose, a new series of yearly meetings was
organized under the name of *Workshops on Hadrnoic Mechanics.*
The first meeting was held at the I.B.R. in Cambridge, U.S.A., in
August 1983, and resulted in the publication of proceedings
[127]. (The second meeting, scheduled for August 1984, has
been moved to Europe, as anticipated in Figure 1.6.2).

A considerable editorial effort was also promoted (despite
well known, limited marketing potential*) consisting of the re-
printing of collected works in salient segments of particle physics
under the editorship of experts in the field [128–133]. More
recently, these efforts permitted the funding and organization of
a new journal in pure mathematics [134].

The Institute for Basic Research, the Journals, and the
various Workshops and Conferences, have proved to be invaluable for advances in the limitations and possible generalizations
of current relativities, mechanics and related mathematical structures. In fact, they have permitted the coordination of efforts
by independent mathematicians, theoreticians, and experimentalists. Lacking this coordination, the advances would have been
improbable. The understanding stressed earlier is that the studies
are still at the beginning.

The progressive increase of the opposition.

---

*To have an idea, in the U.S.A. there are about 130 advanced research
libraries interested in high energy physics (those of colleges with graduate
schools in physics and of a few national laboratories). These libraries
can generally purchase only a fraction of the new titles printed every year.

The existence of opposition, interference or shear suppression of due scientific process on our studies by vested, academic—financial—ethnic interests in the U.S.A., is beyond any reasonable doubt, in my personal view and experience.

The opposition was initiated by senior high energy physics at Harvard University with the prohibition for my drawing my salary from my own grant for one academic year (1977—1978). After my passing to Harvard's Department of Mathematics, the opposition continued with a number of ducumented episodes, such as the written prohibition to hold at Harvard our Third Workshop (which was in fact held elsewhere), despite the fact that it was an important part of my research contract. The opposition then continued with the refusal by Harvard to continue in the administration of my contract (despite the implied, considerable, financial loss of the related overheads). Harvard's refusal evidently propagated to other colleges, leaving no other choice than passing the administration of the contract to a non-academic corporation.

As we shall see, the organization of the I.B.R. was made necessary by the refusal of local colleges to provide even hospitality for me, let alone a regular academic job paid by my own governmental contract.

Opposition, interferences, and shear suppression of due scientific process continued in a variety of ways, such as: the prohibition to list I.B.R. seminars in the Boston Area Physics Calendar; the impossibility to publish papers in journals of the A.P.S.; the open warning to members of our group "to keep a distance from Santilli's studies" or to discourage their visiting our institute; the systematic rejection of all research grant applications filed by the I.B.R.; and other rather incredible (but documented) occurrences.

Admittedly, some of the episodes may have been due to my temperamental character, or to my firm determination NOT to accept gracefully academic manipulations on fundamental physical issues. I admit to these possibilities and assume all possible responsibilities. Nevertheless, the shear volume, number and diversification of the hostilities I have experienced are such to relegate my personality to a secondary role.

As far as the future is concerned, I shall gladly collaborate, most humbly, with the most humble colleague, on all topics reviewed in this chapter. The understanding is that arrogance will be met with magnified arrogance, and manupulatory practices on Einstein's ideas will be openly identified for what they are: scientific crimes.

The risk of turning physics into a farce.

Where ever the responsibilities lies, the end results are incontrovertible. The opposition by vested interests has succeeded in preventing the conduction of comprehensive research at the I.B.R. on the inconsistencies and/or limitations of Einstein's ideas. The same research, however, is not conducted at other research institutions in the U.S.A. Whether intended or only accidental, the opposition has therefore succeeded in preventing the conduction of comprehensive research in the sector throughout the U.S.A. Any person aware of the international power of U.S. physics, will then see the propagation of the condition abroad.

This book intends to establish a record of the danger of a situation of this type.

A typical illustration may be the available experimental information on Pauli's exclusion principle in nuclear physics reviewed in Section 1.7 (Figure 1.7.2). As well known, the principle is ASSUMED in the data elaboration. The end results are then in agreement with the assumptions (see the lack of mutual overlappings of the wave—packets of the incident neutron on the tritium core in the upper right corner of Figure 1.7.2). It is evident that this situation could repeat itself ad infinitum, in the sense that new experiments could be done and never show an overlapping of the wave—packets because of the underlying assumption of the exact validity of Pauli's principle.

On the other side, one could re—elaborate exactly the same data under the assumption of a (small) violation of Pauli's principle due to the conceivable mutation of spin during the collision of the incident neutrons with the tritium core (Section 1.6). This would evidently result in overlapping wave—packets, that is, in exactly the opposite experimental conclusion of the upper—right corner of Figure 1.7.2.

The danger of suppressing, ignoring or otherwise discrediting dissident views is then evident. In fact, if we ignore the possibilities of sufficiently small deviations from Pauli's principle, we risk turning nuclear physics into a farce.

Along fully similar lines, if we ignore the critical literature of Einstein's gravitation (Section 1.5), we also risk turning gravitation into a farce.

If we ignore the irreconcilable incompatibilities between the established non—Hamiltonian character of our macroscopic world and the presumed Hamiltonian character of the particle descriptions (Figure 1.6.3), we risk turning research on irreversibility also into a farce.

If we ignore the impossibility of achieving an identically null probability of tunnel effects for free quarks under conventional, internal, quantum mechanical laws (Section 1.6), we also risk turning quark theories into a farce.

And so on.

If we do all these things simultaneously, and with one common root, the preservation of Einstein's theories, the risk is compounded. In fact, we risk the implementation of a scientific obscurantism.

This is, after all, a rather natural consequence of any totalitarial scientific organization, where "physical truths" are imposed via shear academic power, rather than a scientifically democratic consideration of all possibilities, whether aligned or against Einstein's theories.

The financial dimension of the scientific accountability of Einstein's followers.

The continuation or correction of the current scientific scene in U.S. physics is up to you, fellow taxpayer. In fact, the research is conducted with your money. It is therefore time to have an idea of how much public money is involved in the sector.*

★In FY 1983, N.S.F. spent $ 4,900,000 of public funds in gravitation. A major portion of this sum has been spent on Einstein's theory of gravitation, that is, on a theory which is manifestly incompatible with physical reality according to numerous articles published in different refereed journals (Section 1.5). Papers published in the field under N.S.F. contracts have ignored the technical literature on the inconsistencies of Einstein's gravitation. Also, no self—correcting process of the governmental—academic complex is foreseeable, as stressed in Section 1.5. In FY 1984, N.S.F. plans to spend $ 6.1 million of public funds in gravitation and $ 7.9 million in FY 1985. Fellow taxpayers, shall you permit the continuation of N.S.F. dispersing public money on Einstein's gravitation under the ignorance of the technical literature on its inconsistencies?

★In FY 1983, N.S.F. and D.O.E. spent a combined sum in particle physics exceeding $ 100,000,000. A major portion of this sum has been spent in strong interactions under the assumption of the exact validity of Einstein's special relativity. At the same time, papers in the field published under governmental contracts have ignored the now vast literature on the expected approximate character of the special relativity. If this critical literature is correct, a significant portion of the $ 100,000,000 has been wasted. In FY 1984, N.S.F. and D.O.E. plan to spend over $ 110 million in particle physics, and over $ 121 million are scheduled for FY 1985. Fellow taxpayer, shall you permit N.S.F. and D.O.E. to continue in the dispersal of public funds under a totalitarian scientific condition aligned with the exact validity of Einstein's special relativity?

*The financial information below has been derived from *Physics Today,* April 1984, pages 55—60.

★In FY 1983, D.O.E. spent $ 461,300,000 in magnetic fusion. If the magnetic moments of protons and neutrons change under the fusion conditions (Section 1.2 and 1.7), a significant portion of this public sum has been wasted. $ 477.5 million are scheduled for FY 1984 and $ 483.1 for FY 1985. The test of the possible alteration of the magnetic moments under the fusion conditions via neutron interferometers costs less then $ 100,000 (Section 1.7). Fellow taxpayer, shall you permit D.O.E. to continue in the dispersal of public funds in magnetic fusion while ignoring the possible alteration of the magnetic moments?

My list of public expenditures in FY 1983 by Einstein's followers that are rendered questionable at least in part by the inconsistencies and/or limitations of Einstein's ideas could easily pass the mark of one billion dollars in the U.S. alone, particularly when military research is included. But I see no point in entering into such a detailed presentation, because the sole issue of scientific ethics is sufficient here. After all, we are talking about a totalitarian conduction of research in the ultimate foundations of physical knowledge.

IL GRANDE GRIDO

IT IS THE DUTY OF EVERY PERSON TO HONOR THE MEMORY OF ALBERT EINSTEIN AS ONE OF THE SINGLE GREATEST CONTRIBUTORS TO HUMAN KNOWLEDGE.

BUT THE LIFTING OF EINSTEIN'S IDEAS TO THE LEVEL OF RELIGIOUS DOGMA, TO BE PRESERVED INDEFINITELY VIA THE ORGANIZED SUPPRESSION OF POSSIBLE FUNDAMENTAL ADVANCES, WOULD BE A CRIME AGAINST HUMANITY.

CHAPTER 2

THE PERSONAL EXPERIENCE

2.1: HARVARD UNIVERSITY.

I now pass to the presentation of my personal experience beginning with my stay at Harvard University in 1977—1980. The fellow taxpayer should keep in mind that a true understanding of the various episodes reported in this chapter requires a sufficient knowledge of the scientific profiles reviewed in Chapter 1, which are and remain the most important ones. The episodes presented in this chapter will then be used in Chapter 3 for the submission of constructive suggestions to improve the scientific ethics in U.S. physics.

September 1, 1977.

The day started early, with my being in line at the unemployment office of Galen Street, in the town of Newton, Massachusetts. A nationwide search for an academic job in 1976—1977 had turned out to be a complete waste of time and money.* A number of hours passed while waiting, first, for the open-

---

*
According to the guidelines set forth by the American Association of University Professors and other bodies, by 1977, I could not be hired by a U.S. college for a regular teaching job without a joint permanent position (tenure). This is due to the fact that by 1977, I had reached the maxium of seven academic years of teaching functions in U.S. colleges (the year of teaching in Italian colleges prior to leaving for the U.S. and the years of research employment in the U.S. without teaching did not count). This "numerology" evidently created substantial difficulties in my securing an academic job in the U.S. beyond 1977 which still persists to this day. The problem of "numerology" here considered is evidently not restricted to myself. Instead, it has invested and continues to invest so many scholars, to constitute a problem of national proportion. The search for a tenured position during the period 1967—1977 turned out to be fruitless. The best job I could obtain was the sadly known one—academic—year—TERMINAL—appointment, with the customary letter of remainder in mid year of the TERMINAL nature of the employment.

ing of the doors of the unemployment office, and then for the completion of all the formalities. I was told to have 33 weeks of unemployment benefits providing funds essentially sufficient to pay the rent of my two—bedroom apartment. With this I had to support my two children then in tender age and my wife (then a graduate student) while having virtually no savings and no other income.

Soon after completing my unemployment formalities, I went to the Lyman Laboratory of Physics of Harvard University to initiate a visit there under the unsalaried position of "Honorary Research Fellow" for the academic year 1977—1978. Steven Weinberg, then at the Lyman Laboratory, had expressed interest in certain papers of mine (on the conditions of variational self-adjointness in field theory; see ref.s [135]), and kindly offered the opportunity of spending a year at Harvard (Doc., pp. I—3—6).* After presenting myself at the departmental office, I visited Weinberg who received me quite cordially, and indicated that Howard Georgi (then a junior member of the department) would be my reference person. I left Weinberg sincerely pleased.

I therefore visited Howard Georgi, who also was quite cordial with me. In fact, I sensed positive feelings and the anticipation that our acquaintance could lead to a rewarding collaboration (a few months later Georgi and I founded the Hadronic Journal). While conversing on topics of disparate nature, the phone rang. On the other line there was David C. Peaslee of the Energy Research and Development Agency (ERDA), in Germantown, Maryland, near Washington, D.C., which became a few months later the U.S. Department of Energy (DOE). Peaslee was searching for the Harvard officer supervising my visit to invite my application for a research contract with ERDA. Georgi was visibly pleased by the invitation.

My plea to Weinberg.

The following day I phoned Peaslee. I told him that all my preceding applications to ERDA, filed from another college, had been systematically rejected, and that these rejections had been a significant reason for my inability to secure a tenured academic job. I frankly told Peaslee that, as a result of this history, I was not ready to reapply unless I received assurance that, this time, ERDA was seriously interested. Peaslee indicated his awareness of the preceding rejections and stressed the seriousness of ERDA interest at that time.

I had met Peaslee before. I trusted him and initiated all the various steps needed for the new application. First, I revised

---

* It should be indicated for future needs that, while Weinberg's letters clearly refer to the title of "Honorary Research Fellow", the formal letter of appointment I received from the university secretary refers to "Research Fellow in Physics" (p. I—3).

and updated the scientific part of the application, which essentially consisted of research underlying possible generalizations of available mechanics for contact/nonpotential forces (Section 1.3). The proposal was expected to result in a number of papers, monographs and scientific activities.

On September 5, I wrote to Weinberg a very respectful, hand written letter (p. I—5) in which I asked for his help in filing the research grant application to ERDA. In the same letter, I indicated that I was not aiming to remain at Harvard. Instead, I wrote Weinberg that I was merely interested in having the contract administered by Harvard the first year, and then move it to another college where I had some chance for tenure. The letter concluded by saying: *"I am currently unemployed; I have two children of tender age to feed and shelter; my wife is a graduate student; our savings are non—existent; and the unemployment benefits last only a few weeks."* I personally placed the letter in Weinberg's mailbox.

A few days later, I went to see him. He had seriously considered the case, by verifying the existence of the invitation, (one of the very few he had eyewitnessed, as he jockingly told me), and confirmed his help for the administrative formalities. Weinberg was aware of the topic of the application (which included papers [136]). In particular, he was aware that I had been working at the drafting and re—drafting of monographs [9, 10] which were then under consideration for publication by one of the most prestigious editorial houses in physics, Springer—Verlag of Heidelberg, West Germany.

The administrative difficulties in filing the invited application to ERDA/DOE.

Weinberg showed me Harvard's faculty manual indicating that only full professors qualified as principal investigators of research contracts. Being a research fellow, I could not therefore apply alone, but had to search for a full professor interested in serving as principal investigator of the contract with me as co—investigator.*

Weinberg did a genuine effort for that. In fact, he personally contacted a number of administrators in the department and in the Dean's Office; he introduced me to potentially interested colleagures; and tried other avenues. Regrettably, it was impossible to locate any full professor in physics who could serve as principal investigator. Steven Weinberg, Shelly Glashow and Sidney Coleman were principal investigators of a contract with the National Science Foundation (NSF), and could not serve in the same capacity for a contract with ERDA. Other colleagues

---

* The manual did allude at the possibility of waiving the restriction and permitting research fellows to be principal investigators, but this possibility was not considered in my case.

we contacted, such as Roy J. Glauber, even though under ERDA support, were not interested or had other reasons to decline.

ERDA independently explored other avenues. A senior Italian experimentalist at Harvard, C. Rubbia, was part of an experimental team operating under ERDA support. To my understanding, Peaslee contacted Rubbia proposing the incorporation of my contract into his via a budgetary increase of the funds, plus other benefits. Rubbia apparently refused the proposal (and the money, including the considerable overheads for Harvard) on grounds unknown to me. I had never met Rubbia, nor I believe that he had ever heard my name before. What struck me was his rejection without even bothering to call and talk to me. After all, my office was not that distant from his. What an ackward behaviour, particularly from a compatriot! What a difference with other ethnic groups!

In the meantime, months were passing by and my financial situation was becoming more critical. Nevertheless, the scientific qualifications for my research activities with or without ERDA support, were increasing. For instance, I delivered at Harvard an informal seminar course in the topic of my monographs, which was attended by a number of graduate students from the local universities (p. I—8). Subsequently, W. Beiglböck, Editor of Springer—Verlag for the series "Textbooks and Monographs in Physics", sent me the formal acceptance of the publication of my volumes (p. I—10). In addition, I had written a paper in "Harvard style"readily accepted by Phys. Rev. D (ref. [136]; see p. I—55 for the front page of the Lyman preprint) and was working at several other projects.

By October, 1977, I had exhausted all possible avenues for filing the invited application with a principal investigator from the Department of Physics (Georgi was not qualified because not a full professor at that time).

I therefore attempted to file the application under the administration of Boston University, where I would have no difficulty to be principal investigator under my title of Associate Professor of Physics. Boston University readily accepted the proposal, which was prepared and signed by the necessary administrative officers (p. I—15). Unfortunately, this change of administration was not well received by ERDA, and that application was never filed in Washington. In fact, all the preceding rejections I had received from ERDA regarded applications filed precisely under the administration of Boston University.

After this last episode, my personal situation deteriorated considerably. I was left with a few additional weeks of unemployment benefits to pay the rent, while the lack of savings began to affect visibly my family. I had no other alternative but initiate suitable scientific actions. That meant to put in black and white the insufficiencies and limitations of Einstein's theories.

In my "last progress report" to S. Weinberg, M. Tinkham (the departmental chairman of that year), and H. Georgi of December 4, 1977 (p. I–16), I disclosed my second series of monograph [11, 12], with copies of the statements by colleagues released by a new publisher (p. I–18). To be as clear as possible, I entitled the first volume "Nonapplicability of the Galilei and Einstein Relativities?" and the second volume "Coverings of the Galilei and Einstein Relativities?"

I had crossed my scientific Rubicon for the first time. At any rate, I had no other alternative. The monographs were my only hope for some income.

The filing of the invited application to ERDA with S. Sternberg as principal investigator.

In mid December, 1977, an unexpected event occurred. Shlomo Sternberg, a professor of mathematics at Harvard (and that year chairman of the department), was aware of my papers on the topic of the invited application to ERDA and indicated interest in being the principal investigator. Sternberg is a renown geometer. As such, he qualified in full for the position.

Sternberg and I had a brief meeting on the matter in which we readily reached a full agreement on all aspects. After that, everything moved quickly. My part of the application had been written and rewritten countless times and was ready. It took a few hours for Sternberg to prepare his own part, its enclosures and the front page. After that, I asked authorization from Tinkham, in his capacity as chairman of the physics department, to file the application with Sternberg as principal investigator and with me as co–investigator, UNDER MY AFFILIATION WITH LYMAN LABORATORY OF PHYSICS. I emphasized this last point because, since I am a theoretical physicist and not a mathematician, I was not expecting to qualify for an association with the mathematics department. Independently from that, Sternberg contacted the senior members of the Lyman Laboratory to have the go ahead under the same terms, which was readily given (see copy of the front page of the application on p. I–45). In this way, it took very few days to complete the application; to have it signed by the various administrative officers; and to have it shipped by Harvard's Office of Research Contracts (ORC) to ERDA. In turn, it took only a few weeks for the scientific office of ERDA in Germantown to approve the application and send it to ERDA's administrative office in Argonne, Illinois, for funding. Each and every one of Peaslee's words turned out to be correct, as expected.

The impossibility of receiving a salary under my own grant.

Always alert for possible things that could go wrong, and with deteriorating family conditions, I kept checking on the progress of the contract. In early April, 1978, I discovered that I COULD NOT DRAW MY SALARY FROM MY OWN GRANT because, according to university regulations, I had an appointment as "Honorary Research Fellow", that is, an appointment without compensation, while I needed an appointment at least as "Research Fellow" to draw a salary.

On April 6, 1978, I therefore wrote a formal application to Tinkham asking for the removal of the word "Honorary" in my title, so that I could draw a salary under my contract (p. I—24). That application signaled the initiation of a crisis that, a number of years later, rendered unavoidable the writing of this book.

On personal grounds, my unemployment compensation would end in April, 1978. In turn, this raised the spectrum of: possible eviction of my family from our apartment because of lack of payment of rent; lack of money to buy food; etc.

On administrative grounds, the remaining formalities had been completed by ERDA and Harvard's ORC; the contract was operative under number ER—78—S—02—4742; and the money was sitting in a bank somewhere, including the money for my own salary.

On scientific grounds, my research on the limitations and possible generalizations of Einstein's theories had become better known to the members of the Lyman Laboratory (see Figure 2.1.1 and, later on, Coleman's case).

The chain of repetitious rejections by Coleman, Glashow, Weinberg and possibly other senior physicists at Harvard to prevent my drawing a salary from my own grant.

The months of April, May and June, 1978, saw repetitious rejections of my appeals to senior physicists at Harvard with a predictable deterioration of the relationship.

The affair evolved like this. By the end of the week, I would phone the chairman of the physics department to inquire about the status of my application for the removal of the term "Honorary" from my title. Tinkham would generally tell me that the case would be considered at the senior faculty meeting of the following week. The day after the meeting, Tinkham would usually call me to indicate that the senior faculty had voted against my appointment as "Research Fellow", that is, against the removal of the word "Honorary" from my title, which implied my inability to draw a salary from my grant*.

---

* The fact that my official appointment had the title "Research Fellow in Physics" (Doc. p. I—3) remains a mystery to me to this day. In fact, I have been unable to figure out why with this title I was prohibited to draw a salary from my grant.

At the beginning, I was as courteous as permitted by the circumstances. It should not be forgotten that Harvard had formally approved and filed a governmental contract with my affiliation to the physics department (p. I–45). Now that the grant had been funded by the U.S. government, the physics department was preventing, opposing or otherwise jeopardizing its actuation.

By May, 1978, my unemployment benefits had expired; my family was truly risking eviction and lack of money to buy food; while the senior physicists at Harvard were still preventing my drawing a salary from my own grant. This situation should be kept in mind while passing judgment on anything I did during (and after) that period, such as the letters I wrote to directors of National Laboratories (p. I–360 and ff.), or my exchanges with officers of the American Physical Society (APS), notoriously aligned with vested interests at Lyman.

Some of the dates of the repetitious rejections have been documented in the front pages of ref.s [8] and [14]. I had planned to release these memoirs several years later, under the evident assumption of having my salary supported by the DOE contract. The prohibition to draw my salary compelled me to anticipate their publication. Thus, every time that Tinkham would call me to report the negative decision of the senior faculty, I would improve ref. [8] and [14] and resubmit them to the Journal, thus resulting in the indicated partial record of negative decisions (see the dates of pp. I–56 and I–57).

On May 10, 1977, Tinkham wrote me a letter (p. I–43) communicating the final negative decision by the physics department.* In that letter, he expressed the view of his department according to which, since the principal investigator of my contract was a member of the department of mathematics, I should seek an affiliation with that department.

There is little point in indicating my surprise. In fact: (a) I had asked and obtained authorization to file the grant application with my affiliation to Lyman and the same result had been independently reached by Sternberg (p. I–45); (b) copy of the research grant application had been passed to the Physics Department in January, 1978; and, last but not least, (c) I had expressed to Tinkham my impossibility to apply for a position at Harvard's mathematics department simply because I am not a mathematician.

Why S. R. Coleman, S. L. Glashow, S. Weinberg and other senior physicists at Harvard had collegially changed their commitment with the U.S. Government? Why had they waited so many months to tell me to apply for a position at the mathe-

---

* Howard Georgi was not part of this decision, to my knowledge, because a junior faculty at that time, while the various meetings on my case had been restricted to the senior faculty.

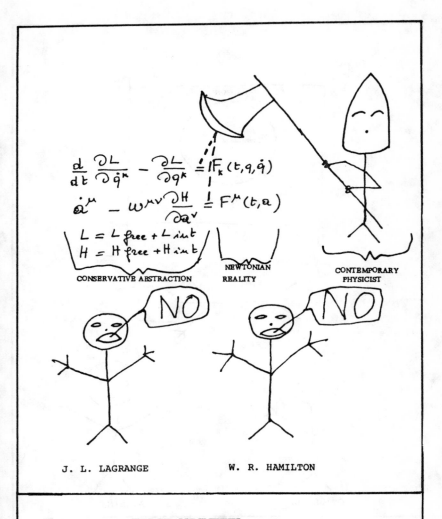

FIRST VIGNETTA:

THE TRUNCATION OF

LAGRANGE'S AND

HAMILTON'S EQUATIONS

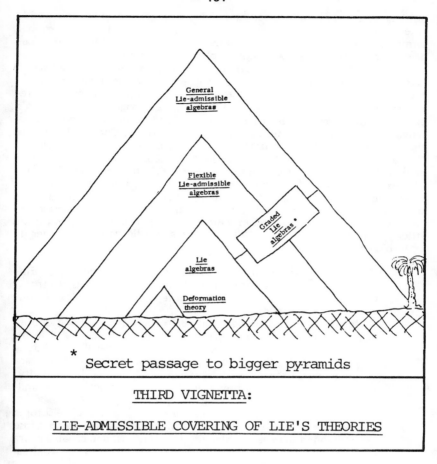

Figure 2.1.1. The three "vignette" appended to a presentation dated April 26, 1978 I submitted to the senior members of the Lyman Laboratory of Physics of Harvard University (p. I–26–32), following a request of additional information of my research by the departmental chairman M. Tinkham. The information was needed for action on my application for the removal of the term "Honorary" from my title, so that I could draw a salary from my own contract then in full administrative standing (DOE contract number ER–78–S–02–4742). The senior physicists at the Lyman Laboratory were aware of the topic of my monographs with Springer–Verlag (the first volume was in print at that time) and related papers, but they had no specific idea how the underlying techniques would be used in particle physics. My presentation to the Lyman Laboratory of April 26, disclosed the intended use of the techniques: to conduct a study of the limitations and possible generalizations of Einstein's theories in the interior of nuclei, or of strongly interacting particles (hadrons) or of stars along the lines essentially reviewed in Chapter 1. The three vignette were appended in the hope of toning down the topic and stimulating a friendly atmosphere. The first vignetta depicts the historical roots of the contact/nonpotential forces among extended particles. The founders of contemporary analytic mechan-

ics, Lagrange and Hamilton, had formulated their celebrated equations with external terms representing precisely the forces considered. These external terms had then been "truncated" since the beginning of this century because not needed in the description of planetary trajectories or of the evolution of electrons in the atomic clouds. The same external terms, however, had to be added for more complex trajectories of non—perpetual—motion—type, such as the motion of a proton within the core of a star. The resurrection of the historical external terms in Lagrange's and Hamilton's equations then implied the irreconcilable abandonment of Einstein's relativities for a number of technical reasons reviewed in Chapter 1 (such as the breakdown of the Lie character of the underlying algebraic structure). The second vignetta depicts a rather heated discussion I had sometime in early 1978 at the Lyman Laboratory with F.F.F., a firm believer of the unlimited applicability of Einstein's theories. The third vignetta presents a schematic view of the mathematical tools I was using for the construction of possible generalizations (the Lie—admissible algebras). The presentation stressed the scientific iterim which, as the reader can see, has been strictly implemented in the outline of the scientific case of Chapter 1, and which consists of

1— Identification of an arena of unequivocal applicability of Einstein's special relativity (point—like particles, such as electrons, moving under electromagnetic interactions, as originally conceived by Einstein);

2— Identification of broader physical conditions implying doubts on the exact validity of the special relativity (extended/deformable particles such as protons and neutrons under the conditions of mutual overlapping of the strong interactions, which were unknown at the time of formulation of the special relativity, and which imply the presence of contact/nonlocal/non—Hamiltonian forces);

3— Identification of mathematical tools (such as the Lie—isotopic and Lie—admissible algebras) which are broader than those underlying the special relativity (Lie algebras) and capable of incorporating non—Hamiltonian forces at least in local approximation;

4— Attempts to construct a generalization of the special relativity for the broader physical conditions considered via the use of the broader mathematical tools, under the conditions that the new relativity contains the old as a particular case (see ref. [8] for the Galilean case; ref.s [12, 33] for the special relativistic case and ref.s [50, 51] for the gravitational case).

5— Formulation of experiments for the resolution of the problem of exact or only approximate character (or, strictly speaking, the validity or invalidity) of the special relativity under the broader conditions considered.

This scientific iterim was submitted to the senior physicists at Harvard not only with the presentation of April 26, 1978, but also in a variety of other ways, such as: the submission of a draft of memoir [8] to S. Coleman for review (see below in the main text); the presentation to departmental members of the subsequent memoir [14] on the need to test the special relativity under strong interactions; and other ways. Despite the friendly and respectful tone, the presentation of April 26, 1978, did not achieve the intended objectives. In fact, I never received any scientific assistance and/or comment whatsoever from Harvard's physicists on my efforts, while the primary reason for my going to Harvard was precisely that of receiving a minimal, but scientifically professional assistance on such a manifestly difficult problem. Second, the senior physicists of the Lyman Laboratory of Physics voted against the removal of the term "Honorary" from my title, or, equivalently, against my appointment as "Research Fellow", by therefore preventing in this way that I draw a salary from my own grant.

---

matics department? Why had they done these things in full awareness of the consequential hardship on my children?

The most probable answer is evident: they opposed the actuation of my DOE contract at their department, that is, they opposed studies on the limitations and possible generalizations of Einstein's ideas in the interior of strongly interacting systems.

Needless to say, my personal opinion is insignificant. What is important is the opinion of the fellow taxpayer who has provided large financial support to Weinberg, Glashow, Coleman and other members of the Lyman Laboratory on research in particle physics under the (tacit) assumption of the exact validity of Einstein's theories under unlimited physical conditions.

More on Sidney Coleman.

In late 1977, Howard Georgi and I founded the Hadronic Journal. The first issue was scheduled for printing at the end of April, 1978. In early 1978, we were carefully selecting the papers for the first issue (mainly by invitation). Also, as editors, we had decided to print in the first issue one paper each. By April, Georgi had completed his paper [137] (on soft CP violation), while I was working at the drafting and redrafting of a memoir on a conceivable Lie—admissible generalization of Galilei's relativity [8].

However, as indicated earlier, my plans were to work at that memoir for a number of additional years before releasing it for printing, in case my salary had been finally authorized. In place of ref. [8], I could have readily prepared for the first issue of the journal another paper written in "Harvard style", such as ref [136]. In short, I was waiting for the physics department to resolve the issue of my salary, so that, in turn, I could decide whether or not to publish memoir [8] in the first issue of the Hadronic Journal. I had submitted several drafts and redraftings to colleagues, experts in the essential topics (mechanics, algebras and geometries). But I still lacked a critical inspection of the memoir from a competent fellow at Harvard.

For these reasons, in early April, 1978, I visited Sidney Coleman, indicating the case, and asking for the courtesy of a critical review of the manuscript. Coleman indicated interest, and actually stressed that I should give him a copy, but he could look at it only after filing his tax returns.

On April 15, 1978, I therefore wrote a very courteous note to Coleman asking for a critical examination of the manuscript and for counsel (p. I–25). I had selected Coleman because he was one of the few physicists at Harvard with the necessary mathematical knowledge to understand, first, the proposed generalized algebras and geometries, see how corresponding generalized mechanics follow, and finally, see how a generalization of Galilei's relativity was inevitable within such a setting.

Regrettably, I never heard or saw Coleman again after my petition of April 15, despite a number of solicitations such as those of April 27 (p. I–33) and May 5 (p. I–38). Nevertheless, I was told that Coleman, while being totally silent with me, had been quite generous of criticisms on my memoir at the senior faculty meetings on my case.

Subsequently, in a letter to Tinkham of July 19, 1978, (p. I–47), I expressed my "extreme disappointment" for Coleman's behaviour "because contrary to centuries of scientific traditions to which I have been educated, and contrary to the confidentiality of the formal referee process". In fact, the memoir had been clearly submitted to Coleman for refereeing, with a clear mark on the front page indicating "Rudimentary draft for confidential communication" (p. I–26). As chairman, Tinkham treated the case with manifest disinterest.

Centuries of traditions in scientific ethics should have definitely prevented Coleman from expressing his criticism to others while keeping silence with me.

But, again, my personal opinion is immaterial. The important opinion is that by the fellow taxpayer who has financed Coleman's research for years.

The appointment at Harvard's mathematics department.

In this way, I was left with no other choice than apply for a position at the Department of Mathematics, which I did on May 16, 1978, (p. I–45). The mathematical content of my monograph [9] was considered sufficient for a position; my application was accepted in a matter of a few weeks; and, FINALLY, in June, 1978, I drew the first salary from my DOE grant.

The entire affair at Lyman remained, for me, substantially beyond a rational explanation, as it remains today. During the entire period of the affair, I was indeed a formally appointed member of the laboratory and, as such, I was regularly publishing articles and books with my affiliation to the Lyman Laboratory. Under these circumstances, which was the rational explanation underlying the decision by the senior faculty there to prevent my drawing a salary under my own grant, while jointly preventing Harvard from cashing the related, considerable, overheads? How could such a behaviour under said circumstances be rationally explained, if one keeps in mind the fact that the case had been pushed to such extremes, to be very close to the filing of multimillion dollar law suits?

The most plausible explanation I could find is that the senior faculty at Lyman apparently intended to use the hardship on my children and my wife as a possible means of bending my complete independence of scientific thought into a form compatible with their research lines. If that was the case, Coleman, Glashow, Weinberg and the other senior faculty there incurred into in a major misperception. I am a committed free person, humanly and scientifically. My complete independence of scientific thought simply has no price.

Judging in retrospect, I am happy to see that the episode was one of the most instructive of my life. For instance, I learned the way to conduct an intense financial activity while owning nothing, in such a way to be able to inflict the maximal possible damages permitted by law, while suffering the minimal conceivable damages. Also, in the long run, the episode turned out to be most productive for me, in the sense that it forced my undertaking of a number of scientific initiatives that otherwise would not have seen the light. In fact, I am happy to admit that I own a number of my achievements to the obstructions I experienced from Coleman, Glashow and Weinberg.

Final report to the Lyman Laboratory.

At the time of expiration of my honorary appointment at the Lyman Laboratory on June 30, 1978, I presented my final report according to customary departmental practice. The report summarized my scientific activities for the past academic year which include (pp. I—49—61):

a— The reception of a DOE research contract;

b— The funding of the Hadronic Journal;

c— The publication of two monographs [9, 11] and the preliminary drafting of additional ones;

d— The writing of a number of articles and memoirs in Physical Review D [136] and in the Hadronic Journal [8a, b; 14];

e— The delivery of an informal seminar course on the Inverse Problem at Lyman;

f— The delivery of a number of formal or informal seminars (at: the International Center for Theoretical Physics, in Trieste, Italy; the Institut voor Theoretische Mechanica of the Rijksuniversiteit, Gent, Belgium; the Institut für Theoretische Physik der Universität, Zürich, Switzerland; the Department of Physics of Northeastern University, Boston; and the Department of Physics of Queens College, New York); and,

g— The conduction of referee work for a number of

journals, besides the Hadronic Jouranl, such as: Physical Review Letters; Physical Review D; Annals of Physics; and others.

All this was achieved while being unemployed.

The first comprehensive report to Derek C. Bok, President of Harvard University, on December 27, 1978.

After leaving Lyman for the mathematics department, I though that my problems were over, and that I would have been left in peace to conduct research under the DOE contract.

I was wrong.

The opposition by Coleman, Glashow, Weinberg and possibly others against the conduction of studies on the limitations of Einstein's theories continued, propagated outside the university; and eventually rendered the writing of this book unavoidable.

The first, outside, negative, intervention of which I am aware,* occurred when senior physicists from Lyman indicated to senior mathematicians that "Santilli's studies have no physical value". In turn, this created evident, apparently intended problems for my appointment there, clearly, because I was a physicist. Mathematicians had to consider the judgment of their physical colleagues to appoint me. It was only thanks to the mathematical content of my research that this additional problem was by–passed.

The situation deteriorated substantially in December, 1978. In essence, Sternberg was interested in continuing the contract. As a result, I was not in a position to move it to another college, as originally planned. My only possibility to keep the contract was therefore that of remaining at Harvard. At that time, Sternberg and I had a sincere, scientifically and humanly rewarding relationship.☆ He had no personal objection on my continuing under our DOE contract for one additional (although terminal) year.

By December, 1978, the application for the renewal of the

---

* The episode of the denial of hospitality under contract with the U.S. Department of Energy by the European Organization for Nuclear Research (CERN) of Geneva, Switzerland (Appendix A), should be kept in mind. In fact, it is evidently unlike that CERN reached a negative decision on an application for hospitality originated at the Lyman Laboratory without first consulting senior members there.

☆See my letter to Sternberg of p. I–66 while he was at Tel–Aviv. It concerns the sudden death of one of my best personal friends, the Jewish musician, John Boros of Brandeis University, and his Italian wife Emy. We had joined forces here, organized a fund raising, and succeeded in doing a record of John's (beautiful) musics. I asked Sternberg to donate one sample of the record to any public collection in Israel preferably, that of Tel–Aviv University.

contract for one second year had to be filed. Its renewal from the part of the DOE was expected to present no problem. I had contacted David C. Peaslee at the DOE in that respect, and he had explained to me that the second year renewal was normally done without external refereeing. All the books and papers Sternberg and I had published during the first year were more than sufficient, in Peaslee's view, to warrant the renewal of the contract for one additional year.

The problems for the renewal were at Harvard, that is, they were at the Lyman Laboratory of Physics. In fact, one day in the second half of December, 1978, Sternberg came to me saying that he was experiencing extreme difficulties in securing the renewal of my appointment at the department of mathematics under the DOE contract, because of the insistence on the "lack of physical value" of my research from the senior members of the physics department. As a result of that, Sternberg was proceeding alone with the renewal of the contract without my participation. This meant for me, again, unemployment a few months later on.

Two things then happened, almost simultaneously. On December 27, 1978, I wrote my first, comprehensive, ten—page report to Derek Bok, in his capacity as President of Harvard University, with copy to Richard G. Leahy, in his capacity as Associate Dean in the Faculty of Arts and Sciences. The report (pp. I–72–81) was studiously written in a language as candid as possible for the intent of identifying the implications and potential danger for Harvard of the posture by Coleman, Glashow, Weinberg and possibly others. The objective was to prevent that the apparent opposition against the study and experimental resolution of the validity or invalidity of Einstein's ideas in the interior of hadrons would propagate from individual faculty to the entire university. Stated differently, my objective was to prevent that the personal problems of scientific accountability vis–a–vis the U.S. taxpayers by Coleman, Glashow and Weinberg extend to the entire university.

This time, I intentionally became repetitious by conveying and reconveying again the same message to Bok a number of additional times, such as those of January 11, 1979, (p. I–82), May 6, 1979, (p. I–100), September 23, 1979, (p. I–127), May 1, 1980, (I–172), May 8, 1980, (p. I-175), and even telegrams just a few days before leaving Harvard (see below). The clear objective of all these letters was to make absolutely sure that Harvard's administration knew in all the necessary details the ethical implications for the suppression of studies on the verification of Einstein's theories.

One thing I studiously attempted to convey to Bok with this correspondence, is that I was not a "Harvard man" as customarily intended in the Yard. In fact, I studiously avoided the use of "Harvard's language" (a concoption of allusory remarks which: avoid the direct consideration of the case at hand; are formulated in the most concise possible terms; and are expressed only in case of extreme necessity — ignorance being the most dominant "language" in the college). Instead, I consider it a question of principle to be as specific as conceivably possible, owing to the gravity of the case and of its implications.

At any rate, it was clear that I was at Harvard to attempt the free pursuit of novel physical knowledge and NOT a career in the University, with full knowledge that these two pursuits, in my case, were irreconcilably incompatible.

I believe that I did succeed in conveying the necessary information. However, Derek Bok turned out to be substantially uninterested, to use an euphemism, as we shall see. Back to my first report of December 27, 1978, it remained unacknowledged.

Independently from this report, Sternberg had contacted the DOE office indicating his decision to submit the renewal application for one second year without my name. Peaslee discouraged quite firmly such a renewal, indicating that the likelyhood of its funding would have been very small. I still remember when Sternberg came to my office reporting this phone conversation and indicating his embarassment.

In this way, we reached the decision to apply for the renewal of the DOE contract with my affiliation this time to the Department of Mathematics. Sternberg evidently followed the administrative iterim with all due care, beginning with the formal approval by the mathematics department, and then passing to the approval by the appropriate administrative bodies, and finally releasing the contract to the ORC.

I thought that my problems were over for at least one more year. They were not. The DOE contract was soon renewed. However, when time came for the renewal of my appointment, the senior physicists created additional difficulties at the mathematics department. The case has been reported in Section 1.6, pages 132—136 (of this volume), and resulted in a paper of criticisms on quarks I wrote and distributed worldwide in 15,000 copies (see Doc. p. I—97 for copy of the front page).

The subsequent moratorium at the Hadronic Journal for the publication of papers on nonrelativistic quark conjectures because of excessive inconsistencies (Section 1.6, pages 136—140), also belongs to that period.

The proposal to President Bok to organize a new center of research within the university.

The scientific initiatives of 1977 and 1978 had created a considerable interest in the physical and mathematical communities. By late 1978, an increasing number of scholars were becoming interested in the Lie—isotopic and Lie—admissible generalizations of Lie theory, and their applications to classical mechanics, statistical mechanics, particle physics and other disciplines.

This information originated not only from the papers routinely arriving at my editorial desk, but also by the ongoing organization of our *Second Workshop on Lie–admissible Formulations,* as well as from the requests of scholars to visit me at Harvard.

It was clear that I could not effectively relate to such a growing activity while being a member of the department of mathematics. The most effective way would have been to organize a new center of research, for the conduction and coordination of research on generalizations of Lie theory and their applications (including possible military applications; see Section 1.6, pp. 120–123).

In early January, 1979, I therefore proposed to President Bok the consideration of the possible founding of a new branch of the university under the name of "Center for Hadron Physics" or any other more preferable name, such as "Center for Applied Mathematics" (pp. I–82–83). As an incidental note, I made it clear that I was not a candidate for an executive position. I was merely interested in being a member.

The proposal soon received encouraging, although informal, support from mathematicians at Harvard, such as Sternberg and the new chairman for that year, Heisuke Hironaka. The proposal was also informally communicated to DOE in Germantown. Pleaslee had a meeting with Hironaka on the project, confirming the best possible consideration of possible research proposals. To stress the feasibility of funding this possible new center, Peaslee indicated that, in case needed, it could get started with my existing contract (which would have implied no financial disbursement from the University, but actually the acquisition of new overheads). Everything looked quite promising at that time, until . . . .the proposal reached the senior physicists at Lyman. In fact, Hironaka subsequently communicated to me the existence of an "extreme opposition" conveyed through Dean Paul Martin from Pierce Hall. Associate Dean Leahy subsequently indicated in a letter of January 24, (p. I–85), that the proposal was solely in the hands of the faculty, who had to approve it, formally endorse it, and then submit it collegially to the administration. By late January, the proposal was evidently dead.

I still wander how much America has lost with the suppression at birth of this new center of research in pure and applied mathematics, and what scientific (as well as military) contributions the center would have achieved in case truly permitted to pursue novel advances in disrespect of vested, academic–financial–ethnic interests.

The unsuccessful attempt to interest Harvard's Center

for Astrophysics.

I had promised to Sternberg first, and then later to Hironaka NOT TO APPLY to the department of mathematics for a third year and I kept my promise.

Sternberg still wanted to continue the grant and, therefore, I could not move it elsewhere. I was then left with no other choice than attempting to interest Harvard's Center for Astrophysics. My research had in fact direct gravitational implications (Section 1.5). A possible research position at the Center for Astrophysics would have been fully sufficient for the continuation of the DOE contract with Sternberg.

I therefore contacted Fred L. Whipple first, then Director of the Center (p. I–107), his successor G. B. Field (p. I–111), and R. Giacconi (p. I–144), one of its members, by conveying the main scientific aspects of the program. I received from all of them courteous acknowledgments, but no true interest materialized.

For me, this meant to leave Harvard.

For the Center for Astrophysics, it meant the continuation of a considerable problem of scientific accountability vis–a–vis the taxpayer. In fact, to my best knowledge, research at that Center has been continuing on conventional, Einsteinian, gravitational theories, without any consideration and/or quotation of the literature on their manifest inconsistencies or disproof of dissident views (see Section 1.5 for scientific details and Section 3.3 for suggestions to the taxpayer).

Harvard's refusal to house on campus the Third Workshop on Lie–admissible Formulations under governmental support.

As indicated in Section 1.9, we held, under DOE support, our *First Workshop on Lie–admissible Formulations* in early August, 1978, in a very informal way, at the office kindly provided to the (three) participants by G. Birkhoff (the mathematician, son of the mechanicist to whom I named the "Birkhoffian mechanics" [8, 10]).

The *Second Workshop* was held, under DOE support, at the Science Center of Harvard in early August, 1979. The participation this time was considerably greater. The meeting resulted in two volumes of proceedings (see ref.s [124] or pp. I–118–122 for reproductions of their Table of Contents).

Throughout the last year at Harvard, I worked at the organization of the *Third Workshop on Lie–admissible Formulations.* The meeting had to be scheduled in early August, 1980, because of the inability of the participants to attend at an earlier date.

But . . . ., my contract at Harvard expired on May 31, 1980. I therefore wrote the following letter (p. I–156):

Professor H. HIRONAKA   *April 25, 1980*
Chairman
Department of Mathematics   *UNIVERSITY MAIL*
Dear Professor Hironaka,
I acknowledge receipt of your recent note confirming the termination of my appointment on June 1, 1980, and indicating the possibility of my continuing to use the current office for a limited additional period of time (and definitely not beyond August 15, 1980).
For your information, and as a rather important part of my current research under DOE support, the THIRD WORKSHOP IN LIE—ADMISSIBLE FORMULATIONS was tentatively scheduled in Cambridge (from August 4 to 9, 1980) several months ago.
The organization of this workshop is now close to completion. A list of participants is enclosed. In addition, we contemplate to have a number of distinguished guests (such as editors of physics Journals).
I assume you have no objection for having this scientific event at Harvard, and I am continuing the organization under this assumption.   *RMS/ml*
Very Truly Yours,   *ecls.*
Ruggero Maria Santilli   *cc: Ass. Dean Leahy*

The list of participants indicated in the letter included a considerable number of distinguished, senior, mathematicians, theoreticians, and experimentalists from the U.S.A. and abroad, including "corresponding participants" from Eastern Countries (for specific names and addresses, see the three volumes of proceedings [125] or the Table of Contents reproduced on (p. I—176—184).

On May 2, 1980, I received the following answer (p. I—174).

Dear Dr. Santilli,   *May 2, 1980*
According to my letter of February 12, 1980, which you clearly received and acknowledged in your letter of April 25, 1980, your status at Harvard is to be totally ceased on May 31, 1980.
Therefore you have no right whatsoever to call for a meeting or conference, academic or otherwise, to be held on the premises of Harvard University after the date of the termination of your appointment, unless you were to obtain special permission from the appropriate administrative board of Harvard University. In any event, you have no authorization and no recommendation from our Mathematics Department for the Hadron Workshop to be held at the Science Center during the summer after May 31.
Sincerely yours,   *HH/mjm*
Heisuke Hironaka   *cc: Dean Richard G. Leahy*
Chairman   *Enclosures*

As one can see, my status had "to be totally ceased on May 31, 1980", and this included all scholars who had been contacted to be hosted by Harvard as part of research under a contract with the U.S. Government!

Evidently, the case was too serious to leave it to Hironaka and Leahy alone. I therefore reported the case to President Bok with a letter of May 8 (p. I–175).

Subsequently, during the last days of my stay I sent to Bok two telegrams soliciting his intervention for the holding of the meeting as originally scheduled at Harvard.

Bok did not acknowledge these last communications.

At 11 p.m. of the night of May 31, 1980, I dismantled my office and left Harvard.

The *Third Workshop* was held at the New Harbour Campus of the University of Massachusetts in Boston. Copy of Hironaka's letter was evidently circulated at the meeting when the participants asked me the reasons why the workshop had not occurred at Harvard as scheduled one year earlier (virtually all participants had their Hotel reservations near Harvard in Cambridge and rather far from the U–Mass campus in Boston).

The opposition by the Lyman Laboratory of Physics at Harvard to list seminars by the Institute for Basic Research in the Boston Area Physics Calendar.

After leaving Harvard and founding our independent Institute for Basic Research (I.B.R.—see next section for details), I thought that FINALLY, I would be left in peace to conduct my research. AGAIN I WAS WRONG! In actuality we were only at THE BEGINNING OF THE PROBLEMS. I shall report below only one case, and present others in the remaining parts of this presentation.

In April, 1982, G.G.G., a distinguished, senior, U.S. mathematician, co—author of a famous book in Lie theory among numerous other works, and member of the Division of Mathematics of the I.B.R., came to visit his "second scientific house" in Cambridge. He wanted to deliver a seminar on certain applications of the Lie—admissible generalization of Lie theory.

The Boston Area Physics Calendar (see Section 1.5, page 74 of this book, for a description) was run that year by the Department of Physics of Tufts University. I therefore wrote a letter to the Editor of the Calendar, Celia Mess at Tufts, on April 19, 1982, (p. I–189), well in advance for the listing of G.G.G.'s seminar scheduled for April 30, under the (studiously innocuous) title of "Algebraic identities, vector fields, and coordinate changes".

TO MY ENORMOUS SURPRISE, TUFTS UNIVERSITY REFUSED TO LIST G.G.G.'S SEMINAR! I heard this first from Celia Mess when phoning on April 20 to verify that everything was in order. It was not. I was told to contact the chairman of Tufts' physics department, Jack Schneps, which I did immediately. Schneps openly told me that:

- the prohibition to list G.G.G.'s seminar had been specifically voiced by the chairman of the Lyman Laboratory of Physics, Karl Strauch, and other senior physicists there (S. R. Coleman, S. L. Glashow and apparently others);*

- the prohibition would persist for all other seminars of our Institute, irrespective of their authors and irrespective of the wording of the announcement; and,

- the prohibition would persist until lifted by the Lyman Laboratory of Physics.

Numerous things happened after that. First, the fellow taxpayer can understand G.G.G.'s rage. I do not know what he did, nor did I ask to know, but we can expect that he did not remain inactive. Second, I immediately submitted a second request to list in the Calendar an I.B.R. seminar. The request was mailed this time via certified letter, return receipt requested. I was the speaker now for a talk under the title "Experimental and theoretical reasons why I do not believe in quarks".☆ I was evidently expecting the rejection of the listing. In fact, Tufts University rejected this second listing too. I gained, in this way, an unequivocal confirmation of the refusal to list I.B.R. seminars even when of strictly theoretical character. Thirdly, I wrote a confidential memo to selected members of the I.B.R. Evidently, I had to inform them of the "iron curtain" the Lyman Laboratory was apparently committed to build around its neighboring, independent, much younger, institution.

A number of possible actions were considered to bring the physicists at Lyman to scientific reason, ranging from the disclosure of the occurrences to the international press, to the filing of (duly publicized) law suits. Nevertheless, the I.B.R. decided to do nothing in the hope that time would bring to reason the senior physicists at Harvard.

---

*Weinberg at that time had left Harvard for the University of Texas at Austin.

☆For physicists who are aware of my research, this title is referred to quarks conceived as elementary particles, as conjectured at Lyman during that period. The paper underlying the proposed talk is that distributed in 15,000 copies, and subsequently published in Found. of Phys., ref. [49]. As indicated in Section 1.6, the conjecture that quarks are truly elementary has been lately abandoned, and it is not considered viable any more, although ref. [49] has never been quoted in the orthodox literature on quarks at Lyman and elsewhere (see Section 1.6, pp. 132–140 for details).

The recent rejection by the Boston College to list an I.B.R. seminar by H. Yilmaz on the inconsistencies of Einstein's general theory of relativity (Section 1.5, pp. 74–77) confirmed the continuation of the problem in 1984.

The writing of IL GRANDE GRIDO was then unavoidable.

Epilogue

I must express my gratitude to Harvard University for the hospitality that, despite all, was provided to me in 1977–1980. In fact, a number of scientific initiatives I undertook during that period could materialize because I was at Harvard.

I would like also to express my respect and consideration for Harvard University which is and remains one of the most prestigious academic institutions throughout the World.

Nevertheless, my dedication and commitment to America are much bigger than my sentiments toward Harvard. I therefore feel obliged to express my disagreement with Derek C. Bok, President of Harvard University, on grounds of scientific ethics.

During the last decades, Harvard University has used large amounts of public money in mathematical, theoretical and experimental research in particle physics under the assumption of the exact validity of Einstein's special relativity. Once doubts on such exact validity under specific physical conditions are voiced in refereed journals, as they have been, and brought to the direct attention of the university administrators, as done repeatedly, those administrators have the ethical duty to promote active research on campus on the resolutions of the doubts either in favor or against established Einsteinian doctrines, the understanding being that such resolutions must also occur via articles published in refereed journals (rather than talks in university corridors).

The existence of such an ethical duty for Harvard is manifest and incontrovertible. In fact, to this day (June 18, 1984), Harvard could be continuing research under governmental contracts for which Einstein's special relativity is violated, with consequential risk of misusing public funds. Until Harvard uses university money ONLY, outsiders do not necessarily have the right to pass judgment on university decisions. However, the moment Harvard uses one penny of public money, outside taxpayers such as myself or my neighbor, have the right to pass judgment on the ethical soundness of university decisions, and voice their concern as effectively as possible.

S. R. Coleman, G. B. Field, R. Giacconi, S. L. Glashow, P. Martin, C. Rubbia, K. Strauch, M. Tinkham, S. Weinberg, F. L. Whipple and other physicists and astrophysicists at Harvard University have accumulated throughout the years a sizable PERSONAL problem of scientific accountability vis–a–vis the U.S. taxpayer, for conducting or otherwise supporting research under Governmental contracts crucially dependent on the exact validity of Einstein's special and   general relativities, or part of them, under physical conditions for which numerous, at times historical doubts have been voiced and published in the technical literature, and without the appropriate quotation of the dissident views.

Again, as stressed earlier, physicists and astrophysicists at Harvard have the right to believe in the exact validity of Einstein's theories under unlimited physical conditions, but they have the ethical duty, first, to quote dissident views, and, second, to support the resolution of the problem, whether in favor or against their personal opinions and interests, whenever operating under support from the U.S. taxpayer. The numerous episodes reported in this book and in the related documentation, indicate beyond a reasonable doubt the opposition by senior members of Harvard University against such resolution, while the lack of quotation of dissident views on Einstenian ideas by Harvard's papers can be readily verified in research libraries.

Furthermore, the backing provided by Derek C. Bok, President of Harvard University, and/or his administration, to the senior physicists and astrophysicists, or the mere lack of interest on the issue, has propagated the ethical problems, from individuals, to Harvard University AS AN INSTITUTION. The size of the public funds involved, the duration in time of the episodes, the international academic weight of the campus, and other factors indicate beyond a reasonable doubt that Harvard University cannot suppress research on the insufficiency and possible invalidation of Einstein's theories without infriging fundamental codes of scientific ethics, and, at the extreme, without putting the premises for a potential, future, threat   to National Security, particularly in case the action is done in support of vested, academic—financial—ethnic interests of individuals or of organized groups of individuals at Harvard, in disrespect of the interests of America.

It should be stressed that my personal contributions are insignificant here. There are many physicists more qualified than myself to conduct a better job on dissident research on Einstein's theories. The point is that by backing the senior physicists at Lyman, and by permitting the suppression of my feeble voice, Bok has endorsed the suppression of dissident research at Harvard thus creating the university problem of scientific ethics indicated earlier. In fact, after I left that campus, no paper explicitly treating the possible invalidation of Einstein's theories has been published under Harvard's affiliation ('evidence to the contrary would be appreciated).

But there is more. The international academic power of Harvard University is well known to outsiders and certainly well known to its president. By merely tolerating the actions

perpetrated by Coleman, Glashow, Weinberg and other physicists against myself and my associates during our efforts to
identify the limits of applicability of Einstein's theories, Derek
C. Bok has created the potential prerequisites for a scientific
obscurantism in physics, based on the suppression of dissident
views on Einstein's theories via academic power, rather than
papers in technical journals.

In fact, the mere tolerance of the actions by the university president and/or his administration following my detailed
reports, rather than containing has multiplied the confidence
and impunity in questionable behaviour, by reaching extremes
such as the direct interventions to suppress the listings throughout the years of dissident I.B.R. seminars on the (seemingly
democratic) Boston Area Physics Calendar. The possible premises for a scientific obscurantism then become plausible for
anybody who is really aware of the international academic
power of senior faculty at Harvard.

This is a true, ultimate reason for my writing this book.
In fact, until the opposition by Coleman, Glashow, Weinberg
and others against my dissident research remained contained at
Harvard, I did carefully avoid any release of the information
outside the Yard. The propagation of the opposition to outside
peers in the U.S.A. and abroad (see the remaining presentation)
indicated to me the possible initiation of a scientific obscurantism on Einstein's ideas. The writing of this book was then
rendered absolutely unavoidable.

Even ignoring the evident, fundamental character of the
scientific issues, there are military aspects (touched in Section
1.6 evidently without any detail) that simply cannot be treated
too lightly. Hadrons are the biggest energy reservoir known to
mankind. The possible invalidation and generalization of Einstein's ideas in their interior may permit the conception of new
weapons which are simply unthinkable under Einstenian laws.
The risk that such weapons might be conceived first by enemies
of America must be prevented. This should indicate the reasons
why the backing of vested, academic—financial—ethnic interests at Harvard University on Einstein's theories not only would
be antiscientific and in violation of scientific ethics, but could
constitute a potential threat to the free world.

But . . . . my personal opinion on these matters is insignificant. Equally insignificant is the personal opinion by Derek C.
Bok and other members of Harvard University. The only important opinion is that by the taxpayer who supports the research at Harvard.

Fellow taxpayer, the passing of judgment on the matters
is therefore released to you. For that, I beg you not to be
blinded by the notorious brillance of Harvard's parlance. As
recalled in Section 1.4, physics is a science that will never admit
terminal theories. No matter how good Einstein's theories are

today, one day they will be replaced by more general and more accurate descriptions. The sooner these generalized theories are achieved, the better it is for America and mankind.

2.2: MASSACHUSETTS INSTITUTE OF TECHNOLOGY

The primary reason of scientific dispute with colleagues at Harvard was the exact or approximate character of Einstein's special relativity in the interior of hadrons. The primary reason of scientific dispute with colleagues at the Massachusetts Institute of Technology (MIT) was the exact or only approximate character of a central part of the special relativity: the symmetry under rotations.

For a better understanding of this section, it is useful to review the following scientific aspects considered in Chapter 1.

1.) Victor F. Weisskopf, a senior physicist at MIT, was one of the first scholars to acknowledge in his book [2] of 1952 the hypothesis formulated in the early stages of nuclear physics according to which the intrinsic magnetic moments of protons and neutrons could experience a deviation from their conventional values, when the particles are within a nuclear structure.

2.) After being ignored for decades, studies of the hypothesis were resumed in 1978. It was then understood that the alteration (called "mutation") of the intrinsic magnetic moments of protons, neutrons and all hadrons under strong interactions is expected to be a consequence of the deformation of the extended charge distributions of the particles. In turn, such deformation implies a breaking of the (conventional) rotational symmetry (one can think of a sphere which, because of collisions or external forces, is no longer spherical and, therefore, no longer rotationally invariant; see Figure 2.2.1). It was furthermore understood that the maximal conceivable conditions of mutation of intrinsic magnetic moments (rotational asymmetry) were expected to be due to the alteration of the intrinsic angular momentum (spin) in the conditions considered (sufficiently energetic hadrons under EXTERNAL STRONG interactions). In turn, the alteration of spin under these extreme conditions would imply the alteration of the statistical character of the particles. Thus, Bosons or Fermions were not expected to remain exact Bosons or Fermions, respectively, under the extreme physical conditions considered, and Pauli's exclusion principle (a pillar of quantum mechanics) was not expected to be exactly valid [14].

3.) In summer 1981, it became known that, for sufficiently low energies, the alteration of the magnetic moments could occur under deformation of shape/rotational asymmetry, but in such a way to preserve the conventional values of spin and, therefore, of Pauli's exclusion principle [65]. These were evidently some intermediary conditions prior to the more general deformation/rotational—asymmetry AND mutation of spin of point 2.)

4.) The Austrian experimentalist H. Rauch and his collaborators had been conducting, since 1975, direct experimental tests of the intrinsic magnetic moment/rotational symmetry of (low energy) thermal neutron [96—99]. In 1981, Rauch announced re—elaborations of preceding tests indicating a possible 1% mutation/rotational—asymmetry exactly along points 1.) and 3.) (but not necessarily 2.). Rauch announced his measures at an international conference in Orléans, France, of 1981 [100], and subsequently confirmed the same measures at an international workshop in Tokyo, Japan, in 1983 [139]. To this writing, these measures remain the ONLY available DIRECT measures on the rotational symmetry.

5.) In the same contribution [100], Rauch indicated the experimental plausibility of sufficiently small deviations from Pauli's exclusion principle for sufficiently energetic neutrons colliding with the tritium core.

To this writing (June 19, 1984), the problem of the rotational symmetry is still fundamentally open on theoretical and experimental grounds. In fact, the resolution of the problem needs considerable, additional, theoretical study, as well as a sufficient number of diversified experiments, such as those identified in Section 1.7. Most importantly, the fellow taxpayer should keep in mind the current orthodox position according to which Pauli's principle is exact under strong interactions. This conclusion, however, is supported by data elaborations of experiments which are based on the assumption of the exact validity of the principle. To prevent turning nuclear physics into a farce (Section 1.9, pp. 178—180), current experiments on neutron—tritium scattering should also be re—elaborated under the assumption of a (generally small) violation of the principle. The two different elaborations should then be confronted, and the differences resolved via specific experiments. Most of all, to understand the content of this section, the taxpayer should keep in mind that the possible extablishing of the breaking of the rotational symmetry in physics (whether only for conditions 3.) above or for the full conditions 2.), would imply the irreconcilable invalidation of Einstein's special relativity (Section 1.4).

The beginning of my contacts at MIT.

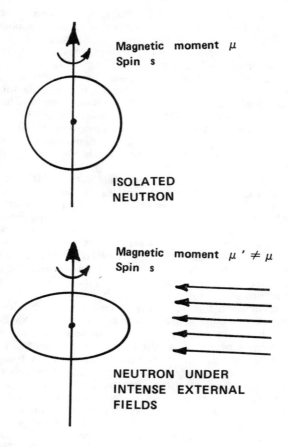

Figure 2.2.1. A schematic view of the primary reasons of dispute with senior physicists at MIT. Protons and neutrons are not point–like particles, but possess an extended charge distribution with a radius of about 10^{-13}cm. Assume for implicity that such distribution is perfectly spherical and therefore rotationally invariant (an assumption that is already debatable to begin with). Under sufficiently intense external forces and/or collisions, protons and neutrons are then expected to experience a deformation of shape, trivially, because perfectly rigid objects do not exist in the physical reality. The amount of deformation for given external conditions is unknown at this time. But the existence of the deformation itself is out of the question on strict physical grounds (although not on grounds of academic politics!). The deformation of shape has a number of scientific, economic and military implications. First, it implies an alteration of the intrinsic magnetic moments of the particles, as it can be inferred from mere classical considerations. In turn, the alteration of the magnetic moments has important implications for controlled fusion (e.g., for magnetic confinement) trivially, because the value of the intrinsic magnetic moments of the particles to be confined magnetically may change pre-

cisely at the time of the initiation of the fusion process. Second, the deformation of shape of protons, neutrons and all hadrons implies a breaking of the symmetry under rotations, trivially, because the particles are no longer rotationally invariant. In turn, such breaking implies that of Einstein's special relativity (see Sections 1.4 and 1.6). The political implications for vested, academic—financial—ethnic interests on Einstein's theories at MIT and other campuses are simply unavoidable for the problem under consideration. The possible military implications cannot evidently be detailed here. The fellow taxpayer should however know that, if the intrinsic characteristics of protons and neutrons change when the particles are in the interior of nuclei, improvements of existing weapons or even new weapons could become conceivable. At any rate, these possibilities simply cannot be dismissed too lightly. Despite: the manifest plausibility of the deformation, the availability at MIT of all equipment for speedy experimental resolutions (see below), and the scientific—economic—military implications, senior MIT physicists showed no interest in the problem. In fact, this section is a report of my repetitious attempts to suggest an active involvement by MIT, which were followed by equally repetitious dismissals over several years. The fellow taxpayer should be aware of the "rebuffal" often voiced by academicians in the hope of by—passing the deformation/rotational—asymmetry/violation—of—the—special—relativity depicted in this figure. The argument goes by saying that protons, neutrons, and all hadrons are made of quarks which are point—like and therefore fully invariant under rotations. Stated in different terms, the argument attempts to recover the exact rotational symmetry and the exact validity of the special relativity, by performing the transition from a proton as a whole, to its constituents. The theoretical plausibility of the argument cannot be denied by a true physicist. Nevertheless, the use of the argument for the purpose of suppressing the need for the experimental resolution of the problems considered, is so questionable, to raise a host of issues of scientific ethics. Quark theories are still conjectural to this writing for a variety of reasons, such as the fact that the quarks themselves have never been isolated and physically detected in a direct way; the achievement of a model of true confinement of quarks is still lacking; etc. (see the end of Section 1.7). **The physical phenomena under consideration here (deformation of shape; alteration of magnetic moment; breaking of the rotational symmetry; etc.) are referred to and must be referred to one proton or one hadron as a whole, irrespective of what the constituents are. It is then the task of any structure model to recover these data on the particle. For these and other reasons, the mere mention of the word "quarks" can be potentially unethical, particularly when used for the intent of voiding the experimental resolution of the deformation of shape of hadrons, with related breaking of Einstein's special relativity.**

As predictable, my contacts at MIT initiated under the best possible auspices and mutual respect. I had been an (unsalaried) personal guest of Francis E. Low at the MIT Center for Theoretical Physics from January, 1976, until August, 1977 (while jointly holding a salaried faculty position elsewhere). During that period, I wrote the preliminary drafts of monographs [9, 10] papers [125], and the preliminary versions of a number of other works. To have an idea of how smooth my contacts at MIT were at that time, I reproduce below the referee report of papers [135] published in Annals of Physics (which is a journal edited by MIT faculty) (see Doc. p. I–680)

> "Santilli has performed a real service in reviewing beautiful old ideas and extending them to field theories. Such scholarly virture is rare these days and is very important".

At the termination of my stay, I left MIT for Harvard sincerely grateful to Francis E. Lǫw, then Director of the Center for Theoretical Physics, Herman Feshback, then Chairman of the Physics Department, and several other colleagues.

But . . . . . in all my scientific activities at MIT of that time, I had carefully avoided the mentioning of doubts on the possible invalidation of the rotational symmetry and Einstein's special relativity in particle physics.

The founding of the Hadronic Journal.

On October 20, 1977, I submitted to Annals of Physics five papers on the need to test rotational symmetry and Pauli's exclusion principle under strong interactions (p. I–681). In the subsequent correspondence with H. Feshback, as Chief Editor of the journal, I pointed out the immaturity of the papers and my need for help. Unfortunately, months and months passed without any editorial decision. In fact, the papers were formally rejected only on May 22, 1978 (p. I–685), and it was only after several subsequent requests, that I finally succeeded in having copy of at least part of one referee report (p. I–687–688).

Verbal communications in the meantime gave me the clear impression that senior physicists at MIT were not interested in the experimental verification of Pauli's exclusion principle in nuclear physics, despite its evident fundamental character, not only for basic knowledge, but also for energy related issues (see the implications for controlled fusion of the possible alteration of the magenetic moments of hadrons of Section 1.1, pp. 8–10), not to ignore for military profiles.

The delay at MIT in the consideration of the papers was determinant in my decision to found a new journal with a specific emphasis on the publication of plausible conjectures expressed in a theoretically and mathematically mature way, irrespective of their implications for academic politics. In fact, my search for funds to initiate production of the Hadronic Journal began exactly at that time. The submission of the papers on the tests of Pauli's principle to Physical Review D (Particles and Fields) had to be excluded owing to the notorious attitude of that journal against the publication of speculative ideas (see Section 2.4).

My plea to H. Feshback, F. E. Low, P. Morrison, V. F. Weisskopf, and other senior MIT physicists to conduct the tests at MIT on Pauli's exlusion principle under strong interactions.

I spent the entire day of October 10, 1979, at my typewriter writing individualized letters to Feshback, Low, Morrison, Weisskopf and other senior physicists at MIT, each letter being several pages long (pp. I–213–243). As one can see, the letters pointed right to the heart of the scientific issue. For instance, after seven pages of presentation, the letter to Weisskopf concluded by saying (p. I–232)

"I am appealing to you for support in my proposal to Philip Morrison and other friends at MIT to initiate studies at MIT in the experimental verification of Pauli's principle in nuclear physics".

As recalled earlier, Weisskopf had been among the first to acknowledge the hypothesis of the possible alteration of the intrinsic magnetic moments. I therefore thought that he would be interested in the experimental resolution of this historical open problem. Also, I thought that everybody could see evident physical aspects such as: (a) the plausibility of the deformation of the extended charge distributions of protons and neutrons under sufficiently intense external forces and/or collisions (recall that absolutely rigid objects do not exist in the universe!); (b) the consequential alteration of the intrinsic magnetic moments exactly as predicted by the historical hypothesis; and (c) the equally evident breaking of the rotational symmetry. I thought that Victor Weisskopf and the other senior physicists at MIT would see these things, and initiate an active scientific role or at least be receptive.

But I was wrong.

No acknowledgment of my proposal of October 10, 1979, was ever voiced to me verbally or in writing by any of the senior members I had contacted. The only comment that unidentified MIT physicists made later on to DOE was that "Santilli writes long letters".

The availability at MIT of the equipment for a speedy experimental resolution of the issue.

The fellow taxpayer should know the background reasons for my writing several "long letters" to MIT physicists. In 1979, MIT possessed capabilities to conduct the suggested tests in house. By 1979, I had become acquainted with the experiments conducted by H. Rauch and his team on the rotational symmetry of neutrons via interferometric techniques [95–99]. I had also become aware of the fact that all the interferometric equipments (perfect crystals, detectors, etc.) used by Rauch were already available at the MIT nuclear physics laboratories. MIT therefore had the capability to repeat Rauch's tests on the rotational symmetry under strong nuclear interactions in about two months running time; all this, if and only if desired or otherwise permitted by the senior physicists there.

But . . . . . ., an MIT acknowledgment of the need to test the rotational symmetry would have implied the official acknowledgment of the existence of authoritative doubts on Einstein's special relativity. In turn, the mere acknowledgment of doubts would have been manifestly damaging to the large interests surrounding Einsteinian theories at MIT, throughout the U.S.A. and abroad.

The MIT declination of my proposal was therefore consequential, no matter how plausible the violation is, and no matter how important the implications are.

The visit at MIT to inspect the equipment.

On March 19, 1980, I visited the neutron interferometry facilities at MIT with H.H.H., a European scholar then visiting me at Harvard. The head of the neutron interferometric experiments, Clifford G. Shull, was in Europe. His junior collaborators, J. Arthur, D. K. Atwood, and M. A. Horne were there. They received us quite cordially, by showing the experimental facilities; by providing a detailed presentation of the experimental set ups; and by outlining experiments running there at that time.

After completing the tour of the facilities, we had a meeting in which H.H.H. and I proposed to Arthur, Atwood and Horne the conduction of the experimental test of Pauli's exclusion principle. The subsequent day, I summarized the proposal in a letter (p. I—251) also including a list of references on the proposal (pp. I—252—253).

H.H.H. and I came out of this visit with the confirmation of the conviction that MIT had already in house all that was needed to resolve experimentally the historical hypothesis of the possible alteration of the intrinsic magnetic moments of protons and neutrons under nuclear conditions. H.H.H. was, of course, aware of the solicitations I had made to senior physicists at MIT to conduct these evidently fundamental tests. He was also fully aware of the implications for controlled fusion. I still remember H.H.H.'s surprise to see that so eminent physicists were not interested in testing the rotational symmetry despite all these aspects. It was in this way that H.H.H. reached, in his own independent way, the conclusion that the lack of interest at MIT in the tests was due to academic politics. I still remember my uneasiness with H.H.H., and my worrying of the comments that this fellow scholar would have expressed on MIT when back to Europe.

The appeal to C. G. Shull.

In my view, the implications of the case were too serious to be left only at the level of junior experimentalists at MIT. On August 27, 1980, I therefore wrote a personal appeal to the senior physicist in charge of the neutron interferometric experiments, Clifford G. Shull (p. I—259—260). For clarity, the full letter is reproduced below.

Dear Professor Shull,
On March 19, 1980, during your leave, I visited your associates M. A. HORNE, D. K. ATWOOD, and J. ARTHUR for the purpose of indicating that your neutron interferometer equipment appears to be particularly suited for the experimental verification of the SU(2)—spin symmetry as well as of Pauli's exclusion principle under strong interactions. Copy of the correspondence with Mike Horne is enclosed.
I am referring, for instance, to suitable modifications and/or improvements of the initial tests on the 4π spinor symmetry already done by the European experimental group headed by Professor RAUCH (a copy of his last paper on the subject is enclosed).
On experimental grounds, the need for additional measurements are numerous. For instance, (1) the exact symmetry value of 720° barely makes it within experimental data (716.8 ± 3.8 deg); (2) the median angle in the latest as well as in the preceding experiments has a tendency to be below 720 deg; and (3) the best fit does not appear to be provided by a sinusoidal curve, as necessary for the exact symmetry (see the diagram of fig. 3 of Rauch's paper, p. 284).
On theoretical grounds, the need for additional measurements are equally numerous, and they have been discussed in detail in the specialized literature on the topic (see the enclosed list of references, copies of which were released to your associates). In its most rudimentary form a primary argument is as follows. For the case of the electromagnetic interactions, the exact validity of the SU(2)—spin symmetry is incontrovertible, as established (for instance) by the property that the angular momentum of a charged particle under an external elm field is conserved. For the case of the strong interactions the situation does not appear to be necessarily the same. As clearly indicated by available experimental data, strongly interacting particles are actually constituted by wave packets in condition of mutual penetration or overlapping (which is absent for the elm case, in general). This confirms the rather old expectation that one component of the strong interactions is constituted by a nonlocal, nonpotential (non—Hamiltonian) force. In turn, this

is expected to imply the lack of applicability in an exact form of the entire Lie's theory, let alone that of the SU(2)—spin case. Irrespective from this aspect (or as a complement to it), the angular momentum of a particle under strong interactions is not expected to be conserved (to avoid the perpetual—motion—type of approximation that, say, a proton orbits inside a star with a conserved angular momentum. . . .). In turn, this is expected to imply a form of breaking of the SU(2) symmetry. Needless to say, such a possible breaking can be only an internal effect of closed strong systems and, as such, not observable via external elm interactions. Also, for the case of the nuclear forces the effect can at most be quite small.

These ideas have been subjected to a quantitative study by a number of mathematicians and physicists via the so—called Lie—admissible generalization of Lie's theory. In essence, the approach studies the generalization of the Lie algebra/enveloping algebra/Lie group in such a way to permit the representation of nonpotential forces.

Also, the approach is applicable to the quantitative treatment of a broken Lie symmetry, and admits the conventional Lie theory as a particular case. The application of these new mathematical tools to the case of a strongly interacting particle under condition of penetration with other particles and expected nonlocal forces has provided: (A) the prediction of a conceivable deviation from the exact SU(2) symmetry of the order of at least 5×10^{-4} for the case of low energy nuclear processes; (B) the apparent interpretation of the "slow down effect" of the median angle; and (C) the apparent improvement of the fit of the experimental data by Rauch and his collaborators.

In conclusion, and to our best understanding at this time, the current experimental data appear to be compatible with both the exact and the broken SU(2) spin symmetry. The fundamental character of the symmetry for theoretical as well as applied physics (e.g., the problem of the controlled fusion) then warrants, in my view, additional experiments.

Since the time of my visit to your laboratory, several developments have occurred, such as

— a number of experimentalists have answered my call for the initiation of a feasibility study for more refined experiments;

— I have delivered an invited talk at the recent Conference in Differential Geometry and Applied Mathematics held from July 23 to 25 at Clausthal-Zellerfeld with encouraging results; and,

— we recently had our Third Workshop in Lie—admissible Formulations here in the Boston area from August 4 to 9 with the participation of some 30 scientists, including mathematicians, theoretical and experimental physicsts. The workshop was virtually devoted to the study of the

problem.
In case you are interested in more detailed information, I would
be happy to visit you either for an informal meeting or for de-
livering a seminar on the subject (I could essentially repeat my
presentation at Clausthal—Zellerfeld). I can be reached more
readily at my home address given below.
Best Personal Regards,   *cc: Professor FRANCIS E. LOW, MIT*
Ruggero Maria Santilli   *encls.*
RMS/ml

Shull never acknowledged this appeal, by remaining totally silent with me, despite the explicitly stated offer to meet "informally", that is, to avoid any official announcement by MIT of
our possible meeting.

What a difference between the real MIT, and the MIT I
had imagined as the temple of pursuit of novel scientific knowledge, while being a high school student thousands of miles away!

**The firm continuation of support by DOE after my leaving
Harvard University.**

The fellow taxpayer will recall that my status at Harvard
had to be "totally ceased" (In Hironaka's words) on the night of
May 31, 1980. I knew this end well in advance and, therefore, I
initiated, in time, all the necessary action.

It was at this point that the Division of High Energy Physics of the U.S. Department of Energy gave concrete proof of determination (at that time) to continue the support of my research irrespective of academic dances that might occur at local
institutions. Also, the way DOE conducted the case, and the informal support I received were such that I felt proud of being
the father of American children.

In short, by late 1979, I knew that the opposition at Harvard against my research would readily propagate to other
campuses, by therefore preventing any realistic possibility of continuing the administration of my DOE contract by an academic
institution. I therefore contacted the DOE in Washington asking
for the administration by a non—academic corporation. This
proposal was accepted by DOE upon due consideration, scrutiny
and qualification of the corporation as the administrative conduit
of federal contracts.

It is regrettable that such a beautiful independence of the
DOE Division of High Energy Physics from high ranking U.S.
physicists was short lived. In fact, the DOE subsequently had to
succumb to the mounting of pressures intended to suppress
the funding of my research. Ironically, this subsequent truncation of support occurred exactly at the time of conclusion of the
classical research and initiation of specific studies in particle physics, not excluding military profiles.

The offer of guest status by Gian–Carlo Rota at the MIT Center for Applied Mathematics.

Once I had achieved the removal of the administration of my DOE contract from the academic world, I thought that my problems were indeed finally over, and that I could finally plunge myself into the study of basic experiments without wasting unnecessary human energies in mumbo–jumbo academic dances.
BUT, AGAIN, I WAS WRONG!
One technical aspect of my new DOE application, I knew well since late 1979, was that, even though the administration was of non–academic type, I still needed an academic institution to conduct my work because of the need of library and other research facilities.

For this reason, on January 9, 1980, I wrote to Gian–Carlo Rota, a senior mathematician at MIT, asking for hospitality under my own, independently administered, DOE contract (p. I–248). I specifically indicated in this letter that any possible visiting status would be formally included in my grant application to the DOE (see the last lines of p. I–248).

On January 18, 1980, Rota kindly answered with a formal offer of a guest status for the academic year 1980/1981. In this way, the DOE approved a new research contract (DE–AC02–80ER10651) under a number of provisions, including the administration by the corporate, non–academic, conduit AND my guest status at the Center for Applied Mathematics at MIT.

The printing of the cover of the Hadronic Journal of June, 1980, with my MIT affiliation.

Journals must meet certain production deadlines. To do so, it is a rather frequent practice to print in advance the cover, and then the contents itself. The Hadronic Journal is a bimonthly journal and, as editor, I must confirm or otherwise modify my affiliation and full address for the cover of the journal at least every two months. The last issue with my Harvard affiliation was that of April, 1980. The subsequent issue of June, 1980, had to carry a different affiliation owing to the termination of my status there on the night of May 31.

In early May, 1980, the printer contacted me requesting the affiliation and address for the cover of the June issue. Always suspicious of political maneuvrings, and despite having a written authorization, I phoned Louis Howard, in his capacity of Director of the Center for Applied Mathematics at MIT. G. –C. Rota had previously informed him of all details. He therefore was fully aware of my imminent guest status. I explained to Howard the advance printing of the cover of the Hadronic Journal, and asked for the confirmation of the authorization to disclose the MIT affiliation in my editorial address, which he gladly did.

There were considerable financial matters involved in the printing of the cover. I was not satisfied with the additional phone authorization I received from Howard. I therefore wrote him a detailed letter summarizing our phone conversation (p. I–254) and again asking for an immediate communication in case of any objection. No objection was raised. On May 18, I therefore authorized the printing of the cover of the Hadronic Journal of the June, 1980, issue and of the additional issues of the academic year 1980/1981.

The revocation of the guest status by the MIT Center of Applied Mathematics on the day of initiation of the visit.

TO MY ENOURMOUS SURPRISE, ON JUNE 1, 1980, JUST AFTER HAVING LEFT HARVARD AND WHILE PREPARING TO GO TO MIT, I RECEIVED A LETTER FROM L. N. HOWARD REVOCATING MY GUEST STATUS AND PROHIBITING THE INDICATION OF ANY MIT AFFILIATION IN MY EDITORIAL ADDRESS (p. I–255)!!!

The letter is evidently the result of what is sadly known as "MIT politics". It uses academic parlance deprived of any contents, while avoiding the disclosure of the real issues. For instance, Howard cites the lack of office space as a reason for the decision, while I had stated, restated, and repeated again that I did not need an office. I only needed the use of the libraries and an academic address.

Why this sudden change? Why had MIT done this in full knowledge that the guest status was part of an official document with the U.S. Government? Why had MIT done this despite the full awareness of the fact that the June, 1980, issue of the Hadronic Journal had already been printed with my MIT affiliation? Which was the force behind the decision? Was it due to isolated individuals or to organized academic—financial—ethnic interests in the Cambridge area?

The most plausible answer is rather simple. I had kept silence on my guest status at MIT; I had asked DOE to keep the information as confidential as possible (by going as far as asking for the courtesy of NOT submitting my application for review in the Boston area), and I have reason to believe that the confidentiality was indeed kept by DOE; Rota, apparently, also kept the information to himself; and Howard did not apparently inform his colleagues of the occurrence. When the time of the initiation of my visit arrived, the information had to be communicated to MIT mathematicians. We must then expect that the information propagated rapidly to the physics department at MIT and/or to Harvard's mathematics and physics departments. Under these circumstances, the gathering of vested, academic—financial—ethnic interests in the Cantabridgian academic community to suppress my guest status at MIT would have been an extremely easy task covered by total impunity.

Whatever the truth, the fact remains that an incontrovertible, drastic change occurred in a matter of days, from a very nice, friendly and cordial attitude by L. Howard toward me up to the end of May, to the suddenly rigid position of suppressing the visit at whatever cost. It is evident that: (a) Howard did not revoke the guest status by acting alone; (b) the decision must have been the result of a sufficient quorum at MIT; and (c) the diversification and amount of pressures on Howard to suppress my visit must have been proportional to the implications.

I then visited Howard in his office for the purpose of identifying as clearly as possible the financial implications of the revocation. I told Howard that, not only the corporation producing the Hadronic Journal had to destroy the covers of the journal, but my DOE application, even though approved, might well be revoked because based on the assumption of MIT providing the needed use of research facilities. I furthermore indicated the rapidly increasing interest in the studies of the Lie—admissible generalization of Lie theory, by pointing out the gain for his center in adding this line of inquiry. I finally asked him authorization to stay there at least a minimum time for my securing another guest status elsewhere. As a gesture of courtesy, I gave Howard a complimentary copy of my monograph with Springer—Verlag with a dedication.

Howard kept mostly silent during my presentation; he accepted the gift of my monograph; and answered my last question with the confirmation that I was absolutely prohibited to initiate my visit there.

My plea to Francis E. Low, then Provost of MIT.

I could readily foresee the subsequent events. In fact, under the circumstances, the corporation producing the Hadronic Journal would have been forced to file a law suit for damages against the Massachusetts Institute of Technology. Additional law suits against MIT could also be anticipated in case anything would have goon wrong with the DOE contract.

At that time, I was still sincerely interested in avoiding gestures that could damage local institutions. I therefore called Francis E. Low, then MIT Provost, by reporting to him the case at least in a summary way (as I attempted to enter into details, Low would remind me that he was very busy). I then asked Low to intervene, in order to prevent a completely unnecessary crisis.

Apparently, Low did intervene in this particular instance. On June 13, 1980, L. N. Howard wrote me a letter confirming the original authorization to print the June issue of the Hadronic Journal with my MIT affiliation, but he kept silent on the guest status, thus implying that his preceding letter on the matter was still standing, that is, I would be prevented from being formally authorirized to use the MIT libraries and other facilities essential for the actuation of my research under the DOE contract.

The founding of the Institute for Basic Research.

After the episode of the guest status at MIT, I resolved myself to organize a new research center under the name of THE INSTITUTE FOR BASIC RESEARCH. In fact, while waiting for the initiation of the new DOE contract (which occurred in the subsequent month of September, 1980), I worked virtually full time on the organizational preliminaries (raising of the necessary seed money; charter; operations; etc.). The Institute was incorporated on March 2, 1981, as an academic non—profit institution; a building adjacent to Harvard University, the Prescott House, was purchased on July 29, 1981, to provide permanent housing for the Institute in the heart of the Cambridge academic community; and the official ceremony of inauguration occurred on August 3, 1981 (see Appendix B).

To understand the decision, the fellow taxpayer must know that MIT was not the only U.S. institution to have rejected hospitality to me. In fact, several other colleges had formally declined a temporary guest status with all expenses supported by my DOE contract. This is the case, for instance, of the Department of Physics of Tufts University (p. I—188), the University of Rochester,* and others.

In addition, a number of colleges had rejected my request of administration of the DOE contract. This is the case, for instance, of the Department of Physics of Virginia Polytechnic Institute & State University (p. I—302). As an incidental note, a detailed letter written to R. E. Marshak at the physics department there (to inform him of the status of the studies on the fundamental tests) remained completely unacknowledged, without even a word of thanks for the gift of my monographs accompanying the letter.☆

But the Virginia Polytechnic Institute at least had acknowledged my application and indicated the negative decision!

---

*Regrettably, the documentation of the Rochester case was misplaced and could not be found at the time of the release of this book for printing. Note that I am referring to declination of guest status made following the declination of an academic position by both Tufts and Rochester.

☆R. E. Marshak subsequently became the President of the American Physical Society for 1982–1983. I then absteined from communicating to him, in his capacity as APS president, additional evidence on the need to verify Einstein's special relativity in the interior of hadrons, because an expected, total waste of time without scientific feedback.

Other U.S. institutions did not even bother to communicate the negative decision. This is the case of the Department of Physics of the University of California at Berkeley, which was formally considering me for a faculty position, but which never acknowledged its evident negative outcome (p. I–310–332); or the Institute for Theoretical Physics of the University of California at Santa Barbara (p. I–303–309) where I was formally considered for a position, and which had received a rather considerable amount of (free) scientific material, including volumes of proceedings of our conferences!

Still other U.S. institutions did not even bother to acknowledge my application, despite the amount of appended material. This is the case, for instance, of the Nuclear Science Division of the Lawrence Berkeley Laboratory, in Berkeley, California. In fact: a formal letter of application for a position there to its Director, Bernard G. Harvey, dated October 10, 1979, (I–334); a subsequent letter to the Director of the Physics Division of the same laboratory, Robert W. Birge, dated October 22, 1979, (I–339); and subsequent letters of January 9 and 30, 1979, (I–346–348); they ALL remained totally unacknowledged! It is impossible for me not to think that the reason for this rather unusual and uncollegial behaviour was due to the fact that I had applied, specifically, to study the test of Pauli's principle under strong interactions, as clearly stated beginning from the very first pages of my application. Yet, while I was predicting opposition by members of the laboratory against the experimental verification of Pauli's principle, I still cannot figure out how so many individual letters and thousands of pages of scientific material could remain totally unacknowledged!*

---

* This lack of acknowledgment of my job applications propagated to other academic activities, including my formal invitations to U.S. physicists for a variety of functions. As a result of this experience, I now issue invitations to U.S. physicists only under truly exceptional circumstances for the simple reason that the greatest majority of the invitations remain unacknowledged. I see no point to present here a list of documented cases. The following one, however, is particular, and must be brought to the attention of the taxpayer as an example of current professional custom in U.S. physics. In mid 1981, Howard Georgi had to leave the post of editor of the Hadronic Journal for a number of reasons, including the fact that he had been promoted to a tenured position at Harvard University. I therefore initiated the search for a colleague from the U.S.A. sufficiently qualified to substitute Georgi as editor of the Journal. After due search, and a number of consultations with physicists from different ethnic groups, I issued a formal invitation to Sidney Meshkov of the National Bureau of Standards in Washington, D.C. The letter, dated July 4, 1981 (pp. I–416–418), invited Meshkov to consider the post of editor of a journal whose Editorial Council comprised distinguished scientists (including two Nobel Laureates). As one can see, the invitation was written in a most respectful form. Time passed and Meshkov did not acknowledge the invitation. We subsequently reached the time of the inauguration of our new Institute in Cambridge (which would have housed part of the editorial activities of the journal). I therefore mailed

I hope the fellow taxpayer understands why, whether right or wrong, I had the feeling that the opposition against the experimental verification of Einstein's special relativity in the interior of hadrons I experienced at Harvard University, after having been backed up by MIT members, had propagated throughout the U.S.A.

The founding of a new, INDEPENDENT, institute of research was then the only possibility left for the continuation of the studies in the U.S.A. by our group.

The MIT refusal to participate in the experimental test of the rotational symmetry via a joint Austria—France—U.S.A. collaboration.

When MIT turned down my appeal to repeat Rauch's tests on the rotational symmetry under external nuclear interactions, I was evidently left with no other choice than contact Rauch himself. I thought that MIT was not interested in doing the experiment in house, but would have no objections in others doing the

---

an additional invitation to Meshkov for participation at the inauguration ceremony of the I.B.R. (p. I—419). But . . ., months and months went by, the I.B.R. was inaugurated, and no acknowledgment whatsoever was received by Meshkov. I therefore attempted to contact common friends in the hope of soliciting any resolution. The fellow taxpayer should know the common practice of scientific ethics according to which, when one individual physicist is invited to become the editor of a scientific journal, no additional invitation must be issued to other physicists for the same post. Ethical standards demand that you simply wait for that physicist to consider the invitation and communicate his/her decision. Additional invitations should then be issued only after declination of the original invitation. Sidney Meshkov, being a senior physicist at a U.S. National Laboratory, knows these things well or, at any rate, he must be expected to know them well because of his post. According to established ethical standards, Meshkov should have communicated his lack of interest with a simple note of declination, thus permitting the continuation of the search with other physicists. In fact, because of the lack of answer by Meshkov, the search for the editor of the Hadronic Journal had to be delayed for over half a year, thus creating predictable scientific damages. The lack of acknowledgment by Meshkov evidently created a host of unanswered questions. After all, invitations for an editorial post of the type I issued in writing (with total and independent editorial authority) are not received every day. But then, why did Meshkov have to damage the Journal? Was he acting for himself, or was he acting on behalf of his peer group? Was the unusual uncollegiality of Meshkov's behaviour due to personal reasons, or was it due to the primary objectives of the journal explicitly recalled in my letter (THE PROMOTION OF THE EXPERIMENTAL RESOLUTION OF THE VALIDITY OR INVALIDITY OF EINSTEIN'S SPECIAL RELATIVITY UNDER STRONG INTERACTIONS)? Nobody will ever know the TRUE answers to these and many more questions. One visible consequence however occurred. The Meshkov case occurred after a number of similar ones in the U.S. physics community. Therefore, subsequent invitations had to be issued to foreign physicists.

experiment elsewhere.

Again, I was wrong! The story of Rauch's experiment is reviewed in detail in Section 2.5 because of its rather crucial scientific, economic and military implications. In this section, I want to report only the following episode.

As a true scientist and a gentleman, Rauch accepted immediately my appeal for the continuation of the experiments, and offered a mutual collaboration between his Atominstitut and the IBR. I therefore proposed to Rauch to apply for partial support at the Division of Nuclear Physics of the National Science Foundation and the U.S. Department of Energy. He stressed the need of minimal funds because the experimental apparatus had already been constructed, while the essential personnel was under employment either of the Atominstitut, in Wien, Austria, or of the Institute Laue–Langevin in Grenoble, France (which provided the nuclear reactor). Nevertheless, he gladly accepted my recommendation. We therefore prepared a proposal for a joint Austria–France–USA collaboration to be submitted to NSF and DOE for partial funding.

To my extreme dismay, I subsequently learned that A. Zeilinger, one of Rauch's collaborators for the experiments on the rotational symmetry, and a proposed co–investigator of the grant application to U.S. Governmental Agencies, HAD LEFT WIEN TO SPEND ONE YEAR AT THE MIT NUCLEAR PHYSICS DIVISION, AND, IN PARTICULAR, TO WORK WITH SHULL'S INTERFEROMETRIC GROUP!!! As soon as I was informed of this, I called Rauch and attempted to convey the idea that it would be better to remove Zeilinger's name as a co–investigator of the application, because, in my expectation, his MIT affiliation could create unnecessary problems. I stressed that this administrative change would leave the scientific profile completely unaltered, including Zeilinger's participation in the new tests. But Rauch, in his kindness and unawareness (at that time) of the Cantabridgean academic politics, dismissed my view as excessively pessimistic, and insisted that Zeilinger should deserve a chance. Evidently, I could not insist. As IBR president, I therefore provided my full services to the experimental team for the completion of the application.

By mid 1981, the application had been completed under the title, "Experimental verification of the SU(2)–spin symmetry under strong and electromagnetic interactions by a joint Austria–France–U.S.A. collaboration". The application was signed in two continents, including administrative formalities in three Countries, and mailed to Zeilinger at MIT for the last missing signature, his.

By keeping in mind all the preceding episodes, the fellow taxpayer can now predict what happened. Nothing happened. That is, MIT did nothing, and released no information whatsoever, whether or not Zeilinger would be permitted to sign the front page of the application under his MIT affiliation, despite the numerous signatures already there (p. I–263)! Months passed by and no information could be obtained from MIT, whether verbal or in writing. I had a meeting with Zeilinger at the IBR on the matter, which resulted to be fruitless. A subsequent formal letter I wrote to Zeilinger at MIT on October 29, 1981, with copy to C. G. Shull and H. Feshback (p. I–268–269) soliciting "any" decision, whether favorable or unfavorable, was left unacknowledged.

In this way, several months passed by with the application sitting on my desk, without being able to submit it to NSF and DOE because of the lack of Zeilinger's signature. It was only ONE YEAR LATER that Rauch finally acknowledged my original prediction to be verified by the reality of the events. We then prepared a new application by repeating again the entire administrative iterim in two continents, but this time WITHOUT Zeilinger as co–investigator. In this way, the application was finally submitted in Washington with over one year of delay.

But . . . ., as the fellow taxpayer can readily anticipate, the application was rejected (Section 2.5).

Zeilinger's seminar at MIT on the experimental tests of the rotational symmetry and other laws.

In the third week of November, 1981, the Boston Area Physics Calendar brought the information that A. Zeilinger would deliver a seminar at MIT on neutron interferometry experiments (which, as the fellow taxpayer will remember from Section 1.7, are precisely the experiments used by Rauch, Zeilinger himself, and others to test the rotational symmetry [96–99] and other basic, quantum mechanical laws).

At that time, I had already made a formal commitment with myself NOT TO ATTEND ANY SEMINAR AT ACADEMIC INSTITUTIONS OF THE BOSTON AREA, evidently because of the formal prohibition by these institutions to list IBR seminars. In the case of Zeilinger's seminar, the need for my absteining was even more compelling. In fact:

- on one side, I expected Zeilinger to be silent on the recent experimental data [100] and theoretical studies [65] indicating the plausibility of about 1% breakdown of the rotational symmetry; and,

- on the other side, under these premises, it would have been necessary for me to disrupt the seminar in a way as forceful as possible.

For these reasons, I asked the courtesy of a number of other physicists attending the seminar (and familiar with the scientific issues) to report to me the essential elements of Zeilinger's presentation. This was indeed done by a number of friends, including members of the IBR, such as I.I.I., a European scholar.

The reports I received in the evening of the seminar (November 18, 1981) confirmed the most pessimistic of my predictions. In fact, Zeilinger had essentially told a rather numerous audience (for which the use of a larger lecture hall had been necessary) that everything was fine with the rotational symmetry, as well as with other quantum mechanical laws. In particular, Zeilinger had absteined from quoting the new experimental data [100] from his boss at the Atominstitut in Wien, and the theoretical studies [65] from his senior colleague at the same institution, not even as a marginal, incidental, curiosity! Note that Zeilinger's awareness of these publications at the time of his seminar was absolutely unquestionable, not only because the papers had been mailed to him from Wien, but also because they were an essential part of the research grant application he had not signed.

I hope the fellow taxpayer begins to consider a bit more seriously my fear of a scientific obscurantism potentially on the way in U.S. physics due to vested, academic—financial—ethnic interests. In fact, what Zeilinger had done is a genuine act of scientific obscurantism under the formal backing of the Massachusetts Institute of Technology!*

The additional seminar at MIT on the rotational symmetry by L. Grodzins.

The Boston Area Physics Calendar of the same week had also announced a seminar by the senior MIT physicist L. Grodzins on the "Measurement of magnetic moments of high spin rotational state". Again, I could not attend any seminar at MIT because of my selfcommitment. Nevertheless, I was interested in listening to the impression by friends and IBR members who attended the meeting.

---

*
The climax of the irony was subsequently reached in 1983 when A. Zeilinger, C. G. Shull et al. from MIT presented a paper at the *International Symposium on the Foundations of Quantum Mechanics* held in Tokyo, Japan, under the seemingly illuminated title of "Search for unorthodox phenomena by neutron interference experiments" (see p. 289 of the Proceedings edited by S. Kamefuchi and printed by the Japanese Physical Society). Despite the illusory title, the paper carefully avoids the problem of the fundamental test of the rotational symmetry. The fellow taxpayer should keep in mind that the crucial measures (715.87 ± 3.8 deg) on the LACK of achievement of the 720 deg needed for the establishing of the rotational symmetry via neutron interferometry, originally presented by H. Rauch at our First International Conference in Orléans, France, of 1981 [100, 126], had been represented by Rauch at the same Symposium in Tokyo a short time before the exploit by Zeilinger, Shull et al. And in fact. one can read in the proceedings of the same symposium the value 715.87 ± 3.8 deg on page 281, only eight pages before the Zeilinger—Shull contribution.

I still remember I.I.I. returning from this seminar full of scientific excitement because the experimental results presented by Grodzins appeared to be out of the predictions of conventional quantum mechanics and, in particular, of the rotational symmetry. I.I.I. had warned me that, under questions posed by MIT colleagues, Grodzins had made all conceivable efforts to indicate the possibility of reconciling his measurements with the exact rotational symmetry.

Nevertheless, the data persisted. Evidently, Grodzins views on the compatibility of his measures with orthodox doctrines could not be dismissed. The point is that, on similar scientific gounds, one could not dismiss the interpretation of the same data via the VIOLATION of the rotational symmetry (Section 1.6 and 1.7). Furthermore, Grodzins tests could shed light on the historical hypothesis of the possible alteration of the magnetic moments embraced by V. F. Weisskopf at MIT in 1952.

I.I.I. and other colleagues therefore urged me to contact Grodzins. Even though highly skeptical on any scientific outcome because of the evident affiliations, I did contact Grodzins via a letter dated November 30, 1981, (p. I–272), indicating the great similarities of his experiments with Rauch's measures [100]. In fact, both Grodzins and Rauch had performed measures directly related to magnetic moments although for different cases (one for high and the other for low spin values). Also, in both cases the agreement with orthodox predictions was too dubious to be fully convincing. Thus, Grodzins' measures could be a back–up of Rauch's measures and vice versa.

L. Grodzins answered on December 4, 1981, with a few, dry, scientifically uncooperative lines, indicating that *"there is no connection between these studies [his] and those by Professor Rauch on the test of the spinor symmetry of neutrons via neutron interferometers. I regret that members of your institute who heard my talk came away with the wrong impression."* (p. I–273).

On December 9, 1981, I answered Grodzins with one of the scientifically most dissonant letters I have ever written (p. I–272).

The last little academic dance.

Despite everything that had happened, in early 1983 I was still willing to keep some form of contact with the Cantabridgean academic community. After all, I was the president of a growing institute of research, as well as the editor of a scientific journal, and an active researcher.

On February 5, 1983, a paper authored by two scholars from a far away Country was submitted to me for publication in the Hadronic Journal. The paper developed research originally conducted by V. F. Weisskopf and his associates at MIT, which were indeed quoted first. I therefore submitted the paper to Weissopf for refereeing, with a respectful letter (p. I—275) recommending him to provide a "generous refereeing", of course, not in the sense of scientific leniency but in scientific help and assistance, as requested by our journal. After all, the authors belonged to an important foreign Country; they had worked hard on the subject; and, in the final analysis, the research was on Weisskopf's own topics.

On February 23, 1983, I received the following answer (p. I—276)

Dear Professor Santilli:

Professor Weisskopf asked me to look at the manuscript you recently asked him to referee. It appears to me, from the cover letter accompanying the manuscript, that the authors have not submitted the paper for publication but merely sent your institute a copy of one of their preprints.

Sincerely,

Rober L. Jaffe

To understand this letter, the fellow taxpayer must know that IT IS ABSOLUTELY UNCOSTUMARY TO PROVIDE REFEREES WITH COPIES OF THE LETTERS OF SUBMISSION unless containing useful technical information. The editor merely mails to the selected referee one copy of the paper and the request for refereeing. I know this practice well. Jaffe, being a senior MIT physicist, must also know this practice well. At any rate, only the paper and the letter of request of review had been mailed to Weisskopf. But then, how could Jaffe possibly conclude that the paper had not been submitted to the Hadronic Journal?*

The most plausible answer is therefore that Jaffe's letter was an "MIT parlance" to indicate lack of willingness to review the paper, even though the paper was in their own area of vested interests (imagine what would have been the case if I had mailed a paper to MIT for review on the possible violation of Pauli's principle . . .).

In this way I reached the conclusion that CONTACTS WITH LEADING PHYSICISTS AT LEADING U.S. INSTITUTIONS ARE NOWADAY GENERALLY DAMAGING, UNLESS ONE HAS A HISTORY OF SUBSERVIENCE TO THE CURRENT, VESTED, ACADEMIC—FINANCIAL—ETHNIC INTERESTS, IN WHICH CASE CONTACTS CAN BE AT BEST HOPED TO BE INNOCUOUS.

This admittedly sad conclusion is reached not only for individual physicists scattered throughout the world, but primarily for officers of the American Physical Society, members of U.S. Governmental Agencies and U.S. politicians (see Chapter 3),

---

* I personally did not even bother to answer, but simply asked the staff of the Hadronic Journal to mail Jaffe a copy of the formal letter of submission (p. I—277). I have erased the names of the authors in the Documentation to avoid a political and scientific incident.

in the latter case, the manifestation of the expected damage can be less obvious and may take considerable more time.

The hope of this book is that of promoting the return to the only way of doing physics, the traditional way of free, dispassionate communications and contacts among free physicists. But this can only be hoped following a public denounciation of the current situation and its independent appraisal by the taxpayer.

Epilogue.

I would like to express my gratitude to the Massachusetts Institute of Technology for the hospitality granted me from January, 1976, until August, 1977, which was one of the most enjoyable academic periods of my life.

I would like also to confirm my respect and consideration for MIT which is and remains one of the most prestigious academic institutions throughout the world.

Nevertheless, as it was the case for Harvard, my commitment and decication to America and to the advancement of physical knowledge are or otherwise must be greater than my sentiments toward MIT. I therefore feel obliged to express my disagreement on grounds of scientific ethnics with Francis E. Low, Herman Feshback, Victor F. Weisskopf, Philip Morrison, Arthur K. Kerman, Clifford G. Shull, Lee Grodzins, and other MIT physicists.

The Massachusetts Institute of Technology is one of the largest, private, nuclear physics laboratories in the U.S.A. and, as such, it has used during the last decades large amounts of public funds in nuclear research, estimated in the range of billions of dollars.

These large public funds have been spent and are continued to be spent under the assumption of basic quantum mechanical laws which have been experimentally established under electromagnetic interactions, but whose validity in the interior of nuclei is only conjectural at this time.

As a result of this situation, the Massachusetts Institute of Technology has an unquestionable ethical duty to conduct an active role in the direct experimental verification of the validity or invalidity of conventional quantum mechanical laws AND relativities under open—external, strong, nuclear, interactions.

In the final analysis, as stressed in my correspondence with individual MIT physicists, the objective IS NOT that of verifying the violation of the laws. Not at all. The objective is that of establishing the laws in a quantitative experimental way, irrespective of whether valid or invalid. As a consequence, the recommended experiments may well confirm the validity of orthodox laws. Oppositions 'to this type of experiments cannot, therefore, avoid the raising of ethical issues.

Physics is a science with an absolute standard of values:

the experimental verification. Until physical laws are established beyond any reasonable doubt by direct experiments (rather
than indirect information only), those laws are and must be of
conjectural value, no matter how important they are. The Massachusetts Institute of Technology simply cannot continue, nor
can be permitted to continue in the use of large public funds
whenever dependent on the exact validity of physical laws in
the interior of nuclei that are merely conjectural at this time.

Also, experiments themselves have an absolute standard
of values: the more fundamental the tests are, the higher their
priority. This is due to the fact that basic experiments have
much bigger scientific, administrative and ethical implications
when compared to lesser relevant tests. By keeping these known
values in mind, the fellow taxpayer is then recommended to tour
the Massachusetts Institute of Technology. He will see a feverish
experimental activity in a considerable variety of branches of
physics. At times, the experiments attempt the achievement of
new knowledge, but in the greatest majority of the cases, the experiments deal with refinements of existing knowledge. The
value of experiments done or currently under way at MIT is
unquestionable, and not the issue here. The fellow taxpayer is
instead suggested to compare the experiments running at MIT
and those on the basic physical laws, such as the test on the
rotational symmetry or on Pauli's exclusion principle or on
Einstein's special relativity (Section 1.7). Under all standards
of true science (that is, excluding academic politics), it is evident that the importance of the tests of the basic physical laws
is such to dwarf all other conventional experiments that can
possibly be on at MIT. But then, this situation cannot but raise
issues of scientific ethics.*

When, in addition to all that, fundamental tests create a
manifestly large problem of scientific accountability vis–a–vis
the taxpayer, and have potentially important scientific, economic
and military implications, then one cannot but raise severe reservations on the vested, academic–financial–ethnic interests at
MIT that have prevented the conduction of the tests until now.

No American resident or citizen can consider him/herself
a truly free and responsible member of this society, unless he/she
has the courage to denounce publicly the situation, once aware
of it, and participate in its public scrutiny.

---

*
Academicians are known to be capable of masterpieces in the adulteration
of facts. I would like here to recall a crucial scientific profile, from Sections
1.6 and 1.7, according to which the true experimental tests of basic laws demands open strong conditions, such as measures on ONE hadron under
EXTERNAL strong interactions, exactly as it was done to establish the
same laws under electromagnetic interactions. Thus, if the fellow taxpayer
is approached by an academician with a river of evidence on the validity of
conventional laws for a closed–isolated strong system, academic mumbo–
jumbo or scientific corruption should be suspected.

Unfortunately, MIT has inflicted on itself, as well as on the U.S. physics community, considerable scientific damage. All the various episodes reported in this book (and more) are well known to several academic circles in the U.S.A. and abroad. They were known long before the appearance of this book, which has merely brought the episodes to the attention of the taxpayer. As a consequence of this situation, I do not know whether it is appropriate for MIT to initiate, at this time, tests of basic physical laws and relativities. As an internationally known physicist told me: *"I will not believe in possible experiments at MIT on the rotational and other basic symmetries* **even if claiming violation"** [emphasis mine].

What is therefore needed for MIT and other important academic institutions and national laboratories in the U.S. is, first of all, to regain the confidence by independent observers on the implementation of strict codes of scientific ethics via concrete, visible, public actions (such as the firing of members, irrespective of their seniority, rank and ethnic affiliations, in case caught with scientifically unethical behaviour). Only then, after regaining the ethical credibility, the tests of fundamental physical laws can be effectively conducted, and their results accepted by the national and international scientific community.

But . . . ., my personal opinion on the matters is insignificant. Equally insignificant is the personal opinion by F. E. Low, H. Feshback, V. F. Weisskopf and other physicists at MIT. The only important opinion is that of the taxpayer supporting MIT research.

The passing of judgment on the matters is therefore released to you, fellow taxpayer. In this function, I beg you not to be blinded by the renouned MIT authority. Perfectly rigid objects can only exist as a figment of the academic imagination, but not in the physical reality. Once you see this, the violation of the rotational symmetry for protons, neutrons and other hadrons deformed by sufficiently intense external forces and/or collisions is incontrovertible. The amount of violation for given physical conditions and the appropriate generalized theory are evidently debatable at this time. But the existence in nuclear physics of the violation of the rotational symmetry is absolutely out of the question, no matter what MIT physicists may say. At any rate, the only available direct measures are those by Rauch (715.87 ± 3.8 deg) and they DO NOT recover the angle (720 deg) needed for the exact rotational symmetry [100, 137]. This is the physical reality as it stands now, fellow taxpayer. The rest is nothing but MIT politics.

2.3: U. S. NATIONAL LABORATORIES.

When the opposition and/or lack of interest on fundamental tests at Harvard and MIT became clear, I had no other alternative but to contact U.S. National Laboratories. The objective was to solicit the initiation of experimental studies on the
exact or approximate character (validity or invalidity) of Einstein's special relativity and other physical laws in the interior
of strongly interacting particles, or under other suitable conditions.

This action was reason for considerable, additional disappointment to me. I thought that, because of their evident
need for clear accountability vis—a—vis the taxpayer, U.S. National Laboratories would be more receptive than private colleges.

Again, I was wrong.

National Laboratories emerged from these contacts, at
least in my eyes, as being without proper scientific light, and
being instead subservient to vested, academic—financial—ethnic
interests at Harvard University, the Massachusetts Institute of
Technology, Yale University, and other leading colleges in the
U.S.A.

**The gravity of the scientific scene at U. S. National La-
boratories.**

Numerous experimental verifications of fundamental laws
are possible today at National Laboratories (Section 1.7). For
the sake of this section, it is sufficient to recall only one case,
that of the measures of the mean life of unstable hadrons (pions,
kaons, etc.) at different energies (Section 1.4, 1.6 and 1.7). If
Einstein's special relativity is exactly valid in the interior of these
particles, their mean life should behave with energy as predicted
by Einsteinian laws. On the contrary, if internal deviations from
the special relativity exist, they are expected to manifest themselves via deviations from Einsteinian laws on the behaviour of
the mean life.

A number of historical, authoritative voices of doubts have
been voiced throughout this century on the plausibility of internal deviations. The argument is based on the expected nonlocality of the strong forces due to mutual wave overlappings of the
particle constituents (Section 1.7).

After a number of attempts, initial, quantitative predictions of violation began to appear in the 70's. Even though not
necessarily correct, the predictions were nevertheless specific,
quantitative and numerical. As an example, paper [101] by the
Canadian physicist D. Y. Kim predicted 14.3% deviation from
the Einsteinian law for composite particles at 400 GeV. These

predictions have been lately superseded by more accurate predictions, such as those of ref.s [35, 36].*

On experimental grounds, measures of the mean life of unstable hadrons were conducted soon after the discovery of the particles. These measures, however, generally refer to the particles at rest, or at one value of the energy. To reach the experimental information useful for the problem considered, we need the measure of the mean life of at least one hadron (and not a lepton such as the muon) for at least two different values of energies. The understanding is that the experimental resolution of the issue one way or the other will demand measures conducted for a comprehensive range of energies and for a variety of particles.

Now:
— despite the existence of historical voices of doubts;
— despite the availability of specific predictions of violation;
— despite solicitations independently made by a number of scholars;
— despite the feasibility of the experiments;
— despite the ready availability of all the necessary equipment;
— despite their low cost when compared to less relevant experiments done and/or currently under way;

the needed measures of the mean life of unstable hadrons at different energies HAVE NOT BEEN DONE IN U.S. (AND FOREIGN☆) LABORATORIES TO THIS WRITING (June 20, 1984).

The task of passing judgment by the fellow taxpayer now becomes much more complex. In fact, from the judgment of potential insufficiencies in scientific accountabilities by individual U.S. physicists and/or institutions, the task is now shifted to a much more serious subject: the conceivable existence of a conspiracy in U.S. physics perpetrated by vested, academic—financial—ethnic interests to prevent the experimental resolution of

---

*The fellow taxpayer should recall from Chapter 1 that the possible internal deviations have been proved to be compatible with the exact validity of the special relativity for the dynamical evolution of the center of mass of the particles. Stated differently, the well known exact validity of the special relativity for the motion, say, of a pion in a particle accelerator constitutes no evidence whatsoever, not even indirect, on the validity of the same relativity for the interior dynamics, which could therefore follow structurally more general laws. This occurrence can be inferred from a mere observation of our physical reality. For instance, the validity of Galilei's relativity for the dynamical evolution of the center—of—mass of our Earth in the solar system is fully compatible with the manifest violation of the same relativity for interior trajectories, such as satellites during re—entry, damped spinning tops, etc. (Sections 1.3 and 1.4).

☆See Appendix A for the situation at CERN, Geneva, Switzerland.

the validity or invalidity of Einstein's special relativity in the physical reality.

I present below my case with the understanding that it is not unique.

My first appeal to Wolfgang K. H. Panofsky, then Director of the Stanford Linear Accelerator Center (SLAC).

When I arrived at Harvard in September, 1977, one of the first preprints that caught my eyes was paper [101] by Kim. The preprint had been written at SLAC, while Kim was spending a leave from Canada. When, in 1978, I realized the opposition and/or lack of interest in the Cantabridgean physics community on the tests of the special relativity, I wrote a long, passionate appeal to W. K. H. Panofsky to initiate active experimental studies of the problem at SLAC. The letter (seven pages long with numerous scientific enclosures) was mailed on July 19, 1978, (p. I–360).

On July 27, 1978, I received a letter from Panofsky (p. I–373) which, even though courteous, was scientifically vacuous in my view. Panofsky essentially qualified my recommendations to conduct basic experiments with the judgment that I *"profoundly misinterpreted both the experimental status of elementary particle physics and the methods of conducting experimental investigations"*. My specific reference to Kim's paper written at his laboratory; my insistence on the evident, primary relevance of these tests over the experiments then going on at SLAC; etc.; all these appeals resulted to be useless. THE NEEDED EXPERIMENTS WERE NOT CONSIDERED THEN, THE SUBSEQUENT YEAR, AND THE YEAR AFTER THAT, NOR ARE THEY GOING ON THERE NOW.

The true understanding of the passionate character of my letter to Panofsky demands the knowledge of the fact that, at the time of drafting and re–drafting the letter in early July, 1978, I was unemployed since the preceding month of September, 1977, while being the recipient of a DOE contract, and while being prohibited to draw my salary from my own grant by senior Harvard physicists.

My first appeal to R. R. Wilson, then Director of the Fermi National Acceleration Laboratory (FERMILAB).

Essentially the same letter and enclosures mailed to Panofsky on July 19, 1978, were also mailed to Wilson at FERMILAB jointly with additional material and letters to the theoretical division of the laboratory.

Wilson answered on September 27, 1978, (p. I–382) informing me that he was no longer the director of FERMILAB (a position assumed by L. M. Lederman), and that *"there seems to be little point in trying". . ."to answer the questions you have raised".* The remaining part of Wilson's letter dealt with the following, admittedly harsh criticisms of FERMILAB'S theoretical division I had candidly voiced to U. D. I. Abarbanel there, in a letter of July 19, 1978, (p. I–371)

"I do feel obliged to clearly and openly express my utmost concern on the current conduction, operation and policy of the Theoretical Division of FERMILAB. I believe that this division is:

— *monopolistic, in the sense that it has only conducted research based on the conjecture that quarks are the constituents of hadrons;*

— *unbalanced, because of the literal lack of diversification of studies on the fundamental problem of contemporary physics; and,*

— *of marginal effectiveness, in the sense that the virtual entire theoretical production on the problem of hadron structure conducted in this division in recent times is devoted to minute aspects along mere opinions by groups of physicists, without any direct consideration of truly fundamental physical problems.*

For more details on my view, you may consult my recent letter to Professor WILSON, copy of which is enclosed."

To understand these words, one must keep in mind that FERMILAB carries the name of Enrico Fermi. The lab therefore had (and still has) a truly special meaning for me. I was sincerely interested in seeing FERMILAB remain as the forerunner of novel physical knowledge. My language was therefore studiously challenging and provocative in the hope of stimulating some suitable action, by therefore preventing the occurrences I was experiencing at Harvard at that time.

The best way for FERMILAB to remain the leading experimental laboratory in particle physics was given, in my view, by the inclusion of truly fundamental experimental tests, those of basic physical laws. I reasoned that, at that time (mid 1978), we had already discovered what is often called a "zoo" of particles (over one hundred of them). Besides the discovery of a few additional ones (such as the so—called W's and the Z^0), the push toward the discovery of new particles was loosing scientific interest . Whether sooner or later, the search for new particles had to leave the way for more fundamental inquiries. The test of basic quantum mechanical laws and relativities is of evident, much bigger scientific interest than the search of new particles, besides being of comparatively much less expensive.

At any rate, long before 1978, FERMILAB possessed in house all the necessary equipment for the resolution of the existence or lack of existence of deviations from the special relativity in the behaviour of the mean life of unstable mesons at different energy. How could FERMILAB possibly remain insensitive to the experiment, particularly when taking into account the large scientific accountability vis–a–vis the taxpayer?

Above all, I was concerned for the freedom of scientific inquiry at FERMILAB and for its independence of scientific thought from vested interests at outside colleges. I saw such freedom and independence as prerequisites for genuinely novel achievements.

Wilson commented on my letter to Abarbanel by saying that (p. I–382)

"You do make some pretty harsh charges regarding our Theory Department. Generally speaking, we have tried to hire the best people available based on the advice of the best theorists in the country. A broad range of theorists come to visit Fermilab for various periods to supplement the efforts of the Fermilab theorists. Having done that, as Director, it would never occur to me to try to influence or restrict their work. Although the tragic death of Ben Lee set us back, I have been satisfied with and proud of our theoretical department."

This answer confirmed the worst of my fears. In fact, it confirmed that the hiring at FERMILAB was done on the advice of the "best theorists in the country", which is an euphemsim for leading representatives of current, vested, interests in physics. The lack of independence of thought and the subservience to said interests, was then a natural consequence, in my view. Needless to say, I did share in full, Wilson's reason of being proud for past achievements. But the reason for my concern was the future. There was no doubt in my mind that, if the control of FERMILAB by vested interests in primary academic institutions was permitted to propagate to the level of jobs, programming and scientific output, the laboratory would decay with the inevitable decay of the vested interested controlling it or not keep up with the pace of advances, IRRESPECTIVE OF THE AMOUNT OF PUBLIC FUNDS POURED INTO IT. To my sincere disappointment, time is apparently proving me right.

I feel obliged to present my apologies here to Wilson, Abarbanel, and other colleagues at FERMILAB. I would like to appeal to their understanding of the harshness that senior physicists at Harvard were forcing upon my children and my wife at the time of our correspondence. I also want to admit the insufficiencies and decifiencies of my presentation.

Nevertheless, Wilson, Abarbanel, and others at FERMILAB have apparently failed to understand my concern and, at any rate, they made no effort in trying to understand it.

One thing is certain. Exactly as it had occurred at SLAC, FERMILAB DID NOT INITIATE ACTIVE STUDIES OF THE EXPERIMENTAL VERIFICATION OF EINSTEIN'S SPECIAL RELATIVITY AND OTHER BASIC LAWS FOLLOWING MY APPEAL OF 1978, NOR DID THEY FOLLOWING THE SUBSEQUENT APPEALS BY MYSELF AND OTHERS.

The rather perfect alignment between SLAC and FERMI-LAB on one side, and the opposition I was experiencing at private colleges on the other side, creates the difficult task for the taxpayer indicated earlier: to ascertain whether or not we have been facing a conspiracy by vested interests to prevent the experimental verification of the special relativity in particle physics.

My first appeal to G. H. Vineyard, then Director of the Brookhaven National Laboratory.

The same letter of July 19, 1978, mailed to Panofsky at SLAC and Wilson at FERMILAB was mailed also to Vineyard at Brookhaven with additional material. I thought that most of the argumentations, particularly the moderate costs for fundamental tests could re—propel Brookhaven to the frontier of advances.

My appeal to Vineyard was perhaps even more pertinent than those to Wilson and Panofsky. In fact, Brookhaven was suffering from a comparative decay in scientific output and relevance, not only with respect to comparable foreign laboratories, but also with respect to other U.S. laboratories. Also, while SLAC and FERMILAB had been equipped with advanced machines, Brookhaven had been somewhat left behind in technological refurbishing.

As a result, SLAC and FERMILAB had, in 1978, a realistic possibility of remaining at the forefront of advances in particle physics via conventional tests (this possibility more lately proved to be erroneous). Brookhaven, however, was lacking even such a possibility evidently because of lack of the machines.

As a result of this situation, the ONLY possible rebirth I foresaw for Brookhaven National Laboratory was the return to the true values of physics: test the fundamental physical laws. In fact, the cost of basic experiments was minute when compared to those of others, while the scientific output could have been potentially substantial. It is appropriate to bring again to the taxpayer's attention the following facts regarding the test of the rotational symmetry via neutron interferometry [100, 139]. The experiment can be done with an amount of money of the order of $ 100,000, which is a fraction of the cost of experiments generally conducted in particle physics. On the other side, a confirmation of measures [100, 139] regarding the breaking of the rotational symmetry (with consequential breaking of the special relativity) would have scientific implications so vast to promote quite likely a new scientific renaissance (recall that a generalization of the rotational symmetry demands a corresponding generalization of the virtual entirety of contemporary physics).

Owing to these evident possibilities, and sincerely committed to provide my contribution for the future well being of the laboratory, I approached Vineyard with a scientific fervor even greater than that I felt for Wilson and Panofsky.

But . . . ., Vineyard did not acknowledge my appeal of 1978. The appeals I submitted the subsequent years, not only to Vineyard, but to each member of the executive staff of the laboratory also remained totally unacknowledged. In my eyes, this indicated only one thing: the lack of scientific courage to conduct fundamental experimental tests even if opposed by senior physicists at Harvard, MIT, and at other leading colleges. My dream of contributing to the initiation at Brookhaven of a scientific renaissance without large budgetary increases was doomed.

The second appeal to Panofsky at SLAC, Wilson at FERMILAB and Vineyard at BROOKHAVEN.

On May 7, 1979, I made a second appeal to Panofsky, Wilson and Vineyard in their capacity of directors of national laboratories, with particular reference to the following passage (pp. I–391–394)

"I would like to take the liberty of warmly encouraging again the initiation [at your laboratory] of studies on the experimental verification of the basic physical laws currently used in strong interactions, with particular reference to Einstein's special relativity and Pauli's exclusion principle. Even the activation of an initial feasibility study at your laboratory would be invaluable, provided that its conduction is not restricted to quark supporters only.

I am confident that you will see that the protraction of the current situation in hadron physics may invite a crisis. I am referring here to the current investments of truly large amounts of money on strong interactions, all based on the mere belief of the validity of the basic laws, without jointly conducting their experimental verification. Quite frankly, I am seriously concerned that the protraction of such a situation may imply a process to our scientific accountability.

I think that we still have time to prevent further deteriorations. But we simply cannot continue to effectively conduct studies in hadron physics on the basis of mere beliefs by individual physicists on fundamental issues. The return to the traditional conduction of physics, that via experiments, is, in my humble view, much needed and needed soon."

No acknowledgment was ever received from any of them. Sometime later, J. Ballam of SLAC resigned as a member of the Editorial Council of the Hadronic Journal (p. I–395).

The last appeal in 1981 to all officers of all U. S. National Laboratories.

On July 2, 1984, I mailed an additional, final appeal to all officers of SLAC, FERMILAB and BROOKHAVEN, as well as of: the Oak Ridge National Laboratory; the Lawrence Berkeley

National Laboratory; and the Los Alamos National Laboratories. The appeal (essentially the same with the same enclosures for all) included the passage (pp. I–398–415)

During the past years, I have contacted you at the rate of less than once per year to solicit the initiation at your laboratory of experimental studies on the validity or invalidity for the strong interactions of the basic physical laws of the electromagnetic ones, with particular reference to Einstein's special relativity, Pauli's exclusion principle, and other basic laws.

This is my letter of soliciation for 1981.

The appeal passed to a number of elaborations and information pertinent to the problem, and added:

"I have recalled these known points to stress the complexity of the problem underlying my proposal to you. In fact, my proposal ultimately calls for direct measures under strong interactions, which is not an easy task. Yet, the need to initiate at least feasibility studies is much pressing, and increasing in time. Following several international conferences on the subject, and countless articles, the open character of the basic laws under strong interactions is too well known to be continued to be ignored by experimentalists in high energy physics; the human and financial resources we currently spend in the development of the theory of the strong interactions are too huge to justify ignorance of the fundamental aspects without risking dangerous administrative unbalances; and the implications of the knowledge advocated (e.g., for the controlled fusion) are too serious to prevent the accumulation of a need of potentially crushing and definitely unpredictable consequences."

Panofsky answered on July 13, 1981, with the following letter (p. I–420)

Dear Professor Santilli:

Thank you very much for your letter of July 2 which you describe as the annual letter "to solicit the initiation at SLAC of experimental studies on the validity or invalidity for the strong interactions of . . ."

You correctly refer to the fact that the experimental information is still preliminary; in fact all experimental information is preliminary in the sense that it can and will be superceded by newer results. You also say "All data could be manipulated to force compatibility with conventional laws." Your principal proposal is that I should convene a meeting of leaders of our laboratory and in the field to consider experiments to specifically test your hypotheses.

Experiments are not conceived or designed in committee; rather, individual initiative arises from the scientific community and from that initiative results a proposal for a specific undertaking which appears technically feasible to the laboratory. The laboratory directors have little and should have little influence over this process. Therefore the only recourse you have is to disseminate your theoretical deliberations to as wide an audience of experimentalists as possible in a manner such that they can extricate easily the experimental implications of the theory. With best personal regards, Wolfgang K. H. Panofsky

I answered by recalling that a number of specific, and clearly identified proposals were available in the literature and had been in fact brought to his attention before, such as the measures of: the mean life of mesons at different energies; the neutron–tritium scattering length; etc., (p. I–421). But my reply was evidently useless.

Leon M. Lederman, the new director of FERMILAB answered on July 28, 1981, with the following letter (p. I–422)

Dear Dr. Santilli:

Your letter of 2 July has raised procedural problems we have no way of addressing. This Laboratory provides facilities for carrying out experiments in High Energy Physics — orthodox or not — as long as the Physics Advisory Committee deems the proposal of sufficient scientific merit.

The main point is that this Laboratory does not do experiments. These are proposed to us by users groups at Harvard, Caltech, and some 100 institutions in the U.S. and abroad. We would be happy to receive unorthodox proposals for research to which we can react. We do not have any mechanism to set up committees to address the kind of tasks you outline. This would have to be done at your initiative outside of the activities of Fermilab.

Sincerely,
Leon M. Lederman

I answered on August 12, 1981, with the following comments (p. I–423)

Dear Dr. Lederman,

I would like to express my appreciation for your kind letter of July 28, 1981. However, permit me the liberty of expressing concern for its content.

Truly large financial and human resources have been spent through the years and are currently spent at FERMILAB in strong interactions, all under the assumption of the validity of conventinal laws, and despite the knowledge, repeated through the years, that possible modifications of the basic laws imply such technical consequences to result in different numbers for the same experiments. The seriousness of the problem is then self–evident.

On my part, I have simply accomplished the scientific duty of bringing to the attention of Fermilab (to Dr. Wilson first, and now to you) the existence of a rapidly growing community of scientists and observers calling for the experimental verification of the basic laws, irrespective of its result (whether in favor or against), as well as, perhaps equally importantly, the achievement of a more balanced use of public funds.

My concern for FERMILAB has been increased considerably by your letter because Harvard, Caltech, and all the other academic Institutions you mention are not responsible for the situation. In fact, these institutions have good reasons to resist any intrusion in their own internal decisional processes. As a result, the entirety of the responsibility of the situation is viewed to rest on you, as well as all the other executives at FERMILAB and other national laboratories. The fact that, according to your letter, FERMILAB does not have mechanisms to set up committees of study, can aggravate the situation, but cannot eliminate your responsibility. To be specific, if fifty colleges propose independently exactly the same experiment, they infringe no rule. It is the responsibility of bodies such as FERMILAB to prevent that public funds are wasted by unnecessarily repeating the same experiment fifty times. If all the colleges affilated with FERMILAB abstein from proposing a needed experiment, they also violate no rule. In fact, if the experiment is needed to provide credibility to others, or for any other scientific reason, its promotion is expected from laboratories such as FERMILAB.

It is usually difficult to predict the future, and it is more so in this case. This means that everything may continue to function smoothly and orderly for years, or a serious crisis may be triggered a few months from now by malcontent or other unforeseeable reasons, particularly in this delicate moment of considerable scrutiny on the use of public funds.

The following point may serve as partial illustration of the interest at FERMILAB in the basic experiments. As everybody knows, FERMILAB is famous for the vastity of its research libraries, including subscriptions to all possible research journals in physics, whether from the U.S.A. or far away places. Despite that, FERMILAB has apparently avoided, for years, the subscription to journals known for their commitment to the promotion of fundamental tests and continues to do so to this day (see p. I–431).

Vineyard and all his executives at Brookhaven totally ignored my last appeal. There is no point therefore in adding further comment on that laboratory.

One point is crystal clear: my appeal resulted to be useless. The tests on Einstein's special relativity, Pauli's principle and other fundamental physical laws were not considered then, were not considered thereafter, and, to my best knowledge, are not running there now.

The appeal of 1981 to National Laboratories was my last. It had been mailed to over eighty officers of the indicated laboratories (their names are provided at the end of each letter on pp. I–398–415). The enclosures were more than sufficient to present the scientific case. I saw further appeals as merely a waste of time and money. No additional appeal has therefore been submitted ever since.

Only a few, marginal episodes occurred thereafter. For instance, Ch. Prescott at SLAC and other physicists had released on October, 1981, a round table discussion entitled "Is spin physics worthwhile?" in which absolutely no mention was made of the experimental tests of the spin symmetry done by Rauch since 1975 or any other experiments that might indicate even minimally possible deviations from orthodox laws. I felt obliged to bring these tests to Prescott's attention as well as to the attention of the other co—authors of the report. After all, and contrary to their conclusion, spin physics could indeed provide truly fundamental advances. Prescott never acknowledged my letter, nor any of the other co—authors ever did.

Further contacts with individuals on specific issues at national laboratories also remained without acknowledgment (see, the case of the TACUP committee pp. I—436—442). The time for IL GRANDE GRIDO was therefore closing in.

The dangerous financial heading of national laboratories.

The failure of the efforts to stimulate a return to basic values in physics, has implied the continuation, completely unperturbed, of the lines preferred by vested interests in academia: the search for newer and newer particles.

But the accelerators currently available at FERMILAB, SLAC and other national laboratories are now essentially obsolete and unfit for the new tasks. As a consequence, the construction of new, truly large accelerators is under way.

As a physicist, I favor any physical advance, no matter how costly it is. But the size of the new accelerators (several miles) and their costs (billions of dollars) are so huge that it is time to compare the scientific output with the financial investments of public funds. In this sense, I cannot justify the expenditures of billions of taxpayers money at this time just to add, in case of luck, a few new particles to the large zoo of particles already discovered, particularly when truly fundamental questions on the already known particles remain ignored by the establishment in physics. Perhaps in the future, when the U.S. economy is such to permit a surplus of funds, at that time I would gladly support the expenditure.

My primary concern is of human nature originating from budgetarial considerations. The billions of dollars to be spent for the new machines will appear, on budgetary grounds, under the heading of physical research. Nevertheless, an unknown percentage of the funds will go to corporations outside the physics community. If the percentage of the funds leaving the physics community is sufficiently higher than the yearly budgetary increases allocated by Congress to physical research, the construction of the new machines will inevitably imply a reduction of funds to the physics community and, therefore, the loss of jobs by young and senior physicists.

This I cannot accept lightly. I must voice my opposition as effectively as I can. The scenario is now no longer that of greedy academic barons suffocating possible fundamental advances at birth to protect their interests. The ethical problems would be much much bigger than that, and proportional to the size of the expenditures under consideration, as well as to the human suffering because of the termination of jobs. Senior physicists at leading institutions cannot understand the latter point. Only physicists who have been unemployed with children to support can understand it.

It is a truly incredible story. What will future historians say about the scientific accountability of our society? What will happen in the U.S.A. if foreign laboratories establish the violation of Einstein's special relativity in the interior of hadrons? Will, under these circumstances, directors of national laboratories and their primary executives resign voluntarily from their posts? Or, under the circumstances indicated, will individuals have to initiate actions aiming at the identification of their responsibilities? And what about the responsibility of past presidents and officers?

The number of unanswered questions is endless. But the stakes are simply too high for America to treat them lightly. After all, we are facing a potential manipulation of fundamental human knowledge. As evident from this presentation, my repetitious appeals to executive officers of national laboratories resulted to be a failure on scientific grounds. Nevertheless, the appeals were successful in achieving one objective: to make absolutely sure that executive officers of national laboratories were fully informed of all possible scientific, financial and ethical implications of the case, in order to prevent even the most remote possibility of their saying:

"I did not know!"

Panofsky's last chance.

In March, 1983, the Boston Area Physics Calendar scheduled a talk by Panofsky on general aspects of experimental particle physics to be held at Harvard University. It was against my principles to attend any talk at Harvard for the reasons indicated earlier.

Yet, I wanted to meet Panofsky during his trip to Cambridge. I thought that, perhaps, by meeting each other and by talking to each other, we could reach some common grounds, or, in the absence of a scientifically valuable outcome, we could at least enjoy each others acquaintance.

For these reasons, I wrote Panofsky on March 1, 1983, inviting him for a meeting "possibly outside Harvard", "to exchange ideas on the orderly approach to the problem of the experimental test at national laboratories of the Lorentz symmetry under strong interactions" (p. I—443).

Panofsky never replied. The writing of this book was therefore confirmed.

Epilogue.

Dear fellow taxpayer, I have expressed to you my judgment regarding the subservience of national laboratories to vested, academic—financial—ethnic interests at leading, outside, U.S. colleges. This subservience and the consequential lack of scientific freedom, have prevented the laboratories from considering the conduction of fundamental physical tests. In turn, this has created a rather massive problem of scientific accountability. In fact, the labs could be using hundreds of millions of dollars in experiments depending on the exact validity of Einstein's special relativity, under conditions for which the relativity is erroneous, thus implying a potential waste of large public sums. I have also expressed my judgment that the vested interests apparently responsible for this situation are so powerful, that no self—corrective measure is conceivable. The vested interests will continue to control national laboratories and they will continue to suppress all possible nonaligned experiments or scientific inquiries, unless . . .you intervene. I have finally expressed the opinion that, from the alignment of various national laboratories among themselves and their subservience to the outside academia, there are sufficient reasons to fear a conspiracy of national proportions perpetrated by leading physicists at leading U.S. colleges to prevent the tests of Einstein's special relativity and other basic laws.

Again, my personal opinions are insignificant. Equally insignificant are the opinions of the past and current directors of national laboratories and their staff. The only important opinion is yours, fellow taxpayer.

In considering the case, permit me to beg you to return to the true physical values: fundamental advances occur in a given society if and only if that society permits their attempts. If a society suffocates the consideration of the experimental verification of basic knowledge such as Einstein's special relativity because damaging to vested interests, that society could be doomed. The ONLY way to establish the special relativity is by verifying it directly, and then verifying it again and again, whenever the slightest doubt arises. When the taxpayer compares these evident physical values with the scientific scene, the emergence of substantial problems of scientific ethics in U.S. physics is simply inevitable. In fact:

THE ONLY DIRECT EXPERIMENTAL DATA CURRENTLY AVAILABLE ON EINSTEIN'S SPECIAL RELATIVITY IN THE INTERIOR OF HADRONS

SHOW CLEAR VIOLATIONS [35, 36]. LACKING
THEIR DISPROOF, THIS IS THE ONLY PHYSICAL
TRUTH AT THIS MOMENT. THE REST IS MUMBO–
JUMBO SCIENTIFIC GREED OF POTENTIALLY
SINISTER IMPLICATIONS FOR AMERICA AND MAN-
KIND.

2.4: JOURNALS OF THE AMERICAN PHYSICAL SOCIETY.

Voltaire taught us to risk our lives so that dissident views
can appear in print. I believe that the journals of the American
Physical Society (APS) are a long, long way away from this illuminated intellectual democracy. I should indicate from the
outset that all my comments and personal experiences refer
specifically to APS journals dealing with nuclear and particle
physics, such as Physical Review Letters, Physical Review D (Particles and Fields) and Physical Review C (Nuclear Physics).
Nevertheless the mounting chorus of protests one can read in
Physics Today, Science, and other general scientific publications
concerning other cases (evidently not reported here), provides
sufficient confidence to extend the main problematic aspects to
all APS journals. In fact, the situation has reached such a point
that attentive observers can readily find quotations of the following type in TECHNICAL papers published in non–APS, RE-
FEREED journals: "This paper was rejected by Phys. Rev. . .";
or "After . . . .months, it had been impossible to resolve the publication of this paper in Phys. Rev. letters"; or "Paper . . .[pub-
lished in an APS journal] had no sufficient novelty to appear
in that journal"; etc.

Statement of the problem.

APS journals have acquired an international reputation of
being against the historical way of pursuing NOVEL physical
knowledge. I am referring to:
- the publication of plausible, sufficiently well presented CONJECTURES, irrespective of whether aligned
or not with predominant lines of inquiries;
- followed by their critical examination by independent scholars, also via published articles.

APS journals are today generally considered the journals most
unsuited for the submission of fundamental, potentially new
ideas.
Publication of a paper in APS journals is today generally
considered to be a qualification of the aligned character of the
paper and/or of the author(s) with vested interests in U.S. physics but not necessarily a qualification of physical novelty.

In short, I believe that the publications of the APS are the ultimate and most visible illustration of the totalitarian condition of the current, U.S. physics community. Apparently, I am far from being alone in this view . . . . .

I should stress that the concern of APS journals is not new. It has been voiced and re—voiced numerous times by several scholars and, as such, it is known in academic circles. Only the fellow taxpayer had been kept uninformed until now. That is why this book was conceived and written.

The dimension of the problem.

The fellow taxpayer should know that the problem is of such a magnitude that, nowadays, entire new branches of physics are born or are at the threshold of birth WITHOUT ONE SINGLE PAPER APPEARING IN APS journals.

Again, I shall abstein from reporting experiences by others and restrict the presentation only to personal cases. The first documented case is the birth of a new classical mechanics called, for historical reasons, "the Birkhoffian mechanics". The fellow taxpayer will recall from Chapter 1 that the systems of our Newtonian environment had been traditionally represented via a mechanics known under the name of "Hamiltonian mechanics". This mechanics is certainly effective for planetary motions and other systems with conservative forces (say, a satellite while moving outside earth's atmosphere). However, the insistence of the use of the same mechanics for Newtonian systems at large generally produces mumbo—jumbo academic abstractions of "perpetual—motion—type". At any rate, the Newtonian systems of our environment violate the integrability conditions for the existence of a Hamiltonian representation in the frame of the observer, as established in the technical literature in all needed rigour.

As a result of this limitation of Hamiltonian mechanics and following over one century of contributions by mathematicians and theoreticians, the Birkhoffian generalization of Hamiltonian mechanics was born. Monograph [10] provides a review of this scientific process.

The fellow taxpayer is now encouraged to inspect the list of references of monograph [10], or that of any contribution in the field (that is, strictly non—Hamiltonian). He/she will note a virtually complete lack of references to papers printed in APS journals.

As a further documentation, the fellow taxpayer may consider the ongoing effort to contruct a generalization of quantum mechanics under the name of "hadronic mechanics" (Section 1.6). Admittedly, the new mechanics has been proved to be mathematically consistent, although its compliance with the physical reality is far from being established at this time. We therefore have the case of a potential new branch of physics at the threshold of birth.

Now, despite the fact that:

— the hadronic mechanics has been studied by a considerable number of mathematicians, theoreticians, and experimentalists for a number of years;

— the mathematical foundations of the new mechanics have been studied at five international workshops (those on the so—called Lie—admissible formulations initiated at Harvard in 1978; see Section 1.9, and proceedings [124—125]);

— a formal presentation of the new mechanics occurred at an international conference in Orleans, France (see proceedings [126]);

— the new mechanics was subsequently studied at two workshops specifically devoted to the physical aspects of the problem (the "Workshops on Hadronic mechanics"; see proceedings [127]);

— despite the appearance of a considerable number of papers in the field;

despite all that, the name "hadronic mechanics" has not yet appeared in print in any APS journal to this day (June 30, 1984).

Papers on the Birkhoffian and hadronic mechanics have indeed been submitted to APS journals by myself and, independently, by several other authors. The point is that these papers were systematically rejected.

The ultimate roots of the problem.

In my view, the roots of the occurrence are the vested, academic—financial—ethnic interests in U.S. academia on Einstein's theories. We are therefore facing always the same, ultimate, roots for ALL the problems considered in this book. I cannot find any other "explanation" which achieves even a comparable credibility.

It is important for the taxpayer to have all the necessary information for the achievement of independent judgment on the matter. The presentation of Chapter 1 and the quoted references provide precisely such information. The taxpayer will therefore recall the following aspects:

— The Birkhoffian mechanics establishes in an irreconcilable way the limitations of Einstein's special relativity in classical mechanics. In fact, the Newtonian limit of the special relativity is strictly Hamiltonian and cannot therefore be compatible with the covering Birkhoffian mechanics. The new mechanics therefore establishes the foundations for a suitable generalization of Einstein's special relativity.

— The Birkhoffian mechanics establishes, beyond any reasonable doubt, the irreconcilable incompatibility of Einstein's interior gravitation with physical trajectories of the real world, those genuinely non-conservative. In fact, Einstein's interior gravitation was built to admit only Hamiltonian, perpetual—motion—type of internal trajectories. Not even this task was truly accomplished by Einstein, as established by Yilmaz (see Section 1.5). The birkhoffian mechanics therefore establishes the need for a suitable generalization of Einsteinian gravitational theories for the interior problem.

— The hadronic mechanics is an operator version of the Birkhoffian mechanics and, as such, it is irreconcilably incompatible with Einstein's special and general relativities. Of course, I am referring only to the arena of its intended use, the INTERIOR of nuclei, strongly interacting particles, and stars, while recovering conventional formulations for the EXTERIOR dynamics.

In summary, the very names "Birkhoffian mechanics" and "hadronic mechanics" are synonyms of nonaligned research. From the preceding presentation of this chapter, the fellow taxpayer can therefore imagine the vigor with which possible publications in the fields at APS journals have been suffocated at birth.

The most plausible reason for the suppression of potentially fundamental advances at the APS journals is that novelty is always threatening to existing, vested, academic—financial—ethnic interests, or at least that is the way possible advances are perceived by vested interests in control.*

The financial implications of the problem.

The fellow taxpayer should also keep in mind the financial implications of the problem. Only then he/she can appraise sufficiently its national character. All research contracts in physics are granted by governmental agencies on the basis of the contents of the application and, mostly, on the applicant's record of publications. The point is that the publications by grant referees are studiously restricted to PUBLICATIONS IN APS JOURNALS.

The suppression of plausible conjectures and/or dissident views in APS journals therefore implies whether directly or indirectly, the denial of federal contracts. APS publications are there-

---

*
The scientific reality is, of course, different. For instance, as elaborated in pp. 126–129 of this volume, the possible invalidation and generalization of Einstein's special relativity in the interior of hadrons may well permit the resolution of some of the most vexing open problems of current quark theories, such as the true confinement of the unobserved quarks in the interior of hadrons, or the identification of quark constituents with physical, experimentally detected particles.

fore a vehicle for the allocation of large public funds, or their shifting from one research line to another.

My own experience is sufficient to document the occurrence. In fact, as we shall see in the next section, the rejection of I.B.R. research grant proposals for mathematical, theoretical and experimental developments of the hadronic mechanics often occurred on the basis of the claim that myself and the other applicants did not publish articles in the field in APS journals. The fact that we have published articles in the field in several other REFEREED journals had no value. Thus, the systematic rejection of the papers submitted to APS journals on the conjectural physical value of hadronic mechanics, subsequently implied the systematic rejection of a rather considerable and diversified body of grant applications.

The national character of the problem.

The American Physical Society is an independent, private organization which, as such, is not subjectable to external interferences unless requested by law. As a result, I can voice here my concern as an APS member, but it could likely be inappropriate for me to express the same concern in other capacities.

Nevertheless, the problem at APS journals constitutes, in my view, a problem of clear national proportions. No informed person, genuinely interested in the well being of America, can deny this. In fact, the systematic suppression of plausible physical conjectures at APS journals necessarily implies the suppression of the birth of advances of potentially national interest , including military profiles. After all, most classified physical research started via articles in APS journals to achieve the needed credibility.

The standard of reference for excellence in APS publications.

As anticipated in Section 1.7, all papers rejected by APS journals should be compared with the current standard of excellence in the field. It is given by the so—called quark theories that have dominated particle physics soon after their original proposal by Gell—Mann [92] , Zweig and others in 1964.

An outsider would therefore expect that these theories, being the standard of excellence in the field, are non—conjectural and fully established beyond reasonable doubts. Nothing could be more fallacious than that. **Quark theories are among the most CONJECTURAL theories of our time, for a litany of reasons, each one of rather fundamental character** (see, for instance, dissident paper [49]). It is sufficient to recall here that the quarks themselves are purely conjectural at this time, having escaped direct experimental detections conducted for almost two decades at a cost of hundreds of millions of dollars, fellow taxpayer. Also, quark theories have not yet achieved the so—called strict—confinement of quarks, that is, a formulation possessing an IDENTICALLY NULL AND EXPLICITLY PROVED probability of tunnel effects or of inelastic production of free quarks, as needed to comply with experimental evidence. Current theories generally have a "qualitative confinement" thus being in direct disagreement with the experimental reality in their current formulation.*

In short (and on this point I intend to be repetitious) by no means APS journals reject plausible conjectures because of insufficient physical evidence. Not at all. If this rule were truly applied, APS journals should terminate their publications. Instead, APS journals publish selectively only certain types of plausible conjectures, and reject others.

How this selection is done and by whom? The selection is done on grounds of whether or not a given conjecture is aligned with vested academic—financial—ethnic interests. The decision is taken by the usual groups of people controlling local physical institutions and national laboratories: leading physicists at leading U.S. institutions.

It is all a totalitarian machination conceived, organized and operated in the interest of a few, in basic disregard of scientific democracy, that is, in disregard of the interest of the Country. It is mostly academic politics, only conducted on the ultimate foundations of human knowledge.

Ironically, the paper that started this editorial dynasty at APS journals, Gell—Mann's paper [92], was rejected by Phys. Rev. Letters, as well known in academic corridors. According to insisting rumors, the rejection was done via such offensive reports, to force the author into a plea not to submit further papers to the same journal.

This case, rather than being the exception, fits perfectly into the appraisal presented above, and in actuality it could have been predicted by the attentive reader. Paper [92] was one of those rare, seminal papers that can change the course of physics, of course, when seeded in a scientifically fertile community. This implies that paper [92] was not aligned

---

* In my capacity as editor of the Hadronic Journal, I received in 1979, a paper on quark conjectures whose lack of confinement was excessively manifest. I therefore submitted the paper to two referees, one with a notorious (financial) alignment with vested interests on quark lines (a theoreticians), and the other with an impeccable record of ethical standards (an applied mathematician). The former recommended publication (upon the implementation of marginal improvements grossly irrilevant here). The other indicated that "the publication in a physical journal of a paper in quark theories without a rigorous confinement of quarks, would be equivalent to the publication in a mathematical journal of a paper stating that $2 + 2 = 318$".

with the vested interests of the time. Rejection in the most vigorous possible form was then an absolute necessity, under current APS operations.

This is exactly what happened. That is the way totalitarian systems operate. We are merely facing their specialization to the case of physical inquiries.

The means for the actuation of APS editorial policies.

The fellow taxpayer can readily anticipate that the people responsible for the current situation at the APS journals are not naive. And in fact, the realization of the scenario depicted above is so sophisticated, to be impeccable at a superficial inspection.

To begin with, the fellow taxpayer should know that, in general, APS journals do not reject papers. The editors merely send the referee reports to the authors for their consideration. After reception of the revised version of nonaligned papers, the process is repeated again, and again, and again at times for years, until the authors are tired of wasting their time, and submit the paper to another journal outside the APS.

As everybody can see, this technique is indeed impeccable, but only on the surface. In reality, the technique hides the violation of a number of basic editorial principles, as well as a sizable scientific accountability by APS editors vis—a—vis the Country.

To begin, a primary duty of editors and referees alike is that of being SCIENTIFICALLY CONSTRUCTIVE, particularly in their criticisms. To fulfill this societal function, a rejection must therefore contain the detailed identification and itemization of the aspects that should be improved by the authors to reach the necessary maturity of publication. Lacking such specific guidelines for improvements, authors face an endless variety of possible, different, revisions. The chances of their selecting exactly the revision desired by the referees is virtually null. Under these conditions, the re—submission of a new version of the paper revised by the authors without specific guidelines by the referees generally results into a waste of time.

A primary means for rejecting nonaligned papers by APS journals is via the absence of scientifically constructive suggestions in the referee reports, with particular reference to the studious avoidance of the indication of the revisions needed to achieve maturity of publication. I can provide, alone, a considerable number of APS referee reports to establish the existence of this antiscientific practice at APS journals beyond reasonable doubts. Additional documentation can be obtained by numerous other physicists in the USA and abroad. The studious, specifically intended nature of the occurrence can also be documented beyond reasonable doubts, because the requests of identification of specific improvements needed to achieve maturity of publication were not honored in a meaningful way.

I have been a referee of a number of journals in the USA and aborad for almost two decades, and an editor of a physics journal for over seven years. I therefore have sufficient experience to identify the above technique of rejection with a mere glance at the report.

But, the lack of scientifically constructive contents in APS referee reports is only the tip of the iceberg. The ultimate responsibility rests, and otherwise must rest with the editors. In fact, the editors are PERSONALLY responsible for:

— the selection of the referees;
— the formal acceptance of their reports and their mailing to the authors; and,
— the selection of the subsequent procedure, e.g., whether to consult another referee.

When APS journals reject a paper via referee reports lacking any CONSTRUCTIVE scientific contents, the primary responsibility rests with the editors. Referee reports are scientific material exactly like the manuscript submitted for publication. The editor is therefore personally responsible for the acceptance of the referee report, or its rejection and return to the referee for improvement PRIOR to its official acceptance by the journal and mailing to the authors. Therefore, when authors receive scientifically vacuous reports, the primary responsibility rests with the editors.

But we are still at the surface of the problem. Anybody with a minimum of knowledge of the structure and organization of the American Physical Society knows that potentially important papers are passed to leading members "in good standing" at the society. This is a known euphemism to indicate leading representative of vested, academic—financial—ethnic interests in control of the field. The rejection of the paper, under these premises is then inevitable.

At any rate, mature editors know sufficiently well the academic, the financial and the ethnic interests of primary referees. As a result, they can judge in advance in the greater majority of the cases whether given, nonaligned papers will be rejected or have a chance of reaching the light with the selected referee. In this sense, the suppression of the publication of unaligned papers, let alone dissident views, is often decided by the editor at the time of the selection of the referee (in full parallelism of what happens for grants — see next section).

The problem, however, is so deep and articulated, that we are still far from its end. The next issues are those regarding the ethical responsibilities of the editors. However, the appraisal of this, as well as of a number of other aspects, demands the consideration of specific cases, and cannot be treated on general grounds.

My first dissident paper submitted to an APS journal.

Back in 1972, I worked with a graduate student of mine on a project in particle physics and submitted a joint paper to Phys. Rev. D entitled "Generalization of the PCT theorem to all discrete space—time symmetries in quantum field theory". The central tools of the paper were the so—called Wightman's axioms, which essentially represent the ultimate embodiment of Einsteinian ideas within the context of quantum field theory.

Since the time I studied Wightman's axioms several years earlier, I was convinced that they were evidently valid under appropriate physical conditions. Nevertheless, I had doubts on the universal validity of Wightman's axioms under unlimited physical conditions of particles, simply because theories of this type exist in academic politics, but not in the real world. The value of the possible identification of the limitations of Wightman's axioms is evident. In fact, such an identification would have stimulated the search for more general axioms, possibly valid under broader physical conditions.

My graduate student and I therefore initiated a laborious work aimed at extracting as many consequences of the axioms as possible, with particular reference to those with a potential capability of direct experimental verification. We did indeed succeed in this task, inasmuch as we generalized one of the central theorems of quantum field theory, the so—called PCT theorem. Upon achieving sufficient maturity, we therefore submitted a paper to Phys. Rev. D which essentially presented our generalized theorem, and a number of comments indicating the purpose for which the paper had been written: identify consequences of Wightman's axioms suitable for their experimental test.

The paper was immediately rejected. Yet, the referee could not disprove our theorem. So I wrote back asking for specific indications where the paper was wrong, while making marginal improvements. This type of submission—and—rejection—followed—by—a—revised—version—followed—by—rejection, went on and on, and on, for ABOUT TWO YEARS, without any flaw being identified by the referees in the central theorem. So much time passed by that, following the submission, my graduate student received his Ph. D. degree; he spent one year (unsuccessfully) looking for a job in the U.S.A.; and then left America for an academic job in Europe!

At that time, I was still very naive. In particular, I rejected the idea that academic politics could dominate the publications of the APS. It took therefore years for me to understand what was really going on. When I did, things changed drastically and rapidly. In fact, I merely removed from the paper any scientifically valuable passage aimed at the use of the results for the verification of the validity or invalidity of Wightman's axioms in the physical reality. As soon as I did that, the paper was published immediately (see ref. [140]). The price I had to pay is the suppression of its primary physical contents.

Correspondence in 1979–1980 with R. K. Adair of Yale University as editor of Physical Review Letters.

On January 26, 1979, R. K. Adair, G. L. Triggs, and G. L. Wells, editors of Phys. Rev. Letters, mailed a memorandum to all members of the APS Division of Particles and Fields regarding general editorial policies (Doc., Vol. II, p. 481). I thought that this was an excellent opportunity to voice my concern on the editorial policies of the APS journals, and to present my suggestions for possible improvement, whatever their value was.

I did present my views, but the action was a total waste of time. The reading of the correspondence with R. K. Adair on the topic (pp. II–288–507) is instructive. It starts with the most polite possible mutual language; it goes through a crescendo of identification of the problems and the scientific action needed for their containment; to reach a point of irreconcilable disagreement. The correspondence was closed via the following dry note by Adair stating (p. II–507)

"Dr. Santilli, I have received your insulting letter of Oct. 23, and I write this note as a termination of our correspondence. R. K. Adair."

Let me state that my language was as scientifically aggressive as possible, but not offensive, as the interested reader can verify. Whether I was offensive or not, that is of no relevance here. The substance of the issue is the point of real interest.

My concern was (and still is) that papers on quark theories routinely published in APS journals did not identify, even minimally, the conjectural character of the basic physical laws and relativities used for the strong interactions, nor they provided a clear separation of experimentally established facts from theoretical beliefs, thus creating the prerequisites for the conduction of physics via totalitarian authority, rather than physical veritas.

The issue was therefore the following: what are the conditions for a paper on quarks to be sound on grounds of scientific ethics and accountability? The lack of direct experimental verification of Einstein's special relativity under strong interactions is an incontrovertible scientific reality of our times. Silence on this situation MUST therefore constitute an issue of scientific ethics and accountability.

Adair never agreed that papers on quark theories had to indicate, at least indirectly or marginally, the conjectural character of Einstein's ideas under strong interactions. The grounds were therefore confirmed for the potential obscurantism that I fear to be under way in U.S. physics.

The moratorium of 1980 on the publication of papers on nonrelativistic quark theories at the Hadronic Journal.

The next episode is that reported on pp. 136–140 of this

book. the fellow taxpayer should perhaps reconsider it at this point. In fact, the moratorium followed the correspondence with R. K. Adair on questions of scientific ethics and accountability. As the taxpayer will recall, the moratorium was suggested by excessively big inconsistencies of the nonrelativistic quark theories of that time. As the taxpayer will also recall, G. L. Trigg, as APS editor, dismissed the moratorium on grounds that the deficiencies were of "questionable mathematics" (while they were instead of fundamental physical relevance, such as the violation of Galilei's relativity; the violation of the conservation of the total energy; etc.).

At any rate, my efforts to inform APS editors of the moratorium at the Hadronic Journal, with disclosure of all needed information (including an invitation to participate at a subsequent meeting where the issue would be discussed by mathematician experts in the field), all this resulted in a complete waste of time. APS journals continued to publish papers on nonrelativistic quark theories without any apparent consideration of their excessively big inconsistencies, or at least a remote indication of the technical literature accumulated in the field.

But then, one cannot but raise doubts of subservience by APS journals and their officers to the vested, academic—financial—ethnic interests currently controlling the U.S. physics.

The rejection of a paper by Phys. Rev. D to recommend the test of Pauli's exclusion principle under strong interactions.

When, on June 1, 1980, L. H. Howard, director of the MIT Center of Applied Mathematics revoked my visit there under my, independently administreed, DOE contract (Section 2.2), it became a question of principle for me to write a paper of strict nonaligned character under my MIT affiliation. In fact, after a number of draftings and re—drafting, the paper was submitted to Phys. Rev. D on October 4, 1980.

The topic of the paper was to recommend the direct experimental verification of the rotational symmetry via the repetition of Rauch's experiments [96—99] along alternatives essentially reviewed in Section 1.7, pp. 148 and following (such as, the repetition of the tests as originally conducted although with a better accuracy; the repetition of the tests with a multiple of 720 deg in the spin precession; etc.).

The paper was evidently rejected, and then rejected again, and then rejected again, via a step—by—step realization of the technique outlined above in this section. The studiously nonscientific content of the referee reports is very instructive in this case. As an excerpt of the documentation (pp. II—516—530), one can read the following motivation for rejection: *"None of the proposed experiments are substantive. Anyone can ask for better accuracy or for a thermal beam of neutral kaons. The*

Physical Review need not publish idle dreams. (We need con-structive suggestions)."

Evidently, the establishing of the rotational symmetry in particle physics in a quantitative way via direct experimental measures was an "idle dream" for this referee as well as for the responsible APS editor. The specific, detailed, experimental suggestions one can read on p. 148 are not substantial in the view of this referee—editor pair. Nevertheless, the plausibility of the deformation of protons and neutrons under sufficiently intense external fields and/or collisions is simply out of the question, and so is the consequential breaking of the rotational symmetry (see Figure 2.2.1 for a review). The validity of the rotational symmetry in strong interactions is today essentially imposed via academic power, rather than a quantitative experimental process. This situation cannot but raise "sustantive" questions of scientific ethics and accountabilities. I therefore answered with (typeset) comments as scientifically heavy as possible (pp. II–523–524).

The paper was rejected again, as expected, and, also as expected, the rejection was based on the total absence of any scientifically constructive process. In fact, the two, additional referee reports amounted to a total of seven (typed) lines, and concluded with the statement, evidently backed in full by the responsible APS editors (p. II–527), that: *". . the author's remarks on spin are totally unfounded and seriously flawed".*

All this, DESPITE THE FACT THAT THE BEST AVAILABLE MEASURES (715.87 ± 3.8 deg [100]) DID NOT (I REPEAT, DID NOT) CONTAIN THE ANGLE NEEDED TO ESTABLISH EXPERIMENTALLY THE ROTATIONAL SYMMETRY, AS EXPLICITLY INDICATED TO THE REFEREES AND THE EDITORS (SEE p. II–528). APS EDITORS THEREFORE ACCEPTED THE ABOVE REFEREE REPORT IN FULL KNOWLEDGE OF THE FACT THAT THE SOLE DIRECT EXPERIMENTAL DATA AVAILABLE AT THAT TIME (AND NOW) SHOW THE VIOLATION OF THE SYMMETRY!!!

It is evident to all that we are facing rather incredible excesses of questionable scientific practices. The natural question for the fellow taxpayer is then: How can such excesses occur these days in America? The answer is crucial for the contents of Chapter 3: The excesses occur, quite routinely, because the U.S. physics community is structured, organized, and operated under conditions of total impunity. No matter what editorial action an APS officer perpetrates against the interests of America and of human knowledge, that officer is absolutely certain of enjoying total impunity as things stand now (exactly the same situation occurs for officers of governmental agencies reviewing research grant applications; see the next section).

In this way, we begin to approach the roots of the suggestions submitted in Chapter 3 for the improvement of the scientific ethics and accountability in the U.S. physics community, beginning with all the necessary means to terminate the current state of total impunity, as a prerequisite for individuals to face and fulfill their personal responsibilities.*

The handling by APS journals of a potentially fundamental, experimental papers on the origin of the irreversibility of our macroscopic world.

At this point, the fellow taxpayer is encouraged to reconsider the case of the experimental measures by the Québec—Berkeley—Bonn experimental group on the apparent origin of irreversibility in the most fundamental and elementary level of nuclear interactions (their spin component), ref. [103]. The case was reported on pp. 160—168 of this book. Most importantly, the fellow taxpayer should recall that the experimental confirmation of measures [103] would have implied sooner or later the need to generalize Einstein's special relativity beginning with its most fundamental part, the time component.

This case is the experimental background of the following theoretical case at APS journals. In particular, the taxpayer should recall that two papers were submitted by the experimenters to APS journals, the first to Phys. Rev. Letters (which was published [103] only after the iterim reviewed on pp. 160—168). The second paper was submitted to Phys. Rev. C (Nuclear Physics), following the appearance of the experimental rebuffal by a Los Alamos group [104], and following a repetition of the original measures which confirmed findings [103]. This latter paper was rejected by Phys. Rev. C, although it was readily published in a European journal [105].

The way APS journals handled the experimental papers by the Québec—Berkeley—Bonn group on the apparent time—asymmetry of nuclear interactions is so grave and its societal impli-

---

* I should indicate for fairness that, out of the scientific production reviewed in Chapter 1, APS journals did indeed publish ONE single paper in the field, ref. [123]. This publication, however occurred after about two years of refereeing fights. Also, the acceptance of the paper was preceded by a phone call from a colleague I knew (who was not an APS editor), indicating quite clearly the extreme improbability that APS journals would publish additional papers of mine in the same field for the foreseeable future. This prediction resulted to be prophetic. In fact, the prediction was confirmed by the rejection of the paper on Pauli's principle under consideration in this paragraph. The prediction was subsequently confirmed by the rejection of the theoretical paper on the origin of irreversibility treated below. Finally, the prediction was confirmed by a number of additional episodes I did not report here for brevity, such as the submission in 1983 of a paper to Phys. Rev. D UNDER LEGAL ASSISTANCE because dealing with a rather considerable editorial insufficiency of a paper on the test of the rotational symmetry that had been previously published in the same journal (the paper, even though on the experimental verification of the rotational symmetry, had not quoted Rauch's crucial measures [100], Eder's contributions [64—66] and other papers in the field). The interested reader may find the documentation of this additional case in Vol. II, pp. 682—689.

cations so vast, in my view, to justify at least some appropriate governmental investigations. After all (and as indicated in Chapter 1.7) there are reasons to expect that, following numerous independent solicitations (including mine), the case is under monitoring by the Nobel Committee and other foreign bodies.*

Rejection of a crucial theoretical paper on the possible, interior time—asymmetry of particle interactions.

A most serious episode, which was crucial for the decision to write IL GRANDE GRIDO, and which resulted in the requests of resignation of two members of the APS editorial staff, occurred in 1982—1983. It referred to the stubborn rejections of a theoretical paper I submitted on the use of the hadronic mechanics for the possible identification of the origin of irreversibility, and the regaining of unity of thought. The documentation of this case alone exceeds the mark of 1,000 pages when inclusive of the technical aspects. It has been summarily reproduced in pp. II—516—679. In the following, I can therefore only review some of the most salient aspects. A knowledge of the background technical profile is essential for an in depth understanding of the case (see Section 1.6, pp. 101—109 and Section 1.7, pp. 160—168 on the theoretical and experimental aspects of irreversibility).

A summary of the case is the following. The paper was originally submitted to Phys. Rev. Letters on April 16, 1982 (p. II—532) under the first title: "Use of the hadronic mechanics for the best fit of the time—asymmetry recently measured by Slobodrian, Conzett, et al"; APS ref. No. LR2111 (cited numerous times in the documentation). The paper was rejected on May 20, 1982, by the editor G. L. Trigg (p. II—533). The paper was re—submitted on May 26, 1982, in a revised form (p. II—536), including rather comprehensive information. Trigg rejected the paper again on July 2, 1982 (p. II—542). A second revised version with additional information was re—submitted on July 21, 1982 (p. II—544), which was rejected by Trigg again on September 3, 1982. A third revision was re—submitted with an improved title on September 9, 1982 (pp. II—551), which was rejected again by Trigg soon thereafter. A further, this time final revision was re—submitted for the fifth and last time to the APS Editor in Chief, David Lazarus, on December 14, 1982 (p. II—568), with: additional material; the list of several experts in the fields of the paper; and the recommendation to conduct a comprehensive review, by consulting as many experts in each field touched by the paper as possible. The paper was considered a "new" one and identified with the new ref. No. LZ 2206. It was rejected by Trigg on April 6, 1983 (p. II—580)

---

*A presentation to the Nobel Committee is reproduced in pp. II—620—622. D. Lazarus was informed on July 6, 1982 (p. II—612).

The rejections implied a number of consequences reviewed later on in this section. As far as the paper is concerned, I became tired of wasting my time with APS journals, and submitted the paper to a European journal where it was received, reviewed, typeset, and printed in about three weeks (see ref. [59]).

Paper LR2111/LZ2206 therefore constitutes a beautiful documentation of the techniques of rejection of nonaligned papers apparently in effect at APS journals, that of tiring the authors via rejections followed by rejection followed by further rejections, all without any scientifically constructive contents, until the authors send their papers elsewhere. In this sense, APS editors and referees can claim victory for paper LR2111/LZ2206. Who the real loser is will be decided by the fellow taxpayer upon understanding the implications for America of the editorial practices in effects at APS journals.

The scientific scene in APS journals underlying the topic of the paper.

The fellow taxpayer should be aware of the fact that, at the time of the episode of paper LR2111/LZ2206, as well as now, publications in APS journals were suffering from a truly incredible lack of unity of physical thought and underlying mathematical structure. In fact, APS journals were (and still are) routinely publishing papers in different segments of physics with a manifest, irreconcilable, mutual incompatibility. This situation has been reviewed in Section 1.6 (see in particular Figure 1.6.3). At this point, I merely recall for the taxpayer's convenience the following facts:

A— the Newtonian systems of our enviornment (missiles trajectories in atmosphere; damped spinning tops; holonomic systems with evidently frictional hinges and constraints; etc.) possess a rigorously established NON—HAMILTONIAN analytic character; they evolve in time according to a NONCANONICAL law; and they are irreversible in the sense of violating the symmetry under inversion of time;

B— the statistical systems of our macroscopic world are also demonstratedly NON—HAMILTONIAN and NONCANONICAL because of well known collision terms which simply cannot be incorporated in the Hamiltonian; also the systems are irreversible, this time in the statistical sense (e.g., entropy);

C— elementary particle systems routinely treated in APS journals are, instead, strictly HAMILTONIAN (or, equivalently, Lagrangian); they evolve in time according to the so—called UNITARY law; and, last but not least, are generally time—reflection invariant.

In particular, while the characteristics of systems A and B are established beyond any possible doubt, those of systems C are strictly conjectural at this time (e.g., based on the conjecture that quarks are physical particles, complemented by the additional conjecture that quark confine; supplemented by a litany of additional, even more fundamental conjectures, such as that Einstein's special relativity is exactly valid within hadrons; etc.; etc.; etc.).

The point that the fellow taxpayer should recall to reach a mature judgment of the case is that elementary particle systems C are IRRECONCILABLY INCOMPATIBLE with macroscopic systems A and B, thus resulting in the indicated lack of unity of physical thought in APS publications. The lack of mathematical unit is a direct consequence. In fact, the brackets of the time evolution of systems A and B are NON—LIE, while those of papers in elementary particle physics published in APS journals are LIE.

The fellow taxpayer will recall the case of Skylab during re—entry (pp. 28—29 of this book). The system was strictly non—Hamiltonian, non—canonical, and time—asymmetric. As such, Skylab simply could not be reduced in any credible way to a large collection of constituents with a dynamics which is Hamiltonian—Lagrangian, unitary and time—reversible.

The contents of paper LR2111/LZ2206.

With the understanding that the regaining of the unity of physical and mathematical thought will demand the participation of the scientific community at large over a predictably long period of time, the primary objective of paper LR2111/LZ2206 was that of simply initiating the traditional scientific process needed for the future resolution of the issue: the publication of plausible conjectures followed by the publication of independent appraisals.

The idea of the paper was simple and inspired by direct observation of nature (rather than consideration of academic politics). Look at our Earth. Its dynamical evolution within the solar system is fully time—reflection—invariant. To see the irreversibility, you have to enter into our atmosphere and examine OPEN, NONCONSERVATIVE, INTERIOR trajectories such as Skylab during re—entry. Paper LR2111/LZ2206 presented a particle model exactly along the same lines, that is, such that the time—reflection—symmetry is exact for the exterior, closed, center—of—mass treatment, while the interior dynamics is intrinsically time—asymmetric.

The paper (quite brief, being intended for a letter journal) then worked out generalizations suitable for the experimental verification of the theory (the generalization of the so—called theorem of detailed balancing and of the ratio between the analyzing power for the forward reaction with respect to the polarization of the backward reaction).

The paper finally concluded with the apparently full agreement of the theory with the measures by Slobodrian, Conzett, et al [103], under the assumption that they refer to OPEN, NONCONSERVATIVE nuclear reactions, where the nonconservative character is due to the external nature of the target used in the experiments.

The possible regaining of the unity of physical thought was studied in paper LR2111/LZ2206 via the non—Hamiltonian generalization of the interior dynamics. In fact, this reduced all the Newtonian, the statistical and the particle layers to the same class of underlying forces: superposition of action—at—a—distance/potential/Hamiltonian forces and contact/non—potential/non—Hamiltonian forces. Equivalently, the unity of physical thought was recovered by admitting the extended character of systems at all levels, the Newtonian, the statistical and the particle one. The existence of contact/non—Hamiltonian forces at all levels was then consequential.

The unity of mathematical thought was trivial for the theory of the paper. The reader will recall from Sections 1.3, 1.4 and 1.6 the direct universality of the Lie—admissible formulation of the dynamics in Newtonian and statistical mechanics. The theory of paper LR2111/LZ2206 then generalized the interior dynamics of particles also into a Lie—admissible form. In this way, different layers of Nature resulted to be nothing but different realizations of the same, single, unique, abstract mathematical axioms.

In summary, the theory presented in paper LR2111/LZ2206 combined two well established physical truths. On one side, it embodied the well known time—reflection—invariance of the center—of—mass of closed—isolated systems of particles. On the other side, the paper embodied another well established property, the time—asymmetry of nonconservative (e.g., dissipative) nuclear processes. This is a trivial consequence of the non—unitarity of the related time evolution, as well known since the birth of quantum mechanics.

Thus, the physical facts presented in paper LR2111/LZ2206 are simply incontrovertible. The theory presented merely reformulated known nonconservative, nonunitary time evolutions for the interior dynamics via mathematically more consistent and more modern tools (the Lie—admissible generalization of Lie's theory; see Figure 1.6.2, particularly p. 95).

And indeed, no APS referee could even remotely prove that ANY of the arguments of the paper was wrong, as confirmed by the APS editor in chief in our correspondence. The novelty of the paper was evident (see also next paragraph). Its fundamental character is established by the underlying generalizations of basic quantum mechanical laws. The stubborn, repetitious rejections by the APS editors and referees cannot therefore be supported by scientific grounds in any credible way, and must be expected to be due to nonscientific motivations of academic politics.

The implication for APS journals NOT to participate in the ongoing efforts to construct the hadronic generalization of quantum mechanics.

Paper LR2111/LZ2206 was crucially dependent on the use of the hadronic generalization of quantum mechanics under construction by an increasing number of scholars [127, 133] following the original proposal at Harvard back in 1978 [14]. In fact, the interior dynamics of the theory is time–asymmetric in an intrinsic, dynamical way, e.g., irrespective of any invariance property of the Hamiltonian. In particular, the theory is based on certain generalizations of the most fundamental dynamical laws of contemporary theoretical physics, Schroedinger's and Heisenberg's equations, precisely, according to the Lie–admissible lines of the original proposal of 1978.

Paper LR2111/LZ2206 was therefore a crucial test: to ascertain whether or not APS journals were willing to participate in the laborious scientific process of trial and error which is needed to construct a new discipline. This point was stated, restated, and repetitiously indicated again, not only to the APS editors, but also to the APS Editor in Chief, D. Lazarus (see also below).

The stubborn rejections of paper LR2111/LZ2206 confirmed the apparently studious intent by APS journals NOT to participate in this ongoing scientific process, and to prevent the appearance of the words "hadronic mechanics" in their publications, as stated earlier. After having wasted so much of my time, it is a question of principle for me to avoid the submission of any paper to APS journals, until evident, concrete proof of serious ethical purges have either occurred spontaneously but publicly at APS journals, or are forced by suitable governmental bodies. Apparently, all other researchers in the field have also reached independently the same conclusion.

A taste of the antiscientific nature of the APS referee reports.

To reach a mature judgment, it is important for the taxpayer to inspect the referee reports which were formally accepted by APS and used for the rejection of paper LR2111/LZ2206. To have a first taste of them, let me recall that, at the time of the first submissions, there were only two experiments directly relevant to the topic considered:

- paper [103] by the Québec–Berkeley–Bonn experimental group claiming the existence of the time–asymmetry in nuclear physics; and,
- paper [104] by the Los Alamos group claiming a full time–reflection–invariance.

As a result of this situation, the case was unsettled, that is, lacking further runs of the measures, the experimental information was insufficient to claim which of the two papers was right and which was wrong.

As one can see, the first rejection (p. II—534) was based on the referee statement that: *"the data shown by Slobodrian et al. . . . . are not correct. A repetition of . . .[measures 103] by Hardekopf et al . . . .[ref. 104] yielded data in disagreement with the measurements by Slobodrian, and found agreement between the polarization and analyzing power, as one would expect from time—reversal—invariance."*

The antiscientific nature of this statement is such to raise doubts of potential scientific corruption in this editorial process at APS journals. In fact, no true Scientist could have claimed then, nor could claim now, PARTICULARLY IN A REFEREE-ING PROCESS, that one of opposing measures [103, 104] is right and the other is wrong. Only an intentional manipulation of basic human knowledge, perpetrated for the protection of vested, academic—financial—ethnic interests, can reach any "claim".

As a further taste of the scientific stature of the APS refere-eng process, I may recall a further reason of rejection by a referee consisting of the view that the central equations of the paper were of *"exceedingly general and elementary aspect[sic] , expressed in a bizarre notation."* (p. II—534) Besides the evident lack of relatedness of such a view, the fellow taxpayer should be aware of the fact that the paper submitted a generalization of the celebrated Heisenberg's equations $idA/dt = AH - HA$ into the co-covering form $idA/dt = ARH - HSA = A \triangleleft H - H \triangleright A$, where the symbols " $\triangleleft$ " and " $\triangleright$ " expressed the forward and backward character in time, as needed to treat irreversibility (Section 1.6). Now, Heisenberg's equations are some of the most fundamental equations of contemporary physics. Their possible generalization of any type would have equally fundamental, far reaching implications. The referee's report solicited by APS editors and backed up by the same editors did not care whether or not the proposed generalization of Heisenberg's equations was right or wrong. The referee only cared about the fact that the equations were written in a "bizarre notation"! But then, APS journals should not expect credibility from the international physics community!

Numerous additional, highly illustrative aspects can be identified in the refereeing process of paper LR2111/LZ2206. Regrettably, I am forced for brevity to refer the interested taxpayer to the Documentation, Vol. II, pp.531—588.

The lack of qualification of referees selected by APS editors.

A point that transpares quite clearly in the documentation is the manifest lack of qualifications of the referees selected by the APS editors on paper LR2111/LZ2206. The fellow taxpayer should recall that, to qualify as referee of a paper submitted to an APS journal, a physicists must (on the surface) be an "expert" in the field of the paper. Now, **the only possible qualification for being an "expert" in a given field is that the physicist has PUBLISHED AT LEAST ONE PAPER IN A REFEREED JOURNAL IN THAT FIELD.**

It is evident from the documentation that the referees selected by APS for the FIVE submissions and resubmissions of paper LR2111/LZ2206 were not experts in the field of the paper (isotopies and genotopies of enveloping associative algebras, Hilbert spaces and dynamical laws of quantum mechanics). Besides being transparent from the several nonsensical comments in the reports, the lack of expertise was often explicitly admitted by the referees themselves. Yet, the APS editors studiously accepted their reports and rejected the paper.

Note that the APS editors have no excuse here. In fact, owing to the novelty of the fields of the paper, I had provided them with a considerably list of senior mathematicians and theoreticians in the U.S.A. and abroad who were true experts in at least some of the areas of the paper (pp. II–568–573). The APS editors apparently decided to avoid the consultation of true experts and selected instead other non–experts. This illustrates the point made in the introductory remarks to the effect that the rejection of a non–aligned paper may be decided by the editor at its submission, via the appropriate selection of referees with a notorious academic–financial–ethnic non–alignment with the contents of the paper and/or of its authors.

At any rate, the demonstrable lack of qualification of the referees (see also the next paragraph) automatically implies the lack of a scientific process in favor of a nonscientific/political one.

The bottom line is that, despite the manifest lack of expertise, non–aligned papers are equally sent to leading physicists at leading U.S. institutions. This results into a further mechanism for the perpetration of current scientific control. In fact, leading physicists become arbiters, not only of papers in their true field of expertise, but also in other fields in which they have absolutely no qualification whatsoever.

The correspondence with D. Lazarus, as Editor in Chief of the American Physical Society.

As evidently predictable, I reported each and every aspect to the APS Editor in Chief, David Lazarus, beginning with the first rejection, and then continuing thereafter, until the closing of the case. This correspondence alone is per se rather voluminous (pp. II–589–645). The additional time I spent in writing all these letters to Lazarus, and gathered for him the rather voluminous scientific material, also resulted to be a waste of time.

I did however learn a lot on how APS operates. For instance, my insistence on the referees being true, qualified and documented experts in the field of the paper met with the clarification by Lazarus that APS referees have to be qualified only as far as their APS standing is concerned. For instance, one can read the following passage by Lazarus (p. II—639)

"I have read through the comments of the three reviewers of this paper [version LZ2206] with some care, particularly since I do know their identities. All three are very respectable physicists, and referee no. 2, who dismissed the paper summarily, is a Nobel laureate. . . . . . Note carefully that referees 1 and 2 feel that there is probable merit in the work but clearly cannot themselves understand it sufficiently to pass judgment on it [sic!!]. Referee 2 cannot even read the paper, and clearly finds it completely 'obscure'."

The fellow taxpayer should know that theoretical physics has become so specialized that, to understand a paper in Phys. Rev. Letters, one must be a true expert, specifically, in the field of the letter and possess a detailed technical knowledge of ALL quoted references.

My reply could not possibly be graceful, if I had to be in peace with my own ethical principles. In fact, I replied to Lazarus with numerous, rather heavy comments, including the passage (p. II—641)

"In the final analysis, the selection of a (US) Nobel laureate as a referee of my paper may be seen as demonstrably unethical because no (US) Nobel laureate has any meaningful knowledge and record of expertise in the field of the paper (isotopies and genotopies of Hilbert spaces and Lie algebras)."

Another point I learned in the correspondence with Lazarus is that the APS editor in chief is not an editor! This was clearly stated by Lazarus in his letter of January 6, 1983 (p. II—637). But then, the title of the post, "editor in chief" should be changed to something else because grossly misrepresentative for the general APS membership.

The rejection of paper LR2111/LZ2206 against the recommendation of qualified referees.

A further aspect of this episode is that not all referees rejected the paper. In fact, a senior, "leading physicist at a leading U.S. institution", Susumu Okubo of the University of Rochester, New York, did indeed recommend the publication of paper LR2111/LZ2206. In fact, Okubo acknowledged to me that (p. II—567) *". . .I was one of the referees of your paper as you rightly guessed. Although I did not recommend its publication*

*to the [Phys. Rev] Letters, I suggested that it should be publish-
ed rather in Phys. Rev."*

Publication in Phys. Rev. was perfectly acceptable to me,
as stated and restated in the correspondence with the editors.
In fact, the ongoing test was to see whether or not APS journals
should participate or be excluded by the scientific adventure
under way in the construction of the hadronic mechanics. The
selection of the specific APS paper was immaterial.

**As one can see, APS editors rejected paper LR2111/
LZ2206 despite favorable recommendations such as that by a
physicist as senior and as renowned as Okubo. This evidently
confirms the apparent, firm, determination at the EDITORIAL
LEVEL to reject the paper for reasons of academic politics.**

**The request of resignation of Charles M. Sommerfield of
Yale University as Divisional Associate Editor of Physical
Review Letters.**

One day in October, 1982, in the midst of the rage of the
scientific battle on paper LR2111/LZ2206, I received the following UNSOLICITED letter from Sommerfield at Yale in his capacity as associate editor of Phys. Rev. Letters (p. II−646)
*"Dear Dr. Santilli:
The dossier on your manuscript LR2111 on time asymmetry has
been sent to me in my capacity as Associate Editor of Physical
Review Letters. My task is to determine if the referees have properly performed their jobs in evaluating the paper. In the present case, the referees, all of whom are well known and respected
physicists, have done just that. Thus, I can find no grounds for
reversing their unanimous recommendation that the manuscript
not be published in the Letters.
Best regards,
Charles M. Sommerfield
Divisional Associate Editor
Physical Review Letters"*
I immediately answered with the following   certified letter,
return receipt requested (p. II−648)
*"Dear Dr. Sommerfield,
As a member of the American Physical Society, I am hereby requesting that
     you tender your resignation from your position of divisional
          associate editor of the Physical Review Letters,
and terminate all your editorial functions at the Journals of the
APS as soon as possible.
This request is the result of your unsolicited letter of September
30, 1982, (which reached me only on October 14, 1982) in
which you misused your editorial position, you violated basic
codes of our profession, and created doubts on the editorial processing which are damaging to the APS.
In fact, you passed judgment as a physicist on my paper LR2111*

submitted to Physical Review Letters dealing with the vast field of non–Lagrangian/non–Hamiltonian, Newtonian, statistical, and particle dynamics in which you have no established record whatsoever of expertise. In addition, the contents of your letter indicates that you did not take the responsibility to become acquainted, even minimally, with this vast new field.

Episodes of this type generally admit the explanation that the editorial action is taken in the sole, intended, specific benefit of particular academic interests, or because of recommendations from members of the same group of academic interests, in disrespect of National interests for the pursuit of novel physical knowledge. In order to prevent even the remote possibility of shadows of this type on the editorial sector of the APS, you are hereby requested to resign.

You must be fully aware that this is a formal request of resignation and that, in case of its lack of due consideration, all necessary action will be implemented as vigorously as possible, as permitted by the codes of laws and of the APS, not to exclude individual and/or group action, in order to protect National interests as well as the image of the APS throughout the World.

Ruggero Maria Santilli
Member of the American Physical Society
96 Prescott Street, Cambridge, Massachusetts 02138
cc: Dr. D. LAZARUS, Editor in Chief, APS
Observers
P.S. You should be made aware that, jointly with your letter of September 30, 1982, rejecting my paper LR2111 on a theoretical treatment of time–asymmetry, I received not one, but two copies (apparently because of a mailing mixup) of the recent paper by the Québec experimental group submitted to PR–C which confirms the original measures of time–asymmetry, by therefore providing a beautiful EXPERIMENTAL confirmation of my own paper."

Sommerfield did not resign from his post. D. Lazarus (who had been immediately informed of the case) did not suggest Sommerfield to resign. A. B. Giamatti, President of Yale University, and F. W. K. Firk, Chairman of the Physics Department at Yale, who were immediately informed of the occurrence (pp. II–675–676), did not even acknowledge my letter. The writing of IL GRANDE GRIDO, as a first step toward the removal of Sommerfield from his editorial APS post, was for me absolutely unavoidable.

The request of resignation of R. K. Adair also of Yale University as editor of Physical Review Letters.

In October, 1982, I subsequently received the following additional, also UNSOLICITED, letter from Adair (pp.II–649–650), in his capacity as editor of Phys. Rev. Letters and chairman of the divisional associate editors. Adair evidently supported the action by Sommerfield on the reason that, in his view, *"Sommerfield acted, as he should, not as a referee but as an editor."* The letter furthermore specified that *"In your letter to David Lazarus, you speak of the possibility of submitting a revised version of your paper to Phys. Rev. Letters. I must point out to you that paper LR2111 has been rejected, and we will not consider again a paper which is quite similar to LR2111."* This evidently confirmed the predetermined decision of preventing the appearance of the paper in an APS journal, irrespective of any improvement I could conceivably achieve.

Adair's letter had initiated with the statement that *"I am not writing to you to object to your request (?) that he [Sommerfield] resign. The first Amendment to the U.S. Constitution gives you the absolute right to ask anyone, President, Pope or Editor to resign. And President, Pope or Editor can ignore you."*

I immediately answered with the following letter, also certified, return receipt requested (p. II–651):

"Dr. Adair,

It was instructively edifying to read in your letter of October 27, 1982, that you associate yourself and Dr. C. Somerfield with popes and presidents.

I am under the impression that you understood absolutely nothing of the entire issue of my paper LR2111 submitted to Phys. Rev. Letters. However, the position that Yale University continues to give you presupposes you have the full mental capacities to understand the issue. In this latter case, a more probable occurrence is that you simply mimic lack of understanding for the pursuance of objectives to be identified at the appropriate time.

As said countless times by now, PRL has the following two alternatives for paper LR2111.

ALTERNATIVE I. Paper LR2111 is rejected because of the clear identification of scientifically credible errors, inconsistencies, or incompatibilities presented in due scientific language. In this case, you should expect nothing more than my respectful and graceful acceptance.

ALTERNATIVE II. PRL continues to reject the paper on the basis that the available referee reports are credible. In this case, I shall oppose the decision in any conceivable way permitted by law, beginning with the filing of law suits to you and Dr. Sommerfiled, first, as individuals, and second, as associate editors.

All my efforts have been devoted to the implementation of the best possible scientific process in this case, owing to the number of observers, and of international implications, in the best possible interest of the American Physical Society.

Your letter is a total uncompromisable rejection of this orderly scientific process, on mere grounds that 'the professor says so, and therefore it is so'.

The action by you and your friend Dr. Sommerfield could be tolerated if it occurred in countries under totalitarial control, whether of political or ethnic color. It appears you forget that we are in the United States of America. If aspects of questionable conduct occurred within public offices are brought to the attention of the public at large, the persons involved are socially dead here, sooner or later. It is only a matter of time. You associate yourself to presidents, but you forget President Nixon.

Your letter constitutes the second, completely unsolicited intervention in the case. As such, it can only prove your personal, uncontrollable desire to prevent the publication of the paper, as well as to support your personal friend Dr. Sommerfield, in complete disrespect of the interests of the American Physical Society, as evidentiated by your presumptuous assumption that PRL will not consider again paper LR2111.

In addition, your letter constitutes the second, unsolicited attempt intended to falsify or otherwise annul specific agreements in regard to paper LR2111 reached with Dr. Lazarus as Editor in Chief of Physical Reviews and Physical Review Letters.

In view of these and other circumstances, I am hereby requesting (sic) that you also resign from your editorial post at the Physical Review Letters, and terminate all your associations with the Journals of the American Physical Society.

Finally, I must take all possible precautions, in the interest of the American Physical Society, to truncate this insanity of unsolicited interventions in the orderly scientific process regarding paper LR2111, beginning with formal requests to the appropriate bodies to initiate investigative committees.

Ruggero Maria Santilli, Member of the American Physical Society cc: Drs. A. B. GIAMATTI and F. W. K. FIRK, Yale University; Drs. D. LAZARUS, G. TRIGG, G. J. DREISS, and D. NORD-STROM, Phys. Rev. and Phys. Rev. Lett.; selected observers."

Adair answered with a letter dated November 12, 1982 (pp. II–652–653), containing the following passages

"I rejected your paper because I decided that the objectives of the journal would be better served by other selections.". . ."the final responsibility for the acceptance or rejection of papers is mine and you may conclude that what disagreements you have with the Editors —— and Associate Editors —— are disagreements with me. As for your 'request' that I resign; after more than four years at this job I have asked to be relieved in the fullness of time but, for the moment, I have more work to do and must reluctantly reject that request."

Thus, Adair confirmed in writing what I had suspected since the beginning, that Trigg was merely serving his name, while Adair was the true, ultimate editor responsible for paper LR2111/LZ2206. This multiplied the reasons of my determination to undertake any action permitted by law so that Adair and his friend Sommerfield terminate all their present and future editorial functions at the APS. IL GRANDE GRIDO is only the first step intended to inform the widest possible scientific community in all different languages, as well as to set the necessary record for the only judgment that truly counts in scientific matter: that by posterity.

Evidently, I did not even bother to write again to Adair. Nevertheless, I did write to Lazarus at the APS and to Giamatti and Firk at Yale University, by providing all the necessary information and documentation.

The elaboration of one aspect of my request of resignation to Adair may be of relevance for the fellow taxpayer. It is the passage indicating that the actions by Adair and Sommerfield annulled specific agreements I had reached with the APS editor in chief. In essence, during a phone conversation in September, 1982, I had proposed Lazarus to pause in the consideration of paper LR2111/LZ2206 for a couple of months or more, to give time to Phys. Rev. C (Nuclear Physics) to consider the new experimental paper in time–asymmetry submitted by the Québec–Berkeley–Bonn experimental group to rebuff the Los Alamos measures [104]. I had been informed of this submission directly by the authors. Also, this is exactly the experimental paper that Sommerfield's letter had inadvertently included.

Since there were experimentalists in three Countries (Canada, U.S.A. and West Germany) submitting an EXPERIMENTAL PAPER WHICH SUPPORTED PAPER LR2111/LZ2206, Lazarus could not evidently reject my proposal to pause. At any rate, it would have made no difference to the vested interests to reject my paper in September or two months later. Thus, Lazarus gladly agreed to my evidently moderate proposal.

Sommerfield AND Adair could not evidently control their desire to suppress the publication of paper LR2111/LZ2206 as soon as possible, and therefore ignored the two months "truce" I had agreed with Lazarus. They "had" to convey their unsolicited rejection of the paper as soon as possible.*

---

* By no means the present section exhausts all aspects related to Adair and Sommerfield at Yale University, of which I am aware. As an example, Yale is renowned for the vastity of its libraries, by possessing one of the most vast collections of research journals on a world–wide basis. The care with which Yale's libraries are provided with funds for the updating of this record is also well known. Despite that, Yale University has always declined the subscription to the Hadronic Journal, apparently because of opposition originating from within the department of physics (where Adair and Sommerfield belong), beginning from the first announcement of late 1977, and continuing with announcements mailed to Yale libraries every subsequent year (for an excerpt, see pp. III–677). The fellow taxpayer should recall that the Hadronic Journal is one of the few journals permitting, and actually promoting, explicit studies on the insufficiencies, limitations and inconsistencies of Einstein's theories. The lack of subscription to the Hadronic Journal, which is not evidently due to budgetary restrictions, has evidently implied the suppression of the possible exposure of young minds at Yale to dissident physical thought.

Whatever the truth, a number of things are established: the APS journals, not only rejected my theoretical paper LR 2111/LZ2206 on the time—asymmetry, but also the EXPERIMENTAL paper supporting my arguments. In fact, this latter paper too, like mine, had to be published elsewhere (see ref. [105]).

It is impossible not to suspect that the reason for such a truly unusual vigor in rejections is due to the fact that papers [59, 105] are irreconcilably incompatible with Einstein's special relativity, by therefore being manifestly damaging to vested, academic—financial—ethnic interests in U.S. physics.

The specter of a conceivable conspiracy at APS journals.

But above all, the fellow taxpayer should keep in mind the rumors I have heard in more than one continent, that the rebuffal of experiments [103] by R. A. Hardekopf, P. W. Keaton, P. W. Lisowski, and L. R. Veeser at Los Alamos [104] had been commissioned by vested interests during the consideration process of paper [103], as indicated on pp. 163—168 in this book. If these rumors are even partially true, they provide credibility to the idea that the same group of people, whether APS editors or members, are responsible for the chain of events reported in this section, such as:

1— The lack of cooperation in 1979 for the identification, in the papers published in APS journals, of the unverified character of Einstein's special relativity in the interior of hadrons;

2— The lack of interest in the moratorium at the Hadronic Journal of 1980 on nonrelativistic quark conjectures because of excessively big inconsistencies;

3— The repetitious rejections of my paper of 1980 indicating the need to test the rotational symmetry while the only available direct measures show violation;

4— The apparent editorial misconduits in the handling of experimental paper [103] on the origin of irreversibility;

5— The apparent commissioning of the Los Alamos rebuffal [104] rushed up during the consideration process of paper [103];

6— The rejection of experimental paper [105] confirming the original measures [103];

7— The rejection of the theoretical paper [59] on irreversibility;

etc., etc., etc.

In turn, all these alleged, scientifically evil actions create serious doubts on the existence of a CONSPIRACY at the journals of the American Physical Society for the purpose of suppressing the achievement of potentially fundamental, novel, human knowledge that is contrary to vested interests in U.S. physics, or jeopardize the orderly scientific process of acquisition of novel physical knowledge, that via the PUBLICATION of plausible conjectures, followed by the PUBLICATION of their independent critical appraisals. The complete alignment of behaviour among Adair, Sommerfield, Trigg and possibly other APS editors, the demonstrable lack of qualifications of the referees, the lack of credible scientific criticisms in the rejection of papers [59, 105], and numerous, additional, scientifically evil aspects, are per se sufficient prerequisites for a conceivable conspiracy at APS journals.

Whatever the truth, one thing is certain: the current editorial—refereeing practices at the journals of the American Physical Society are undignifying for the United States of America.

The crossing of the Rubicon.

In one of my last letters to the APS "editor" in chief, D. Lazarus, I stressed that paper LR2111/LZ2206 was my scientific Rubicon (p. II—642). The American Physical Society should identify credible errors and/or insufficiencies in the paper, in which case I would be only grateful. Lacking a true scientific process, I had to follow what I considered necessary for the future of my children: inform the fellow taxpayer. In fact, I stressed to Lazarus that his action (p. II—642)

> *". . . .contains absolutely no light, by therefore confirming the only alternative left to physicists concerned for the future of their children: GO PUBLIC, GO PUBLIC, GO PUBLIC."*

And that is exactly what I did with IL GRANDE GRIDO. In fact, this book is my Rubicon.

Epilogue.

I feel obliged to express my disagreement with A. B. Giamatti, president of Yale University, on a number of grounds of scientific ethics and societal accountablility. My requests that R. K. Adair and C. M. Sommerfield, of the Department of Physics of Yale University, resign from all their editorial functions at APS journals because of apparent editorial misconduits, should have been, ABOVE ALL, subjected to an in depth, comprehensive, and public investigation by Yale University. Following my detailed reports, their considerable enclosures, and my offer for additional information and assistance (pp. III—675—676), Giamatti elected to conduct no action visible from the outside of his campus. This implied a *de facto* backing by Yale University to the faculty members Adair and Sommerfield in regard to their APS functions. In turn, such a *de facto* backing implied, on one side, the unperturbed continuation by Adair and Sommerfield of their editorial–scientific practices and, on the other side, the dilation of the responsibility from Adair and Sommerfield as individuals, to Yale University as an institution.

No administrator of a leading U.S. academic institution can, or should be permitted to, ignore even minute shadows of ethically questionable behaviour of his/her faculty, particularly when such behaviour invests a public function. When this function consists of public activities so vital to the scientific, economic and military interests of America, such as editorial functions at primary scientific journals, the silence by college administrators simply cannot but be interpreted as potential complicity.

For these and other reasons, no *bona–fide* member of a truly free society can remain in peace until full light is thrown, not only on the apparent editorial misconduits by R. K. Adair and C. M. Sommerfield AS INDIVIDUALS, but also on the apparent responsibility by Yale University AS AN INSTITUTION.

My scientific disagreement with D. Lazarus, editor in chief of the American Physica Society, is so manifestly irreconcilable, to demand no additional comment here. According to his own communication, and contrary to his title, Lazarus is not an editor. If this is correct, Larazus cannot therefore be charged with editorial responsibilities on the several cases reviewed here (and numerous others I could not possibly review for brevity). Nevertheless, Lazarus himself admitted to the administrative responsibility of his post (p. II–637). This is the function for which I had contacted him in the first place, and that is the function in which he disappointed me most. In fact, a primary reason for my contacting Lazarus as APS editor in chief (pp. II–590–623) was to recommend an in depth investigation to ascertain whether or not a scientifically evil conspiracy was under way within his journals along the lines reviewed above. Besides expressing his personal belief on the lack of existence of such an alleged conspiracy (p. II–623–624), Lazarus failed to conduct any credible consideration of the allegation, that is, he failed to organize a public investigation of the allegation conducted by credible persons, such as persons OUTSIDE THE APS AND WITH A NOTORIOUS LACK OF ALIGNMENT WITH THE VESTED, ACADEMIC–FINANCIAL–ETHNIC INTERESTS INHERENT IN THE CASE. Lacking a suitable action at least minimally commensurate to the seriousness of the allegations, Lazarus has done nothing but create a further deterioration of the case, by multiplying the unanswered questions everybody can readily formulate independently.

But again, my personal opinion is insignificant. Equally insignificant is the personal opinion by Giamatti at Yale, or Lazarus at the APS. The only important opinion is that by the fellow taxpayer. This book merely provides information useful for the taxpayer's achievement of independent judgment.

During the consideration of the case, I beg the fellow taxpayer to go back to the true values of this Land. **The future of America, that is, the future of our children, is heavily dependent on the capability of the Country to achieve NOVEL physical knowledge. But such a knowledge can be best achieved via the traditional scientific process: PUBLICATIONS of plausible conjectures followed by PUBLICATIONS of their independent appraisals. Particularly essential for the effective achievement of novel knowledge is the implementation of a true intellectual democracy, where the PUBLICATION OF PLAUSIBLE DISSIDENT VIEWS is lifted to a sacred level. By keeping in mind that ALL PUBLICATIONS AT THE FRONTIERS OF KNOWLEDGE ARE CONJECTURAL, if editors of nationally relevant journals organize themselves to publish selectively only certain classes of conjectures and reject all the others, they become arbiters of the direction along which the research will be conducted, thus acquiring immense scientific power with commensurate responsibility and accountability. If, in addition, the same groups of editors systematically suppress the publication of all plausible dissident views, then they commit a crime against society which, even though permitted by the current code of laws, implies societal damages far greater than those produced by ordinary crimes. The end result under these premises will certainly be beneficial to the vested, academic—financial—ethnic interests preferred by said groups of editors, but it can only be of sinister value for America and mankind.***

---

*By no means, the problems of scientific ethics at physics' journals occur only at the American Physical Society. In fact, similar problems exist also at other journals scattered throughout the world. A rather visible case is that of PHYSICS LETTERS B, a letter journal in nuclear and particle physics which is considered to follow closely PHYSICAL REVIEW LETTERS in academic prestige. As one can read in the cover of the journal, the sole editor for countries outside Europe is Howard Georgi of the Department of Physics of Harvard University. This implies, in particular, that Georgi has a totalitarian control of ALL submissions from the U.S.A. I believe that this situation is damaging the scientific process and, consequently, Georgi himself as well as the journal. I had a first taste of Georgi's refereeing in 1982 when he rejected a paper of mine via unconvincing arguments (the paper was readily published in another refereed letter journal). A documentation of Georgi's refereeing at PHYSICS LETTERS B is presented in pages II—734—745. It regards a second paper which was rejected without any visible or otherwise credible, technical and/or editorial reason. I submitted the paper to R. Gatto, an European editor of the journal, precisely to avoid Georgi's review (p. II—735). But Gatto promptly remailed the paper to Georgi, thus confirming his totalitarian control of submissions from the U.S.A. The exchange of letters that followed between Georgi and I (pp. II—736—744) are useful for anybody interested in an independent appraisal of the soundness of Georgi's (or Harvard's?) review. Predictably, the topic of the paper was essentially that considered of "no physical value" by senior physicists at Harvard University during my visit there in 1977—1980 (Section 2.1). On a rather aligned basis, Georgi rejected the

2.5: U. S. GOVERNMENTAL AGENCIES

I now pass to the outline of my personal experience with U.S. Governmental Agencies in charge of the consideration, acceptance or rejection of research grant proposals. I should indicate from the outset that the terms "Governmental Agencies" refer only to the National Science Foundation (NSF) and the Department of Energy (DOE). The National Areonautics and Space Administration (NASA) should be excluded for the reason that I have never applied to NASA for a research contract. Military Agencies should also be excluded. Furthermore, the considerations of this book apply solely to the NSF Divisions of Physics and Mathematics, and to the DOE Divisions of Nuclear and High Energy Physics, and they should not be construed as being necessarily applicable to other divisions of the same Agencies. This is due to the fact that my personal experience is limited to the divisions specified above.

The achievement of a mature, independent, and in depth appraisal of the operations of Governmental Agencies demands, among others, information on FUNDED research and on REJECTED applications. The need for both is evident. In fact, only a comparative analysis between funded and rejected applications can provide the necessary elements to achieve an independent judgment, that is, a judgment independent from vested, academic—financial—ethnic interests in the U.S. physics.

---

paper with the statement (p. II—738), among others, that *"I do not know whether your whole program makes any sense because I have not studied it deep enough (although people I respect have studied it and claim that it doesn't)"*. The paper, rather brief and concise (being intended for a letter journal), essentially indicated the possibility of regaining the space—reflection symmetry in weak interactions via the generalization of the quantum mechanical unit, from its current (constant) form, to the generalized operator form of hadronic mechanics. I sincerely regret the eipsode and my impossibility to prevent it. Indeed, owing to my former editorial association with Georgi, Gatto should have reviewed the paper himself. As an incidental note, I should indicate here that the HADRONIC JOURNAL has an editorial organization conceived precisely to avoid territorial control by individual editors. In fact, authors can select the editor they prefer, thus permitting papers written in the USA to be reviewed by European editors and viceversa. Additional journals deserving an independent appraisal of their practices are: NUCLEAR PHYSICS (pp. II—690—699); JOURNAL DE PHYSIQUE (pp. II—700—706); LETTERS IN MATHEMATICAL PHYSICS (pp. II—734—745); and others. Regrettably, I cannot review my personal experiences with these latter journals to avoid excessive length. I must therefore refer the interested reader to the above quoted documentation. The bottom line is however always the same: selective publication of plausible conjectures aligned with vested interests in the field, and suppression of equally plausible, but non—aligned conjectures, in disrespect of scientific democracy and the advancement of human knowledge.

The gathering of the information on FUNDED applications is easy. This profile will therefore be ignored hereon. The scanning of articles in physical and mathematical journals will provide the necessary information (Governmental support must be listed in the front page of each article). At any rate, the information is expected to be of public domain and, as such, to be available from each Agency. The scope of this section is to provide the fellow taxpayer with a documentation of REJECTED applications which, unlike that of funded ones, is much more difficult to obtain from both applicants and Agencies alike.

I shall begin by providing the fellow taxpayer with a "taste" of NSF's processing of research grant applications in theoretical physics not aligned with fashionable trends. I shall then pass to an outline of rejections I have experienced over a fifteen year period at NSF and DOE, first, as an individual, and then as president of a research institution. These personal experiences are important to appraise the constructive suggestions submitted in the next chapter. A knowledge of the scientific issues outlined in Chapter 1 is essential for an in depth understanding of this section.*

By no means, my experiences constitute isolated cases. In fact, if we exclude the few leading physicists at leading institutions and their direct pupils, the malcontent in the physics community on the current structure, operations and staffing of Governmental Agencies has reached widespread manifestations in departmental meetings, international conferences, journals, etc. We have now reached such a point that the preservation of the *status quo* may imply lack of political sensitivity in the Country. We may disagree on what to do, but one thing is certain: profound revisions of current structure, operations and staffing of Governmental Agencies MUST be implemented.

2.5.1: DIVISIONS OF PHYSICS AND MATHEMATICS OF THE NATIONAL SCIENCE FOUNDATION.

An old, rather incredible rejection by NSF in 1977.

During the fall of 1977, while at the Lyman Laboratory of Physics of Harvard University, I received almost simultaneously:

---

*
As indicated in Section 1.6 (pp. 120–123), I did apply or contact Military Agencies for potentially classified research originating from the studies reviewed in this book. All I.B.R. applications submitted to the Defense Advance Research Project Agency (DARPA), a Division of the Department of Defense, and to the U.S. Air Force Office of Scientific Research (USAFOSR) were rejected, while other Military Agencies even discouraged the applications. As indicated earlier, all the correspondence regarding these rejections have been removed from the Documentation of this book because of potentially sensitive material.

(a)   the acceptance by Springer—Verlag (a publishing house from Heidelberg, West Germany, which is renowned for postgraduate books in physics and mathematics) for the publication of monographs [9, 10] ; and,

(b)   the rejection by the National Science Foundation of a research grant application I had submitted to its physics division in October, 1976 (Doc. pp p. III—755), precisely for the completion of monographs [9, 10].

The application (NSF number PHY77—03963) evidently included a draft of the monographs. It was processed by Boris Kayser, NSF Program Director for Theoretical Physics. Kayser's processing was formally reviewed and accepted by Marcel Bardon, Acting Division Director for Physics (pp. III—756—774). The rejection was based on referees' reports of the following type solicited, reviewed, accepted and released by Kayser and Bardon (p. III—771):

"I have examined the proposal by Dr. Ruggero M. Santilli PHY7703963 (returned under separate cover). My reaction to it is rather negative. I also thought that Santilli was on the borderline between being a third rate scientist and a crack pot and I do not think that the monumental work can change substantially my opinion. The idea of reading it thoroughly produces in me an incoercible revulsion and if you insist on it I am going to resign as a reviewer. The book is written in a pompous, immodest, self-glorifying style which I detest given also the absolute lack of physical content. In view of this criticism I find the total figure asked for the project quite extraordinary."

The recollection of my first contact with Americans, while I was a young boy in Italy, during World War II.

When I received the above referee's report, my mind instinctively turned back in time, to my recollections as a young boy, when I was among the first to greet American Soldiers who had liberated my town (Agnone, currently in the province of Isernia) during World War II. That was the birth of my sincere admiration and devotion toward the U.S.A. which subsequently grew in time. In fact, during my high school studies I noted that, having been conquered in war, Italy should have been a country controlled by the U.S.A. at least in the same measure as that existing at Eastern European countries. Instead, I was seeing around me free people among free, democratic institutions. The voluntary relinquishing of the control of Italy by the U.S.A. could only indicate to my young eyes a superior nobility in the conception of life.

The reception of the above quoted referee's report brought

me to the reality of the facts that the U.S.A. is not perfect. Nevertheless, the eipsode did not weaken, even minimally, my faith toward the country. Instead, the episode reinforced the determination to provide my own contribution to America, for whatever its value, which lead later on to the decision to write IL GRANDE GRIDO.

America is a Country founded by immigrants that continues to be shaped by immigrants to this day. As an immigrant, I intend to raise my voice as loud as conceivably possible to denounce the current NSF operations as undignifying for the U.S.A., let alone scientifically damaging to the Country.

The senseless character of the episode.

To begin the understanding of the case, the fellow taxpayer must know that, at the time of filing the application, I was an obscure young physicist working alone in my own corner. Also, at that time, I still had the illusion of reaching a "tenured" (permanent) academic job in the U.S.A. I therefore avoided any conflict with colleagues inside and outside my campus. Finally, I am referring to a period of time prior to the publication (or even informal release) of my doubts on the validity of Einstein's ideas in the interior of hadrons. In short, at the time of application PHY77–03963, I could not possibly have represented a threat to anybody.

But then, why did the application have to be rejected via offensive language such as that above? After all, the application could have been rejected via a few dry lines without any need for additional comments.

The affair remains, for me, beyond a rational explanation. Its senseless character is much similar to my experience at that time, when I was a formal member of the Lyman Laboratory at Harvard, yet I was prevented by my senior colleagues to draw a salary from my own grant (see Section 2.1, pp. 194–195 of this book).

The necessarily ungraceful reaction.

I am convinced that it is the duty of any responsible member of the U.S. physics community NOT to accept gracefully offensive language in referees' reports on technical material, whether from Governmental Agencies or the American Physical Society.

As soon as I received the above referee's report, I therefore initiated a number of intentionally ungraceful actions. First, I consulted a law firm in the Boston Area and initiated the search of a corresponding law firm in Washington, D.C., for the purpose of FILING LAW SUITS, PERSONALLY, AGAINST BORIS KAYSER AND MARCEL BARDON AS INDIVIDUALS, AND NOT AGAINST THE NSF AS AN INSTITUTION. The NSF statute is not expected to authorize its officers to accept offensive language in the review of technical material. The sole responsibility of the case therefore appears to rest, personally, on Kayser and Bardon as individuals.

Furthermore, I applied to NSF for a reconsideration due to manifest improprieties in the processing of the application itself. The hot ball was passed by Bardon to James Krumhansl, NSF's Assistant Director, via Ronald E. Kagarise, NSF's Deputy Assistant Director. In this way, the reconsideration process was formally initiated (pp. III—776—802).

Jointly, I expressed my indignation to the NSF Director General of that time, and to the highest Officer of the Country. This action lead to the appointment of Wayne R. Gruner, NSF's Special Assistant to the Associate Director for Mathematical and Physical Sciences, as the officer in charge of my case.

When, in early 1978, Harvard University finally filed the necessary documents to the DOE following its offer to support my research (Section 2.1), I contacted Gruner to withdraw the reconsideration of the case (p. III—791). Gruner reacted promptly (p. III—792) by indicating *"my pleasure and the pleasure of the Foundation"* in regard to the DOE support.

The roots of the affair.

It is evident that the rejection of the application is not the issue here. After all, NSF routinely receives qualified physical applications for sums exceeding its physics budget. My indignation was due to the senseless use of offensive language in the rejection. In fact, I saw it as a sign of decay of the Country in one of its most vital function: the pursuance of novel physical knowledge.

At the peak of my protests, I pounded Gruner with letters and phone calls to obtain more information so that I could reach the roots of the affair. I wanted to know more about the criteria for selection of the referees, and the NSF processing of their reports. In particular, I wanted more information on the referees' academic status and affiliation.

At one point, during a rather heavy phone conversation, Gruner acknowledged that the auther of the report reproduced at the beginning of this section was *"a truly renowned physicist at a leading U.S. institution"*. My pressures to know whether that institution was Harvard evidently remained without confirmation (but also without denials).

As a result of a considerable experience accumulated over more than fifteen years, I believe that officers of the physics divisions of U.S. Governmental Agencies are servants to leading physicists at leading academic institutions, not only collectively, but also individually.

Whether this is true or false, one thing is certain: manifestly offensive referees' reports must be returned to the referees, rather than being released to the authors. After all, authors are not permitted the use of offensive language in their papers, books or grant applications! It is evident that Boris Kayser and Marcel Bardon should have rejected the above referee report and terminated the use of this referee because of its manifestly offensive language, let alone the total lack of scientific content needed to pass judgment on the application. The issue left to the taxpayer is the identification of the most probable reasons why Kayser and Bardon DID NOT reject the report and submitted themselves to the referee's threat: "... *if you insist on it I am going to resign as a reviewer.*"

The litany of NSF rejections; Part A: Rejections prior to the founding of the IBR.

NSF has rejected ALL research grants applications I have submitted, first, as an individual, and then as IBR president on behalf of fellow mathematicians, theoreticians and experimentalists. I am referring to a considerable number of rejections over a period of about fifteen years. The list of rejections provided below is therefore only partial because the documentation of the early applications has been lost.

NSF REJECTION NO. 1 dated September 22, 1972, (p. III—752), of an application entitled "Investigations on a new analytic extension of the scattering amplitude". The application was connected to the paper submitted to Phys. Rev. D regarding the identification of the limitations of Wightman's axioms (p. 251—252 of this book).

NSF REJECTION NO. 2 dated July 16, 1975, (p. III—753), of an application entitled "Investigations of generalized analytic, algebraic and statistical formulations for interacting systems". The proposal was preparatory to the studies that lead to the Birkhoffian generalization of Hamiltonian mechanics (Section 1.3).

NSF REJECTION NO. 3 dated June 28, 1976, (p. III—754) of an application entitled "Investigations on the origin of the gravitational field". The application dealt with: the possible electromagnetic contribution to the origin of the gravitational field; the possible, consequential, elimination of the vexing problem of the unified field theory; and the proposal of experiments conceived to test, at some future time, the foundations of current gravitational theories,* along the lines discussed in Sec-

---

*As one can read in ref. [40], the proposal included the submission of experiments on the "creation" of the gravitational field of matter, via a suitable distribution of electromagnetic fields patterned along the electromagnetic structure of material bodies without any mass contribution. Once the mechanism of creation of the gravitational field is understood, far reaching advances are conceivable at the frontier of imagination and beyond. The truncation of research indicated below in the text refers to all these developments.

tion 1.4 (ref. [40]). The rejection lead to my decision to terminate research in gravitation, owing to the extremes of the problems of scientific ethics in the field as outlined in Section 1.4.

NSF REJECTION NO. 4 dated June 30, 1977, (p. III–769), of an application entitled "Necessary and sufficient conditions for the existence of a Lagrangian in Newtonian mechanics and field theory". This is the sample rejection reviewed at the beginning of this section.

NSF REJECTION NO. 5 of support for the "Third Workshop on Lie-admissible formulations"(see p.III–803 for the application; the papers of the rejection could not be identified at the time of printing this book and are not present in the Documentation). For the taxpayer's convenience, let me recall that this is the international meeting that Harvard University prohibited to keep on campus (pp. 200–202 of this book). Also, this is the meeting that initiated our experimental study of the insufficiencies of Einstein's ideas in the interior of hadrons (see the contributions by experimentalists in the third volume of the proceedings, ref. [125]). The application was processed by L. P. Bautz, as Deputy Director of the NSF Division of Physics. Boris Kayser, however, was still in charge of the NSF theoretical physics programs. A short time before the initiation of the Workshop, certain of the NSF rejection because of the lack of decision with sufficient notice,* I called Kayser at NSF pressing for a resolution of the case. Kayser acknowledged the rejection. I asked him whether he was aware of the fact that the application dealt with the SOLE meeting in the U.S.A. which was critical of orthodox doctrines for hadrons. Kayser answered *"Yes".* I still remember vividly my comment: *"If NSF were to disperse 99% of the budgetary funds in strong interactions to research aligned with quark conjectures, and 1% to non–aligned research, I see no problem. However, since NSF disperses 100% of the funds to quark oriented research and absolutely nothing to dissident views, I see the existence of a BIG, BIG PROBLEM OF TOTALITARIAN DISPERSAL OF PUBLIC FUNDS AT THE DIVISION OF PHYSICS OF NSF."*

---

*A rather peculiar aspect of NSF operations is that of delaying the communication of rejections of applications for scientific meetings in physics. This forces the organizers to solicit a resolution, so that they can, in turn, communicate the decision to the participants. I have experienced this occurrence a sufficient number of times (see below) to suspect a repetitive pattern. The antiscientific nature of this practice is evident. In fact, it leaves the entire organization of the meeting in suspended animation, thus providing evident scientific damages. Apparently, the practice is not implemented for meetings which, even though not funded, are nevertheless aligned with vested interests in academia. Instead, it appears that the practice is implemented specifically for meetings, such as those I applied for, which are manifestly non–aligned with vested interests. This aspect alone is so diversified, to require a separate, detailed investigation.

The litany of NSF rejections; Part B: Rejection of the primary IBR application.

NSF REJECTION NO. 6 dated March 3, 1983, (p. III—861), of the primary, I.B.R. group application entitled "Studies on Hadronic Mechanics", NSF number PHY83—00195. The NSF officer in charge of the application was this time S. Peter Rosen, Program Associate of the Theoretical Physics Program. The NSF officer that reviewed and accepted Rosen's processing of the application was, again, Marcel Bardon, this time as Director of the Division of Physics (pp. III—847—868).*

The application dealt with comprehensive, mathematical, theoretical, and experimental studies on the construction of the so—called hadronic generalization of quantum mechanics (a new mechanics specifically conceived for the interior of hadrons as outlined in Chapter 1, Sections 1.6 and 1.7 in particular). The application involved a number of senior mathematicians, theoreticians and experimentalists, whether formal members or only affiliated to the I.B.R. Part of the application included the organization of workshops and conferences, as done for the preceding, fully successful research program that lead to the construction of the Birkhoffian generalization of the classical Hamiltonian mechanics. The application was divided into branches, essentially dealing with nuclear physics, particle physics and experimental physics, each branch with its own leader. The application indicated the possibility that hadronic mechanics, rather than being against physical knowledge acquired via quark conjectures, could be of assistance in the future resolution of some of their problematic aspects, such as the achievement of a strict confinement of quarks or the identification of the quark constituents with physical, directly detected, particles (see pp. 126—129 of this book). As I.B.R. president, my role would have been essentially that of coordinator of the various branches of the project and co—organizer of the various meetings.

The note of rejection, signed as usual by Marcel Bardon, was dated March 3, 1983, (p. III—861). The reading of the referees' reports (pp. III—862—863) is quite instructive.

An excerpt from the first referee's report (p. III—862):

". . . I fail to see any results that are remotely persuasive or inspiring to the physicists at large. The author [sic] quotes one experimental paper on time reversal violation as a support for his ideas, but that paper is now discredited . . . [by] Hardekopf et al. Phys. Rev. C25, 1090 (1982)."

To understand this comment in full, it is essential for the fellow taxpayer to have a knowledge of the scientific background considered previously with particular reference to: pp. 101—109 (lack of unity of contemporary physical and mathematical thought); pp. 160—168 (the apparent commissioning by vested

---

*All names of I.B.R. applicants have been deleted in the Documentation.

interests of the experiment by Hardekopf et al quoted by the referee, during the consideration process by Physical Review Letters of the original results of the Québec—Berkeley—Bonn group, ref. [103]); pp. 257—273 (rejection by APS journals of a theoretical and an additional experimental paper on time reflection violation); pp. 261—262 (the potential scientific corruption in the APS referee process because of the impossibility of deciding at this time which of the opposing experimental data are right and which are wrong); etc.

To see further the alignment of the above NSF referee report with the APS referee reports reviewed in Section 2.4, it is sufficient to recall that the rejection by APS journals of the theoretical and experimental papers on time reflection violation, and the NSF rejection of the primary I.B.R. research grant proposal occurred one after the other, the APS rejections being evidently the first.

But, above all, the fellow taxpayer should know that the irreversibility of proposal PHY83—00195 was referred to OPEN, NONCONSERVATIVE conditions of particles, that is, conditions whose irreversibility has been established since the early days of quantum mechanics. The reference to Hardekopf et al. in the above referee report, not only was a manifestation of potential scientific corruption (for the reasons indicated earlier), but also of total lack of scientific appropriatedness for the case considered (in fact, Hardekopf et al aim at CLOSED, CONSERVATIVE conditions).

Despite these aspects, conveyed repetitiously to NSF officers during the consideration process, S. Peter Rosen and Marcel Bardon accepted the above referee's report to reach a formal decision of an Agency of the United States of America involving the dispersal of public funds!

An excerpt from the second referee's report (p. III—863): "... In the past five years, he [Santilli] and his followers have produced no solid achievement worth mentioning." I detest to be vane. Yet, the fellow taxpayer must know as an example that our group has produced an entire new branch of classical mechanics, the Birkhoffian generalization of the conventional Hamiltonian mechanics along the lines reviewed in Section 1.3. The new mechanics was named after Birkhoff (father) because of historical reasons reviewed in the original publications. While the old Hamiltonian mechanics can effectively treat Newtonian systems only of perpetual—motion—type, the new mechanics is "directly universal" for ALL Newtonian systems verifying certain topological conditions, thus including the realistic systems of our environment. The new mechanics was assumed at the foundation of the hadronic mechanics in the NSF application. Thus, the NSF referee AND officers simply cannot deny its knowledge. Yet, this scientific event was not considered a "solid achievement worth mentioning".

At this point, to reach a minimum of credibility, the U.S.

National Science Foundation should exhibit AT LEAST ONE EXAMPLE of a "solid achievement worth mentioning" reached under NSF support DURING THE SAME PERIOD OF PROPOSAL PHY83—00195. This latter point is evidently crucial to conduct a meaningful comparison among the applications REJECTED and those FUNDED by NSF during the same period.

An additional excerpt by the second referee's report: ". . . None of their papers, except for one, were published in regular refereed journals where most of major mathematical and physical works have been published." This is a documentation of the point raised in the preceding section, regarding the deep interdependence of editorial processing at APS journals and review processing at Governmental Agencies. Often, the same leading physicist at a leading academic institution suppresses, on one side, the birth of plausible fundamental advances in APS journals, while, on the other side, rejects research grant applications in the same topic, on grounds that the argument has not appeared in "regular refereed journals"!

An excerpt of the third referee's report (p. III—864): ". . .this research has been founded by DOE for the past four years. The results of this DOE supported work appear to have been nil." I must be vane here and claim that our group has indeed achieved: (A) the identification of numerous reasons leading to the invalidation of Einstein's relativities in the interior of hadrons as well as under strong interactions at large; (B) preliminary, and tentative, yet SPECIFIC AND CONCRETE GENERALIZATIONS of Galilei's [8, 10], Einstein's special [32] and general [50] relativities verifying theorems of direct universality; and last but not least, (C) the formulation of experiments for the resolution of the validity or invalidity of Einsteinian theories under the conditions considered (to avoid the quotation of others at this point, see, for instance, the experiments proposed in ref.s [49, 62] printed prior to proposal PHY83—00195).

All these aspects were reviewed and itemized in the proposal as well as in the various correspondence. Yet, the NSF referee/officers claim that these results are "nil". The task left to the fellow taxpayer is therefore that of reaching an independent judgment whether these results are indeed truly "nil", or they are "nil" only because contrary to the vested academic—financial—ethnic interests of the referee and/or of the NSF reviewers.

An excerpt from the third referee (p. III—865): "The principal investigator, R. M. Santilli, has a very poor reputation among mathematical physicists and elementary particle physicists." To appraise this statement, the fellow taxpayer should differentiate the community of mathematical and particle physics into two categories, a first one with vested interests on the preservation of Einstein's theories for personal gains, and a second one with a view of their possible generalizations for the advancement of human knowledge. There is little doubt that I am one of the few, independent, theoreticians who have proved to possess sufficient courage to PRINT their view on the possible invalidation of Einstein's ideas in the interior of hadrons. The fellow taxpayer can then decide whether my "poor reputation" is established in both groups or only in one of them, evidently the first. Speaking on personal grounds, I feel praised by the fact that I have a poor reputation among vested, academic—financial—ethnic interests on Einstein's theories. In fact, such a "poor reputation" is a NECESSARY QUALIFICATION FOR INDEPENDENCE OF INQUIRY AND NOVELTY OF THOUGHT.

The termination of contacts with Larry C. Biedenharn, Jr., of the Department of Physics of Duke University, Durham, North Carolina.

The second referee concluded the report with the following statement (p. III—863): *"I recognize only two names of theoretists among those quoted by Santilli. They are [S.] Okubo [of the University of Rochester, New York] and Biedenharn. The latter declined joining Santilli according to a copy of the letter. [A rather mysterious blank space occurs at this point prior to the resumption of the report]."*

The fellow taxpayer should know that Biedenharn was an advisor of the proposal, that is, he would have been consulted on specific technical aspects in his field. Evidently, Biedenharn had been listed in the proposal following his formal, written, authorization. I never received any communication by Biedenharn whether verbal or in writing of his intention to withdraw from the project. The referee's statement quoted above therefore leads to the idea that this referee had not stopped short of recommending rejection, but had additionally attempted to discredit the proposal and its authors at NSF, by going further ahead to the point of contacting directly one of the senior members of the proposal (Biedenharn) and securing a copy of his (apparent) withdrawal from the project.

The fellow taxpayer should then decide whether or not the affair verifies all the standards of scientific ethics needed for the dispersal of public funds at an Agency of the United States of America, or we are facing corrupt practices. As far as I am concerned, I see in the too many episodes of this type the completion of the cycle of information indicating the existence of a scientific obscurantisms on Einstein's theories under way in the U.S. physics, as illustrated in my preceding experiences at leading academic institutions, Federal laboratories, and journals of the American Physical Society.

In regard to Biedenharn, despite my sincere regrets and contrary to my best desires, I evidently had no other choice than to terminate all contacts, as I did with a certified letter, return receipt requested (p. III—876).

The rather incredible alignment of the five NSF reviewers.

Besides the apparent scientific corruption in the referees' report and their total lack of scientific content, a most visible aspect is the rather incredible alignment of all the reports toward the rejection of the application. To understand this point, the fellow taxpayer should keep in mind that:

(1) The application had been filed by a new institute of research founded by individual scholars without any governmental support. The decision to fund or reject the application would therefore have had a clear, large, bearing on the decision whether to maintain or suppress the new institution.

(2) The application was not filed by an individual. Instead, it was a group application involving an international team of senior experimentalists, theoreticians, and mathematicians in some seven different Countries.

(3) Even ignoring points (1) and (2), the topic of the application was TO DEVELOP A NEW MECHANICS, THAT IS AN ENTIRE NEW BRANCH OF HUMAN KNOWLEDGE. To understand this point, the fellow taxpayer should keep in mind that new mechanics are created quite rarely through the course of a century. Also, the hadronic mechanics submitted for development, was not the dream of a "crackpot". Instead, its mathematical existence and consistency had been independently proved by mathematicians at the Orléans International Conference of 1981, as recalled in the proposal itself. Finally, the hadronic mechanics, being a covering of quantum mechanics, not only contains the latter as a particular case, but the latter can be approached as close as desired, thus rendering inevitable physical applications in the interior of nuclei, of hadrons and of stars.

Despite these manifestly unique aspects, all five different referees aligned themselves in a truly incredible way toward the vigorous rejection of the proposal. Only inepts and accomplices will see in this a normal routine. Persons who care about the Institutions of this Land and what they represent to the Free World must do much better and be alert, if they are truly committed to the preservation of these Institutions. We must acknowledge that the chances for five seemingly independent reviewers to reject the proposal vigorously are virtually null under premises (1), (2) and (3). We must acknowledge the possibility that something was done by the NSF officers at least to facilitate, if not to encourage the alignment. For that, it would have been sufficient that the NSF officers first, selected for reviewers known representatives of vested, academic—financial—ethnic interests; and, second, the officers informed at least ONE of them (say, the most representative) of the names of the others. The strict alignment of all of them toward the suppression of due scientific process at an agency of the U.S.A. would be a trivial consequence under these premises. In fact, the mutual loyalty among members of said interests is known to be so strong to dwarf the mutual loyalty within circles of organized crimes.

One thing is certain: when an NSF referee contacts a member of the team of applicants (L. C. Biedenharn, Jr.), to discourage his participation and to secure the documentation of his withdrawal while putting all this in plain light, THAT REFEREE MUST BE CONSIDERED CAPABLE, IN THE DARK, OF ANY CONCEIVABLE SCIENTIFIC CRIME.

The litany of NSF rejections; Part C: Rejections of applications by individual IBR members.

NSF REJECTION NO. 7 undated (received sometime in September, 1982) of an application by L.L.L., a senior IBR physicist, entitled "Variational method of calculating structural properties of solids". The rejection was signed by Lewis H. Nosanow, Acting Division Director of NSF Material Research (p. III–886).

The field of the application is outside my expertise and, as such, I cannot pass any judgment here on the possible scientific merits of the proposal. There is however a human aspect that is worth bringing to the attention of the fellow taxpayer. After all, advances in human knowledge are not made by machines, but by human beings. No society has a true, long term, scientific future unless the human aspect is provided with priority over all technical issues.

L.L.L. is a senior jewish physicist who had managed to leave the U.S.S.R. with his wife and son. When he came to me, he was unemployed with a family to support. He therefore reminded me of the experience at Harvard, when the triplet Coleman—Glashow—Weinberg prevented my drawing a salary under my own grant for feeding and sheltering my family. I therefore provided L.L.L. with my best assistance, which included: contacting all possible Governmental Agencies interested in considering his proposal; paying personally all duplicating and other expenses for the various submissions (three different applications were finally selected, all rejected); contacting jewish foundations in the Boston area for possible assistance to L.L.L. (only, WITHOUT overheads to the IBR); etc. I must admit that I failed on all these counts, by therefore resulting in the impossibility of providing any financial support to L.L.L. The fellow taxpayer must decide whether this was my personal failure, or a failure of the current U.S. physics community.*

---
* As an incidental note, L.L.L. had reached a senior status as a physicist

NSF REJECTION NO. 8 dated June 13, 1983 (p. III— 911), of a proposal entitled "Fifth Workshop on Lie—admissible Formulations". The proposal was authored by four senior mathematicians of the IBR (each holding a joint full professorship in mathematics at other, large, U.S. academic institutions). The proposal was processed by Alvin Thaler, Director of Special Programs at the NSF Division of Mathematics (this is the division handling workshops and conferences). The rejection was signed by E. F. Infante, Director of the NSF Division of Mathematics and Computer Sciences.

The fellow taxpayer should be aware of the fact that in the preceding four meetings of the series, we had conducted jointly mathematical and physical research. However, as clearly stated in the proposal, the fifth workshop of this series was restricted to pure mathematics. In particular, since I am a physicist, I was strictly excluded in the presentation and in the program.

The application was evidently rejected. Again, it is not the rejection per se, but rather some of its rather peculiar aspects that are suitable for reflections. First and above all, the seniority and qualification of the applicants were absolutely impeccable. Second, the topic dealt with a generalization of a truly fundamental part of contemporary mathematics, the Lie—admissible generalization of Lie's theory (see Section 1.8). Rejections under these premises, particularly when compared to the modest amount of funds requested (a few thousand dollars), are already sufficient to motivate the suspicion of possible scientific manipulations at NSF. A number of additional elements do nothing but reinforce such a suspicion. Unlike other programs, the NSF budget for mathematical conferences was fully funded in the period of the proposal, to the point that NSF regularly advertized the availability of funds and solicited the submission of proposals in the Notices of the American Mathematical Society. **Under these premises, the rejection does not appear to have been motivated by the lack of funds.**

The fellow taxpayer would then expect that the rejection was motivated by poor referees' reports. This is not true. Each and every referee report rated the proposal "GOOD" as the fellow taxpayer can verify (pp. III—912—915). **As a result, the proposal does not appear to have been rejected because of lack of qualifications of the applicants, or because of lack of positive referees' reports, or because of lack of funds.**

---

while in the U.S.S.R. As such, he had acquired a considerable, if not unique knowledge of the condition of the research in the field in that Country. In his application he had made a reference to this aspect, by indicating his willingness to cooperate for his new Country. The last NSF referee commented on this delicate, tastefully presented point of the application with the statement: ". . .the Russian Menace can safely be ignored in the field for quite a while." Fellow taxpayer, do you think that this represents a responsible way of processing your money at the U.S. National Science Foundation?

BUT THEN WHY, AND ON WHAT GROUNDS, NSF REJECTED THE PROPOSAL?

The most plausible answer under these premises is evident: because of what is sadly known as "NSF politics" (see the comment at the end of this sub–section).

As an incidental note, I should report how we finally received the communication of rejection. The NSF Division of Mathematics had indicated the need of six months for the processing of the application. In 1983, well over the expiration of six months and close to the initiation of the meeting, I was forced to call Thaler in Washington and pressure him to release at least a verbal decision on the application. The entire organization of the meeting had been suspended, evidently because of lack of knowledge whether or not the organizers (I was NOT one of them) would have some minimal funds to support the travel expenses of a few, highly selected mathematicians in the field. After some pressure, Thaler finally acknowledged that, not only the application had been rejected, but the rejection had been decided sometime before, EXACTLY AS I HAD SUSPECTED FROM MY PRECEDING EXPERIENCE OF NSF OPERATIONS IN SIMILAR CASES. I therefore expressed my complaints to Infante, in his capacity of NSF Division Director and officer ultimately responsible for the case (pp. III–908–908). Infante reacted in a way that can only stimulate smiles. He first acknowledged my complaints with a letter in direct disagreement with the statement by Thaler (p. III–910), in which he claims that "At this time, the review and evaluation process of this proposal has not been completed." A few dozen hours later, Infante communicated the rejection of the proposal via a second letter (p. III–911).

In the consideration of the affair, the fellow taxpayer should keep in mind ABOVE ALL the fact NOT STATED IN THE PROPOSAL that the "Lie–admissible generalization of Lie's theory" means the generalization of the mathematical structure of Einstein's theories. As stressed in Section 1.8, once this mathematical generalization is achieved in sufficient diversification, the generalization of the physical part is only a matter of time, as well known to any NSF referee and officer sufficiently qualified for these functions. There is no doubt that vested, academic–financial–ethnic interests on Einstein's theories have benefited by the rejection of the proposal. The issue left open for the fellow taxpayer is to ascertain who is the loser. The applicants, being senior, tenured, renowned mathematicians, cannot possibly be the losers. The answer can then only be one: the U.S.A. is the loser.

Predictably, the episode implied visible consequences. In fact, following this rejection, all IBR workshops and conferences were moved to Europe. It was indeed foolish to dream that other IBR meetings could have a better chance of being funded by U.S. Governmental Agencies.

NSF REJECTION NO. 9 dated April 14, 1983 (p. III—921) of an IBR application by two senior, U.S. mathematicians entitled "Mathematical studies on reductive Lie—admissible algebras and H—spaces with applications to the geometry of nonpotential dynamical systems". The application was processed by a number of officers of the NSF Division of Mathematics, beginning with Harvey Keynes, Program Director of Modern Analysis. The final review and approval of the consideration process was conducted by E. F. Infante as Division Director.

An inspection of the referees' reports and of the individualized comments provided by the IBR for the NSF, is quite instructive, particularly to reach a mature understanding of the true, ultimate criteria according to which NSF operates and disperses public funds.

Again, the qualifications of the applicants were impeccable (one of them is the co—author of a book in Lie algebra which is rather famous in mathematical and physical circles). Again, the fundamental mathematical relevance of the research program was simply out of the question.* The requested budget was not a problem for anybody with a minimum of knowledge of the procedures used by Governmental Agencies in funding research proposals (the only meaningful budget is that the Agency is willing to pay, while that requested by the applicants has only a vague meaning for a theoretical proposal). The NSF Division of Mathematics was fully stocked with taxpayers' money to support valuable mathematical research, and the availability of funds was not a problem.

BUT THEN, WHY WAS THIS PROPOSAL REJECTED TOO BY THE U.S. NATIONAL SCIENCE FOUNDATION?

On the surface, and judging from the referees' reports, the proposal was rejected on PHYSICAL AND NOT ON MATHEMATICAL GROUNDS, with the motivation that (see referee's report "C", p. III—931) "*. . .general classes of nonpotential interactions of the type to which the proposed formalism nontrivially applies are not clearly relevant, if indeed they exist at all. The*

---

*Virtually all spaces of mathematical and physical relevance (such as the Euclidean or the Minkowski space) are reductive within the context of the conventional mathematical formulation of Lie's theory (that expressed via the trivial unit element and the simplest conceivable Lie product; see Section 1.8). The proposal under consideration recommended the generalization of reductive spaces via the use of the Lie—admissible generalization of Lie's theory. The mathematical implications are truly far reaching (e.g., the turning of a nonlinear structure into an isotopic linear form). The physical implications are simply outstanding (e.g., the technique permits the representation of the transition from the exterior to the interior problem of gravitation for realistic interior trajectories, those of non—perpetual—motion—type; or the representation of the variation of the speed of light in the transitin from one medium to another, which is representable exactly via different Minkowski—isotopic spaces, that is, via different generalizations of reductive spaces).

principal interactions of physics are constrained by symmetry and/or causality considerations, and it is not shown that the proposed formalism has anything useful to offer in connection with them." A number of comments are here in order. First, everybody knows that macroscopic systems are potential only in special circumstances (such as planetray motion), while they are generally nonpotential in the physical reality. Different views would imply the existence of the perpetual motion in our environment (Section 1.3). Similarly, everybody knows that a proton cannot orbit in the core of our sun with a conserved angular momentum. The interior problem of gravitation is therefore intrinsically nonpotential (Section 1.5). Also, everybody knows that open, nonconservative particle reactions have nonunitary time evolutions. ALL these systems and countless more are outside the technical capabilities of potential dynamics. The review of these points was studiously avoided in the proposal, first of all because of their physical nature (the proposal being of pure mathematical character) and, secondly, because offensive to the reader (any NSF referee, to possess sufficient qualifications for this post, is expected to know that the perpetual motion does not exist in our environment). Nevertheless, these points and numerous others were presented, reviewed and repetitiously itemized to the reviewers and, in particular, to Infante, via letters, comments on referees' reports, IBR memos and papers, etc. (for instance, the IBR comments on referee's report "C" – see pp. III–928–930– reviewed the "direct universality" of the Lie–admissible approach for the representation of nonunitary time evolutions, as outlined in pp. 94–96 of this book).

As a result of these and other aspects, it is evident that the referee's report under consideration was inappropriate (rejection of a fundamental mathematical application on physical grounds) and, if indeed appropriate, totally deprived of any credibility.

I must therefore encourage the fellow taxpayer to **see the motivations of the rejection outside the lines of the referees' reports, that is, in the unspoken parts of the proposal and of the review process. In fact, every qualified physicist and mathematician knows well that NONPOTENTIAL (NONLAGRANGIAN– NONHAMILTONIAN) DYNAMICAL SYSTEMS ARE IRRECONCILABLY INCOMPATIBLE WITH EINSTEINIAN THEORIES. This is the point in which the proposal was silent. This is the point that none of the referees had the courage to raise explicitly.** The fellow taxpayer must then reach his/her own appraisal of the TRUE, ULTIMATE reasons why NSF rejected this beautiful proposal by two outstanding, senior, U.S. scholars. To reach a deeper judgment, the fellow taxpayer must know that the generalized mathematical tools submitted in the proposal do indeed constitute a generalization of the mathematical structure of Einsteinian theories. **The ultimate issue is not, therefore, that of a mere rejection, but rather whether or not the case constitutes a** documented illustration of an intentional, organized effort TO PREVENT THE ACHIEVEMENT OF THE GENERALIZATION OF THE MATHEMATICAL STRUCTURE OF EINSTEIN'S THEORIES, or at least to prevent its achievement under the NSF backing. In different terms, the ultimate issue is whether or not we are facing a conspiratorial obscurantism on Einstein's theories by vested academic—financial—ethnic interests in a U.S. Governmental Agency. After all, we are treating here only the last link of a chain of similar indications in academic institutions, Governmental laboratories and journals of the American Physical Society.

NSF REJECTION NO. 10 dated April 21, 1983 (p. III—950), of an IBR application by three senior, U.S., mathematicians entitled "Studies on Lie—admissible algebras". At this point, the fellow taxpayer will see a repetitive pattern. The proposal was processed by Judith S. Sunley, NSF Program Director for Algebras and Number Theory. Sunley's processing was reviewed and approved by Infante, again, as Division Director. The qualifications of the applicants are simply out of the question (each of them is the holder of a full professorship in mathematics at a large U.S. university with graduate school). The mathematical relevance of the proposal was equally out of the question for the reasons indicated earlier. The NSF mathematical division was stocked with taxpayer's money to support valuable research. Etc.

BUT THEN WHY WAS THIS ADDITIONAL MATHEMATICAL PROPOSAL ALSO REJECTED BY THE NSF?

Again, the reading of the referees' report solicited, inspected, and approved by NSF officers is instructive (pp. III—951—953). Again, the fellow taxpayer WILL NOT necessarily find in these reports the true reasons for the rejection. After all, even though not stated in the application, the proposal dealt with the mathematical generalization of Lie algebras, that is, of a central part of contemporary mathematics and physics. Again, the TRUE, ULTIMATE, reasons must be searched in the unspoken parts. The end result cannot but be the same as before: a reinforcement of the doubts on the existence of a conceivable conspiratorial obscurantism at a U.S. Governmental Agency on Einstein's ideas in an apparent full alignment with corresponding vested interests in leading academic institutions, Governmental laboratories, and APS journals.

After all, the fellow taxpayer should not forget the extremes attempted by senior Harvard faculty to prevent my studies on the conceivable invalidation of Einstein's theory in the interior of hadrons under Governmental support (Section 2.1), or the rather incredible lack of interests at National laboratories on the tests of Einsteinian theories DESPITE THE FACT THAT ALL AVAILABLE DIRECT ELEBORATIONS OF EXPERIMENTS SHOW VIOLATION (Section 2.3); or the incredible stubborness by APS journals to prevent the publication of papers in the field (Section 2.4).

The proposal under consideration here had one peculiarity that is worth reporting to the fellow taxpayer. In late January, 1983, I received a rather unusual letter by Judith S. Sunley (p. III–940). She announced having contacted DIRECTLY AND WITHOUT ANY PRIOR NOTICE the highest administrative officers of each primary affiliation of the applicants, asking for their formal authorization of the IBR administration of a possible NSF contract, as well as a number of additional administrative commitments, all this PRIOR TO THE ACTUAL, FORMAL, APPROVAL OF THE APPLICATION. Each administrative officer contacted by Sunley immediately provided all the needed authorizations (see pp. III–941–947, where all names of individuals and of institutions have been evidently deleted). AND THEN, SOON AFTER THAT THE PROPOSAL WAS REJECTED!!!

A host of unanswered questions are raised by such unorthodox behaviour (U.S. Governmental officers are notoriously cautious on matters of this type). I have my personal theory and I intend to pass it to the fellow taxpayer for whatever its value. Judging from phone calls and other elements, I believe that the proposal had been INFORMALLY ACCEPTED at the time when Sunley contacted the primary administrative officers of the three large U.S. colleges (plus the IBR). At that time, the information was still restricted within a limited circle of the NSF Division of Mathematics. As soon as the informal decision of support propagated to other branches of NSF, such as the Division of Physics (see below for what happened there), pressures by representatives of the apparent, organized, scientific obscurantism on Einstein's ideas initiated their action for the intent of suppressing the funding of the proposal. Success under impunity was assured by the current structure and organization of the U.S. science.

Admittedly, this is my undocumented, personal, theory of the affair. Nevertheless, one thing is certain: a rather drastic change occurred soon after Sunley implemented her unorthodox initiative, and that change was in the negative. The forces of the spider's web that lead to such a change are unknown to me.

NSF REJECTION NO. 11 dated June 8, 1983 (p. III–967), of an IBR application by a senior physicist as principal investigator, entitled "Theoretical, experimental and applied studies on a possible pulsating structure of the Coulomb force of individual electrons". The proposal was processed by David Berley of the Elementary Particle Program, for the experimental profile, and (AGAIN!) Boris Kaiser for the theoretical part (p. III–962). Such a dual processing was reviewed and approved by Rolf M. Sinclair, Acting Director of the NSF Division of Physics.

The proposal was rejected with manifest, vulgarly offensive language, in the referees' reports, such as that of the third reviewer (p. III–970) stating that

"Under no circumstances should precious resources be wasted on such TRASH [emphasis mine]".

I hope the fellow taxpayer sees the reasons why I had no alternative then launching a worldwide denounciation of the current ethical status of the U.S. physics. If this book is not sufficient to promote the deep changes that are needed for the improvement of scientific ethics and accountability, all conceivable initiatives permitted by law will be undertaken, beginning with the promotion of suitable class actions against the U.S. National Foundation to prevent further damages to the dignity of the Country.

The seemingly corrupt character of the NSF referee here considered is clear. On technical grounds, the research project (not reviewed previously in this book) referred to a conceivable pulsating structure of the electrostatic force among two elementary charges, such as the electrons, although the hypothesis could evidently be referred to other elementary charges, such as the quark constituents. Now, suppose that the referee can prove the erroneous nature of the hypothesis for two electrons.* But then, the same referee has absolutely no reliable information to reach any conclusion for the case of quark constituents, whether in favor or against the hypothesis. The corrupt character of the referee, that is, his/her studious adulteration of scientific facts for nonscientific motivations, simply cannot be ruled out.

NSF REJECTION NO. 12 dated June 8, 1983 (p. III—985), of an IBR proposal by a senior physicist entitled "Studies on nonpotential scattering theory". The processing of the application was done by S. Peter Rosen, NSF Program Associate of the Theoretical Physics Program. The review and approval of Rosen's processing was done by Rolf M. Sinclair, Acting Director of the Division of Physics.

The reading of the referees' reports accepted and released by Sinclair (pp. III—986—990) is quite instructive. For example, the first referee begins with the claim (p. III—986): *"I have no confidence in the soundness of . . .the institution with which he*

---

*This is already debatable. In fact, the consistency of the hypothesis for two ordinary electrons has been proved in the literature beyond a reasonable doubt for the case of nonrelativistic dynamics. The consistency or inconsistency of the hypothesis for the relativistic case as well as for the additional quantum electrodynamical case had not been studied at the time of the submission of the proposal, as clearly stated in the proposal itself (which recommended exactly that study among others). The point is that, traditionally, all hypotheses which are consistent at the nonrelativistic level have been proved sooner or later to admit a consistent relativistic extension. Also, the electromagnetic coupling constant is so large, and the effects of the hypothesis are comparatively so small, to render the hypothesis quite natural. After all, its physical basis is the old idea that electrons are oscillations of the geometry of space. If this is true, the current theories of the electrons' field are irreconcilably insufficient to represent nature (although I do not call them "trash").

[the principal investigator] is associated." Lack of confidence in an institution evidently means lack of confidence in its members. This referee therefore claimed lack of confidence in the 39 members of the Institute for Basic Research, scattered throughout the (western) world, WITHOUT KNOWING THEIR NAMES!!! In fact, their names have not been disclosed by the IBR, because such a disclosure is discretionary to each member (Appendix B). This referee therefore had no information on IBR members, except those of the principal investigator and of the administrative officers. How can Governmental officers have confidence in the credibility of this referee? It is evident that this person pursues schemes of academic politics, rather than science. Yet, U.S. Governmental officers DID consider the report as valid, and they DID use it in the decision making process regarding the dispersal of public funds. The report also claims that the Lie–admissible differentiation used is nonexistent. The Lie–admissible approach is a mere mathematical re–formulation of known NON-UNITARY time evolutions of OPEN systems according to the elementary rules reviewed on p. 95 (of this book). If the seemingly "technical" argument of this referee were correct, non-unitary time evolutions would be prevented to exist, and we would have the perpetual motion everywhere in the universe!

The remaining reviews are plus or minus, of the same caliber of the first. I shall therefore avoid boring the fellow taxpayer with the repetitious illustration of their lack of scientific content.

Quite likely, NSF officers selected as referee representatives of the circles of vested, academic–financial–ethnic interests controlling the U.S. physics. The suffocation of non–aligned research under these premises was then a mere consequence.

The comments made in pp. 169–170 however persist. **The conventional (potential) scattering theory has huge financial implications inasmuch as it is used for the data elaboration of most of current experiments in nuclear and particle physics. If strong interactions do indeed have a nonpotential component (Section 1.6), these data elaborations are incorrect, as established in ref. [113]. The proposal under consideration suggested the development of the nonpotential generalization of the potential scattering theory as a NECESSARY PREREQUISITE for the future resolution of the issue. The existence of huge problems of scientific accountability at the U.S. National Science Foundation is then consequential.**

In fact, the study submitted in the proposal MUST be conducted. The only debatable issue is the institution where the research has to be conducted. Now, I would have accepted with grace the NSF backing of the claim of lack of soundness of the IBR, PROVIDED THAT NSF WOULD HAVE FUNDED THE PROJECT AT SOME OTHER INSTITUTION. The reality is that, to this writing (July 10, 1984), NSF has not funded the research elsewhere (evidence to the contrary would be welcome). The existence at NSF of huge problems of scientific accountability is then unavoidable. **Large public funds (estimated in the range of hundreds of millions of dollars per year) continued to be spent to this day on data elaboration of strongly interacting experiments, in total ignorance of the critical literature PUBLISHED IN REFEREED JOURNALS (such as Nuovo Cimento, Hadronic Journal,* and others).**

NSF REJECTION NO. 13 dated December 16, 1983 (p. III—999), of an IBR proposal entitled "Studies of quantization of systems with gauge symmetries". The proposal was processed by Su—Shing Chen, Program Director for Geometric Analysis. The processing was reviewed and approved by E. F. Infante, as Division Director of Mathematical Sciences.

This rejection represented the climax of all NSF rejections of the IBR applications. In fact, it was perpetrated AGAINST the referees' reports. As the fellow taxpayer is encouraged to verify (pp. III—1000—1004), all referees praised substantially the principal investigator (a senior, foreign, applied mathematician), and his outstanding record of achievements (including a prestigious monograph on the topic of the proposal). The proposal was therefore rated by the referees as "Excellent", "Very Good", etc.

This last rejection did indeed have visible consequences. When combined with some fifteen years of experiences with NSF all of the same nature, it confirmed to me the apparent existence at NSF of an organized mandate to prevent our group of scholars to conduct research under NSF backing.✰ I therefore withdrew the last two IBR applications pending at DOE and, a few days following the reception of Infante's last rejection, I initiated the writing of IL GRANDE GRIDO.

> **Lack of consideration by the NSF of a comprehensive experimental—theoretical—mathematical proposal to test the validity or invalidity of Einstein's ideas under strong interactions.**

Understandably, I did not intend to terminate in a graceful

---

*Another corrupt statement that repeatedly appeared in NSF reviews is that the Hadronic Journal is not a refereed journal. The erroneous nature of the statement is well known to the authors who have published or attempted to publish a paper in that journal. The corrupt character of the statement is evident, because based on the venturing of a judgment with full awareness of the lack of any solid information on the subject.

✰ Note that money was not a factor in most of the applications, inasmuch as a few thousand dollars would have been sufficient. The ultimate, objective seems to be that of preventing the appearance of papers dealing with the possible invalidation of Einstein's ideas, under the official backing of the U.S. National Science Foundation.

way my contacts with the current NSF officers. I therefore studiously left at NSF a sort of "time bomb". In fact, I collected into a single document all the experimental, theoretical and mathematical proposals rejected by NSF with a coordinating preface and the new title "EXPERIMENTAL, THEORETICAL, AND MATHEMATICAL STUDIES ON A POSSIBLE GENERALIZATION OF EINSTEIN'S SPECIAL RELATIVITY FOR EXTENDED, DEFORMABLE, STRONGLY INTERACTING PARTICLES" (pp. III–1122–1131).* The insidious aspect is that I did not submit to NSF this huge document as a proposal. Instead, I submitted it to E. F. Infante as an "advance consultation" via a detailed letter of presentation mailed in copy to some 31 senior scholars who had been involved in the research in one form or another (their names have been evidently deleted in the Documentation).

As I had predicted, Infante passed the hot ball from his desk to the NSF Division of Physics, where the material truly belonged and, in particular, to Marcel Bardon. Exactly as predicted, Marcel Bardon ignored this document in violation of NSF's statutory obligations. To this day (July 15, 1984), no communication has ever been received from NSF on this advance consultation since the notice of reception and referral by E. F. Infante dated May 20, 1983 (p. III–1127).

Lack of interest by Edward Knapp, NSF Director General.

It is the duty of every member of a free society to inform the highest possible officers of any, even minimal, doubt of ethically questionable practices involving public funds. I therefore informed Edward Knapp, NSF Director General, of each and every aspect reviewed in this section (and more), via copies of all various letters, documents, complaints, comments on referee reports, IBR presentations, papers, memos, etc. This process was done with the same repetitious intent I had studiously implemented for Derek Bok, President of Harvard University (Section 2.1), or for Leon M. Lederman, Director of FERMILAB (Section 2.3), or for David Lazarus, Editor in Chief of the American Physical Society. Again, this pattern was intended to prevent Knapp's statement: "I did not know!"

These (unilateral) contacts concluded with a summary letter (p. III–867), which reviewed: (a) the primary scientific objectives of the studies (resolutions of the validity or invalidity of Einstein's theories under strong interactions), and the NSF responsibilities on the topic; (b) the rejection of technical proposals by qualified senior scholars via approved referees' reports with vulgarly offensive language; (c) the rejection of proposals

---

*The fellow taxpayer should remember here the plausibility of the deformation of hadrons under sufficiently intense collisions, with consequential breaking of the rotational symmetry and invalidation of Einstein's special relativity (see Chapter 1, or Figure 2.2.1, p. 209, for a brief outline.

at times against the totality of the recommendations of the referees; (d) the rejection of proposals while NSF did not fund at other institutions similar projects specifically referred to the possible invalidation of Einstein's theories; (e) the causing of unnecessary damage to the applicants by NSF officers, beyong the mere rejection of the proposals; (f) the NSF repetitious pattern in delaying the communication of rejections of funding for nonaligned meetings, for the apparent intent of damaging their organization; (g) the case of the rejection of the primary, IBR, group proposal whereby one of the referees had contacted directly one of the advisors of the project, L. C. Biedenharn of Duke University, had apparently succeeded in pressuring him to withdraw from the project, and had even secured copy of an (apparent) letter by Biedenharn to this effect; etc.

This final report to Knapp concluded with the following passage: *"As indicated to you in preceding correspondence, I am considering a National campaign aimed at having the American Physical Society formulate and adopt a much overdue CODE OF ETHICS, as well as having the judical and political systems create independent means for its strict enforcement. This letter is intended to give you and your officers all the necessary prior knowledge of the possibility that the totality of the documentation regarding our research grant applications, jointly with individualized comments, of course, might be released to the appropriate Committees of the U.S. Senate and House of Representatives, as well as to the press. In case you and/or your officers have any objection to such a release, you should let me know immediately. However, in case no objection exists (or can be raised), no acknowledgement of this letter is needed."* To make sure of the propagation of the information, I mailed a copy of this final letter to R. M. Sinclair at the NSF physics division, and to E. F. Infante at the mathematics division.

No reply was ever received from Knapp, not even a gesture of courtesy!

Whether Knapp ever did anything following my reports, or he ignored them altogether, is of no relevance here. **The important point is the lack of any investigation of the cases organized by Knapp IN A WAY AS PUBLIC AS POSSIBLE AND AS VISIBLE AS POSSIBLE OUTSIDE THE NSF.** The point is evident for anybody with a minimum of knowledge of the operations of Governmental Agencies. In fact, the lack of a public investigation fully. visible to the outside, is a de facto backing of the action by the NSF officers. This is nothing else than, again, a repetition of what happened at Harvard University, at National laboratories and at journals of the American Physical Society.

These considerations have a crucial constructive role. It is of the essence for the fellow taxpayers to understand that **such extremes of disinterests at the highest administrative levels of the U.S. physics community, are routinely conducted because of the current, absolute, total, and guaranteed impunity.** In turn, this is essential to understand the potential effectiveness of the constructive suggestions submitted in the next chapter for the improvement of the conditions of the physics community.

Epilogue.

I have expressed my personal views that
- Officers of the U.S. National Science Foundation are servants to leading physicists at leading academic institutions.
- The condition of servility leads to the impossibility by NSF officers to reject questionable reports by leading physicists and to accept them no matter what their content is. This, in turn, implies the inevitable use of corrupt referees' reports* in the Governmental process of dispersing public funds.
- The use of manifestly questionable reports and/or practices in the decision—making process has created a huge problem of scientific ethics at the National Science Foundation which has been growing constantly during recent years, by multiplying the concern in numerous segments of the physics and mathematics communities in the U.S.A. and abroad.
- The National Science Foundation has accumulated throughout the years a monumental problem of lack of scientific accountability in the dispersal of public funds on Einstein's special and general relativities, by avoiding the funding of research on the apparent invalidation of Einstein's theories in the physical reality. The preceding outline and the related documentation establish beyond any reasonable doubt the existence at NSF of a mandate to prevent the funding of IBR research proposals in mathematics and physics. Nevertheless, this was not sufficient reason for writing this international denounciation. The staggering problems of scientific accountability at NSF have been created by the joint LACK of funding the needed research on the invalidation of Einstein's relativities at some other institution.
- The seemingly deep interconnection between NSF officers and leading physicists at leading academic institutions, Governmental laboratories and journals of the American Physical Society, has provided sufficient elements to suspect the existence of a conspiratorial obscurantism in the U.S. physics for the intent

---

*The fellow taxpayer should keep in mind that my documentation is only a minute fraction of that available by other NSF applicants scattered throughout the world. Also, I should report that the terms "crackpot", "trash", "no achievement worth mentioning" and the like have been formulated with respect to my person and my work only within the rings of greed surrounding NSF. Outside those rings, my work has been appraised beyond my best expectations, with terms such as "Truly epoch—making" [Journal of Applied Mathematics], "outstanding" [Applied Mechanics Review], and numerous, similar reviews in several languages, printed in journals scattered throughout the world [as obtainable from the publishers of my monographs in theoretical physics].

of suppressing, discrediting or otherwise jeopardizing qualified research on the insufficiencies, invalidation and possible experimental disproofs of Einstein's theories, in the sole benefit of vested, academic—financial—ethnic interests in the U.S.A., and in basic disrespect of the societal need for advancements in basic knowledge.

But, again, my personal opinion is insignificant. Equally insignificant is the personal opinion of Edward Knapp, NSF Director General, Marcel Bardon, Boris Kayser, Rolf M. Sinclair, S. Peter Rosen and other officers of the NSF Division of Physics, as well as E. F. Infante, Judith S. Sunley, Alvin Thaler, and other officers of the NSF Division of Mathematics. The only important opinion is that by the fellow taxpayer who supports the research funded by NSF as well as the salaries of the above quoted NSF officers.

In the consideration of the case, I beg the fellow taxpayer to initiate appropriate action aimed at a genuine improvement of the pursuit of novel physical and mathematical knowledge via public funds, as well as preventing additional, manifest, damages to the dignity of the Country via senseless refereeing practices. It all boils down to a basic, unreassuring, point: **a Country vitally dependent on the advancement of basic knowledge, such as the U.S.A., which penalizes rather than supports, critial examinations of basic issues, such as the validity of invalidity of Einstein's theory under strong interactions, could be doomed within a sufficient time scale, even though amidst the glitter of temporary technological advances.**

2.5.2: DIVISION OF HIGH ENERGY PHYSICS OF THE DEPARTMENT OF ENERGY.

The original determination by the Department of Energy to support our research.

Under the directorship of William A. Wallenmeyer, and with Bernard Hildebrand as chief of the Physics Research Branch, the Division of High Energy Physics of the Department of Energy (DOE) proved, beyond any doubt, its original determination to support the research reported in Chapter 1. In fact, DOE did indeed succeed in providing support to our group while I was at Harvard during the period 1977—1980, despite the vigorous internal opposition there reported in Section 2.1. Subsequently, during the years 1980—1983, when it resulted impossible to continue the research under Harvard's administration, DOE accepted the administration of a nonacademic corporation even though the research was of purely academic character.

The invaluable function of the DOE support.

It is a truism to say that all the scientific results reported in this volume regarding the insufficiencies, generalizations and experimental resolutions of Einstein's theories, are due to the above DOE support. Despite its limited character,* the support permitted the initiation and conduction of numerous scientific initiatives. This resulted into a significant volume of scientific production by the various members supported by the contract (which includes the publication of: six research monographs, nine volumes of proceedings of conferences and workshops, and a total number of over 150 papers).

The litany of subsequent DOE rejections of IBR applications.

In mid 1981, the relationship with the DOE changed rather substantially, and we began to experience a chain of rejections of IBR applications, which later on became a mere litany. We first experienced the rejection of a rather unique mathematical application signed by five senior, renowned, U.S. mathematicians (pp. III–832–901). The repetitious rejections included all primary group proposals submitted by the IBR to the DOE (pp. III–804–846), and numerous other applications that had been also rejected by NSF.

The possible link of the DOE rejections with the founding of the IBR.

On my part, back in 1980, I could not possibly continue the coordination of a growing, international, group of mathematicians, theoreticians and experimentalists while working in an office at home. On the other part, David C. Peaslee, then at the DOE, had told me the minimal chances for DOE continuing to support my academic research under a nonacademic administration. Also, the possibility of my continuing research on the limitations and possible generalizations of Einstein's theories in a U.S. physics department had to be virtually excluded, as seen in pages 220–222. This left no other choice than to organize a new, independent, research institution, the IBR (Appendix B). Apparently, the change of attitude at DOE initiated precisely with the founding of the IBR. The apparent alignment with vested interests in the Cantabrigian academic community is evident and needs no comment here.

---

*To have an idea of the limited amount of funds, the average DOE support to our group during the years 1980–1983 was of the order of $ 60,000.00, including all administrative overheads and indirect costs, the holding of a yearly conference or workshop, publication charges, travel support, etc.

I still remember vividly when, after a long struggle, we finally succeeded in purchasing the Prescott House within the compound of Harvard University to provide permanent housing for the IBR.* I called David Peaslee at the DOE in Washington from the Cambridge Registry of Deeds the very moment following the registration of purchase, to thank DOE for past support and to invite him to be our guest at the inauguration ceremony of the new Institute. Peaslee declined the invitation, although I sensed a touch of sadness in his voice. He had been the DOE officer in charge of our contract since its initiation at Harvard back in 1977. He knew everything, including the financial and human sacrifices which had permitted the founding of the IBR without any Governmental contribution. I had the impression that, in declining our invitation, Peaslee was performing his duty against his personal wishes. At any rate, he left the DOE soon thereafter.

My gratitude toward Wallenmeyer and Hildebrand of the DOE.

Whatever the reasons for the DOE rejection of so many and so qualified applications on so manifestly fundamental topics, I want to be on record to respect these decisions. In fact, I have nothing but respect, admiration and, most of all, gratitude toward Wallenmeyer and Hildebrand. After all, I owe them everything I have accomplished. It is just that simple. If new situations have forced them to terminate the support, I cannot but accept it with grace.☆

It was regrettable that not even a minute amount of funds could be provided to support the IBR research reviewed in this book. In fact, even a very small support of, say, a few thousand dollars per year, would have at least permitted the continuation in the U.S.A. of our yearly research meetings. Instead, the suppression of funds had to be total, thus forcing the IBR into alternative forms of financing, of which this book is an expression.

---

*To have an idea of the difficulty of the purchase, one should keep in mind that Harvard University has an understandable interest in the purchase of buildings within its compound. The Prescott House had, therefore, to be literally purchased under Harvard's nose, as it was indeed the case. An additional difficulty was created by the fact that Cambridge is under Rent Control with its notorious limit on possible income, and consequential restriction of bank appraisals of the value of certain buildings well below their actual value. As a result of these and other circumstances, the purchase of a considerable piece of Real Estate had to be achieved without any bank mortgage.

☆I should stress the difference with NSF here. My intentionally ungraceful reaction to NSF considerations of our applications is due to the NSF acceptance of vulgarly offensive language in the referees' report, and other aspects which never transpared in the DOE considerations.

2.5.3: DIVISION OF NUCLEAR PHYSICS OF THE DEPARTMENT OF ENERGY.

The climax of IL GRANDE GRIDO.

Among all the various, scientifically evil episodes presented in this book, that which I consider to be, by far, the individual, most distressing episode was perpetrated by Enloe T. Ritter, Director of the Nuclear Physics Division of the Department of Energy. The episode regards the rejection of an IBR proposal submitted to Ritter in June, 1982, under the title (pp. III—1064—1121)

EXPERIMENTAL VERIFICATION OF THE SU(2)—SPIN SYMMETRY UNDER STRONG AND ELECTROMAGNETIC INTERACTIONS BY A JOINT AUSTRIA—FRANCE—USA COLLABORATION

(see pp. 145—150 of this book for a description).

The proposal essentially suggested the repetition of the neutron interferometric experiments done by H. Rauch, Director of the Atominstitut of Wien, Austria, since 1975. It was motivated by the fact that the latest measures show the VIOLATION of the rotational symmetry (see Section 1.7). The proposal dealt with the most fundamental possible experiment a particle and nuclear physicist could conceive these days, as stressed throughout this volume. In fact, the confirmation of the experimental measures on the breaking of the rotational symmetry for extended (and therefore deformable) particles under intense, short range, interactions, would imply the need for suitable generalizations of Einstein's special and general relativities.

The first difficulties in 1981 at the Institute Laue—Langevin (ILL), of Grenoble, France.

The experimental team had conducted the tests of the rotational symmetry at the nuclear reactor of the ILL laboratory since their initiation in 1975. As recalled in Section 1.7, the first experiments were done on neutron beams without short range interactions, and they resulted to be in full agreement with the predictions of the exact rotational symmetry, as expected. No academic difficulty of any relevance occurred during this initial period, to my knowledge.

In 1978, the experimenters repeated the measures, also at the ILL reactor, but this time with the (involutary) inclusion of short range interactions. Initial measures released in 1978 [99] resulted to be still compatible with orthodox doctrines. Nevertheless, a new re—elaboration of the experiment done in 1981 because of improved values of constants and other factors, began to show a violation of the rotational symmetry subsequently announced in ref.s [100, 139] (see Figure 2.2.1, p. 209, for a conceptual review). In turn, the initiation of the detection of violation of orthodox doctrines signaled the initiation of academic difficulties experienced by the experimenters.

In early 1981, a group of mathematicians and theoreticians (including myself) launched the organization of the FIRST INTERNATIONAL CONFERENCE ON NONPOTENTIAL INTERACTIONS AND THEIR LIE—ADMISSIBLE TREATMENT, to be held at the University of Orléans, France, in early January, 1982, under the formal support of the French Government (via local Institutions), as well as a small participation of the DOE (via my grant). The Proceedings of the meetings were published in ref.s [126].

Predictably, H. Rauch was the key, invited, experimental speaker. Rauch and his team therefore applied to the Institute Laue—Langevin in 1981 for the re—run of the measures. The running time was planned not later than November—December, 1981, in such a way to be able to report at the Orléans International Conference of early 1982, at least some preliminary results of the new measures.

To the "astonishment" of the experimenters (p. III—1020), the Institute Laue—Langevin declined authorization for the re—run of the experiment at that time (p. III—1018). The decision had been taken by a committee (apparently)* headed by Otto Shult of the Institut für Kernphysik der Kernforschungslage in Jülich, West Germany. A rather intense scientific crisis then followed which included telegrams, certified mail, and the like (pp. III—1019—1048). The crisis was encouraged by unverifiable rumors such as:

— The rumor that the difficulties in France had originated at leading physics institutions in the U.S.A. Whether this is true or false, it is quite plausible that the information leading to the ILL rejection (to re—run the measures in time for the Orléans International Conference) originated outside the Institute Laue—Langevin. In fact, the proposal had been submitted in the traditional dry style used by experimenters with its notorious paucity of information; or,

— The rumor that irate French scholars had filed detailed reports of the entire affair to high levels of the French and West German Governments (the apparent chairman of the committee, Otto Shult, being from West Germany). Whether this is true or false, it seems sure that

* The decision was communicated by a secretary without any indication of the names of the members of the responsible committee. It took some pressure on T. Springer, Director of the Institute, to finally obtain some information on the names of the committee.

the negative decision at the ILL had not been unanimous.

One thing is certain: the measures were not permitted in 1981, and this most crucial experimental information was missed at the Orléans International Conference of early 1982 with predictable scientific damage. The same measures are missing to this day. In fact, we only have re–elaborations [100, 139] of the 1978 measures [99], as stressed in Section 1.7.

Whether in Cambridge, U.S.A., or in Grenoble, France, the gains by vested, academic–financial–ethnic interests resulting from preventing the re–run of measures [99], have been indicated throughout this volume, and they need no further elaboration here.

The opposition at the Massachusetts Institute of Technology and at the National Science Foundation against the re–run of the experiment.

The Austrian–French experimental team did not need U.S. money to repeat the measures, even though any financial support would have been evidently welcome and valuable. The primary reasons for the experimenters' interest in a possible DOE support was the officiality of such a backing, including the hope that it would contain the political difficulties experienced in the re–running of the experiment at ILL.

With this spirit, the IBR provided full support to the Austrian–French experimental team, to file the above indicated proposal. The understanding was that money was not a factor, that is, the "U.S.A." could be part of the "Austria–France–U.S.A. Collaboration" even with a minimal amount of money at the borderline with decency for an experiment (say, a few thousand dollars).

The proposal was first subjected to one year of delay because of the lack of cooperation by a co–investigator who had joined in the meantime the Massachusetts Institute of Technology (see the report of the affair on pages 222–226 of this book). In turn, this left little doubt as for the apparent opposition at MIT against the re–run of measures [99].

Additional delay was caused by the Physics Division of the National Science Foundation. In fact, after resolving the MIT impasse, the proposal was submitted to NSF. Rather than initiating the consideration process, Rolf M. Sinclair, the NSF program director in charge of the case, commented to our submission with the rather unbelievable view (p. III–1055): *"The proposal is excessively brief in experimental details and fails to describe what would be done and by whom, and would probably be impossible to have reviewed."*

I personally did not believe one word of this statement, as indicated to Sinclair in a detailed letter of comments (pp. III–

1056–1060). The proposal quoted ALL the preceding experimental papers in the field (whose detailed knowledge MUST be assumed by anybody to qualify for NSF reviews). In particular, the proposal identified in all the necessary technical details the improvements intended for the new runs. In this particular instance, there simply was no room for academic dances: the measures had been conducted several times since 1975 and, therefore, THE EXPERIMENT WAS NOT NEW AT ALL. It had simply to be re–done with the indicated higher accuracy which would have confirmed or disproved the latest values showing VIOLATION. Owing to the absolutely fundamental character of the problem, delays in the scientific process because of irrelevant or imaginary details could likely imply the existence of unspoken, non–scientific objectives. In the essence, this was the reason of the crisis at the ILL, and this was the reason of my irreconcilable disagreement with Sinclair at NSF.

At any rate, the items requested by Sinclair simply could not be provided at the time of the submission in a way better than that presented in the proposal.* Thus, I could only interpret Sinclair's position as expressing a negative attitude at NSF against the re–run of the experiment apparently because of its evident damage to vested interests in the U.S. academia caused by the possible, consequential invalidation of Einstein's theories. The NSF proposal was therefore withdrawn by the IBR to avoid a total waste of time and money (p. III–1061).

The thirteen months of consideration of the proposal by Ritter at DOE.

With all this rather incredible (but documented) background, the proposal was finally "accepted for consideration" by Ritter in June, 1982 (p. III–1101). The proposal had remained exactly the same as that submitted to NSF. Nevertheless, to avoid possible criticisms, the proposal was complemented by a rather voluminous amount of scientific and administrative information (see pages III–1068 and ff.). For instance, the minimal need of funds was stressed and reiterated numerous times, in writing and verbally. In particular, the IBR made it clear that possible U.S. funds would have priority in the hiring of U.S. experimentalists to be trained by the Austrian–French team in the experimental measures, for their possible subsequent repeti-

---

*For instance, in regard to personnel, the project contemplated the use of the original team, as well as new U.S. experimentalists. The point is that their hiring could possibly be considered only AFTER the formal approval of the proposal with a budget call specifically intended for the hiring. At the time of the submission, only generic information could be provided, and certainly no name of specific U.S. experimentalists could be voiced prior to a formal announcement of the openings, and the screening of the applicants in conformity with the rule of Affirmative Action Employment and other administrative requirements.

tion in the States. After all, it was very easy to predict that, for a relevant experiment such as this one, the measures have to be done, re—done, and then done again before claiming any final scientific conclusion.

The statutory six months of consideration had passed without any decision at DOE. Then, on November 12, 1982, Ritter asked for authorization to retain the proposal under consideration for another six months (p. III—1112). The IBR gladly accepted the request with an additional, detailed report on various aspects, including the formal authorization that the Institute Laue—Langevin had provided in the meantime for the re—run of the tests (p. III—1048).

On July 25, 1983, after thirteen months of consideration, Ritter communicated his rejection of the proposal with a few dry lines, by therefore reaching a decision manifestly aligned with the negative attitudes previously experienced at MIT and at NSF.

Predictably, the arrival of Ritter's letter of rejection in mid July, 1983, marked my formal decision to write this book.

Epilogue.

As indicated earlier, I believe that Ritter's rejection of the U.S. participation in the experiment to test the validity or invalidity of the rotational symmetry, is the individual, scientifically most evil act I have ever experienced in my academic life for the following reasons (among others):

★ **The needed funds were or otherwise must be absolutely insignificant for the budget of the Nuclear Physics Division of the U.S. Department of Energy. In fact, only a few thousand dollars would have been sufficient (at one point, I was tempted to donate myself this small sum to DOE, so that, in turn, DOE could support the U.S. participation in the project). Financial considerations must therefore be excluded from any meaningful or otherwise credible reason for the rejection.**

★ **The towering value of the proposal as compared to ALL other proposals under consideration by Ritter at that time, and the high qualifications of the experimenters, were simply out of the question. It is a truism to say that the virtual entirety of particle physics is in suspended animation because of the lack of resolution of the issue (including relevant military profiles touched earlier in this book). Also, after having done and re—done the experiment since 1975, the experimental team is universally recognized as THE most qualified in the field on a worldwide basis. Thus, insufficient scientific values and/or insufficient qualifications of the applicants must be also excluded by any meaningful or otherwise credible motivation underlying the rejection.**

★ The gains by vested academic—financial—ethnic interests in the suppression of the U.S. participation in the tests and, possibly, in the suppression of the tests altogether, are self—evident. In fact, lacking an experimental resolution of the validity or invalidity of the rotational symmetry, corrupt academic barons at leading U.S. institutions can continue to pocket large public funds via contracts (estimated in the range of hundreds of millions of dollars per year; see Section 1.9) which are centrally dependent on the exact validity of the rotationally symmetry, without any consideration whatsoever of its possible violation.

As a result of all this, I believe that Enloe T. Ritter, Director of the Nuclear Physics Division at the Department of Energy, has acquired a staggering PERSONAL problem of scientific accountability vis—a—vis the fellow taxpayer. As I wrote him in a letter of January 15, 1983, mailed in copy to D. P. Hodel, Secretary, and S. Brewer, Assistant Secretary of DOE (p. III—1119):

". . .no ethically sound scholar can silently accept the scientific, economic and military implications caused by the indefinite deferral of the tests. The rotational symmetry is at the foundation of the contemporary physical knowledge. The suppression of its direct verification which has been successfully achieved until now by vested, organized, academic—financial—ethnic interests, has all the ingredients of a scientific crime against this beautiful Land, against our children who have to live in it, and against the pursuit of novel human knowledge."

As in other cases, my personal opinion is insignificant. The sole important judgment as to whether or not Enloe T. Ritter has indeed committed a "scientific crime", is that by the fellow taxpayer. In turn, the sole judgment which can possibly be even more important, is that by posterity. In fact, posterity can and will unquestionably appraise, one day, whether or not we are currently experiencing in the U.S.A. an organized conspiratorial obscurantism on Einstein's theories and its foundations, beginning most importantly with the rotational symmetry.

CHAPTER 3

CONTAINING THE PROBLEM OF SCIENTIFIC ETHICS IN U. S. PHYSICS

I now pass to the constructive role of my experience: its value for the identification of means to contain the problem of scientific ethics in the U.S. physics community.

The attitude which appears recommendable to all members of the community, including physicists, administrators, governmental employees and officers of professional associations, is that of mutual forgiveness of past wrongdoings, and a commitment to join forces to build a better future.

Since the American Physical Society (APS) has not adopted a *CODE OF ETHICS* until now, all judgments regarding issues of scientific ethics in physics have a strictly personal character, and should not be expected to be necessarily shared by others [this evidently includes all judgments passed or considered in this book]. As a result of this situation, the only value of past experiences, including mine, is that of possible assistance in the building of a better future.

This is the spirit for which IL GRANDE GRIDO was written and this is the spirit here submitted to all members of the physics community.

The insufficiencies of the proposed recommendations.

In the following, I shall submit a number of recommendations inspired by my personal experience, as well as by the experiences of other colleagues I know. In essence, I asked myself the question: what are the improvements in the organizational structure of the U.S. physics community which would have rendered this report unnecessary?

To prevent excessive expectations, I would like to stress from the outset that this constructive part of IL GRANDE GRIDO is insufficient in content, diversification and presentation. To achieve sufficient maturity, each recommendation should be investigated by a team of experts and would require other resources which I simply do not have. I only hope that the recommendations originating from my personal experience as a physicist will be of some value for the appropriate legislative, governmental and societal bodies.

A rudimentary definition of "scientific wrongdoing".

For the sake of the following presentation, I shall assume the preliminary definition of "scientific wrongdoing" as "any act which is committed or omitted by one or more individuals and/or institutions with the awareness that it is harmful to society because detrimental to scientific knowledge".

An important aspect the fellow taxpayer should keep in mind, is that scientific   wrongdoings, in general, DO NOT con—stitute "crimes" according to the current code of law.   In fact, they do not refer to stealing of money and other conventionally unlawful acts (which are not addressed in this book).   This book therefore addresses the paradoxical situation in which given acts by individuals and/or institutions are fully legal; yet they may be, by far, more damaging to society than ordinary crimes.

3.1:   RECOMMENDATIONS TO THE U. S. CONGRESS.

RECOMMENDATION # 1:   LEGISLATE A *BOARD OF SCIENTIFIC REVIEW* (BSR) FOR THE CONSIDERA-TION OF CLAIMS OF SCIENTIFIC WRONGDOING IN PHYSICS, MATHEMATICS, BIOPHYSICS AND OTHER BASIC SCIENCES.

The tragedy of individual scientists who believe to have been the victims of scientific wrongdoings, is that there is no "court" where to file their complaints.   As indicated earlier, sci-entific wrongdoings are generally permitted by the current code of laws.   The filing of scientific claims in ordinary courts is there-fore, generally ineffective, if not inappropriate.   The filing of complaints to the appropriate committees of institutional, pro-fessional or Governmental organizations is equally ineffective for a variety of reasons including: the lack of guaranteed considera-tion of the claim; the lack of organizational guidelines for the proper appraisal of the wrongdoing; the general secrecy of the consideration; etc.*

---

*As a specific example, when I became convinced that the editorial handling by Physical Review Letters of theoretical and experimental studies on the violation of the time—reflection symmetry for open nuclear reactions (re-ported on pp. 160—168 and 256—271 of this book; and pp. II—531—660 of the Doc.) provide vast scientific, economic and military damages to America, I contacted the chairman of the Publication Committee of the American Physical Society, P. W. Anderson of Princeton University. During a phone conversation, Anderson stressed the fact that his committee could consider only cases of papers that had received a "final rejection" by an APS journal.   This organizational structure of the committee implied the

In addition, a reason for the current decay of scientific ethics is the guaranteed complete impunity for any act, decision or omission whatsoever, provided that it is permitted by the current code of laws. This un—reassuring situation is evidently due to the current lack of a "scientific court". The recommendation here submitted, most respectfully, to the U.S. Congress is precisely that of legislating this essential, currently missing, scientific institution.

MAIN ORGANIZATIONAL LINES SUGGESTED FOR THE BSR:

AFFILIATION:	To the Office of the Attorney General in Washington, D.C.*
COMPOSITION:	Five members appointed by Congress, from any suitable layer of society (not necessarily of scientific background)☆ including the Attorney General, the tenure of each member being limited to a maximum non—renewable period of four years, with the possible exception of the Attorney General.
CHAIRPERSON:	The Attorney General or a person designated by the same.
ADVISORS:	The BSR should appoint Advisory Committees from within the (National and international) scientific community

virtual impossibility of even filing a complaint, let alone receive a fair consideration. In fact, as elaborated in Section 2.4, APS journals do not generally provide "final rejections" (or even "ordinary rejections" for that matter), because the editors merely mail, re—mail, and then mail again to authors the negative referees' reports on undesired papers without any indication as to when the rejection becomes "final". After ascertaining the organizational insufficiencies of the APS Publication Committee, I searched for other committees, both within and outside the APS, without any result. In fact, I was unable to identify one single committee, and/or appropriate body, whether in Government or in the Courts of Law, which was sufficiently staffed to even understand my claim, let alone act on it.

*The Attorney General of the United States of America is the chief law officer of the Federal Government, whose primary duty is that of protecting public interest. As such, the Office of the Attorney General is particularly suited to house the Board of Scientific Review.

☆The fellow taxpayer should remember the reason of scientific dispute with the Massachusetts Institute of Technology (Section 2.2): the possibility that the charge distributions characterizing protons and neutrons are not rigid, but experience deformations as a result of external forces. This possibility was readily understood by my neighbors (who belong to walks of life other than science). However, the same possibility was not readily admitted by MIT physicists apparently because of its political implications, such as the breaking of the rotational symmetry and the violation of Einstein's special relativity. Because of this sadly known academic politics, scientists ARE NOT recommendable as executive members of the BSR.

FUNCTION: and act on specific cases following non—binding advice by the appropriate Committee. The BSR should have legislated authority to consider any claim of scientific wrongdoing, whether filed by individuals or warranting consideration in the opinion of the Attorney General and others. The BSR should furthermore have legislated authority to impose suitable punishment, compensation and remedy to any individual and/or institution found guilty of erroneous conduit, such as the termination of an existing Federal research contract, or the prevention of Federal contracts for a given period of time. Finally, the entirety of the proceedings of the BSR should be published and made available to the public (with the evident exception of cases of National security).

Needless to say, a considerable amount of research by a team of differentiated expertise is needed to bring the proposal to maturity, particularly in the organizational and operational details. A few aspects, however, should be firm. First, to be effective, the Board should be legislated OUTSIDE professional organizations, such as the APS as a NECESSARY CONDITION FOR CREDIBILITY. Second, The BSR should take into consideration *CODES OF ETHICS* if and when adopted by individual scientific organizations. Nevertheless, the BSR decisional guidelines should not be restricted to comply necessarily with said Codes. Third, the so—called "leading academic institutions" should be permitted to have their representatives on the Advisory Committees, but the control of any Committee by representatives of said institutions would imply the lack of credibility of the Board's action. In fact, the leading academic institutions are expected to be the primary reasons of concern of the Board. At any rate, qualified advisors can be readily found in "lesser leading", that is, "lesser politically entangled" institutions throughout the U.S.A. and abroad.

RECOMMENDATION # 2: MANDATE THE ROTATION OF EMPLOYEES AT GOVERNMENTAL AGENCIES PROVIDING FEDERAL RESEARCH SUPPORT

One of the strengths of the U.S. Constitution is the wisdom to limit the period of time one individual can serve as President. One of the current weaknesses of Governmental Agencies is the unlimited permanency of their employees. This has resulted in a life—long tenure by specific individuals in the dispersal of public funds in specific sectors of research. The un-reassuring nature of this situation is evident, because of the in-evitable, voluntary or involuntary associations of said Govern-mental employees with outside circles of interests. For in-stance, Marcel Bardon, Boris Kayser, Rolf Sinclair and others have been running the Division of Physics of the National Sci-ence Foundation as far back as my memory can go, since I landed here as an immigrant in the late sixties.

The damage to science of such life—long tenures in the dispersal of public funds in research contracts may be stagger-ing. One of its visible forms is the ABSTENTION by a grow-ing number of individuals to apply for research support. Until this occurrence was made up of isolated cases, it was of no con-cern. But the occurrence is now widespread throughout all sectors of research, with an evident damage to the Country.

The only way to break the sadly known circles of "in-siders" and "outsiders" in Federal research contracts is to man-date the rotation of governmental employees in charge of the consideration process. This can be only accomplished by a Con-gressional legislation on the limitation of the duration of perma-nency by governmental employees in each given Agency division. This can be done in a way compatible with current laws on civil service, e.g., by shifting the personnel to different divisions.

The ineffectiveness of the current means to cope with the problem is well known. Typically, the burden of attempt-ing a rejuvenation of the personnel at Governmental Agencies is passed from one given Administration to the Director of the Agency. This burden generally results in creating a barrier (rather than an atmosphere of cooperation) between the Dir-ector and the personnel. The end result I have observed re-peatedly is the permanency of the employees, and the rapid termination instead of the directorship itself.* In fact, the change of Directorships at the various Governmental Agencies (e.g., the NSF) is a rather frequent event in Washington, D.C. and, per se, an un—reassuring fact. The point is that Directors do not pro-cess research grant applications. Only individual officers do that. The frequent change of Agency Directors, therefore, has no impact on the problem.

RECOMMENDATION # 3: MANDATE IN THE YEAR-LY BUDGET OF EACH GOVERNMENTAL AGENCY THE TOTAL AMOUNT OF FUNDS TO BE DISPERSED TO SCIENTISTS AS INDIVIDUALS AND THE MAXI-MAL AMOUNT OF EACH GRANT PER EACH SECTOR OF RESEARCH.

A further deficiency of the current organization of the U.S. science is the general impossibility for scientists to apply for federal research support AS INDIVIDUALS, without any unnec-

---

*See the case of E. Knapp, former NSF Director, as reported a number of times in Science in 1983.

essary academic and/or corporate conduits. I am referring to the numerically largest percentage of support, that for theoretical research conducted by one individual and possibly one or more associates. These grants essentially provide support for salary, travel and publication charges, by therefore requiring no special administrative skill. The contracts can therefore be handled by the Principal Investigator under the Agency guidelines without any need of wasting public sums in unnecessary administrative conduits, whether academic or corporate.

It should be indicated here that my practical inability to apply for research support as an individual has been a primary reason for the appearance of this book. As well known, the NSF statute does indeed permit scientists to apply for support as individuals. However, as equally well known, the cases of actual NSF grants to individuals are extremely rare. At any rate, the very submission of a proposal to NSF without a "qualified" administrative backing by an "established" academic or corporate entity, is generally considered as disqualifying. The content of the application and the qualifications of the applicant are notoriously of secondary relevance.

These are essentially the reasons why the direct support to individuals is an insignificant element of the current scientific organization in the U.S. These are also the reasons why Congress should mandate the total yearly amount of funds to be dispersed to individuals. In fact, lacking a mandatory quota, we remain at the current *status quo,* where the item "grants to individuals" is essentially a curiosity line in the budget of Governmental Agencies.

The need for Congress to mandate a ceiling on the maximal possible amount of each individual grant is equally evident. In fact, it is needed to avoid disequalities occurring when physicists belonging to "leading" institutions receives sums disproportionately higher than those granted to physicists belonging to lesser prestigious affiliations or no affiliation at all.

In numerical terms, I would like to recommend the mandatory dispersal into contracts to individuals of a minimum of 50% of the annual budget in theoretical physics, with a ceiling of $ 50,000 per each individual contract for FY 1985 (with different numerical percentages for other sectors, such as experimental physics)✩ As a more specific numerical example, the NSF budget for theoretical physics for FY 85 contemplates the dis-

---

✩The percentage of grants to individuals for experimental physics should be evidently lower than that for theoretical physics, because of the usefulnes in this case of academic administration, e.g., for the realization of complex equipments. Yet, a number of grants to experimentalists do not warrant any academic administration, e.g., when modest equipment is required. For this reason, Congress should mandate the percentage of grants to individuals also for the experimental sector (30% of the total experimental budget is recommended here), as well as to all other segments of basic research.

persal of $ 13.9 M (excluding gravitation)*. The proposal here submitted would mandate the dispersal into contracts to individuals in FY 85 of a total of $ 6.9 M. With an average grant of $ 25,000 per individual, the proposal would permit the support of 276 theoretical physicists in FY 85. The residual $ 6.9 M would be dispersed as currently budgeted (for research contracts under academic and/or corporate administration). Assuming a minimum of 50% overheads,☆ and the same average of $ 25,000 per individual, the remaining $ 6.9 M would support 138 additional theoretical physicists for a grand total of 414 supported individuals.

The improvements of support are evident. In fact, by assuming that the entire amount of $ 13.8 M is dispersed as currently budgeted (with an irrilevant percentage to individuals),‡ by assuming again (for mere illustrative purposes) that the administrative conduits pocket 50%, and that the average individual support is $ 25 K, we would reach a total number of 276 supported individuals, versus 414 for the above proposal. Recommendation # 3 therefore implies a 150% increase in the number of supported scientists WITHOUT INCREASING THE BUDGET ONE SINGLE PENNY.

The predictable opposition by vested academic interests.

It is evident that academic interests will oppose the proposal because it implies their loss in FY 85 of at least $ 1.8 M in overheads for the NSF theoretical physics budget alone. The pertinent issue for the U.S. Congress is not what pleases or displeases academic administrators, but rather what serves or disserves National interests. When public funds are allocated for research in theoretical physics, they should not be used as a form of charitable contribution to academia. In fact, the administrative function provided by academia is not necessary for the contracts considered.

Finally, the most negative point discouraging academic support, unless of proved necessity, is the amount of academic politics each individual scholar has to overcome for the mere purpose of reaching all the necessary approvals to apply. These political difficulties are generally interpreted at Governmental Agencies as a guarantee that the proposal has passed the review by the local "peers". In the reality of the academic world, however, this implies that, often, the original proposal had to be

---

*See Physics Today, April, 1984, p. 58.

☆This estimate may result to be conservative, for academic institutions have pocketed overheads of up to 75% of a given total grant, thus leaving only the residual 25% to the Principal Investigator for direct use in the project.

‡An instructive reading is, for instance, the yearly book *"National Science Foundation Grants and Awards"* available from the U.S. Government Printing Office.

adulterated in such a way to comply with the vested interests of the local peers. The advantage of eliminating altogether the academic or corporate administration, whenever unnecessary, is therefore evident.

The more balanced conditions of basic research existing in several Foreign Countries.

A further point which should be brought to the attention of the U.S. Congress is that the funding of basic research at a number of foreign Countries appears to be considerably more balanced than that currently in effect in the U.S.A. on numerous counts. The study of these foreign organizations is therefore recommended.

As a specific example, the Canadian physics community is known to be smoother than its counterpart in the U.S.A. One of the reasons is the wisdom of the Canadian Government to LIMIT THE TOTAL AMOUNT OF INDIVIDUAL SUPPORT, thus permitting the support of a proportionately higher percentage of physicists, with the evident decrease of internal tension. By contrast, the current emphasis in the U.S. is in the so—called "excellence", that is, in the maximization of competition in the hope of stimulating quality. The end result is a proportionately smaller number of supported physicists, as compared to Canada, with the consequential, inevitable, multiplication of internal tensions of which this book is a direct manifestation.

The illusory nature of the current emphasis on "excellence".

To appraise whether or not the current organizational structure of funding basic research does stimulate "excellence" or not, we must recognize openly the following facts.

1) Qualified proposals for Federal research support exceed available budgets at all Governmental Agencies.

2) The selection, among all qualified proposals, of which one should be funded and which one rejected is generally made on the basis of NONSCIENTIFIC elements, such as the academic affiliation of the applicant, the aligned or non—aligned character of the contents and/or of the authors with vested academic—financial—ethnic interests in the field, and other factors not even remotely connected to the technical contents of the application.

3) Few "leading" institutions pocket, by far, the greatest majority of Federal research funds.

Under these premises, the current emphasis on "excellence" is a mere mask for the uninformed. The emphasis evidently serves well the interests of the few "leading" institutions and, according to some observers, the emphasis has been conceived precisely for that purpose. Nevertheless, the idea that the current organizational structure in the funding of basic research truly stimulates "excellence" has today lost all grounds of credibility.

The constructive function of *IL GRANDE GRIDO.*

Once this first point is acknowledged, the understanding of the loss for America is a mere consequence for anybody with a minimal knowledge of the way these "leading" colleges operate. It is at this point where the disclosure of my experience becomes useful. In fact, one can see that, within these leading institutions, the chances of filing an application on a research topic non—aligned with vested interests there, are absolutely null, no matter how relevant the application is.

Consider, for instance, Harvard University. As recalled in Section 2.1, only full professors there qualify as principal investigators of federal research grants. This means that, if a junior member at Harvard has an idea which is brilliant, but contrary to the vested interests of his/her direct, senior, supervisor, that junior faculty has no realistic possibility whatsoever of applying to a Governmental Agency for support.* The only hope for that junior faculty to be a truly free scientist within a truly democratic scientific society, is for the U.S. Congress to pass suitable legislation (the chances that Harvard modifies its statute should be dismissed because unrealistic, with similar situations occurring at the other "leading" colleges currently pocketing the majority of research funds). For that, it is sufficient that ANY member of Harvard faculty, whether junior or senior, has the dual option of, either applying under Harvard's administration (whenever ADMINISTRATIVELY NECESSARY) or as an individual. In turn, this is practically meaningful if and only if Congress mandates the minimum total amount of funds to be dispersed on research contracts to individuals per each Agency, jointly with the maximal individual amount (Recommendation # 3). In addition, Congress should pass legislation intended to break possible rings of alliances within the academic—governmental complex (Recommendation # 2), as well as provide effective means for individual scientists to voice their complaints (Recommendation # 1).

Lacking suitable Congressional legislation, the future scenario of the U.S. science is readily predictable. Governmental Agencies will continue to serve the vested interests of "leading" institutions, with an evident loss of scientific resources outside said institutions. Second, the "leading" institutions will continue

---

*The submission, say, to the NSF Division of Physics of an application as an individual would be immediately disqualified under these premises evidently because the application had been internally rejected at Harvard.

to permit only grants under their administration, even when such administration is basically unnecessary and un—warranted, with evident waste of public money. Third, only these applications compatible with vested academic—financial—ethnic interests in control of each given sector of a "leading" institution, will be permitted to be filed for federal research support, with an evident loss of scientific resources, internally, within said institutions.

The damages to science are multifold.

The moment of truth.

If we are truly sincere in the intent to serve the future of America, rather than that of minoritarian groups, it is time to
recognize the current totalitarian character of the scientific organization in the U.S.A.;
admit the fact that the current governmental funding of research favors and actually encourages such totalitarian conditions; and,
legislate all the necessary improvement conceived to break such an academic—governmental complex, as a condition to guarantee true freedom of scientific inquiry.

3.2:   RECOMMENDATIONS TO THE AMERICAN PHYSICAL SOCIETY.

RECOMMENDATION # 4:   FORMULATE AND ADOPT A *CODE OF ETHICS* IN PHYSICS.
By inspecting the latest (December, 1980) Professional Ethics Project report of the American Association for the Advancement of Science (AAAS) authored by R. Chalk, M. S. Frankel and S. B. Chafer, one can see that VIRTUALLY ALL U.S. SCIENTIFIC ORGANIZATIONS, INCLUDING THE POTATO ASSOCIATION OF AMERICA (p. 134), SUBSCRIBE TO A *CODE OF ETHICS,* EXCEPT THE AMERICAN PHYSICAL SOCIETY (and a few others). This is an evident, most unreassuring situation. In fact, the physics community at large, including the academic, corporate and military sectors, has been using billions of dollars of taxpayers money for decades without any *CODE OF ETHICS* (as well as any genuinely effective control by the political or the judicial systems). A situation of this type is simply untenable. Further delays in the formulation and adoption of a *CODE OF ETHICS* can only substantiate the suspicion that the lack of the Code is the result of a specific intent by opposing, high ranking, vested interests within the society.

RECOMMENDATION # 5: THE AMERICAN PHYSICAL SOCIETY COUNCIL SHOULD ESTABLISH A STANDING COMMITTEE ON THE *CODE OF ETHICS.*

The APS has a number of standing committees on various matters (publications, international freedom of scientists, education, applications of physics, etc.), but NOT on ethics. This situation is also un—reassuring and must be corrected.

Article VI–5 of the current APS Constitution states:

"The Council may establish such other committee as it may deem desirable in the management of the activities of the Society. The Council shall appoint, or delegate to the President the appointment of, the Chairperson and members of each such committee".

Recommendation # 5 is therefore submitted to the APS Council for the establishing of a Standing Committee on the *CODE OF ETHICS* with the following duties:

a) to assist the APS membership at large in the formulation of the *CODE OF ETHICS;*

b) to have the *CODE OF ETHICS,* so formulated, formally adopted by the Society with related revision of the Constitution and By–Laws; and,

c) to continue thereafter the standing function of overseeing possible future updatings, modifications and improvements of the *CODE OF ETHICS;*

as well as any additional function considered recommendable by the Council.

I DO NOT recommend that the committee should review claims of scientific wrongdoings. In fact, such review, to be genuinely effective, should be done by a Federal body OUTSIDE the Society (Recommendation # 1). This is the reason for the suggested name "Committee on the Code of Ethics" rather than "Committee on Ethics".

RECOMMENDATION # 6: THE AMERICAN PHYSICAL SOCIETY PUBLICATIONS COMMITTEE SHOULD REVISE CURRENT REGULATIONS PERTAINING TO THE REFEREEING OF PAPERS IN APS JOURNALS.

One of the most visible and insidious problems of current editorial practices at APS is the life—long tenure as referees by leading physicists at leading institutions. This guaranteed status has implied the practice that everything goes, as far as the contents of the referee's report is concerned. It is evident that a serious improvement of the refereeing process (that is, one beyond a powdery mask for inepts) must imply the termination of refereeing status at APS by dishonest referees, NO MATTER HOW HIGH THEIR STANDING IS AT THE SOCIETY, whenever caught in scientifically unethical or inappropriate practices. Other weaker forms, even though superficially more democratic, may hide schemes intended to preserve the impunity of corrupt refereeing, or serve vested, academic—financial—ethnic interests.

More specifically, the recommendations I submit for considerations are the following.

SUGGESTED REVISIONS PERTAINING TO REFEREES:

6—1)   Referees' reports should comply with the *CODE OF ETHICS* (as soon as adopted by the society);

6—2)   Referees' reports should not contain offensive comments or non—scientific comments on the technical contents of the paper submitted;

6—3)   Referees' reports should be constructive in their criticisms, that is, in case of rejection, they should itemize the improvements recommended in all the details needed for their actuation by the authors, and down to the individual passage, formula and/or word, whenever appropriate;

6—4)   Referees should accept the review of papers if and only if they are not reviewing, at the same time, research grant proposals by any of the authors;

6—5)   Referees should accept the review of a paper if and only if they have a documented record of expertise in the specific topic of the paper (and not in the field at large).

Referees who violate any of the above rules should be terminated or suspended in their function by the society for a period of time commensurate to the violation. As a specific example, consider the report claiming that one of the opposing experiments [103, 104] on time—reversal symmetry is wrong and the other is right without any third, independent repetition of the SAME experiment (pp. 261—262 of this book). That referee committed a manifest violation of scientific ethics and its refereeing function should have been terminated by the society, irrespective of its academic, ethnic and other affiliation. The termination and/or suspension of the refereeing function, particularly if made public, would be a major deterrent of scientific wrongdoings in refereeing.

SUGGESTED REVISIONS PERTAINING TO EDITORS:

6—6)   Editors should inspect each referee report for compliance with conditions 6—1/6—5 above. In case of any major default, upon consultation with the Editor in Chief, the editor should have authority to terminate or suspend the referees in their function for the appropriate duration of time. The referees' reports found in major default of conditions 6—1/6—5 above should then be ignored in the consideration process, and new reports solicited.*

---

*In case of lack of adoption of the revision here proposed by the APS, the editors are recommended to implement revision # 6—6 on their own and have a documentation of it. After all, the editors have the power to select

6—7) In case of mere insufficiencies of the reports with respect to conditions 6—1/6—6 above, the editor should mail the reports to the referees (AND NOT TO THE AUTHORS) for all the necessary improvements to comply with said conditions (PRIOR TO THE RELEASE OF THE REPORTS TO THE AUTHORS).

The effectiveness of a *CODE OF ETHICS* at a given society is as deep as the encouragement for its compliance which is provided by the society itself. A well known deficiency of the current editorial practices at APS journals, is the powerless condition of individual authors for whatever scientific wrongdoings and/or abuses they experience during the submission of their papers.

This deficiency must be resolved as a necessary condition to dissipate the current dark shadows of totalitarian conditions of the U.S. physics community. It is evident that authors must be empowered with, and actually encouraged to use, much more effective means of filing their complaints, particularly when exposed to manifestly corrupt referees and unresponsive editors.

SUGGESTED REVISIONS PERTAINING TO AUTHORS:
6—8) The APS should support authors in their possible claims at the BSR and/or other appropriate bodies outside the society.
6—9) The organization of the Publication Committee should be revised to permit authors to file their complaints DURING the consideration process.

An illustrative example: the current conspiratorial obscurantism on irreversibility.

An illustration is useful here to appraise the constructive potential of the recommendations submitted so far. The fellow taxpayer should recall the case of the experimental paper [103] by the Québec—Berkeley—Bonn group on the apparent violation of the time—reflection symmetry for open nuclear reactions (possible origin of the irreversibility of our macroscopic world). As recalled on pp. 160—168, the paper had been submitted to Phys. Rev. Letters (a letter journal for rapid publications) where it was kept for over one and one—half years, for the apparent intent of permitting an experimental group at Los Alamos National Laboratories to rush disproving measures [104] and have them quoted in paper [103]. Vested, academic—financial—ethnic interests controlling the sector in the U.S.A. immediately claimed measures [103] wrong and their rebuffal [104] correct, prior to

---

or avoid any given referee. The documentation of the practice is here recommended in the editors' own interests, in the event the case is considered by the Board of Scientific Review for possible editorial misconduits.

the availability of any third, independent, experimental resolution of the issue. The world wide acceptance of the U.S. orthodox position routinely followed, thus resulting in the apparent conspiratorial obscurantism in this fundamental aspect of human knowledge.*

Assume now that the recommendations submitted until now were implemented and in effect back in 1981. What would be the scientific scene today? I can readily tell you, fellow taxpayer, that the scientific scene today would have been substantially better.

The mere POSSIBILITY that the Québec–Berkeley–Bonn experimental group (or any other person) could have filed a complaint to a Federal board of scientific inquiry (Recommendation # 1) would have forced the editors of Phys. Rev. Letters to the proper editorial processing of the case, that is, RAPID PUBLICATION of paper [103], followed by a subsequent, equally rapid,

---

*See Sections 1.4, 1.6 and 1.7 for a review of the technical aspects. Certain aspects are crucial for the understanding of the conspiratorial nature of the obscurantism, such as the fact, well known to all physicists, that center–of–mass trajectories of closed–isolated systems are indeed, in general, time–reflection invariant (this is the case of our Earth, to begin with). To see the irreversibility, one must enter within the structure of a system and study open reactions. Corrupt academicians support their claim via papers on the time–reflection invariance of the center–of–mass treatment of closed–isolated systems, in full awareness that this information has no bearing whatsoever on the problem of irreversibility in the interior structure of the system, that is, for each open–nonconservative constituent. Other scientific wrongdoings occur on the technical means to truly claim existence of lack of existence of irreversibility (analyzing power of the forward reaction as compared to the polarization of the backward reaction). Corrupt academicians base their claim of exact time–reflection invariance in nuclear physics via experimental data on the so-called cross–sections, in full awareness of the fact that these means imply averaging processes that eliminate the effect, as stressed, elaborated and repeated again in the literature. As a result of all these (and much more) facts, the only possible scientific conclusion at this time is that the problem is basically unresolved. In the transition from nuclear to hadron physics (the structure of protons, neutrons, and other strongly interacting particles), we abandon Science even more and enter into the realm of personal beliefs without any possibility of experimental resolutions in sight for the foreseeable future. In fact, the current lack of irreversibility within the interior of a proton or a neutron is today imposed via shear academic power based on a pletora of assumptions, none of which is established via direct experiments (such as that quarks exist; that Pauli's principle is exact; that Einstein's special relativity holds; etc.). The lack of resolution of the problem of irreversibility within this finer layer of nature is more unresolved than ever. Yet, academic barons suppress its unresolved character in violation of the most elementary rules of scientific ethics and accountability. The fellow taxpayer should be aware of the consequences of a passive acceptance of this situation, including those for the security of the United States of America. If the time–reflection invariance is truly violated in the INTERIOR of protons and neutrons, potentially new weapons may be conceived by foreign countries.

publication of rebuffal [104] whenever scientifically mature. Second, the very existence of a Federal board of scientific inquiry would have forced the Los Alamos experimentalists to repeat ALL the measures originally conducted in paper [103] PRIOR to venturing any claim, rather than conducting only a small portion of them, as permitted by the APS editors. Third, the very existence of said Federal board would have forced vested interests in the U.S. academia to acknowledge the only possible scientific truth: WE DO NOT KNOW AT THIS TIME WHICH OF MEASURES [103, 104] IS CORRECT AND WHICH IS WRONG, UNTIL ALL MEASURES [103] ARE REPEATED BY THIRD INDEPENDENT PARTIES A SUFFICIENT NUMBER OF TIMES. In turn, the confirmation of the open character of the problem would have, on one side, prevented the rest of the scientific world to follow the position of the U.S. orthodoxy, and, on the other side, would have stimulated new studies. Rather than the current conspiratorial obscurantism, we would have had a beautiful intellectual democracy in which ALL possibilities are duly explored and appraised prior to the final settling of the issue. The remaining recommendations would have assisted in the achievement of the same goals (such as the adoption by the APS of a *CODE OF ETHICS*), or permitted complementary improvements, such as the funding by governmental agencies of proposals on BOTH the preservation AND the violation of the symmetry, by preventing the current monopolistic restriction of federal funds only to research projects based on the conjecture of the exact validity of the time—reflection symmetry in the particle world.

In short, the existence back in 1981 of appropriate means to contain the problem of scientific ethics, would have permitted a genuinely democratic scientific process, resulting today in basic advances at the foundations of scientific knowledge.

As a final point, the fellow taxpayer should be aware that the problem under consideration is not an esoteric one of no practical relevance. Not at all. The problem is of such fundamental physical relevance that can affect YOU, let alone your children, economically and militarily. In fact, the resolution of the problem of the origin of the irreversibility of our macroscopic world could permit far reaching advances, from particle physics to solid state physics, including new military applications.

All this has been lost because of manifest deficiencies in the current organizational structure of the U.S. science, with particular reference to the lack of effective means to contain excesses of academic greed.

3.3: RECOMMENDATIONS TO DIRECTORS OF FEDERAL AGENCIES.

RECOMMENDATION # 7: ENCOURAGE EMPLOYEES OF FEDERAL AGENCIES GRANTING RESEARCH CONTRACTS TO DISCLOSE THEIR ETHNIC BACKGROUND.

A strength of America is the variety of its different ethnic groups, all coexisting with the same rights under one Flag. A weakness occurs whenever one individual ethnic group is permitted to acquire control of any given sector of the Federal government, for that sector will likely operate in the interest of the ethnic group in control, and to the detriment of the Country. Another weakness occurs whenever one individual ethnic group is excluded from a given sector of the Federal Government over a sufficiently long period of time. Participation to Federal activities by as many ethnic and/or minoritarian groups as possible should therefore be encouraged, but the two extremes should be opposed. I am referring to the opposition in equal measures of one specific ethnic group being prevented from participating in a given public sector, or taking over numerical control of a public sector.

The value of these evident rules of democracy becomes magnified when referring to the dispersal of public funds. If a given division of a given Federal agency is permitted to be controlled by ANY ethnic group, that division will likely disperse the majority of public funds to the ethnic group in control, in disrespect of the need to serve the Country via more equanimous practices.

The ONLY way to prevent, or otherwise identify the problem is that each governmental employee participating in the dispersal of public funds via federal contract should disclose his/her ethnic background. As a specific example, each and every member of the Division of Physics of the National Science Foundation (including the secretarial employees) should disclose his/her ethnic background in order to ascertain whether or not ANY ethnic group has acquired control of the division, or whether or not ANY ethnic group has been excluded over a sufficiently long period of time.

The task of each Federal Agency soliciting and making available to the public a disclosure of ethnicity by its employees, can be best performed by the Agency Director.

My ethnic origin is Italian. I am proud of it and I foresee no conditions and/or circumstances whatsoever that would prevent me from disclosing VOLUNTARILY my ethnic origin. I expect ALL other members of a free society to have the same feelings toward their own ethnic origin.

To state it differently, I recognize the right to the confidentiality of the ethnic background to an individual living in a country oppressed by totalitarian regimes, and other circumstances. However, when that individual lives in a free, democratic society such as the U.S.A., and becomes a Governmental employee dispersing public funds, that individual has the moral obligation to disclose his/her ethnic background. The lack of such voluntary disclosure under the premises indicated, can only imply an evil scheme to me. How about you, fellow taxpayer?

RECOMMENDATION # 8:   IMPROVE CURRENT OPERATIONAL RULES FOR THE CONSIDERATION OF GRANT PROPOSALS ALONG LINES SIMILAR TO THOSE RECOMMENDED FOR THE IMPROVEMENT OF THE REFEREEING OF PAPERS AT APS JOURNALS.

I am referring to Revisions # 8–1 through 8–9 pertaining to referees, reviewers and authors essentially along the corresponding Revisions # 6–1 through 6–9.

A number of additional revisions should be implemented, specifically, for the consideration process of research grant proposals, such as:

8–10)   FINAL DECISION SHOULD BE REACHED ON GRANT APPLICATIONS ONLY AFTER THE AUTHORS PROVIDE THE AGENCY WITH THEIR COMMENTS ON THE REFEREES' REPORTS.

The current disparity between the processing of papers and that of research grant proposals is evident and well known (but not acted upon). When an editor rejects papers, the authors have the possibility of commenting on the possible erroneous character of the review. Whenever the author's case is sufficiently founded, the editor can then approve the manuscript without any modification.

For the case of grant proposals, the situation is different. In fact, final decisions are made by the Agency without any consultation with the authors regarding the veridicity of the referees' reports. When these reports are grossly erroneous, offensive, or manifestly corrupt, applicants are practically left with the sole possibility of waiting for a sufficiently long period of time, and then submit a new proposal.

The possibility of applying for a reconsideration, even though existing on paper, is excluded here as an effective means of communication between applicants and reviewers. This is so for a number of reasons, such as: the lack of certainty that the reconsideration will be indeed permitted; the general perception of a reconsideration as an admission of wrongdoing in the review process; etc. At any rate, I did succeed in initiating a process of reconsideration at the NSF (in regard to the vulgarly offensive referee reports for a research grant application pertaining to the writing of monographs [9,10] ; see pp. 276–279 of this book). However, I succeeded only upon reaching the highest Officer of the Country, the Agency Director and other prominent Officers; the reconsideration process demanded the creation of a new post (that of "Special Assistant to the Associate Director for Mathematical and Physical Sciences", see Doc. p. III—792); the officer in charge of the reconsideration soon found himself sandwiched between my relentless accusations of scientific corruption in the NSF refereeing of the proposal, and the predictable support of the referees provided by NSF officers; and similarly unpleasant as well as ineffective situations. Judging from my personal experience, I therefore have no doubt that the current process of reconsideration should be eliminated altogether and substituted with more effective means.

Those recommended here are essentially two. On one side, applicants and reviewers should communicate PRIOR to the Agency reaching any decision. In particular, authors should receive a copy of the referees' reports on their applications and be permitted to express their comments PRIOR to the Agency achieving the final decision. Said comments should then be appraised by the review panel, and be part of the information leading to the final decision. In this way, if a referee makes a statement which is demonstrably wrong, or unfounded, or unethical, the authors have a chance to prove it, and the Agency has a chance of being informed. After all, the scientists who can provide the best, most detailed and elaborated comments on the referees' reports, are the authors themselves.

But . . . . to prevent that the consideration process becomes a farse for uninformed, this is not enough. The organizational structure of science should be complemented with a Federal scientific court, the BSR, where applicants can file claims of misconduits in the reviews of grant applications, with the understanding that said court shall punish reviewers and referees alike found guilty of scientific wrongdoings.

Under these premises, we can expect, on one side, a more cautious attitude by corrupt referees and, on the other side, a more cautious attitude by reviewers with excessive ties to vested, academic—financial—ethnic interests.

8—11) AGENCY DIRECTORS SHOULD HAVE THE AUTHORITY TO TERMINATE OR SUSPEND THE EMPLOYMENT OF REVIEWERS VIOLATING THE CONFIDENTIALITY OF THE REFEREEING PROCESS EVEN AMONG REFEREES.

This is a key point for the set of recommendations submitted in this book. Whether only suspected or actually done, reviewers do have the power of preventing the funding of specific applications. The mechanics for these actions is known to all scholars with a sufficiently deep knowledge of operations of Governmental Agencies, and it is surprisingly simple. In fact, it is sufficient for the reviewer to select, as referees, those academicians who have notorious vested interests opposing the topic and/ or authorship of the proposal.

However, this is per se insufficient to guarantee the rejection of the application. In fact, if some of the referees are "dissident" (that is, not sufficiently aligned in the rejection), the rejection itself is not sure. In order to achieve the alignment of all the referees toward the rejection, it is essential that at least one of the referees (say, that most politically involved) knows the names of the other referees. Once this is done, the unanimous recommendation of rejection is certain. The actual scientific contents of the proposal is only matter for naive people, in my view.*

It is evident that, to better serve America, this possibility must be prevented (or the practive terminated?). Each referee of a research grant proposal of a U.S. Governmental Agency must keep his/her status absolutely confidential. By complement, Agency reviewers must be prevented from disclosing the names of the referees to any of them. In turn, such prevention is effective if and only if embodied in regulations contemplating the termination or suspension of employment for transgressors. Other weaker forms may satisfy inepts and accomplices, but they would leave current practices basically unchanged.

3.4: RECOMMENDATIONS TO INDIVIDUALS.

Recommendations to individual scholars.

Scientific corruption, like any other form of curruption, feeds on three problems: (1) IMPUNITY, (2) COMPLICITY, and (3) SILENCE. The containment of the problem of impunity has been addressed with Recommendation # 1. The containment of the problem of complicity has been addressed with a number of suggestions, such as Recommendation # 4 (the APS should formulate and adopt a *CODE OF ETHICS)* or Recom-

---

*The fellow taxpayer should remember the rather incredible alignment of ALL the referees toward the rejection of the primary group proposal submitted by The Institute for Basic Research to the NSF for experimental, theoretical and mathematical studies on the construction of a new mechanics, the hadronic generalization of quantum mechanics. As pointed out on pp. 385–386, the chances for all referees to be so strongly against the funding of the proposal are minute on all statistical grounds. The ethical standards of the review is qualified by the referee (p. III–865) who contacted one of the senior members of the proposal (L. C. Biedenharn, Jr., of Duke University) to ensure his withdrawal from the project. If that particular referee had been informed by NSF officers of the names of the other referees, the alignment of all of them toward the rejection would have been an easy consequence.

mendation # 7 (Federal employees granting research contracts should disclose their ethnic background).

The containment of the problem of silence is evidently a task of individual members of the community, whether researchers or administrators or governmental officers.

My recommendations to individual scholars are essentially those I have practiced.

RECOMMENDATION # 9: INDIVIDUAL SCHOLARS SHOULD BRING SCIENTIFIC WRONGDOINGS TO THE ATTENTION OF THE HIGHEST RESPONSIBLE ADMINISTRATORS, OR OTHERWISE INFORM THE WIDEST POSSIBLE AUDIENCE, AS SOON AS THEY BECOME AWARE OF THEIR OCCURRENCE.

The form of communication will evidently vary from individual to individual, and much depends on the courage by each individual. But the underlying issue is crystal clear:

WHEN EXPOSED TO APPARENT SCIENTIFIC CORRUPTION, SILENCE CAN BE COMPLICITY IN SCIENTIFIC CRIME.

The newsletter SCIENTIFIC ETHICS.

Another known deficiency of the current organization of the U.S. science is the absence of an editorial vehicle for the rapid, unobstructed, publication of reports on questionable scientific ethics by courageous members of the community. This situation is well known to all scholars who have attempted to publish a comment and/or a letter to orthodox vehicles of the community, such as PHYSICS TODAY (the official vehicle of the American Physical Society), or SCIENCE (the official vehicle of the American Association for the Advancement of Science). Other vehicles do exist and are indeed receptive, but they are generally perceived as being outside academia and, as such, do not carry an appreciable weight in the community.

This situation is also un—reassuring. Suppose that a major scientific wrongdoing occurs somewhere and sometime in the U.S.A. Suppose that individual scholars become aware of such a wrongdoing and are willing to bring the case to the attention of the scientific community. The chances for such scholars of succeeding in having his/her claims published in one of the established vehicles are very small.

I have been aware of this situation for years. In fact, I have tried myself unsuccessfully to publish even moderate appeals on ethical problems of refereeing, without any relevant success. For example, a letter on the topic submitted to PHYSICS TODAY was published with such editorial cuts to the point of compromising its understanding, and definitely not

representing its original intent.* Another letter of denounciation (this time on the offensive language used in the reviewing
of technical books) was rejected altogether by SCIENCE with
the editor's statement that the frequency of the occurrence did
not warrant attention!

Because of the insufficiencies reported above, a newsletter is currently being organized under the title of **SCIENTIFIC
ETHICS.** The newsletter is specifically intended for the rapid
publication of un–adulterated (but refereed) contributions on
ethical issues, and appears to be particularly suited for debating
any of the issues treated in this book.

Recommendations to individual administrators.

When the individual who becomes aware of possible scientific misconduits is a high ranking administrator, the need for
action becomes compelling. My recommendation to individual
administrators is simple:

RECOMMENDATION # 10: WHENEVER AWARE OF
APPARENT SCIENTIFIC WRONGDOINGS, INDIVI-
DUAL ADMINISTRATORS SHOULD SOLICITE OR
OTHERWISE ORGANIZE PUBLIC INVESTIGATIONS
OF THE CASES.

The time when a college president can afford the luxury of
absteining from initiating public action on ethical issues involving
public interests is, or otherwise must be, over because complicity
via silence may have very serious consequences. In fact, the international power of colleges such as Harvard or Yale University,
carries such a weight at other colleges throughout the world, that
the end result could be a conspiratorial obscurantism.

At any rate, if a conspiracy truly exists in the U.S. physics
on Einstein's relativities, the persons that should carry the heavi-
est responsibilities are precisely the presidents and primary administrators of leading colleges. For all legal and practical purposes, they are the "administrators" of public money obtained
via federal research contracts. This implies, in particular, their
responsibility to ensure a well balanced use of public funds, thus
including the encouragement, let alone permission, of dissident
scientific views AT THEIR OWN CAMPUS. In fact, the voicing
of dissident views is notoriously suppressed at departmental
levels, whenever opposing circles of vested interests are in control. The sole possibility for the existence of such dissident

---

*The letter was published in Physics Today, April, 1983. Its objective was
that of putting in black and white the fact that *"the problem of refereeing
does not exist at a remote college in North Dakota. It exists instead at the
colleges where the major refereeing load is carried out, that is, at Harvard
University, at The Massachusetts Institute of Technology, at Yale University, and the like."* This crucial passage was totally omitted by the editor,
jointly with several others.

views, and for the college's fulfillment of scientific accountability, therefore rests where it should be, at the administrative level.

To state it differently, until now, college presidents and leading administrators have implemented the practice of virtually complete lack of interference with departmental research programs. It is now time to reconsider this practice. It is time for leading, or otherwise responsible administrators to appraise departmental research grograms, and undertake all the necessary action to complement such programs, whenever requested for the fulfillment of scientific accountability by the college, vis—a—vis the taxpayer.*

Recommendation to individual taxpayers.

But, above all, the person that should initiate an active role in the conduction of science is that providing the funds: the fellow taxpayer. This is why I have suggested the executive members of the Board of Scientific Review to be selected among ordinary taxpayers, and NOT among scientists (Recommendation # 1). But, even if truly legislated by Congress, the BSR is and remains insufficient. The individual taxpayer, with his/her own initiative, remains the true, ultimate arbiter. The most radical suggestions are therefore submitted in this work to the fellow taxpayer.

RECOMMENDATION # 11: TAXPAYERS ASSOCIATIONS SHOULD FILE CLASS ACTIONS AGAINST ANY INDIVIDUAL AND/OR INSTITUTION SUSPECTED OF SCIENTIFICALLY UNETHICAL CONDUCT.
The most visible illustration for the need of organized action by individual taxpayers is provided by the Program of Gravitation within the Division of Physics of the National Science Foundation. As elaborated in Section 1.5, this Program has, supported for decades, research centrally dependent on Einstein's theory of gravitation, generally without any consideration and/or quotation of the technical literature on its erroneous character.

---

*Derek Bok, President of Harvard University, has acquired a personal problem of scientific accountability, and has propagated such a problem from Harvard's physics department to the entire university, precisely because of his lack of interference with departmental decisions regarding research programs. In fact, once aware of the virtually absolute impossibility of conducting research at Harvard's physics department on the apparent invalidation of Einstein's relativities, Bok should have initiated PERSONAL action, by soliciting, inviting, or otherwise promoting dissident research at some other branch of the university. Then, and only then Harvard would have avoided the current problems of scientific accountability on Einstein's relativities, as reported in Section 2.1. Much similar situations exist, not only at Harvard University in other segments of science, but also at virtually all leading colleges in the U.S.A.

The grip of greed controlling the sector is so strong, organized and diversified, that only one thing can implement an intellectual democracy at NSF: a class action organized by individual taxpayers against the individual officers of the National Science Foundation and their referees who are responsible for the current dispersal of public funds for research in gravitation.

By "intellectual democracy" I am referring to the well balanced condition in which sufficient funding of research based on Einstein's gravitation is evidently continued, but, jointly, NSF disperses a sizable percentage of the budget to dissident research on the incompatibilities of Einstein's gravitation with the physical reality, and on the needed, more appropriate formulations.

I want to be on record here to indicate that, in my view, the situation is so hopeless, that none of the recommendations submitted in the preceding sections of this chapter will permit the achievement of a true intellectual democracy in gravitation at NSF. Only a class action by individual taxpayers can.

3.5: CONCLUDING REMARKS.

Dear fellow taxpayer, permit me to conclude with a few remarks presented in the same spirit as that of the preceding ones, as sincerely felt in the interest of America, and submitted for whatever their value. The remarks below are inspired by a mixture of precautionary pessimism, which is necessary for objectivity, and contained optimism on the capability of the U.S.A. to improve ethics in science.

The first point of contained pessimism I would like to convey, is that scientific corruption has existed since the birth of science, and will continue to exist until the end of academia. The "elimination" of the problem of scientific corruption is, therefore, practically unrealizable. The only realistic goal is that of "containing" the problem within tolerable boundaries, as addressed in this book.

A second point is that scientific corruption exists at the highest levels of academia. It is important that politicians, administrators and the U.S. Government at large become aware of it. We may evidently disagree on the appropriate "definition" of scientific corruption, as well as on the "dimension" of the problem. But, to avoid shadows of hypocrisy or complicity, we must all agree on the "existence" of the problem at the highest, decision making layers of U.S. science.

A further point calling for precautionary pessimism is that the American Physical Society is not expected to be capable, alone, of bringing scientific ethics within contained, acceptable, boundaries. This is due to the fact that the vested interests that have prevented, until now, the formulation of a *CODE OF ETHICS,* not only are still there, but they have actually prospered owing to decades of impunity. It is therefore time for the appropriate political, legislative and other bodies OUTSIDE THE APS, to begin suitable action for the containment of the problem of scientific ethics, IRRESPECTIVELY OF ANY ACTION THAT MAY OR MAY NOT BE UNDERTAKEN BY THE APS.

My primary reason for being optimistic is that the U.S. taxpayer is, today, a well educated and sophisticated person, possessing a rapidly expanding system of information, and capable of identifying, in full, ethically questionable occurrences even with minimal information.

As an example, if a politician appoints, as members of a review panel on National Laboratories, only members from Harvard, MIT, Yale and other leading colleges, the fellow taxpayer will instantly suspect a potentially unethical occurrence, without any need of looking at the wording of the final report. In fact, the fellow taxpayer is sufficiently sophisticated to understand that a serious study on National Laboratories should begin with the critical review of the institutions controlling the laboratories, that is, of the members of the panel itself! At any rate, more qualified members of review panels can be readily found abroad as well as at less politically entangled institutions. Only then, a review panel can be perceived as being truly intended in the interests of science, rather than in the interests of minoritarian groups.

To state it openly, the days when the selection of representatives (or referees, or reviewers) from leading academic institutions was synonymous of credibility, are over because of the relaxation of the ethical standards within the leading institutions themselves. Today, the selection of representatives (referees or reviewers) from said institutions could be a liability for academicians, administrators and politicians alike.

Similarly, if the APS will continue to ignore the need for the formulation and adoption of a *CODE OF ETHICS,* the fellow taxpayer will certainly see in this its most probable cause: the existence of corrupt, high ranking interests within the society which oppose the Code. Even if a Code is eventually formulated and accepted by the APS, but only as a powdery mask for inepts without genuinely effective rules, the fellow taxpayer will be able to see the deficiencies by just looking at the Code.

Above all, my reason for optimism is the fact that the contemporary U.S. taxpayer is fully capable of understanding all the essential TECHNICAL issues, to the point that, if one specific issue cannot be expressed in a form readily understandable by the taxpayer, that issue is not truly important. As a result, I believe that the fellow taxpayer can understand, in full, all the primary technical issues underlying this ethical probe on Einstein's followers in the U.S.A.

I would like therefore to close this book with encouragement toward an appropriate mixture of precautionary pessimism, and contained optimism. in particular, I would like to encourage the fellow taxpayer to initiate an active role in the conduction of U.S. science, such as to call the directors of National Laboratories and inquire whether DIRECT experimental tests of the validity or invalidity of Einstein's special relativity in the interior of strongly interacting particles (pp. 143—170) are running there or not. If these experiments are not going on, and lesser relevant experiments continue to be preferred, the conspiratorial obscurantism suspected in this book on Einstein's relativities would be confirmed, and the grip of greed would still be in firm control of the sector.

If the U.S. taxpayer initiates such an active role in the conduction of the U.S. science, then, and only then, I see reasons for unlimited optimism for the containment of the problem of scientific ethics, as well as the basis for a new scientific civilization founded on intellectual democracy, with potential advances in human knowledge beyond our most vivid imagination.

APPENDIX A: THE EUROPEAN ORGANIZATION FOR NUCLEAR RESEARCH, GENEVA, SWITZERLAND.

In Fall, 1977, while being at the Lyman Laboratory of Physics of Harvard University, I applied to the European Organization for Nuclear Research (CERN) for a one year appointment as Scientific and/or Research Associate. The research program consisted of contacting local experimenters at CERN for the purpose of ascertaining the feasibility of experimental verifications of Pauli's exclusion principle under (external) strong interactions. The reader will recall from Sections 1.6 and 1.7 that the principle is a fundamental pillar of quantum mechanics. It was conceived by W. Pauli for the atomic structure and the electromagnetic interactions at large, under whose conditions it resulted to be strictly verified. The principle was subsequently assumed as valid under the different physical conditions occurring in the interior of nuclei, without any direct experimental verification. By recalling that physical knowledge is established quantitatively via experiments and not by theoretical beliefs alone, the proposal submitted to CERN suggested the initiation of a scientific process (the consultations with local experimentalists) that could subsequently lead to the resolution of this historical deficiency of contemporary physics.*

---

*Pauli himself had stressed in his limpid teaching that his principle had been conceived for physical conditions implying the lack of (appreciable) overlapping of the wavepackets of particles. These conditions are verified for the peripheral electrons of the atomic clouds because of very large mutual distances as compared to the size of the wavepackets. When the physical conditions are such to imply the overlapping of the wavepackets in an appreciable amount, we have the lack of necessary applicability of the principle for a number of well known technical reasons (such as the fact that the conditions imply the lack of necessary separability of the wavefunction, let alone the proof of its totally antisymmetric character). These latter conditions are exactly those in the interior of nuclei where particles are in appreciable conditions of mutual penetration, not only of their wavepackets, but also of their charge distributions. These are the well known historical roots of the doubts on the EXACT validity of Pauli's principle in nuclear physics which have been quantitatively studied by the hadronic generalization of quantum mechanics (Section 1.6). The understanding is that the APPROXIMATE validity of the principle is out of the question in nuclear physics. Thus, the objective of the research proposal submitted to CERN was that of resolving the issue in a quantitative way, that is, by establishing via direct experiment the QUANTITATIVE value of physical conditions in which the principle can be assumed as exact, with the complementary conditions being those within which the principle MAY be exact. The situation for the validity of Pauli's principle within the interior of a proton or a neu-

The application was acknowledged by W. Blair, Head of the Fellow and Associate Service at CERN with a note of January 31, 1978 (See the Docum. Vol. II, p. 445).

On March 14, 1978, I wrote the following letter to Blair (p. II–446):

"Dear Professor Blair,

I would like to express my appreciation for the courtesy of your letter of January 31, 1978, indicating that my application for a Scientific Associate Appointment will be considered at the meeting of April 11, 1978.

In this respect, I would like to indicate that a recent grant application with Professor Shlomo Sternberg, Chairman of the Department of Mathematics here at Harvard, to the U. S. Department of Energy (formerly ERDA), has been recently funded. As a result, I will have financial support for the next two academic years.

Owing to this new occurrence, I would like to confirm my application for a scientific associateship appointment, but modify my application for an appointment without salary."

The letter then continued with the indication that my research project was now part of an official program of the United States of America under administration by Harvard University, with my scientific associate being the chairman of Harvard's Department of Mathematics of that time. I also indicated that, owing to my commitments at Harvard, my visits at CERN could only be sporadic without any need of an office. The letter concluded by stating:

"Clearly, the issue I am referring to goes considerably beyond my capabilities as an isolated researcher. · My interest in a scientific associateship at CERN is therefore twofold: I would like first to attempt to stimulate the awareness of CERN colleagues on the need to conduct the indicated experimental verification, in due time. Secondly, I would like to collect the personal viewpoints of experimentalists (on the technical difficulties for a possible verification) as well as theoreticians (on the reasons for or against such an experimental verification)."

W. Blair subsequently communicated the CERN decision to REJECT MY APPLICATION FOR HOSPITALITY via a letter dated April 18, 1978 (p. II–447).

I immediately contacted L. van Hove, CERN Director at the time, by expressing my doubts, in the strongest possible

---

tron is much more nebulous and not resolvable in a direct quantitative way at this time. Within these smaller physical conditions, the validity of Pauli's principle is essentially inferred via the conjecture of the existence of yet unidentified sixteen, different quarks and sixteen different, unidentified antiquarks, and other assumptions. The validity of the principle then becomes a mere assumption following a primitive set of assumptions, none of which is established in a direct and incontrovertible way. This signals that we have left the arena of SCIENCE and entered the shadowy arena of ACADEMIC POLITICS, which is the ultimate essence of this appendix.

language, of the apparent existence of scientific corruption at CERN in the handling of the affair because:

    ★   I did not need any money (as stated in writing);

    ★   I did not need any office space (as also stated in writing);

    ★   I evidently did not need the use of any CERN equipment and/or facility;

    ★   The reasons for my interest for occasionally visiting CERN dealt with a known, historical, fundamental, open problem of contemporary physics not studied at CERN at that time (or thereafter); and, last but not least,

    ★   the CERN rejection implied the prohibition of occasional visits by a scientist under official support of the U.S. Government.

Regrettably, with the passing of time, I have lost the documentation of these letters with van Hove, as well as several additional exchanges we had throughout the intermediary action of a mutual acquaintance from Belgium. These letters are therefore missing in the Documentation of the case (Vol. II, pp. 444—447). The outcome of my complaints to van Hove are however absolutely incontrovertible and need no documentation. In fact,

    ■   van Hove did absolutely nothing of any value;

    ■   the prohibition for me to visit CERN remained strictly in force; and, last but not least,

    ■   no investigation whatsoever was ever initiated at CERN on the apparent scientific corruption underlying the affair.

Another thing should be crystal clear for the reader of this book. The very existence at CERN of one physicist studying the experimental verification of Pauli's principle under strong interactions, would have provided large damages to the vested academic—financial—ethnic interests there. In fact, the mere "consideration" of the experiments could have been perceived as an acknowledgment of doubts on the exact validity of the principle. In turn, the principle is a pillar of virtually all conjectures on quarks going on at that time at CERN and throughout the world. In fact, the compliance with Pauli's principle was instrumental in forcing quark supporters to invent the so—called notion of "color", which implied the multiplication of the number of conjectured, unidentified quarks (as well as large research contracts, numerous chairs in theoretical physics, and the like).

Years passed by without any event worth reporting here. Then, in 1982, van Hove resigned as CERN Director. His position was subsequently assumed by H. Schopper, a physicists from West Germany. I heard rumors in academic corridors that H. Schopper was bringing a "new wind" to CERN. This and other aspects suggested my contacting Schopper for the purpose of recommending the initiation at CERN of experiments for the resolution of the validity or invalidity of Einstein's special relativity in the interior of hadrons.* The correspondence (reproduced in full on pp. II—465—477) turned out to be, not only useless, but actually damaging.

Regrettably, the problem of scientific ethics and accountability at CERN cannot possibly be treated in this appendix, inasmuch as it would require a separate, extensive report. Nevertheless, in the interest of Europe (as well as of the laboratory itself), it is appropriate to recommend the initiation of the consideration of the problem. Above all, the European press should keep CERN under constant scrutiny for ethical standards and scientific accountability, a task which has not even been initiated to this day, to my knowledge. Without such an independent appraisal of CERN research, the laboratory may well decay in time, despite its historical, outstanding, contributions to human knowledge.

---

*The proposal was essentially that submitted to U.S. National Laboratories, such as the measure of the mean life of unstable hadrons at different energies (Section 1.7 and 2.3). The European taxpayer should be informed of the fact that CERN possesses all the necessary equipment to run this and other experiments in a matter of a few months by therefore resolving this fundamental problem of human knowledge. There must therefore be no doubt whatsoever on the fact that the LACK of experiments of such manifestly basic nature is due to a SPECIFIC, ORGANIZED, INTENT by vested interests in control of the laboratory, and NOT to the lack of equipment or insufficient technology.

APPENDIX B: AN ISLAND OF SCIENTIFIC FREEDOM: THE INSTITUTE FOR BASIC RESEARCH IN CAMBRIDGE, U.S.A.

[Reprinted from Hadronic Journal, Volume 6, 1967–1974, 1983]

1. HISTORY

The mathematicians and physicists who led to the founding of the Institute for Basic Research (I.B.R.) initiated their gathering at the **First Workshop on Lie—admissible Formulations** held at Harvard University in 1978. The group grew considerably in subsequent years. By 1981, it was clear that coordination of the research could be better accomplished by organizing a new, independent, institute.

The I.B.R. was incorporated in Massachusetts on March 2, 1981, as a nonprofit academic institution with a charter similar to, but independent from, that of local institutions. The building known as the Prescott House, adjacent to Harvard University, was purchased on July 29, 1981, to provide permanent facilities for the I.B.R. in the heart of Cambridge's academic community. The building comprises 18 offices in the charming victorian style of New England. This number can be readily increased via suitable remodeling. In the absence of I.B.R. members, the offices are leased to individual scholars and graduate students of local universities.

Inauguration of the I.B.R. occurred on August 3, 1981, jointly with the initiation of the **Fourth Workshop on Lie—admissible Formulations.** The ceremony was attended by the Governors, the Officers, and the Advisors of the Institute; representatives of the firms serving the Institute in accounting, law, and finance; and distinguished scientists from the U.S.A., and from Australia, Austria, Canada, Chile, France, Greece, Israel, Italy, Mexico, Sweden, Switzerland, Venezuela, and West Germany.

To ensure long term stability and independence from fashionable research, the I.B.R. has been organized with a financial backing independent from government support. In fact, the I.B.R. has been founded via private funds, and has been operated via donations and volunteer work by the founders, officers, advisors, members, their spouses and friends.

The I.B.R. is a nonprofit academic corporation with federal tax exemption. All donations to the I.B.R. are, therefore, tax deductible in the U.S.A. under classifications 170(b)(1)(A)(vi) and 509(a)(1) of the Internal Revenue Code. The I.B.R. federal identification number is: 04–2750391.

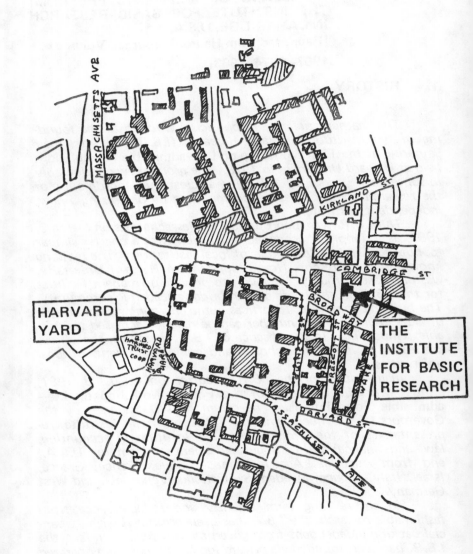

2.   RESEARCH PROGRAMS

Lie's theory, with its diversification into algebras, groups and geometries, constitutes one of the most fundamental branches of contemporary mathematics.

A primary mathematical objective of the I.B.R. is the study of possible generalizations of Lie's theory [beyond grading—supersymmetric extensions]. Priority of research is given to generalizations of Lie algebras that admit generalized group and geometric structures.

A first generalization of Lie algebras of Lie—admissible type was proposed by A. A. Albert at the University of Chicago back in 1948. Additional generalizations of Lie—isotopic and Malcev—admissible type have been proposed by I.B.R. members, and they are currently under intensive mathematical study by a growing number of scholars.

Contemporary physical theories, such as classical mechanics, statistical mechanics and quantum mechanics, constitute a realization of Lie's theory beginning from their most fundamental dynamical part, the time evolution.

A primary physical objective of the I.B.R. is the study of possible generalizations of contemporary mechanics whose existence can be inferred from the generalized forms of Lie's theory provided by mathematical studies. The hope is to achieve a deeper and more refined description of physical systems that admit contemporary descriptions in first approximation.

By combining contributions in mechanics, algebras and geometries beginning from the past century, I.B.R. members have already succeeded in generalizing the contemporary formulation of classical mechanics for conservative systems, into covering mechanics possessing a Lie—isotopic and Lie—admissible structure for the closed and open description, respectively, of the systems of our physical reality, those with potential—Hamiltonian as well as contact—non—Hamiltonian forces. The generalized formulations have been called Birkhoffian and Birkhoffian—admissible mechanics, respectively, because of pioneering contributions made by G. D. Birkhoff in 1927.

The study of a generalization of quantum mechanics as operator image of the generalized classical mechanics indicated above is well under way, for the representation of strongly interacting particles (hadrons) as closed systems possessing an interior dynamics more general than that of the atomic structure. In turn, a generalization of quantum mechanics for the interior strong problem may assist in the resolution of some of the fundamental open problems of the theoretical physical of the last decades; identification of quark constituents with physical, already known particles; etc.

Additional applications of the advanced mathematical

and physical knowledge achieved by I.B.R. members can be foreseen in several other branches of contemporary human knowledge, ranging from theoretical biology to controlled fusion, or to computer modeling.

3.   ORGANIZATION

To minimize costs, the I.B.R. research objectives are pursued via a combination of members actually working at the Cambridge premises, and members residing at other institutions. Therefore, joint membership at the I.B.R. and at other institutions is encouraged. Coordination is ensured by frequent contacts, periodical research sessions, and yearly workshops. Appointments are made under the titles of Full Professor, Associate Professor, Assistant Professor, and Research Assistant. All appointments are on a nontenured, yearly, renewable basis.

The I.B.R. is comprised of a **Division of Mathematics** and a **Division of Physics**. A third **Division of Applied Research** [e.g., for energy] is currently under consideration. In Fall, 1983, the total number of I.B.R. members was 33 [11 mathematicians and 22 physicists]. By 1985, the total number of I.B.R. members is expected to be 50. Presently, 65% of I.B.R. members hold joint full professorship positions at other academic institutions in the U.S.A., Canada, Venezuela, Italy, Switzerland, France, West Germany, Israel and Pakistan.

The I.B.R. is administered by a **Board of Advisors** whenever necessary. General executive authority of scientific character is then invested in the President, while operational authority will be invested in a Director, who is to be appointed in the future.

Several precautionary measures have been implemented by the founders of the I.B.R., beginning with the conception of the Charter, to ensure **genuine freedom in the pursuit of novel scientific knowledge.** For instance, members of the I.B.R. have no authority in the appointments of new members, which are conducted by an outside Committee comprised of distinguished scientists and administrators in the U.S.A. and abroad.

This organizational structure, which is apparently new in the U.S.A., has been implemented to minimize the formation of groups of scholars with vested interests in one given trend, and the not uncommon suppression of research along other trends, whenever said groups are invested with executive authority for new appointments.

4.   EDITING

The I.B.R. considers editorial efforts an important aspect of its contribution to advanced scientific inquiry. Members of *the I.B.R. and non—members alike are involved in the Institute's editorial operations.*

The I.B.R. houses the editorial office of the **Hadronic Journal,** *a journal on basic physical advances which is at its seventh year of publication under the Editorship of J. Fronteau (France), for Statistical Mechanics; R. Mignani (Italy), for Theoretical Physics; H. C. Myung (U.S.A.), for Mathematics; and R. M. Santilli (U.S.A.), as Editor in Chief; with an Editorial Council comprising several internationally known scientists.*

The I.B.R. also houses the Secretarial Office of **Algebras, Groups and Geometries,** *a new journal on fundamental mathematical advances that is scheduled to initiate publication in January, 1984, under the editorship of H. C. Myung (U.S.A.), with an Editorial Council comprising several distinguished scholars.*

Furthermore, the I.B.R. houses the Editorial Office of several yearly reprint series such as:

— **Hadronic Mechanics,**
   A. Schober, Editor;
— **Mathematical Studies on Lie—admissible algebras,**
   H. C. Myung, Editor;
— **Applications of Lie—admissible Algebras in Physics;**
   H. C. Myung, S. Okubo and R. M. Santilli, Editors;
— **A Nonassociative Algebra Bibliography,**
   M. L. Tomber, Editor;
— **Advances in Discrete Mathematics and Computer Science,**
   D. F. Hsu, Editor.

5.   CONFERENCES

The organization of conferences, workshops, and summer schools in physics, mathematics, and other branches of science constitutes an important function of the I.B.R.

During the first year of operation, the I.B.R. organized the **Fourth Workshop on Lie—admissible Formulations,** *held in Cambridge, U.S.A., on August, 1981.*

The I.B.R. also participated in organizing the **First International Conference on Nonpotential Interactions and Their Lie—admissible Treatment,** *held at the University of Orléans, France, in January, 1982. The conference was attended by scientists from around the world, including official convoys from the U.S.S.R. and China. The conference resulted in the publication of four volumes of proceedings, for approximately 2,000 pages of research.*

The I.B.R. subsequently organized the **First Workshop on Hadronic Mechanics** *and the* **Fifth Workshop on Lie—admissible Formulations** *that were held jointly on the premises on August, 1983.*

Currently, the I.B.R. is organizing the **Second Workshop on Hadronic Mechanics** *to be held in Europe in Summer, 1984, and the* **Second International Conference on Nonpotential In-**

teractoins and Their Lie–admissible Treatment *to be held also in Europe in Summer, 1985.*

Additional workshops, and conferences on gravitation, computer science, philosophy of science and other fields are under consideration.

6.   GUEST HOUSE

The I.B.R. is provided with a furnished, four–bedroom **Guest House** *located directly on the water's edge of Allerton Harbor, some 18 miles South of Cambridge. The Guest House has been used by several I.B.R. members, or visitors, their families and friends for brief stays and research sessions, amidst a beautiful natural environment, with stimulating walks on majestic shorelines of the Atlantic Ocean, and enchanting sunsets on the Boston Skyline. The Allerton Harbor houses three marinas, and is an ideal setting for all nautical recreational activities.*

7.   MEMBERSHIP

Applications for I.B.R. membership can be submitted at any time to the

> **Admission Committee**
> **The Institute for Basic Research**
> **96 Prescott Street**
> **Cambridge, Massachusetts 02138, U.S.A.**

To avoid delays, all applicants should
1) *specify whether membership is desired in the Division of Mathematics or of Physics;*
2) *indicate the academic title the application is submitted for;*
3) *include a brief, one–page summary of current research interests;*
4) *provide a curriculum vitae et studiorum with a list of publications; and,*
5) *solicite at least three letters of recommendation to be mailed directly to the Admission Committee.* (**Important Note:** *The I.B.R. does not solicit letters of recommendation).*

Members are initially appointed on a honorary basis without financial support and without any obligation . Appointments are structured to be compatible with pre–existing academic commitments.

I.B.R. membership can be disclosed [jointly with other memberships or individually] in publications, lectures, and all academic activities at large. However, such a disclosure is not obligatory, but only discretionary for each individual member.

I.B.R. membership provides a number of opportunities

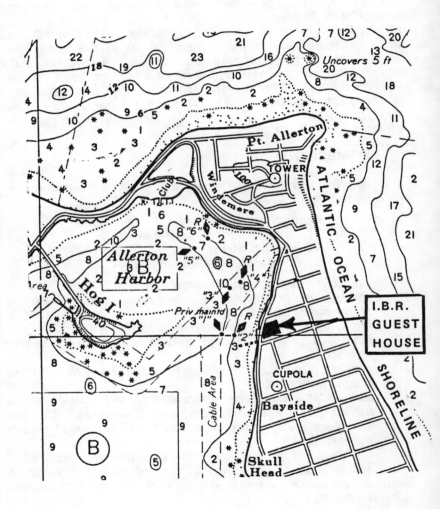

such as:

♦   *participation in ongoing research activities, conferences, and editorial programs of the institute;*

♦   *possibility of initiating new, independent, research programs; organizing new conferences, workshops or summer schools; or launching new editorial programs;*

♦   *seeking financial support from governmental, corporate or private sources under I.B.R. administration whenever appropriate.*

The financing of general logistic expenses is the responsibility of the I.B.R. Board of Governors. The financing of individual I.B.R. members essentially rests in the initiative of each individual member.

The I.B.R. does not require a membership fee. Whenever possible, voluntary, tax–deductible donations depending on the individual capabilities, are welcome.

REFERENCES

1. E. Fermi, *Nuclear Physics,* University of Chicago Press (1949)

2. J. M. Blatt and V. F. Weisskopf, *Theoretical Nuclear Physics,* Wiley, New York (1952)

3. E. Segrè, *Nuclei and Particles,* Benjamin, New York (1964)

4. G. Galilei, *Dialogus de Systemate Mundi* (1638), translated and reprinted by MacMillan, New York (1917)

5. I. Newton, *Philosophiae Naturalis Principia Mathematica* (1687) Translated and reprinted by Cambridge University Press, (1934)

6. V. I. Arnold, *Mathematical Methods of Classical Mechanics,* Springer—Verlag, New York/Heidelberg/Berlin (1978)

7. J. M. Levy—Leblond, in *Group Theory and Its Applications,* Edited by E. M. Loebl, Academic Press, New York (1971)

8. R. M. Santilli, *On a Possible Lie—admissible Covering of the Galilei Relativity in Newtonian Mechanics for Nonconservative and Galilei Noninvariant Systems,* Hadronic Press, Nonantum, MA (1978), reprinted from the Hadronic J. 1, 223—423 and 1279—1342 (1978)

9. R. M. Santilli, *Foundations of Theoretical Mechanics, I: The Inverse Problem in Newtonian Mechanics,* Springer—Verlag, New York/Heidelberg/Berlin (1978)

10. R. M. Santilli, *Foundations of Theoretical Mechanics, II: Birkhoffian Generalization of Hamiltonian Mechanics,* Springer—Verlag, New York/Heidelberg/Berlin (1982)

11. R. M. Santilli, *Lie—admissible Approach to the Hadronic Structure, I: Nonapplicability of the Galilei and Einstein Relativities?* Hadronic Press, Nonantum, MA (1978)

12. R. M. Santilli, *Lie—admissible Approach to the Hadronic Structure, II: Covering of the Galilei and Einstein Relativities?* Hadronic Press, Nonantum, MA (1982)

13. H. H. E. Leipholz, *Direct Variational Methods and Eigenvalue Problems in Engineering,* Noordhoff Intern., Leyden (1977)

14. R. M. Santilli, *Need of Subjecting to an Experimental Verification the Validity Within a Hadron of Einstein's Special Relativity and Pauli's Exclusion Principle,* Hadronic Press, Nonantum, MA (1978), reprinted from Hadronic J. 1, 574—901 (1978)

15.   A Tellez—Arenas, J. Fronteau and R. M. Santilli, Hadronic J. 3, 177 (1979)

16.   G. D. Birkhoff, *Dynamical Systems,* A.M.S., Providence, R. I. (1927)

17.   R. Abraham and J. E. Marsden, *Foundations of Mechanics,* Benjamin/ Cummings, Reading, MA (1978)

18.   R. M. Santilli, "Lie—isotopic lifting of Lie symmetries, I: General considerations", I.B.R. preprint (1983), submitted for publication

19.   R. M. Santilli, "Lie—isotopic lifting of Lie symmetries, II: Lifting of rotations", I.B.R. preprint (1983), submitted for publication

20.   L. C. Biedenharn and J. D. Louck, *Angular Momentum in Quantum Physics: Theory and Applications,* Addison—Wesley, Reading, MA (1981)

21.   L. C. Biedenharn and J. D. Louck, *The Racah—Wigner Algebra in Quantum Theory,* Addison-Wesley, Reading, MA (1981)

22.   H. A. Lorentz, Amst. Proc. 6, 809 (1904) and Verl. 12, 986 (1904)

23.   H. Poincare, C. R. Acad. Sci. 140, 504 (1905) and Rend. Pal. 21, 129 (1906)

24.   A. Einstein, Ann. Phys. 17, 891 (1905) and Jarb. Radioakt. 4, 411 (1908)

25.   P. G. Bergmann, *Introduction to Special Relativity,* Prentice Hall, Englowood Cliff, N. J. (1942)

26.   S. Weinberg, *Gravitation and Cosmology: Principles and Applications of the General Theory of Relativity,* Wiley, New York (1972)

27.   C. W. Misner, K. S. Thorne and J. A. Wheeler, *Gravitation,* Freeman, San Francisco (1970)

28.   A. Pais, *Subtle is the Lord . . ., The Science and the Life of Albert Einstein,* Clarendon Press, Oxford (1982)

29.   G. Yu. Bogoslovsky, Nuovo Cimento 40B, 99 and 116 (1977)

30.   H. Rund, *The Differential Geometry of Finsler Spaces,* Springer— Verlag, Berlin/Gottingen/Heidelberg (1959)

31.   R. M. Santilli, Lettere Nuovo Cimento 33, 145 (1982)

32.   R. M. Santilli, Lettere Nuovo Cimento 37, 545 (1983)

33.   R. M. Santilli, "Lie—isotopic lifting of Lie symmetries, III: Lifting of the special relativity", in preparation

34.   V. de Sabbata and M. Gasperini, Lettere Nuovo Cimento 34, 337 (1982)

35. H. B. Nielsen and I. Picek, Nuclear Physics B211, 269 (1983)

36. S. H. Aronson, G. J. Bock, H. Y. Cheng and E. Fishback, Phys. Rev. Letters 48, 1306 (1982)

37. R. Huerta—Quintanilla and J. L. Lucio, Fermilab preprint 18—THY (1983)

38. W. A. Rodrigues, Hadronic J., in press (1984)

39. R. M. Santilli, *Status of the Mathematical and Physical Studies on Lie—admissible Formulations on July 1979 with particular reference to the strong interactions,* Hadronic Press, Nonantum, MA (1979), reprinted from Hadronic J. 2, 1460—2018 and Errata—Corrige 3, 914 (1980)

40. R. M. Santilli, Ann. Phys. 83, 108 (1974)

41. H. Yilmaz, Phys. Rev. 111, 1417 (1958)

42. H. Yilmaz, Phys. Rev. Letters 27, 1399 (1971)

43. H. Yilmaz, Lettere Nuovo Cimento 20, 681 (1977)

44. H. Yilmaz, Hadronic J. 2, 1186 (1979)

45. H. Yilmaz, Hadronic J. 3, 1478 (1980)

46. H. Yilmaz, Hadronic J. 7, 1 (1984) [note: Volume 7, 1984, of the Hadronic Journal is dedicated to I. Newton in the three—centennial of the inception of universal gravitation].

47. H. Yilmaz, Phys. Letters 92A, 377 (1982)

48. H. Yilmaz, International J. Theor. Phys. 10—11, (1982)

49. R. M. Santilli, Found. Phys. 11, 383 (1981)

50. M. Gasperini, "A Lie—admissible theory of gravity", Nuovo Cimento B, in press (1984)

51. M. Gasperini, Hadronic J. 7, 234 (1984)

52. P. A. M. Dirac, *The Principles of Quantum Mechanics,* Oxford University Press (1930)

53. R. M. Santilli, Hadronic J. 4, 642 (1981)

54. R. M. Santilli, Lettere Nuovo Cimento 38, 509 (1983)

55. R. Mignani, H. C. Myung and R. M. Santilli, Hadronic J. 6, 1873 (1983)

56. R. Mignani, Lettere Nuovo Cimento 38, 169 (1983)

57. A. Jannussis, G. Brodimas, V. Papatheou, G. Karayiannis, P. Panagopoulos, and H. Ioannidou, Lettere Nuovo Cimento **38**, 181 (1983)

58. P. Caldirola, Hadronic J. **6**, 1400 (1983)

59. R. M. Santilli, Lettere Nuovo Cimento **37**, 337 (1983)

60. H. C. Myung and R. M. Santilli, Hadronic J. **3**, 196 (1979)

61. C. N. Ktorides, H. C. Myung and R. M. Santilli, Phys. Rev. **22D**, 892 (1980)

62. R. M. Santilli, Hadronic J. **4**, 1166 (1981)

63. G. Eder, *Nuclear Forces,* M.I.T. Press, Cambridge, MA (1968)

64. G. Eder, Hadronic J. **4**, 634 (1981)

65. G. Eder, Hadronic J. 4, 2018 (1981)

66. G. Eder, Hadronic J. **5**, 750 (1982)

67. R. Mignani, "Lie—isotopic lifting of SU(n) symmetries", Lettere Nuovo Cimento, in press (1984)

68. M. Gasperini, Hadronic J. **6**, 935 and 1462 (1983)

69. J. Fronteau, Hadronic J. **2**, 727 (1979)

70. A. Tellez—Arenas, Hadronic J. **5**, 733 (1982)

71. I. Prigogine, Nobel Lecture (1977) and quoted works.

72. B. Misra, I. Prigogine and M. Corbage, Proc. Nat. Acad. Sci. U.S.A. **76**, 3607 (1979)

73. J. Fronteau, A. Tellez—Arenas and R. M. Santilli, Hadronic J. **3**, 130 (1979)

74. A. A. Sagle and R. E. Walde, *Introduction to Lie Groups and Lie Algebras,* Academic Press, New York (1973)

75. H. C. Myung, *Lie Algebras and Flexible Lie—admissible Algebras,* Hadronic Press, Nonantum, MA (1982)

76. R. C. Tolman, *The Principles of Statistical Mechanics,* Oxford University Press (1938)

77. H. C. Myung and R. M. Santilli, Hadronic J. **5**, 1277 (1982)

78. H. C. Myung and R. M. Santilli, Hadronic J. **5**, 1367 (1982)

79. R. M. Santilli, Hadronic J. **5**, 264 (1982)

80. T. D. Lee, *Particle Physics and Introduction to Field Theory,* Har-

wood, Chur, Switzerland (1981)

81. A. O. Barut, in *Quantum Theory and the Structure of Time and Space*, 5, 122, edited by L. Castell, C. F. von Weizsacker and C. Hansen, Springer–Verlag, Munchen (1983)

82. P. Bandyopadhyay and S. Roy, Hadronic J. 7, 266 (1984)

83. Jiang, Chun–Xuan, Hadronic J. 3, 256 (1979)

84. Z. J. Allan, Hadronic J. 7, 394 (1984)

85. N. Isgur and G. Karl, Physics Today 36, p. 36 (November 1983)

86. R. M. Santilli, Hadronic J. 3, 440 (1979)

87. J. M. Osborn, Hadronic J. 5, 904 (1982)

88. G. M. Benkart, Algebras, Groups and Geometries 1, 109 (1984)

89. A. J. Kalnay, Hadronic J. 6, 1 (1983)

90. A. J. Kalnay, Hadronic J. 6, 1790 (1983)

91. A. J. Kalnay and R. M. Santilli, Hadronic J. 6, 1798 (1983)

92. M. Gell–Mann, Physics Letters 8, 214 (1964)

93. G. W. Mackey, *Unitary Group Representations in Physics, Probability, and Number Theory,* Benjamin/Cummings, Reading, MA (1978)

94. R. M. Santilli, Hadronic J. 3, 854 (1980)

95. K. Bleuler, Helv. Phys. Acta 23, 567 (1950)

96. H. Rauch, A. Zeilinger, G. Badurek, A. Wilfing, W. Bauspiess, and U. Bonse, Physics Letters 54A, 425 (1975)

97. H. Rauch, G. Badurek, W. Bauspiess, U. Bonse, A. Zeilinger; Proc. Int. Conf. Interaction of Nautrons with Nuclei, Lowell Mass. Vol. II, p. 1027 (1976)

98. G. Badurek, H. Rauch, A. Zeilinger, W. Bauspiess, and U. Bonse, Phys. Rev. D14, 1177 (1976)

99. H. Rauch, A. Wilfing, W. Bauspiess, and U. Bonse, Zeit. fur Phys. B29, 281 (1978)

100. H. Rauch, Hadronic J. 5, 729 (1982)

101. D. Y. Kim, Hadronic J. 1, 1343 (1978)

102. R. J. Slobodrian, Hadronic J. 4, 1258 (1981)

103. R. J. Slobodrian, C. Rioux, R. Roy, H. E. Conzett, P. von Rossen,

and F. Hinterberger, Phys. Rev. Letters 47, 1803 (1981)

104. R. A. Hardekopf, P. W. Keaton, P. W. Lisowski, and L. R. Veeser, Phys. Rev. C25, 1090 (1982)

105. C. Rioux, R. Roy, R. J. Slobodrian and H. E. Conzett, Nucl. Phys. A394, 428 (1983)

106. H. E. Conzett, in *Polarization Phenomena in Nuclear Physics,* G. G. Ohlsen et al Editors, A.I.P., p. 1452 (1981)

107. H. E. Conzett, Hadronic J. 5, 714 (1982)

108. R. J. Slobodrian, Hadronic J. 5, 679 (1982)

109. J. Pouliot, P. Bricault, J. G. Dufour, L. Potvin, C. Rioux, R. Roy, and R. J. Slobodrian, J. Phys. 45, 71 (1984)

110. R. K. Adair et al, Phys. Rev. Letters 47, 1032 (1981)

111. R. Mignani, Hadronic J. 4, 2185 (1981)

112. R. Mignani, Hadronic J. 5, 1120 (1982)

113. R. Mignani, "Do cross sections get modified in nonpotential scattering theory?", Nuovo Cimento, in press (1984)

114. N. Jacobson, *Lie Algebras,* Wiley, New York (1962)

115. R. M. Santilli, Nuovo Cimento A51, 570 (1967)

116. L. M. Weiner, Rev. Univ. Nat. Tucuman, Mat. y Fis. Teor. A11, 10 (1957)

117. P. J. Laufer and M. L. Tomber, Cand. J. Math. 14, 287 (1962)

118. M. L. Tomber et al, *A Bibliography and Index in Nonassociative Algebras,* Collected Volumes I, II and III, Hadronic Press, Nonantum, MA 02195 (1984)

119. R. M. Santilli in *Analytic Methods in Mathematical Physics,* R. P. Gilbert and R. G. Newton, Editors, Gordon & Breach, New York (1970) [Proceedings of the Indiana symposium of June of 1968, Bloomington, Indiana].

120. R. M. Santilli, Meccanica 1, 3 (1969)

121. H. C. Myung, Hadronic J. 1, 1021 (1978)

122. C. N. Ktorides, Hadronic J. 1, 194 and 1012 (1978)

123. C. N. Ktorides, H. C. Myung and R. M. Santilli, Phys. Rev. D22, 892 (1980)

124. *Proceedings of the Second Workshop on Lie—admissible Formula-*

tıons, Volume A: *Review Papers,* Hadronic J. 2, 1252—2019 (1979); Volume B: *Research Papers,* Hadronic J. 3, 1—725 (1979)

125. *Proceedings of the Third Workshop on Lie—admissible Formulations,* Volume A: *Mathematics,* Hadronic J. 4, 183—607 (1981); Volume B: *Theoretical Physics,* Hadronic J. 4, 608—1165 (1981); Volume C: *Experimental Physics and Bibliography,* Hadronic J. 4, 1166—1625 (1981)

126. *Proceedings of the First International Conference on Nonpotential Interactions and Their Lie—admissible Treatment,* Volume A: *Invited Papers,* Hadronic J. 5, 245—678 (1982); Volume B: *Invited Papers,* Hadronic J. 5, 679—1193 (1982); Volume C: *Contributed Papers,* Hadronic J. 5, 1194—1626 (1982); and Volume D: *Contributed Papers,* Hadronic J. 5, 1627—1947 (1982)

127. *Proceedings of the First Workshop on Hadronic Mechanics,* J. Fronteau, R. Mignani, H. C. Myung and R. M. Santilli, Editors, Hadronic Press, Nonantum, MA 02195 (1983)

128. *Developments in the Quark Theory of Hadrons,* a reprint collection, Volume I (1964—1978), D. B. Lichtenberg and P. S. Rosen, Editors, Hadronic Press, Nonantum, MA 02195 (1980); Volume II in preparation by new editors.

129. *Applications of Lie—admissible Algebras in Physics,* a reprint collection, Volumes I and II (1978), H. C. Myung, S. Okubo and R. M. Santilli, Editors; Volume III (1984), R. M. Santilli, Editor; Hadronic Press, Nonantum, MA 02195

130. *Mathematical Studies on Lie—admissible Algebras,* a reprint collection, Volumes I, II, III and IV, in press, H. C. Myung, Editor, Hadronic Press, Nonantum, MA 02195

131. *Irreversibility and Nonpotentiality in Statistical Mechanics,* a reprint collection, A. Schoeber, Editor, Nonantum, MA 02195, (in press)

132. *Advances in Discrete Mathematics and Computer Sciences,* a reprint collection, Volumes I, II and III (in press), D. F. Hsu, Editor, Hadronic Press, Nonantum, MA 02195

133. *Hadronic Mechanics,* a reprint collection, Volume I: *Foundations,* II: *Rotational Symmetry* and III: *Time Reversal Symmetry;* in preparation, A. Schoeber, Editor, Hadronic Press, Nonantum, MA 02195

134. *Algebras, Groups and Geometries,* a quarterly mathematical journal, H. C. Myung, Editor, Hadronic Press, Nonantum, MA 02195

135. R. M. Santilli, Ann. Phys. 103, 354 (1977); 103, 409 (1977); and 105, 222 (1977)

136. R. M. Santilli, Phys. Rev. D20, 555 (1979)

137. H. Georgi, Hadronic J. 1, 155 (1978)

138.   R. M. Santilli, Phys. Rev. <u>D20</u>, 3396 (1974)

139.   H. Rauch in *Proceedings of the International Symposium on the Foundations of Quantum Mechanics in the Light of New Technology,* S. Kamefuci, Editor, Phys. Soc. Japan (1983), p. 277

USE OF PROCEEDS

The proceeds from the sale of this book shall be donated to

THE INSTITUTE FOR BASIC RESEARCH (IBR)
96 Prescott Street, Cambridge, MA 02138, U.S.A.

and/or to individual scholars for the continuation of mathematical, theoretical and experimental research on the insufficiencies and generalizations of Einstein's special and general relativities, as described in this book.

The IBR is a nonprofit, academic Institution with Federal Identification Number 04—2750391 under IRS Classifications 170(b)(1)(A)(vi) and 509(a)(1). Donations to the IBR are therefore tax deductible in the U.S.A.

Donations to the IBR are acknowledged with formal nominations, such as *IBR DONOR, IBR SPONSOR,* or *IBR SUPPORTER.*

Special programs are available at the IBR for sufficiently higher donations, such as:

➤ International meetings in the name of the donor.

➤ Summer chairs in physics, mathematics and other disciplines in the name of the donor.

➤ Full chairs in physics, mathematics and other disciplines in the name of the donor.

Interested donors are recommended to contact the IBR Administrative Office for details.

Individual scientists wishing to participate in the IBR research programs are recommended to contact the IBR Admission Committee (See Appendix B for details on applications).

ABOUT THE AUTHOR

RUGGERO MARIA SANTILLI received the (Italian equivalent of the) Ph.D. in theoretical physics at the University of Turin, Italy, in 1966. The subsequent year he moved with his family to the U.S.A. where he remained ever since, by holding research, faculty or visiting positions at a number of academic institutions, including Harvard University, The Massachusetts Institute of Technology, The University of Miami, Florida, and others. Currently, he is the President of The Institute for Basic Research, a new, independent research institution in physics, mathematics and other basic sciences located within the compound of Harvard University. Santilli has taught physics at all levels, from prep courses, to advanced seminar courses for graduate students. His curriculum includes

★   over 100 articles in particle physics published in various journals;

★   seven monographs in theoretical physics published by: Springer—Verlag, West Germany, Hadronic Press, U.S.A.; The University of Turin, Italy; and the Avogadro Institute, also in Turin;

★   Co—founding of a journal in theoretical physics, of a journal in pure mathematics and of numerous other editorial initiatives;

★   Co—organizing of several international workshops and conferences in physics and mathematics;

★   Co—founding of The Institute for Basic Research, Cambridge, U.S.A.

Santilli is a member of several scientific organizations, including the American Physical Society, the American Mathematical Society, and others. He is the recipient of a number of honors, including the Historical Medal of the City of Orleans, France, the Gold Medal of the Province of Campobasso, Italy, and others.

YOUR NEW VEHICLE OF SCIENTIFIC EXPRESSION

SCIENTIFIC ETHICS

A NEWSLETTER PUBLISHED EVERY TWO MONTHS

under the editorship of

I. KAUFFMAN

The Institute for Basic Research

96 Prescott Street, Cambridge, MA 02138, U.S.A.

Yes! Please enter only my subscription to SCIENTIFIC ETHICS at $ 29.50
Name and Address:

☐ *I enclose a check* ☐ *cash* ☐, *or*
☐ *money order*
  for U. S. $ 29.50

(Please type or write in capital letters)

Please charge my credit card number ___ *Credit card name*
Bank's name and address ___ *Signature*

I am interested ☐ *I am not interested* ☐ *in being an Advisor to SCIENTIFIC ETHICS.*
I am interested ☐ *I am not interested* ☐ *in contributing to SCIENTIFIC ETHICS at some future time.*
Tentative date of submission ___ *in the following topic* ___

I am interested ☐ *I am not interested* ☐ *in receiving a quotation for the possible purchase of the*
DOCUMENTATION *of IL GRANDE GRIDO in case printed for distribution to the public.*
Mail this coupon with payment or charge instructions to

ALPHA PUBLISHING
897 Washington Street, Box 82
NEWTONVILLE, MA 02160—0082, U.S.A.

TERMS OF SALE: All shipments are made with pre–payment only. Base prices are inclusive of surface mail and handling
charges for shipment throughout the world. Air mail available at the additional cost of U. S. $ 15. The shipment of the first
issue of *SCIENTIFIC ETHICS* shall be made at the end of March, 1985, and then continue every two months throughout the
year. No subscription can be cancelled. Alpha Publishing shall replace issues damaged during shipment upon reception of the
damaged copy.
**FOREIGN CURRENCIES ARE ACCEPTABLE IF IN CASH OR INTERNATIONAL MONEY ORDER AT THE RATE OF
EXCHANGE WITH THE U. S. DOLLAR ON THE DAY OF THE ORDER.**
Alpha Publishing is a nonprofit, scientific publisher.
Scholars are encouraged to submit their manuscripts.

ALPHA PUBLISHING
897 Washington Street, Box 82
NEWTONVILLE, MA 02160-0082, U.S.A.